CHARACTER AND IDEOLOGY
in the
BOOK OF ESTHER

CHARACTER AND IDEOLOGY
in the
BOOK OF ESTHER

SECOND EDITION
with a New Postscript on
A Decade of Esther Scholarship

Michael V. Fox

WILLIAM B. EERDMANS PUBLISHING COMPANY
GRAND RAPIDS, MICHIGAN / CAMBRIDGE, U.K.

First published 1991 by the
University of South Carolina Press

This edition published 2001 by
Wm. B. Eerdmans Publishing Co.
255 Jefferson Ave. S.E., Grand Rapids, Michigan 49503 /
P.O. Box 163, Cambridge CB3 9PU U.K.

Printed in the United States of America

06 05 04 03 02 01   7 6 5 4 3 2 1

Library of Congress Cataloging-in-Publication Data

Fox, Michael V., 1940–
Character and ideology in the book of Esther / by Michael V. Fox.
p.   cm. — (Studies on personalities of the Old Testament)
Includes bibliographical references and index.
ISBN 0-8028-4881-8 (alk. paper)
1. Bible. O.T. Esther — Commentaries.   2. Bible. O.T. Esther —
Biography.   I. Title.   II. Series.
BS1375.3.F694   1991
222′.9077 — dc20   91-22942

www.eerdmans.com

CONTENTS

CONTENTS

CONTENTS

Contents

ABBREVIATIONS

Addition(s)	(Capitalized): the deuterocanonical Addition(s) A–F that appear in the Septuagint and, subsequently, the Alpha Text, Vulgate, and Old Latin.
Ag. Est.	*Aggadat Esther*, Buber 1897.
AT	The Greek Alpha-Text; see chapter XIV, §2. AT's chapters are given in lower case roman, while LXX's and MT's are given in arabic numerals (e.g., AT's v 1 is the equivalent of MTs 4:1).
AT-end	The ending of the AT (without Adds E and F), namely viii 39–52.
b.	Babylonian Talmud
BH	Biblical Hebrew
BDB	Brown, Driver, and Briggs, *Hebrew and English Lexicon of the Old Testament*
BHS	Biblia Hebraica Stuttgartensia
Est. Rab.	Midrash Esther Rabba
Gen. Rab.	Midrash Genesis Rabba
GKC	Gesenius–Kautsch–Cowley, *Gesenius' Hebrew Grammar*. 1910.
Her.	Herodotus, *The Persian Wars*.
Jos.	Josephus, *Antiquities of the Jews*, XI 184–296 (= chap. vi). References are all to *Antiquities*, ad loc., unless otherwise cited.
j.	Jerusalem Talmud
LXX	Septuagint (the Göttingen text, ed. Hanhart, is used throughout). Manuscript designations are according to Hanhart.
Meg.	Tractate Megilla
MH	Mishnaic Hebrew
Mid.	Midrash

MT	Massoretic Text
NJV	New Jewish Publication Society Version: *The Writings*. Philadelphia, 1982.
NT	New Testament
OL	Old Latin version
R.	Rabbi
R-AT	The redactor who produced the present Alpha Text
R-MT	The redactor who produced the present Massoretic Text
Syr	Syriac version (Peshitta)
Tar^1	Targum Rishon (the first, more literal Aramaic translation of Esther)
Tar^2	Targum Sheni (the second, highly paraphrastic and expansive, translation of Esther)
Vul	Vulgate
//	Parallel to, equivalent to
{ }	Possible later additions
[ ]	In the translation: words added to the translation.

Bibliographical references: In the text, commentaries and some other important works (marked by an asterisk in the Bibliography) are referenced by name of author only; other works are cited by author and date.

CHAPTER I

INTRODUCTION

1. The Art of Simplicity

The characters of the book of Esther, including its heroes, have not always fared well at the hands of their commentators. They have been excoriated for moral failings ("There is not one noble character in the book"[1]), scolded for sexism ("buried in Esther's character is also full compliance with patriarchy"[2]), and put down for flatness and simplicity ("[the] major characters are so superficially drawn that it is difficult to identify very long or intensively with either the book's villains or heroes"[3]). Such strictures do not correspond to my own response to the book, nor do they explain why its characters have lived on, reborn and remolded in numerous retellings of the tale. In many readers—probably most—they have evoked affection and emulation; in some they have aroused disgust and contempt; rarely have they met with indifference.

The issues of morality and sexism will be addressed in the appropriate places[4] (where I will argue that the imputations of immorality and sexism are misreadings). More problematic is the question of literary quality. This problem lies in the book's simplicity; it is more difficult to analyze simplicity than to respond to it.

In fact, much is going on beneath the "artless" surface of these simple but powerful characters. Their surface clarity and vividness make them fascinating and meaningful to children, but these qualities are the products of a sharp and subtle craft that makes the characters intriguing to adults as well, and worthy of repeated scrutiny. These characters become vehicles in conveying a surprisingly sophisticated—in some ways strikingly modern—view of person,

---

1. Paton, p. 96.
2. Laffey 1988:216.
3. Moore, p. LIII. Moore is typical in thinking it a failing that "[n]either Vashti nor Zeresh is a believable life-and-blood individual." But (whatever the validity of this judgment) they are *not* "life-and-blood" individuals, and there is no *a priori* value in making them believable as such. The question is how effective these "unbelievable" individuals are in serving the author's purposes.
4. Chap. XI §§2a-b; chap. X, Excursus.

nation, and religion. With a few episodes, a brief and straight-forward plot, and a few clear-cut characters, the author of Esther says much about the world, humanity, Jews, history, and even God—who is not mentioned at all. To explore all this is the aim of the present study, and it will do so by focusing on character.

2. The Aim of This Study

The name of this series, "Studies on Personalities of the Old Testament," reminds us that we may (and probably must) choose a particular point of focus when reading a literary text, such as the text's story line, its moral and spiritual messages, its historical or social information, its language and stylistic texture, its aesthetic qualities, and more. Or we may decide to concentrate on its characters, the people of the text. The latter is an especially rewarding approach to the book of Esther, where the central ideas are embodied in, rather than merely enunciated by, the persons in the text.

This study approaches the Scroll[5] with a primary guiding question: What are the persons in the story like? This question will quickly lead us to other issues, in particular the ideology of the author—his[6] assumptions, ideas, values, and teachings. Characterization does not, it must be stressed, exist in isolation from a great array of other artistic and conceptual concerns, and these will not be neglected. But as an interpretive strategy I will look at the complex of other features from the standpoint of character and deal with them primarily insofar as they contribute to the shaping and functioning of the book's persons.

There is much that the present study does not attempt to provide, such as an investigation of the origins of Purim, a full textual-philological commentary (but some essential technical underpinnings of my translation and commentary are discussed in the

---

5. The book of Esther is one of the Five Scrolls, each of which is read on a Jewish holiday (Song of Songs, Ruth, Lamentations, Qohelet [= Ecclesiastes], and Esther). In Hebrew, Esther is usually called simply *hammᵉgillah*, "the Scroll"— i.e., the scroll *par excellence*.

6. I refer to the author (and narrator) as "he" because of the overwhelming likelihood that this writer, like virtually all the ones we know about from the ancient Near East, was male and that the narrator too was assumed to be male. I will not, however, make such assumptions about the reader.

Appendix), a survey of the history of interpretation,[7] a discussion of archaeology and realia,[8] and a comprehensive literary-stylistic analysis.[9] For these I refer you to the many fine studies of Esther treating the various historical, literary, and religious issues.[10]

For the most part I will offer my own observations without arguing against others, but even in "neutral" discourse there is often implicit argumentation against other readings, and I will not pretend to neutrality. Beyond the numerous interpretations I simply disagree with, there are other readings that I consider fundamental misapprehensions—some of them quite disturbing—of the characters and their author. To give you an idea of what these readings are, all but one of the chapters describing characters (chaps. VI-XII) have epigraphs that, it must be emphasized, express an attitude that the chapter *repudiates*. Haman alone has evoked no contrary view and so gets no epigraph. These epigraphs and my rebuttal show that the qualities of all the figures in Esther are not a cut-and-dried issue. Like living persons, they can call forth conflicting opinions among different acquaintances.

This study is called "Character and Ideology in the Book of Esther" because it will analyze character portrayal less for its entertainment or aesthetic values than for its role in imparting the author's ideas about realities outside the book. The emphasis on ideology is in accord with the author's own intentions, for the book has little that does not contribute to ideas about religious, moral, and national issues.

The Scroll's principal message is obvious: Jews everywhere in all generations should celebrate Purim. The author succeeded fully in making this point; the holiday is alive and meaningful, and it is celebrated widely and enthusiastically in much the way originally envisioned. But I will be giving less attention to this theme than to

---

7. For which see Herrmann 1986, as well as the commentaries. For Jewish midrashic interpretations see Katzenellenbogen 1933.
8. See the survey by Moore (1975), as well as the commentaries.
9. For this see Berg, Clines, and Striedl (1937). Dommershausen's book (1968) is a painstaking but unproductive detailing of literary and stylistic features.
10. In particular I recommend the literary-ideological studies of Berg and Clines, the solid commentaries of Moore, Bardtke, Meinhold (who has some interesting insights into the book's ideology), and Paton (whose extensive quotation of sources and meticulous, if often misguided, text critical notes keep his commentary useful).

others of subordinate—but by no means negligible—importance. The Purim theme is less a function of characterization than are the others, and it is hafted on to the narrative proper in such a way that it does not permeate and govern its development; in other words, the Scroll's principal theme is not its *central* theme. (Indeed, it is hard, and perhaps artificial, to single out one of the themes in this book as the central one, since they all interlock and overlap.) The Purim message is, moreover, too simple to require much discussion. The ideas that will receive more attention can be conceived of as answers to the following questions, which, I believe, are provoked by the story's own perspectives and emphases:

How can Jews best survive and thrive in the diaspora?

What is the nature of the gentile state?

What must Jews do in times of crisis?

What is the nature of the Jewish community in exile and how does (and should) it work?

How do men and women treat each other?

Where do we see God?

Though something of a synthesis is offered in chapter XIII, where I describe the world that the characters both constitute and inhabit, I omit a standard chapter summing up the "message of the book of Esther." Its messages will be explained and analyzed, but not in isolation from the dramatic substance of the book. The book's themes and teachings will be viewed as expressions of characterization and narrative progression, which is the way they were meant to be seen. In any case, there is already too pervasive a tendency to reduce Bible stories to their "morals," and it won't hurt to take a step away from that habit.

My interest in ideology is not meant to imply that the Scroll is heavily didactic. The author does not seek to drive home most of his perceptions and their attendant lessons, but (what is more effective) to make them the readers' own by re-presenting our world in a miniature literary one. Themes do not always become messages. In some matters—the relations between the sexes and the nature of gentile rule, for example—the author observes without inculcating specific lessons. But taken together his ideas constitute an ideology, for he tries to persuade us to see the world the way he does. The Esther story is a metaphoric world, a concentrated vision of the reality of exile, and the vision itself teaches Jews how to make their way through the life they face.[11]

This study asks about the artistry and function of characterization in the book of Esther, but my interpretation is not meant to give *the* answer—a complete and definitive description of the characters the author intended to create. Such a description is not possible. If it were, Bible studies—indeed, literary study in general—would come to an end or degenerate into transmission of stale doctrines (as happens in orthodoxies, each of which asserts the finality and definitiveness of its own readings). The impossibility of finality is due not to a shortcoming inherent in reading or in criticism, but to the unlimited potential of literary portrayal. As open-ended constructs, literary characters (like real ones) can always evoke new, deeper, and broader speculations, revisions, and reassessments. Hence I am offering only one reading. This reading does, I believe, account for the characters of Esther more adequately and accurately than have previous treatments of the book—largely because it is so indebted to them. But I certainly do not imagine or hope that my reading will exhaust the valid interpretations the text invites.

You will not agree completely with my assessment of the characters in Esther. Even if we were discussing real persons we both knew, especially ones we knew well, we would probably not reach full agreement. We might have different views of their moral strengths, motivations, stability, intelligence, and so on. Moreover, we might agree on some of that person's qualities yet evaluate him or her differently. Nevertheless, our discussion—if conducted in good faith and with a minimum of extraneous presuppositions—would deepen our understanding of those acquaintances, giving it greater nuance, clarity, and subtlety, and making us aware of facets of their character that we had not previously considered.

This book is my side of such a discussion, and although it is obviously not a real dialogue between us, the conversation is not one-sided. This exposition responds to the views of earlier commentators by selectively continuing their ideas, building on them, rejecting them, reshaping them, replacing them, and supplementing them with ideas of my own. I would be pleased if my ideas in turn elicit the response of future commentators. I would also be

---

11. On the truth-claims and teachings of the "metaphoric worlds" of fiction, see Booth 1988:324–73.

interested in learning something of your own views—your reaction both to my interpretations and to the characters in the book we are studying. You can write me at the Hebrew Department, University of Wisconsin, Madison, WI 53706.

3. What Is Character?

I will be speaking about the characters of the book of Esther much as if they were real. This "as if" is an important convention in reading literature. I take it as a given that readers commonly learn about, react to, and speak about the creations of a writer's imagination as if they had intentions, thoughts, feelings, even subconscious minds of their own. We can even imagine them leading lives *outside* the events narrated in the text. And in the book to follow, I will be speaking as a reader not a theoretician.[12]

Of course, while real people may have a "self" that remains the same even through radical changes of character (though the notion of "sameness" quivers a bit under close examination), literary figures do not. They have no space (such as the heart [according to the ancient notion], or the brain, or, more abstractly, a continuous consciousness with a persistent sense of self) that might be considered an organ or a location of character. They have no "core" or "essence" apart from the various things said by and about them. Esther (I mean the Esther of the book, not a woman who might have actually lived in Achemenid Persia) exists solely in the words spoken about and by her.

---

12. The theoretical basis for this approach is a strong one. The best discussions of theories of character and their practical implications are those of Chatman (1978:107–45), Harvey (1965:chap. 1 and passim), Hochman (1985:chap. 2), and Phelan (1989:chap. 1 and passim). The following remarks draw upon and synthesize their approaches (particularly Hochman's), and make use as well of Forster's seminal study (1927).

   Chatman makes a strong case for the affinity between figures in literature and people in life and for the similarity in the ways we "retrieve" character (what Phelan calls the "mimetic component" of character). This affinity allows us to draw conclusions about the past and future of literary figures beyond the scope of the text. Hochman argues that what links characters in literature to people in life, as we fabricate them in our minds, is the "integral unity of our conception of people and of how they operate" (p. 36). Even the clues we use in constructing the image of a person are virtually identical in literature and in life. Thus we "read" life and art in much the same ways (pp. 35–44). This is basically persuasive, though he may be pressing this point too far, not giving sufficient weight to the teleology of traits and even incidentals in literature.

In other words, we have a bunch of pieces, which we must join together into a person who never existed apart from those pieces. But an amazing thing happens: through reading, a person is created (or re-created) who can then even possess a measure of autonomy and exist apart from the text. The proof is the way that Esther can show up in other Esther stories—in the Septuagint, for example, or even the drama of Racine—where she says and does quite different things and yet is somehow the same person with a modified personality. Another proof is the way we can often recall literary figures vividly even after forgetting the words and the events of the text in which they first came alive.[13]

We reconstruct character in reading in almost the same way that we come to know people in "real life."[14] All we know about anyone besides ourselves is pieced together from things they do and say, and even these things we must often construct at one remove, from events that are supposed to have ensued from their actions and from things others say about them. We sort through these bits and pieces, looking for (and creating) order and meaning, linking them together by postulating motivation, and seeking (constantly but usually unconsciously) the patterns or principles by which the fragments cohere. When we find types of behavior that endure and recur, and especially when we can organize the types into patterns, we call the complex of patterns *character*. On the basis of these patterns, especially by reliance on the types of motivation we have inferred, we can deduce a person's thoughts, even subconscious ones, and even speculate on what he or she might yet do. This is a legitimate deduction from type: what is such a person likely to do, based on our knowledge of his or her past actions and those of other persons of this sort? In other words, we continually *read* character in the stories of others' lives. We do the same in reading texts. Literary characters are "images of possible people."[15]

In some ways, as reader-observers we can know literary characters far better than real-life ones. This is one of the sources of literature's power—a power it transmits to its readers. There are several reasons why literary characters are in some ways more knowable than real ones. For the former, the facts are complete. Insofar

13. Chatman 1978:118.
14. The quotation marks, not to be repeated, remind us that the dichotomy is imperfect insofar as it neglects the very real intrusion of literary characters into realms of life outside of literature.
15. Phelan 1989:2, speaking of the "mimetic component" of character.

as the text is intact and we understand its language, we readers have all the data that can and ever will exist, and they will not change. (If anyone adds facts, a different book is created.) Also, these facts stand still for repeated scrutiny and are always available for verification. Moreover, if the narrator is reliable (as in Esther)—and not somehow undermined by his own words—then these facts are reliable. We cannot suspect that the narrator is giving us an untrue picture of the character, because the picture *is* the character.[16] Finally, when the narrator is omniscient (as in Esther), we are often allowed direct access to the characters' thoughts, feelings, and motives—even unconscious ones.[17] We may even be told what might have happened but did not, or what might have been thought but was not. Thus reading can make us privy to information we could never have in real life.[18]

Literary figures exist (and are not only known) *pars pro toto*, meaning that we can extrapolate a whole person from the small part we are given.[19] They live in an organized, purposive world, all of whose parts are, at least potentially, created to constitute the world in just the way it is. This fact charges even minor character traits with potential significance. (This is not the case, however, for faceless "actants" whose only function is to move the plot along, for example the conspirators in 2:21–23; but it is doubtful that they should even be called "characters.")

---

16. We may, however, take a step back and doubt the narrator's or author's *evaluation* of this character. We might say, as some do, that the author considers Mordecai an ideal person but he really is quite arrogant, duplicitous, and so on.
   A reliable narrator is not necessarily telling the truth. The story may be quite different from history—as we understand it. The author may be distorting the facts—as he or she understands them—or simply be mistaken. The reliable narrator is a stance within the text that the author chooses to give to the speaking voice; it is a literary convention; see chap. IV, n. 29. However, with regard to features which are the author's creation—such as literary character— the reliable narrator is, by definition, reliable.

17. Literary figures have an unconscious, about which we can legitimately form hypotheses based on their actions, inasmuch as their characters are constructed on the pattern of people in life. "Language is a key element in this [process], as is the imagery for which language is the vehicle" (Hochman 1985: 71).

18. "[The characters in novels] are people whose secret lives are visible or might be visible; we are people whose secret lives are invisible.
   "And that is why novels, even when they are about wicked people, can solace us; they suggest a more comprehensible and thus a more manageable human race, they give us the illusion of perspicacity and of power" (Forster 1927: 99; see also 74–75, 97–99).

19. For real people, we must reason *pars pro toto*, but we know that the part is not the substance of their being.

How do we judge the adequacy of evidence in proving hypotheses about something that (in our world) never existed? We can only compare literary figures with our own experience of human character. In other words, character analysis is finally a matter of introspection, whereby every reader looks inward to describe, analyze, organize, and interpret what happens when he or she reads this text. Literary criticism is essentially a way of describing the results of this common reflexive act.

As readers and critics we join a community that extends through the centuries and around the world: the community of those who re-create the characters of the book of Esther by reading, thinking, and speaking about them. The author of Esther has projected a world from his imagination, and we can enter it, explore it, explain it, and return yet again for new pleasures and insights.

4. The Texts of Esther

The present study directs its attention primarily to the Massoretic Text (MT), the Hebrew text accepted as authoritative by Jews and most Christians. In contrast to a common usage in modern literary studies of the Bible, I do not speak of this text as "the final form" of the Esther story; rather, it is an intermediate form. The "final" form is, I would imagine, the Septuagint (the authoritative Bible of Eastern Orthodoxy); or perhaps it is the Latin Vulgate (which has canonical status alongside the Hebrew text for Roman Catholics). These "final forms" show certain minor differences from the extant Hebrew version as well as some major ones. Nor is the MT the *earliest* form of the book of Esther.[20] However, the MT is (in my view) the form most rewarding for literary study. Also, being in Hebrew, it has not undergone the distortions inevitable in translation.

Two other forms of the Esther story I will be mentioning for comparative and (occasionally) textual purposes are the Septuagint (LXX) and the Alpha Text (AT), both of them in Greek. The LXX, the standard Greek translation, was finished no later than 78 B.C.E., when (according to a note at its end) it was brought to Alexandria. It is a smooth rendering, usually faithful to the gist of the Hebrew where it attempts to translate, but also flexible, paraphrastic, and

---

20. This will be argued in chap. XIV, esp. §3a.

sometimes innovative, often making adjustments for the sake of clarity and vividness. Hence it can never clearly witness to a different Hebrew text, and I will use it merely as supplemental evidence.[21] The most notable feature of the LXX is the addition of six supplements, Additions A-F. These Additions and other significant changes are surveyed in chap. XIV §4a.

The Alpha Text is a highly variant Greek version. It is very close to the LXX in the Additions and in the ending (viii 39–52, parallel to MT 8:17–10:3); these sections were borrowed from the LXX. Once they are removed (together with a few miscellaneous verses also borrowed from the LXX), there remains an earlier version, the proto-AT, which tells the story of Esther quite differently. The proto-AT is not a revision of the MT, but an independent, collateral version. I discuss it in chap. XIV §2; for full analysis and argumentation see Fox 1990. The AT is nowhere a translation of the MT and has no value in establishing the text of the latter. It does not even help much in establishing the original text of the LXX, since it makes numerous changes, some of them tendentious, in the passages copied from that version.

5. Reading This Book

The Scroll's themes are not the sum of certain statements and symbols; rather, they grow out of the interaction of the story's components in its dramatic progression. Thus I begin with a Commentary that follows the sequence of reading and traces the movement and dynamic shaping of character (chap. II).[22] The Commentary, like the rest of this book (except for the Appendix), requires of the reader no knowledge of Hebrew nor any other technical background. Of course, the translation and interpretation presuppose decisions in philological-textual matters; these are discussed in the Appendix.

Chapters III-V treat matters that pertain to the book as a whole—its historicity, genres, and construction. Chapters VI-XII

---

21. The only place I prefer the LXX reading (though with modification) is 3:7b, and here I recognize that the LXX might have *produced* the right reading rather than *preserving* it. For some sensible remarks about the use and misuse of LXX-Esther, see Wellhausen 1903.
22. Phelan 1989 (passim) shows the importance of narrative progression for character analysis, because progression (rather than, say, binary oppositions) directs the reader's experience and controls thematizing.

describe each character in turn, seeking to offer a picture of each character as a whole. Chapter XIII describes the world they inhabit. Chapter XIV moves to a very different, somewhat more technical, type of literary analysis: a diachronic reading, tracing the growth of the Esther story in three versions and analyzing the changing portrayals of the characters.

Throughout I call upon and react to the views of earlier readers, frequently in footnotes. The footnotes are not extraneous. Their purpose is to help clarify the crucial issue of how we are to read the book of Esther and respond to the persons in it.

6. The Main Thing

The present study addresses a significant aspect of the meaning of the Scroll, but not the most urgent and vital one—its existential bearing on the individual reader. In this matter I cannot speak for you; I cannot even communicate fully my own experience, but I will here attempt to point to it obliquely.

Although I doubt the historicity of the Esther story, and as a critical reader I must make that clear (see chap. III §1), every year at Purim when I hear the Scroll read in the synagogue, I know that it is *true*, whatever the historical accuracy of its details. Indeed, I relive its truth and know its actuality. Almost without an effort of imagination, I feel something of the anxiety that seized the Jews of Persia upon learning of Haman's threat to their lives, and I join in their exhilaration at their deliverance. Except that I do not think "their," but "my."

We are concluding a century blackened by antisemitic horrors. From 1903 to 1906, hundreds of Jews were killed and thousands raped, mutilated, and despoiled in a series of pogroms in southern Russia, particularly around Kishinev and Odessa. These riots were organized by the minister of the interior, V. Plehwe, who, unlike Haman, did not need to deceive his emperor, and were carried out by the bands of the Black Hundreds and deluded peasants, who had been taught to blame the Jews for Russia's self-afflictions. In 1919–1920, the remnants of the hapless Ukrainian nationalist army, along with masses of peasants and opportunists, eased their frustrations by murdering some one hundred thousand of the Jews who came within their grasp. A generation later, the Persecutor of the Jews—now not vizier but supreme leader—no longer had to resort to ruse, but could proceed directly to execute his scheme, with the enthusiastic participation, or at least the criminal complicity, of most of his subjects. One-third of the Jews in the world were wiped out, millions of others tormented beyond telling. Haman's goal, "to slaughter, slay, and destroy all the Jews, young and old," was nearly realized. And other Hamans are always in waiting to revive the attempt.

Although I have not personally faced danger, I, like many Jews, have a sense of narrow, accidental escape: my grandfather left Odessa just before the pogroms, and I happened to be born outside the reach of Nazi power. Too many others whose destinies took a slightly different turn did not escape. The Haman legend has pursued us through history as an ongoing potential. Thus I know the sense of precariousness that impelled Esther's author to insist on the inner powers of a vulnerable people but also—somewhat irrationally—on the certainty of their deliverance.

As the annual reading of the Esther Scroll comes to an end, I breathe a sigh of relief, but this expresses a prayer more than a certitude, for the resolution of the crisis is less believable than its onset. Still, the dramatic intensity of the tale propels us forward from the danger to the deliverance with such momentum that we find ourselves accepting the truth of the latter as well. The literary force of the narrative thus helps us believe, or at least affirm, that "relief and deliverance will arise for the Jews"—even when God is hidden, as he seems to be in the Esther story, and as he has been so often, so inexplicably, so unforgivably, throughout history.

CHAPTER II

COMMENTARY

Preliminary Remarks

To help the reader follow the sequence of events, I date each scene, and, when possible, locate the time of day it took place. Sometimes the author gives a specific date; in other cases, the approximate date can be estimated from hints in the flow of events (see the Excursus on p. 95).

I divide the story into acts, the major clusters of events, as well as scenes, which are segments marked mostly by change of locale. In other words, if this were a play, the curtain would drop and rise to show a shift in time or place.

The Commentary includes a new translation. The translation is fairly literal. It seeks to suggest the rather baroque style of the book (rather than simplifying, as some translations do), and it tries to reflect the quality of the syntax, which is often convoluted (see, for example, 1:1–4; 2:12–13; 9:1–2; and 9:26b-28). I generally maintain the passive constructions in English, because their profusion is part of the book's unusual style, with its courtly, somewhat stiff character. The author likes to use Persian words that were undoubtedly foreign sounding to the Hebrew reader. To suggest the stylistic quality of such usages, I have rendered some of them (especially those that did not enter Hebrew and lose their foreign flavor) with French approximations. These French terms have been used in English but are recognizably foreign—just like the Persian usages in the Scroll. The translation also tries to maintain consistency in the rendering of key words that constitute motifs; for example, "feast" for *mišteh*, "law" for *dat* (which often refers more precisely to edicts). I do not, however, aim for strict correspondence.

Act I: 1:1–22. The Deposal of Vashti. i = 1:1–9; ii = 1:10–22

i

(1:1) It happened in the days of Xerxes—the very Xerxes who ruled from India to Nubia, 127 provinces in all—(2) that in those days, in the third

13

year of his reign, as King Xerxes was sitting on his royal throne in the Fortress of Susa, (3) he gave a feast for all his princes and servants, the forces of Persia and Media, with the high aristocracy and the princes of the provinces in his presence, (4) displaying the opulent wealth of his kingdom and the splendid honor of his greatness, for many days—180 in all. (5) And when those days were over, the king gave, for all the people who were to be found in the Fortress of Susa, from grandee to commoner, a seven-day feast in the courtyard in the garden of the king's pavilion. (6) And oh the cloths of white, percaline and violet, bound with cords of linen and purple on silver rods and alabaster pillars, with couches adorned with gold and silver on a mosaic pavement of porphyry and alabaster, mother-of-pearl and dark marble, (7) with the drinks served in vessels of gold and vessels of various sorts, and much royal wine lavished with kingly bounty! (8) And the drinking proceeded according to law, no one setting restrictions, for thus had the king set down for all the palace butlers, to do as each and every man might wish. (9) Likewise Queen Vashti gave a women's feast in King Xerxes' palace.

Xerxes' banquet.
Date: 187 days during year 3 of Xerxes' rule[1]

(**1:1**) In a long, complex opening sentence (vv. 1–4) characteristic of the baroque style of the book, the narrator looks back to the reign of Xerxes in the indefinite past—"in those days." The narrator takes the stance of a later "historian" speaking from the distance of several generations; he will again remind us of this perspective in 9:28.

The biblical name Ahasueros (Hebrew *ăhašweroš*) has been positively identified with the Persian *xšayāršā*, Anglicized (via Greek) as Xerxes.[2] The narrator identifies the Xerxes of this book as the king of a vast empire, covering virtually all the known world. The historical Xerxes—Xerxes I, son of Darius and grandson of Cyrus the Great—who reigned from 485 to 465 B.C.E., did indeed rule from India to Nubia. He was better remembered, however, by his failure to extend his rule westward, when, contrary to all expectations, he was defeated by the Greeks in a series of battles in 485–479 B.C.E. Herodotus, who traveled the East (though not as far as

---

1. Dates, when available, are given by calendric day, month (in lower case roman), and the year of Xerxes' reign, e.g., 13.xii.12.
2. The Greek translation (LXX), however, misunderstood the name as Artaxerxes. Josephus, surprisingly, uses "Xerxes."

Persia proper) and gathered stories some twenty-five years later, has much to say about Xerxes.

Herodotus' portrayal of Xerxes shows him as an occasionally sagacious and principled, but more often arbitrary, tyrannical, and brutal despot. This picture, held by the Greeks generally, is not necessarily contradicted by Xerxes' substantial achievements in war and administration (Olmstead 1948:230–47).

Whatever the historical validity of this portrayal, in the book of Esther we are dealing not with the historical Xerxes I, but with a literary reworking of the king and his empire. Yet this reworking is certainly not a complete fabrication, but is based on memories, traditions, and tales about the actual Xerxes. Thus the commentary will compare the way that the ancient historians portrayed this king.

In the author's view, the Persian empire comprises 127 "provinces." The standard administrative unit in the Persian empire was the satrapy, of which there were in reality only twenty to thirty. If we rely on the historical accuracy of the count, we must make the book's vocabulary conform with that number and understand "province" (*medinah*) as a district within a satrapy, and we must also take the terms "princes of the provinces" (*sarey hammedinot*) and "satraps" (*ăhašdarpenim*) to refer to officials of a lower order. Those adjustments would, however, run counter to the way the terms are used in Esther. The various edicts in the book (3:12; 8:9) are issued to "satraps and governors who are over each and every province [*medinah*]," and if "satraps" (*ăhašdarpenim*) did refer to subordinate governors, then the more important officials, the actual satraps, would be left unmentioned. Daniel (6:2), of Hellenistic date, speaks of 120 *satraps*, using the Persian term (*ăhašdarpenayya'*). The nature of the satrapies had become vague in historical memory, and their number is here greatly inflated.[3]

(1:2) The phrase "in those days" resumes the temporal clause of v. 1 and again points us back to the distant past.

The fortress of Susa was the acropolis, the palace area distinct from the city proper. Susa was the chief of four capitals of ancient Persia, along with Babylon, Ecbatana, and Persepolis. According to Xenophon, a contemporary of Xerxes, Susa was the royal dwelling for three months of spring (*Cyropaedia* VIII 6.22). For a discussion

---

3. 1 Esdras 3:1–2, a passage clearly imitating Est 1:1–3, refers to 127 satrapies.

of the archaeology of Susa and its bearing on the book of Esther, see Moore 1975:71-73.

Merely as a designation of time, the phrase "As King Xerxes was sitting on his royal throne in the Fortress of Susa," meaning "when he was ruling," would be superfluous, since it goes without saying that by the third year of his reign he had already come to rule. Some commentators take the phrase to imply "sitting firm," "being firmly in power" (thus b. Meg. 11b; Bardtke; Dommershausen), but the expression does not in itself bear that connotation. Perhaps the author was aware, and expected his audience to know, that Susa was one of four Persian capitals, in which case the phrase would be understood to mean: during a period when he was dwelling in Susa and ruling from there. Still, the author does not refer to the other cities.

(**1:3**) Xerxes gives a banquet for the nobility. The author displays his knowledge of Persian words by designating the nobility with a word of Persian derivation, *part^emim*.[4]

(**1:4**) Xerxes flaunts his wealth and splendor during a half year of feasting. The length of the feast is legendary hyperbole showing awe of Persian wealth and luxury.[5] The Persian zest for drinking-bouts reached the ears of Herodotus (I 133) as well as our author.

(**1:5**) Xerxes gives a second banquet, this one for the commoners of Susa, lasting only seven days. This takes place outdoors, in the garden surrounding or before the royal pavilion—also the locale for the climax in chapter 7. The whole population of the city would not fit in the garden at once; hence we may think of the feast as a public reception.

Since we will be looking at the author's attitudes toward women, we might note that "the people" refers to the males: the "people's" wives go to Vashti's banquet.

(**1:6-7**) This is the real banquet of interest, since it is the setting for Vashti's deposal. But the description in 1:6-7 applies, as Ibn Ezra recognized, to the first banquet as well. The description in verses 6-7 is in the form of a one-membral sentence of a sort unusual in Hebrew—actually just a long listing of luxurious appurtenances. Striedl (1937:86) says that the short, exclamation-like

---

4. From *fratama*, "first" (Cameron 1958:162, 166, n.17).
5. The 120-day "feasting" of the Assyrian army in Judt 1:16, to which Xerxes' 180-day banquet is sometimes compared, may also be legendary exaggeration, though there the activity seems to be a time of relaxation and eating well rather than an ongoing dinner.

sentence-equivalents reflect the people's wonder. It would be more accurate to say that this is a long exclamation-like sentence that conveys the *narrator's* wonder. The exclamatory listing creates a mass of images that overwhelm the sensory imagination and suggest both a sybaritic delight in opulence and an awareness of its excess.

(**1:8**) The guests are given as much to drink as they wish. The first part of this verse has caused some perplexity, because *'ones* is almost always translated "forced," and if "no one forced" the guests, in what sense was the drinking "according to law"? Some commentators (e.g., Moore, Baldwin) explain that the drinking was according to special prescription for this banquet, contrary to the usual practice whereby the guests at a Persian banquet drank together whenever the king did (based on Xenophon, *Cyropaedia* VIII 8.18), but now they could drink when they pleased. Josephus (XI 188) believes (probably deducing this from Est 1:8) that the king would usually force his guests to drink continuously. Gerleman says that in the Persian court a strictly detailed ceremony determined social forms, and that "no one forced" (the usual translation of *'eyn 'ones*) means that the banquet master exceptionally allowed the guests to behave as they wished. The LXX solves the problem by simply adding a "not" before "law" to show that the banquet was a dissolute one. The word in question should, however, be translated "hindered" or "set restrictions" (see the Appendix). The point is not that no one was forced to drink, but that no one was kept from drinking when and as much as he wished, and that *this* was the king's "law" or edict: to let everyone do as he wished (v. 8b).

The word translated "law" (*dat*) is used throughout the book of Esther in reference to all royal decisions, from simple directives to servants (as here), to the judicial sentence punishing an illegal action (4:11), to imperial edicts allowing genocide. The empire lives in a rule of "law" for every detail of life.

This verse introduces the motif of "will"—of letting people do as they wish. The plot line will proceed by people attempting to impose their will on others, usually with success. For better or worse, this king tends to let people do as they want, sometimes deliberately, sometimes unawares.

(**1:9**) Queen Vashti gives a banquet for the women. Vashti's party—which rates only one sentence, in contrast to the spacious description of Xerxes' banquet—introduces the motif of the queen's banquet, which will become Esther's proving ground. More important, it makes Vashti's refusal more understandable by segregating the sexes during the merrymaking. If Vashti were to come to the king's banquet at his command, she would be the only woman before a mass of men, whereas a call to a banquet where the wives were present would be less offensive; it would, in fact, be proper and expected.

The opening scene is unusually expansive for biblical narrative. Instead of reporting actions and words, the author scans the venue like a cinematographer, moving at a leisurely pace and describing in lavish detail what one present in the palace would have witnessed. This scene and some others in the book of Esther stand in contrast to the Bible's usually scanty use of description, a quality made famous by Auerbach's assertion that biblical narrative is "fraught with background," meaning "the externalization of only so much of the phenomena as is necessary for the purpose of the narrative, all else left in obscurity; the decisive points of the narrative alone are emphasized, what lies between is nonexistent; time and place are undefined and call for interpretation. . . ."[6] Auerbach's statement highlights the peculiarity of parts of Esther—in particular, this scene and 5:9–6:13. The author is employing a new technique, one probably learned from Hellenistic Romance, which tends to elaborate descriptions of palaces and royal banquets.[7]

ii

(1:10) On the seventh day, when the king was lightheaded with wine, he told the seven eunuchs who attended the king—Mehuman, Bizzetha, Harbona, Bigtha and Abagtha, Zethar and Carcas—(11) to bring over Queen Vashti, wearing the royal diadem, so as to display her beauty to the peoples and princes, because she was lovely to look at. (12) But Queen Vashti refused to come at the king's order conveyed by the eunuchs. And the king became very angry and his wrath burned hot within him. (13) And the king said to the experts who understood the times—inasmuch as that was the king's procedure in the presence of all who knew royal and judicial law (14) (those close to him being Carshena, Shethar, Admatha, Tarshish, Meres, Marsena, and Memuchan, the seven princes of Persia and Media,

---

6. *Mimesis* (1968), p. 11. The continuation of the sentence, which speaks of the fragmentary representation of thoughts and feelings in biblical narrative, does describe Esther.
7. Josephus carried this tendency further; see Feldman 1970:149–50.

who had immediate access to the king[8] and who had a pre-eminent position in the kingdom): (15) "In accordance with law, what should be done to Queen Vashti for refusing to obey the command of King Xerxes conveyed by the eunuchs?"

(16) And Memuchan said to the king and the princes: "It is not only the king whom Queen Vashti has offended, but all the princes and all the peoples who are in all the provinces of King Xerxes. (17) For report of the queen's deed will get out to all the women, making them feel contempt for their husbands, for they will say, 'When King Xerxes ordered Queen Vashti brought to him she would not come.' (18) This very day the princesses of Persia and Media, who have heard what the queen said, are saying this to all the princes of the king, and contempt and anger abound! (19) Should it so please the king, let a royal declaration proceed from him, and let it be written into the laws of Persia and Media, so as never to pass away, that Vashti shall come no more before King Xerxes. And let the king give her queenship to another woman who is better than she. (20) And the declaration the king shall make will be heard in all his kingdom—and magnificent it is!—so that all the women will show honor to their husbands, from grandee to commoner."

(21) The idea pleased the king and the princes, and the king did as Memuchan said, (22) and he sent letters to all the king's provinces, to each and every province in its own script, and to each and every people in its own language, to the effect that every man should be ruler in his household and speak the language of his own people.

Vashti's refusal and her expulsion
Date: the second half of year 3 of Xerxes' reign, seventh day of the second feast.

(1:10) While tipsy, the king calls for Vashti to be brought and put on display. The syntactical link between Xerxes' command and his lightheadedness (lit., "when [his] heart was good") shows that the author views the behavior as not fully rational.[9] The king sends seven eunuchs to bring the queen and display her beauty to his guests. The eunuchs are listed by name, as are the seven princes of Persia and Media in 1:14 and Haman's ten sons in 9:7–9. The author shows a predilection for lists of Persian names. Such listings are probably an attempt to give the narrative historical verisimilitude, to convey the impression that the narrator has the historical

8. Lit., "who saw the king's face."
9. As observed in Est. Rab. V 1, where the rabbis expound at length on the evils of drunkenness.

details well in hand. In fact, however, they prove only that the author knew some Persian names, and we cannot even be sure that they are all genuine Persian.[10] Still, the names do give the story some local color.

The eunuchs are more than mere messengers. One would not need seven servants merely to carry a simple message. Also, the repeated description of the message as "conveyed by the eunuchs" (1:12, 15) suggests that the particular mode of conveyance is significant. The command to Vashti to wear the royal crown also adds to the solemnity and pomposity of the invitation. The affair seems to be formalized, with some significance as a state ritual, but this significance is lost to us. Perhaps, however, it is a phony ritual created for the nonce, to show that in this court, everything, even an invitation to the queen, is thick with pomp and circumstance.

"Peoples" here, set in contradistinction to "princes," seems to refer to the commoners.

(1:12) Why did Vashti refuse to come at the king's bidding? Women were not necessarily separated from men at Persian banquets (see Her. IX 110; Neh 2:6); in Her. V 18, Persian ambassadors to Macedonia declare (though perhaps in guile) that Persians are accustomed to invite women to banquets. A later notion did imagine exclusion of women to be Persian custom (Jos. XI 191), and the author of Esther may share this belief, though Dan 5:2 shows that this it was not universal among Jewish writers. Esther chaps. 5 and 7 also have the queen present at a mixed banquet, but that is a small, private gathering. The segregation of the sexes in the banquets of chapter 1 suggests that the author did assume that this was obligatory or proper. If so, Vashti's motive is clearer. The Vashti episode does not, however, require this assumption. A reluctance to display herself to a gathering of bibulous males, whom the author finds ridiculous, is enough to explain her refusal. I will discuss Vashti's motives and the author's evaluation of them in chapter VI.

(1:13–15) Incensed though he is, Xerxes proceeds carefully, assembling his advisers and inquiring in carefully measured terms what should be done "according to law," which, in this context, means proper, established procedure. His concern for the rule of law is suggested by the highly emphatic positioning of the phrase

---

10. Some have been identified (see Haupt 1908, Gehman 1924, Duchesne-Guillemin 1953, and the commentaries), but most remain doubtful.

"according to law." The king too is constrained by Persian law, even in the most private of decisions.

The seven nobles "who saw the king's face" may be a reminiscence of the seven nobles who were allowed to enter the king's quarters unannounced (Her. III 84), although once Darius came to power, there were actually only six men with that privilege. The seven nobles may also be reflect the council of seven nobles that Cyrus the Younger summoned (Xenophon, *Anabasis* VI 4 (Cook 1985:234).

Those who know the "times" are probably all-around experts rather than astrologers. A close equivalent of this phrase, *yod*ᶜ*ey binah la*ᶜ*ittim*, "those who have [lit., know] understanding with respect to the times," is used in 1 Chr 12:33 with reference to members of the tribe of Issachar. The context implies their legitimacy, and the Chronicler would not view astrologers in that way.

(**1:16**) The king had asked, not unreasonably, how the *law* should direct his treatment of Vashti. Memuchan does not base his advice on any existing law but only warns of the consequences of Vashti's behavior. In actuality, the law will be created ad hoc in 1:19. But lack of an existing law to guide his answer does not keep Memuchan from blundering in and, by a ridiculous overreaction, turning a domestic squabble into an *affaire d'état* and a matter of explicit sexual politics.

Memuchan promptly exacerbates the spat by informing Xerxes that female disobedience shows contempt, in other words, that the king himself is an object of his wife's contempt and will soon be a national—which means worldwide—laughingstock. Memuchan claims that the issue is no longer one woman's deed, but the entire web of relationships between husband and wife. As Dommershausen observes, Memuchan speaks in universals: all princes, all [common] people, all women. In Memuchan's frantic misinterpretation, Vashti's act signals a universal crisis, a rebellion against the sexual and social order, a violation of the harmony of every home and marriage. As he sees it, female contempt is always lurking just below the surface, waiting to pop up whenever the opportunity arises. And he is right, but only because insecure men like him make it so, for if a man's "honor" depends on his ability to dominate his wife, then any failure to enforce obedience is tantamount to male disgrace.

(**1:17**) Hearing that Vashti had the gall to defy the king, other women will dare to treat their own husbands similarly. Their husbands will seem contemptible because men can now be disobeyed, and as Memuchan sees it, a man who can be disobeyed is contemptible.

(1:18) All the women in the empire will eventually hear about Vashti's deed (v. 17), but, Memuchan thinks, the trouble will start "this very day," for the women at the banquet, who have heard what Vashti said, can be expected to throw the incident in their husbands' faces, and there will be much contempt (on the women's part) and anger (on the men's). (Memuchan predicts, literally, "enough" contempt and anger, apparently a facetious understatement.)

(1:19) This expert in "royal and judicial law" urges the king to forbid Vashti to do precisely what she had refused to do—to come to the king. (The motif of "coming" to the king will appear throughout the book. In translation the verb *bo'* must sometimes be rendered "go.") Dommershausen thinks that the concept of talion ("eye for eye") stands behind this passage: the author counteracts Vashti's "not coming" by making "not coming" her punishment and by balancing the "contempt" that she has engendered by the enforcement of "honor" for husbands. But the author is not straight-faced in the narration of this foolish decision and does not present Vashti's punishment as a worthy realization of a fundamental ethical principle.

In order to counteract the danger presented by *dᵉbar hammalkah*, "the word of the queen" (v. 17), a *dᵉbar malkut*, literally, "word of kingship," should be issued (v. 19). Memuchan counsels that Vashti be banished by means of an irrevocable Persian law and that her queenship be given to a "better" woman. By "better" he certainly does not refer to beauty, since Vashti was hardly deficient in that regard. Rather, it is submissiveness alone that constitutes wifely virtue for Memuchan and his fellow wise men. Yet no such virtue will be among the qualities tested for in the search for a bride.

The author uses Vashti's title carefully. Until now she was always "Queen Vashti," the title emphasizing the dignity that would be besmirched by the king's order. Now she is simply "Vashti," for Memuchan has already deposed her in his mind; in 2:1 also she lacks the title, for she is in fact no longer queen. The notion that the Persians and Medes could not repeal their own laws, even ad hoc decrees, is an essential presupposition in the biblical book of Esther. It is found elsewhere only in Daniel (6:8, 12, 15). It is not attested in Persian or Greek sources, and it seems an impossible rule for running an empire.

(**1:20**) The phrase "and magnificent it is" refers to Xerxes' kingdom and is incidental courtly flattery.

Memuchan, identifying with all males of all classes, believes that the news of Vashti's banishment will put a scare into all women, who will then give "honor" to their husbands.

(**1:22**) The author introduces the great Persian system of communications, a pony express described by Herodotus (VIII 98) as the fastest means of mortal communication. It will later be used in spreading the murderous document (3:13), the countermeasure (8:9–14), and, presumably, the letters establishing the holiday of Purim (9:20, 29). Here it is put to service in the dissemination of inanity.

The decree is not exactly what Memuchan called for, which was declaration of Vashti's ouster. Instead, the king issues an unenforceable command that every man shall be boss in his own house and shall speak his own people's language. As R. Huna put it, this decree showed Xerxes to be "completely stupid" (Est. Rab. IV 12).[11]

The last phrase of Xerxes' decree seems to reflect the belief that one's national language is something a man would, or should, *want* to speak (this is the understanding of the older interpreters, for example, Rashi and Ibn Ezra; it is affirmed by Gordis 1976:53). Whether or not other peoples in the Persian empire actually shared that feeling, the phrase is indeed a reflex of a Jewish concern for preserving Hebrew as the Jewish vernacular. Nehemiah was furious with Jews who had intermarried, because half of their children did not know Hebrew, but rather spoke *kilšon ʿam weʿam*, "according to the language of each and every people" (Neh 13:24), that is, of whichever people they were among. (Note the similarity to the phrasing used in Est 1:22; 3:12; and 8:9.) The author of Esther frequently emphasizes that all decrees are issued in every language, as if to say that the Persian empire respected ethnic diversity by maintaining the official status of national languages within the empire.

In Act I we enter a world of crude but cheerful ostentation. The fabled king of Persia shows off his wealth and "honor" (does he distinguish them?) by inviting all the men of Susa to share his

---

11. After all, as R. Huna reasoned, this decree was entirely unenforceable. "If a man wants to eat lentils and his wife wants to eat beans, can he force her? Surely she does what she likes."

largess at outrageously long and lavish and somewhat dissolute parties.

The first two scenes, which function as a single dramatic unit (designated "act"), are framed by an ironic inclusio playing on the theme of the royal and masculine will: The great emperor, who rules "from India to Nubia, 127 provinces" (v. 1), declares by imperial edict that every man shall be "ruler in his own household," in other words, have his wife obey him (v. 22),[12] something the king has proved unable to enforce himself. Near the midpoint too is a royal command—a "law" no less—to the butlers "to do as each and every man might wish" (v. 8).

In a period of prosperity and ease, the court is suddenly inflamed by a clash of wills and silly sexual politics. Things start to sour when the emperor, who has his butlers do "as each and every man might wish," cannot bend his wife to his own wishes and finds himself in a massive—and farcical—dilemma. The king and his nobility are the butt of some rather broad irony. The world-ruler banishes a wife he cannot control, only to take on later a new one who controls him completely. The king is so unsure of his authority that he has a fit when it is defied, and then to prove his strength he allows himself to be manipulated into banishing his beautiful wife. The limpness of the king's masculine authority sends his noblemen into a tizzy, for they believe that his failure will undermine their own status. These paper patriarchs need a royal decree to back them up in their quarrels with their wives. They, like the king, are desperate for honor, and they think they can achieve it by decree. What the decree actually achieves is to broadcast to the entire empire the very news they thought so threatening.

The opening act does not at first seem relevant to the ensuing drama. In fact, it is striking for the *absence* of the chief characters and anything else that bears directly on the crucial events to come. To be sure, the opening act does set the stage for salvation by clearing the way for Esther to reach a position from which she can influence the course of events. But this bare fact could have been stated in a verse or two, so we must ask what the expansive opening seeks to achieve beyond conveying this information.

First of all, the opening gives the story a universal framework, situating it in world history, in the heart of world politics. This universal scope is true to the diaspora experience, in which Jews are

---

12. Different words are used for "rule" in vv. 1 and 22.

caught up in the swirl of events of which they are not supposed to be the center and in which their fate is usually incidental to the concerns—often trivial—that drive the great powers.

The opening introduces us specifically to the Persian empire, which has revealed itself from the start to be rife with instability, conspiracy, and conflict. But these conflicts are as yet more puerile than pernicious. Potentate and nobles affirm the rule of law, though the laws they come up with are less than dignified and just. All this is hardly surprising, since the empire is subject to a weak and unsteady despot. Such a king cannot be expected to care about anything besides his own pride and pleasure. Such a world cannot be expected to trouble itself much about a threat to one of its more obscure peoples.

The initial absence of the book's two heroes shows that these particular persons are in a sense not essential to the events to come; others could have filled the same role (Mordecai himself says as much in 4:14). This is a story of a world crisis in which two individuals who happen to be on the scene rise to the occasion. Their initial absence suggests that their ensuing characterization will serve larger purposes.

The opening sets a tone of humor, even farce. The tale does not at the start seem to be of the sort that will report a supreme Jewish national crisis. We encounter a story that spares the time to describe gentile ostentation and folly. As we move into a tale that reports events of utmost gravity, we bring with us the knowledge that not everything and everyone is to be taken with full seriousness. Buffoons rule the empire (if not the domestic roost), and ironies and confusions are rife. As Clines observes, "Without the rather obvious satire of the first chapter we might well be in more doubt over the propriety of ironic readings in the body of the book. Chapter 1 licenses a hermeneutic of suspicion" (p. 33).

In this way, the first act intensifies the impending shock by making the audience lower its guard. Soon our amusement at the display of wealth and the bumptious machismo of the Persian noblemen will clash with, and thus sharpen, our horror, as we see pride, egotism, and royal instability mutate into murderous hatred and sinister schemes against a people absent from the opening act.

For now, however, the world exhibits a certain stability. The first disturbance to the stasis does not seem threatening; it is a phony crisis of little consequence. But in fact it exposes the seeds of danger. It reveals a society easily destabilized. It shows that be-

25

neath the jovial and trivial surface reside some dangerously tender egos. It introduces men whose need for honor can make them provoke the king into setting in motion the inexorable machinery of empire. It shows us people who try to impose their will on others and who identify strength with rigidity, who fear that flexibility proves weakness and who regard obduracy as the essence of law. Rigidity of this sort will place severe barriers before the book's heroes, who will be forced to work around them in a way that Vashti could not or would not.

Act II: 2:1–23. Esther Becomes Queen; Mordecai Uncovers a Plot. i = 2:1–4; ii = 2:5–7; iii = 2:8–11; iv = 2:12–14; v = 2:15–20; vi = 2:21–23

i

(2:1) Some time later, when King Xerxes' wrath had subsided, he thought back on Vashti and what she had done and what had been decreed against her. (2) And the king's young attendants who served him said, "Let there be sought for the king beautiful young virgins, (3) and let the king appoint officials throughout the provinces of his kingdom to gather every beautiful young virgin into the harem at the Fortress of Susa, under the control of Hegai the King's Eunuch, the Keeper of the Women, and let him administer their beauty treatment. (4) And the maiden who pleases the king shall reign in place of Vashti." The idea pleased the king, and thus he did.

The king decides to seek a new queen
Date: not long after year 3 of Xerxes' reign.

(2:1) This scene is set not long after Vashti was deposed, for it takes place "when [the king's] wrath had subsided," and Xerxes does not seem like the sort of person to persist in his anger for very long. He "thinks back" (*zakar*) about Vashti, what she did, and "what had been decreed against her." The passive verb reminds us that this was not his independent decision. In fact, since this sentence paraphrases *his* thoughts, it suggests that he is transferring blame to his advisers—a habit he will manifest again.[13]
    The servants' quick response to Xerxes' "thinking back" shows

---

13. A midrash (Ag. Est.) tells that when Xerxes was told what had happened to Vashti, he was infuriated at his advisers and banished them. (According to another version, he had them executed.)

that the king in some way revealed his thoughts, and that these were of an unhappy sort.[14] After all, he did love her, after a fashion—she was beautiful, the quality he most prized in women—and, in his clumsy way, he did take pride in her. In the ruckus following their spat he had been pushed into taking a step not of his own devising. But now he is trapped in the web of irreversible law: when he thinks of Vashti, he must also recall "what had been decreed against her," making second thoughts out of the question (Clines, p. 11).

(2:2–3) The "king's young attendants who served him" are his personal servants, available night (6:1, 3) as well as day, rather than the noble counselors called upon in chapter 1.

"King's Eunuch" seems to be an official title, rather than merely a description, because it is obvious that these eunuchs are the king's, and there would be no need to recall this fact repeatedly for the sake of description. Similarly, "Keeper of the Eunuchs" and "Keeper of the Concubines" (v. 14) give the appearance of being titles that are naturally joined to the individual's name. The name of the eunuch is here written Hege, a variant of the name Hegai in verse 8.

The counsel of the young advisers, unlike that of the noble "wise men" of chapter 1, at least is reasonable, and they produce it even before the king asks for advice: he should find another queen— a rather obvious idea, but Xerxes tends to rely on others to supply even his obvious thoughts.

According to the servants' plan, "all" the beautiful virgins in the empire will be gathered by officials appointed for this purpose and brought to the seraglio, where they will be given into the care and supervision of Hegai. The only criteria are virginity and beauty. There is no reason to expect that Esther has anything else to offer.

Though the selection of Esther is commonly thought of as a beauty contest, beauty is the stated criterion only for the first stage of the process, and that stage is not a contest—the desirable girls are simply "gathered," with no regard to whether they proposed themselves for the honor, or even whether they were offered by their fathers. The will of the maidens and their families is not a factor. On the other hand, in the selection of the queen from among the beauties we are to imagine a competition, for not only

---

14. Josephus senses, quite rightly, that the king longed for Vashti: "Now, although the king was in love with her and could not bear the separation, he could not, because of the law, be reconciled to her, and so he continued to grieve at not being able to obtain his desire" (XI 195).

is it desirable to be queen (especially when the alternative is a barren life of imprisonment in the discarded concubines' seraglio), but it is also implied that the other women, by contrast with Esther (2:13, 15), are expending efforts to gain the king's favor by asking for unspecified aids to take with them that night.

The actual competition, to take place after a year of beauty treatments, is a *sex* contest, with the winner being whoever can most please the king during her night with him. Nothing but attractiveness to the king and sexual skills will, in this legendary account, determine who will become queen of Persia. In reality, political and familial factors would undoubtedly have played a major role in the selection. According to Herodotus, the queen of Persia had to come from one of seven noble families (III 84). In this story, the women are not even given the dignity of having political or familial significance, not even of having importance as potential mothers of the heir to the throne. They are merely diversions for the king, truly sex objects.

There are many legendary and literary parallels to the assembling of beautiful maidens for a king's pleasure (see especially Bardtke, pp. 295–296), the most famous of which are King Shekriya's brutal use of a new woman each night in the *Arabian Nights* and King David's search for a beautiful bed- (but not sex-) partner in 1 Kgs 1:1–4. The author of Esther has picked up the motif from the latter source; Est 2:2b is verbally dependent on 1 Kgs 1:2a.

ii

(2:5) Now there lived a Jew in the Fortress of Susa, a Benjaminite by the name of Mordecai son of Yair son of Shimei son of Kish, (6) who had been taken into exile from Jerusalem along with the exiles that were exiled with Jehoiachin king of Judah, whom Nebuchadnezzar king of Babylon had taken into exile.
(7) And Mordecai had been raising Hadassah (known also as Esther), his uncle's daughter, for she had no father or mother. Now the maiden was beautiful and lovely to look at. And upon the death of her father and mother, Mordecai had taken her to himself as a daughter.

Mordecai and Esther are introduced

(**2:5**) The sudden introduction of Mordecai and Esther in this biographical notice, coming after the frilly burlesque of the first chapter, is striking for its businesslike character. It anchors the story in Jewish history and provides background for the events to follow.

In the flow of the narrative, this passage sticks out by its parenthetical character (note how v. 8 follows naturally upon v. 4). Although Esther is the subject of events in the subsequent verses, it is Mordecai who is introduced, with Esther mentioned as a pendant to him. But at this point in the story, that is just what she is.

The notice seems to be influenced, not surprisingly, by the introduction to the Saul story in 1 Sam 9:1, with (1) the general mention of the existence of the man; (2) the name; (3) the genealogy; and (4) the Benjaminite lineage (Bardtke). Mordecai is related, though not by direct lineage, to Saul. Kish (1 Sam 9:1–2) was the father of Saul. A Shimei son of Gera (and thus not actually the "son" of Kish), of the clan of Saul, is mentioned in 2 Sam 16:5. Mordecai's intermediate ancestors are not mentioned. It is of course possible that all the names refer to Mordecai's immediate ancestors, but given the conflict with the Agagite, it is more likely that the names are meant to indicate a relationship to Saul, who fought Agag (1 Sam 15).

(2:6) It is debatable whether the clause "who had been taken into exile" refers to Mordecai or to Kish. The natural antecedent is Mordecai, for he is the one being identified here. Moreover, Haman's Agagite ancestry suggests a contrast with the house of Saul, whose father was Kish, making it likely that the Kish mentioned here is the ancient one, rather than an otherwise unknown man of the sixth century B.C.E. But if it is Mordecai who was exiled with Jehoiachin in 597 B.C.E., he would be over 110 years old in Xerxes' time (485–67 B.C.E.), and his cousin Esther too would be very old. The author probably did not make that calculation but was simply vague on chronological details, not bothering to work these out from the biblical sources. A similar confusion about the end of the Babylonian empire and the early years of the Persian empire pervades the book of Daniel.[15]

---

15. According to Dan 5:2, 11, 18, 22, Belshazzar was the son of Nebuchadnezzer; in fact he was the son of Nabonidus and coregent with him until the fall of Babylon. (To harmonize one must explain "father" as "grandfather.") "Darius the Mede," a historically unidentifiable personage, was supposedly the son of Xerxes I (9:1) (Xerxes' father was Darius I Hystaspes; Darius II reigned four generations later, from 423 to 404. "Darius the Mede" was thought to be the conqueror of Babylon (in fact that was Cyrus I—in 539; Xerxes I ascended the throne 53 years later), and "Cyrus the Persian" is considered Darius the Mede's successor (6:29), whereas Cyrus (539–530) preceded Darius I Hystaspes. Such confusion is the result of the distance between the book and the events it relates. For the chronology see the critical commentaries, e.g., Hartman-Di Lella 1978:29–38.

(**2:7**) We are introduced to Esther, who is characterized by brief, general description only, giving no impression of her features. This sparseness is somewhat peculiar after the prolix description of the banquet hall (1:6–7). What is significant here is the fact of Esther's beauty, not its particular form.

Her cousin Mordecai had taken her "as daughter," though as cousins they could have married.[16] Both Jewish principals have foreign names, Mordecai's derived from the Babylonian god Marduk; the name *marduka* is known from Achemenid documents. The name Esther is derived from either the name of the Babylonian goddess Ishtar or the Persian word *stâra*, "star." (Esther additionally has a Hebrew name, Hadassah, meaning "myrtle.") This is not evidence that Mordecai and Esther were Babylonian deities or even that they were devotees of them.[17] Jews in Babylonia sometimes received foreign names (for example, Belteshazzar, Abednego [Dan 1:7]; Sheshbazzar [Ezr 1:8, 11], Shenazzar [1 Chron 3:18], and Zerubbabel [1 Chron 3:17, e.g.].) Jews in Hellenistic times too were often given non-Hebrew names.

In 597, the Babylonians took the upper classes of Jerusalem into exile with King Jehoiachin; in 587, the commoners were taken. Thus the author is implying that Mordecai was of noble stock (Bickerman 1967:209).

The purpose of the notice in 2:5–7 is primarily to introduce Mordecai, and only secondarily Esther. He is situated in the history and genealogy of Israel, whereas she is defined in relation to him. Her patronymic is given later (2:15).

iii

(2:8) And when the king's word and law were announced and many maidens were gathered into the Fortress of Susa and placed into the charge of Hegai, Esther too was taken into the palace and placed into the charge of Hegai, Keeper of the Women. (9) And the maiden pleased him and gained his favor, so that he was quick to give her her cosmetics and her portions of food and to give her the seven most suitable maids from the palace, and he promoted her and her maids to a better position in the harem.

(10) (Now Esther had not revealed who her people and kindred were, for

---

16. According to the LXX and the midrash in b. Meg. 13a, Mordecai did take Esther as his wife; see the note on this verse in the Appendix.
17. Contrary to Lewy 1939a:130–31.

Mordecai had ordered her not to reveal it. (11) And each and every day Mordecai would walk about in front of the harem courtyard to learn about Esther's welfare and what would become of her.)

The maidens are gathered
Date: ix-x.6

The narrator returns to the story line, which was interrupted for the biographical notice in 2:5–7.

(2:8) The Hebrew text, Paton tells us, "contains no hint that Mordecai was unwilling to sacrifice his cousin to his political ambition" (p. 173). There is also no hint that Mordecai had political ambitions or that he was willing to sacrifice his ward to them, or that either one of them considered this a sacrifice. In any case, the royal officers did not consult either of the cousins. The king had sent out officials with orders to gather *all* beautiful virgins. Moreover, the mention of the king's "law"—the Persian word *dat* is used in this verse, as in 1:19—reminds us of the unalterable law of the Persians and suggests that Esther's induction into the harem was an ineluctable fate, which neither Mordecai nor Esther could withstand (Bardtke).

(2:9) Esther pleases Hegai and "gains" or "takes" (*naśaʾ*) kindness (*ḥesed*). This idiom (found only in Esther) holds a suggestion of activeness in "gaining" rather than, as the usual idiom has it, "finding" (*maṣaʾ*) kindness. Gaining kindness is something she is doing, rather than something being done *to* her.[18] Thus she has some social skills, and not only good looks. But clearly she is almost entirely under Hegai's control. The process of the beauty treatment as well as the "portions" of food depend on his good will, his kindness. And "kindness" (*ḥesed*) is only used to describe an attitude of a superior toward an inferior,[19] which, at this point, Esther obviously still is.

Hegai demonstrates his favor by being "quick" to give Esther her cosmetics and portions. It is unclear how this quickness would have expressed itself. Haupt (1908:116) explains Hegai's alacrity as a display of special interest, but the verb (*bahal*) does not have

---

18. Daniel 1:9 phrases the passive reception of kindness theologically: *wayyitten haʾ ĕlohim ʾet daniyyeʾl lǝḥesed* . . . , lit., "And God gave Daniel for kindness . . . , i.e., made him into an object of kindness (with the chief eunuch).
19. See Fox 1973:443–44.

that sense elsewhere. Hegai could not speed up the process, which took twelve months for everyone, but perhaps he started Esther on it early. On the other hand, he could hardly let any of the girls wait long before giving them their "portions" of food.

These portions (*manot*) are meant to enhance the maidens' attractiveness, perhaps by fattening them up (Ibn Ezra). In Dan 1: 8–16, the portions given to the youths in training in the Persian court are supposed to increase beauty, and when Daniel and his friends reject them in favor of kosher food, it is thought miraculous that they continue to flourish. Joseph gives his favored brother Benjamin a portion of food five times greater than that which he gives to the others (Gen 43:34, though there a different word is used: *maśʾet*, as in Est 2:18, rather than *manot*). This is a sign of favor, not an actual benefit, since Benjamin could not eat five times as much as the others. The portions in Esther too probably have a symbolic function; nutrition would not have been neglected for any of the girls.

Hegai also gives Esther "the seven most suitable maids from the palace." As Paton observes, the use of "the" with "seven maids" shows that every contender received seven maids; the addition of "select" or "worthy" shows that Esther received better ones.

(2:10) This verse and the next supply parenthetical background information. The first explains why Esther hid her Jewishness (which will not be revealed until the day she overthrows Haman). We are left to guess at Mordecai's motive. It is not merely to promote Esther's prospects; nothing suggests that her ethnic background would hold her back, especially since the criterion for advancement is success in bed. Mordecai's command to Esther not to reveal her Jewishness shows him planning and waiting, his caution intimating an atmosphere of danger. The source of danger must be antisemitism, for otherwise public knowledge of Esther's Jewishness would not interfere with her usefulness to her people. The danger that will face them is thus not the unpredictable act of a spiteful individual, but a manifestation of an ever-present—but not universal—hostility, for which one must always be prepared.

Paton too believes that antisemitism lurks in the background— and he aligns himself with it: "Wherever they have lived, the Jews have made themselves unpopular by their pride and exclusive habits. . . ." Therefore, he believes, Esther would not have been treated so well if her Jewishness were known. But this kind of antisemitism—a hostility so pervasive that being Jewish prevents

social success, however that is defined—is not what the book portrays. Mordecai does not seem to have been disadvantaged in his
official life in the palace—until Haman turns against him. The inhabitants of Susa react with sympathy to the Jews' fate (3:15; 8:17).
Antisemitism in this story is not an attitude shared by all people,
but an aberration of certain individuals identifiable as "enemies of
the Jews" (9:1).

(2:11) Mordecai is worried about what might become of Esther
and checks up on her every day. Throughout the book he maintains
communication with her, with apparently little difficulty. Many commentators (especially Paton) consider contact between a woman
of the harem and an outside male implausible and think that such
contact, if it were effected, would expose Esther's origins. But the
preservation of the secret is plausible if one pictures the Persian
palace as a large, bustling compound that allows opportunities for
discreet inquiries facilitated by bribes to maids and eunuchs, who
would maintain discretion or hazard loss of future revenue, not to
mention severe punishment, if their actions became known. It also
seems likely, as Haupt rather confidently asserts, that "the officials
in charge of a royal harem pay very little attention to the race and
faith of an odalisque" (1908:117). In any case, Esther is one of
hundreds of concubines (enough to supply the king with a different
woman each night), and in spite of Hegai's favor, it is reasonable to
think of her doing many things unnoticed in the obscurity of the
crowd, at least before she became queen. After that, she would have
to rely on the discretion of her servants.

In scene iii, Esther is taken into the seraglio to be prepared for
the night with Xerxes. Did she want to go?

We may assume that when the virgins "were gathered" there
was no consultation of the maidens' wishes. The verbs used in
speaking of the girls are passive—they "are gathered," she "was
taken to the palace," then "taken" to the king's bed. Nevertheless,
we cannot conclude that the maidens went only under compulsion.[20] We are probably importing a foreign notion if we imagine
the maidens would have had to be forced into the harem, for life in
the palace would seem desirable to most people. (In any case, the
question is not whether these girls were actually forced against their

---

20. A midrash (Ag. Est. 2:8) says that Esther hid herself for four years until she was
discovered and *taken* by force. The midrash adduces the verb "taken" as evidence of compulsion.

will, for they probably never existed, but how the author imagined their participation.) What is significant—and most oppressive—is that their will, whatever it may have been, is of no interest to anyone in the story. They are handed around, from home, to harem, to the king's bed. Their bodies belong to others, so much so that they are not even pictured as being forced. But not only girls were treated this way. Herodotus (III 92) reports that five hundred boys were taken from Babylonia and Assyria each year and castrated for service in the Persian court. Everyone's sexuality, and not only women's, was at the king's disposal. The brutality of the system in this regard was thus not what we recognize as sexism.

Nor is there any hint that Esther in particular was forced into the harem. On the contrary, when Mordecai says to Esther, "And who knows if it was not just for a time like this that you reached royal station?" (4:14), he seems to assume that her "reaching" royal station was something desirable for her personally and that she sees matters likewise. However degrading we may find such herding of women for royal use, the connection with royalty was perceived as a step up in the world for them; it was no small thing to be queen of the Persian empire. Nor does the author (unlike the Jewish interpreters and translators) seem troubled by the intermarriage or the inevitable violation of Esther's Jewish obligations. In contrast to the authors of Daniel (Dan 1:8–16) and Judith (Judt 10:5; 12:2–5), the author of Esther shows no concern for dietary rules and does not even bother to excuse their violation by appeal to extenuating circumstances. There is not even an awareness that Esther's induction into the harem and the queenhood involved sacrifices on her part, albeit justified by the outcome.

iv

(2:12) Now when each maiden's turn came to go to the palace of King Xerxes, after having completed the women's twelve-month regimen (this being their period of cosmetic treatment: six months in myrrh unguent and six months in perfumes and women's cosmetics), (13) the maiden would go to the king in this manner: Everything she asked for would be given her to take with her[21] from the harem to the king's quarters. (14) She would come in the evening and in the morning go back to the harem again, into the charge of Shaashgaz, the King's Eunuch, Keeper of the Concu-

---

21. Lit., "to come with her."

bines. She would not go to the king again unless the king took a liking to her and she was personally summoned.

The beauty treatment

(**2:12**) The summoning of concubines by "turns" recalls Herodotus' remark: "In Persia, a man's wives share his bed in rotation" (III 69).

(**2:13**) When a maiden's turn came to go to the king, she could equip herself with whatever she wished. What could these things be—garments? aphrodisiac perfumes? love potions? The author leaves this to the reader's imagination.

(**2:14**) If the king took a liking to a girl (*ḥapeṣ bah*), she was "personally summoned"—(*niqr°ah b°šem*) literally, "called by name"—and only then extricated from the anonymity of the harem crowd. This does not mean that she was thereby made queen. From 4:11, where Esther says, "But *I* have not been summoned [or "called"] to go to the king these thirty days," shows that "called" (*niqr°ah*) in 2:14 means being summoned to the king for sex. In other words, for the first visit, the maidens went by "turn" (*tor*; 2:15). A woman who pleased the king sexually was thenceforth called personally. A woman was, so to speak, simply a number, until she received an identity of sorts by titillating the jaded monarch's fancy.

Scene iv gives the rules of the beauty treatment and the night with the king. Each maiden would spend six months in myrrh and six in perfumes and other cosmetics—not "applying" them but "*in*" them, the language suggesting a chemical bath to which the maidens' bodies were subjected. (Albright [1974:31] suggests that the spices were applied by fumigation.) After their night with the king, they retired to the seraglio, still, of course, under the supervision of a eunuch, there to live out a plush but pointless imprisonment unless fetched once again. Did the author see it this way?

The massed detail in the description of harem life reveals an oppressively regulated atmosphere: total dependence on the chief eunuch and a regimen devoted to preparation for someone else's pleasure. Promotion depends on "pleasing" those in charge. The harem is, of course, the world of the Persian Empire in fine.

Just what did Esther do on the night she won the queenship of the world-empire? What wiles and devices did the young virgin use to arouse the interest of a king who had the entire sexual resources of the Persian empire at his beck and call? These rather lurid questions are prompted by the text itself. The patient dwelling on the details of the harem, the preparation of the beauties, their visit to the king and their subsequent return to the seraglio where their life will be devoted to preparing and hoping for a new invitation—all this is scarcely justified by demands of plot alone. It is sensuality primarily for its own sake, like the detailed description of the banquet hall and feasting in 1:6–7. But this sensuality, like the burlesque of chapter 1, also softens the mood and puts the reader off-guard, making the coming danger all the more harsh.

My view of the harem scene and the life into which the maidens were inducted has been colored by Mouffle d'Angerville's description of Louis XV's playground, the Deer Park, a description that serves as the powerful epigraph to Norman Mailer's novel of that name:

> The Deer Park, that gorge of innocence and virtue . . . Indeed who can reckon the expense of that band of pimps and madames who were constantly searching all the corners of the kingdom to discover the objects of their investigation; the costs of conveying the girls to their destination; of polishing them, dressing them, perfuming them, and furnishing them with all the means of seduction that art could provide. To this must be added the gratuities presented by those who were not successful in arousing the jaded passions of the sultan but had nonetheless to be paid for their submission, for their discretion, and still more for their being eventually despised.
>
> *Vie privée de Louis XV*

The author of Esther too perceives how women can be used as toys in the sexual games of the powerful, but he does not condemn the harem setup so harshly. He takes it for granted, as he does all the peculiarities of the gentile state. Both are fields of obstacle and danger—but also opportunity—for the Jews who find themselves thrust into them.

v

(2:15) When it came the turn of Esther the daughter of Abihayil the uncle of Mordecai, whom he had taken as a daughter, to go to the king, she asked for nothing other than what Hegai the King's Eunuch, Keeper of the Women, told her to take; so Esther gained the favor of all who saw her. (16) And Esther was taken to King Xerxes in his royal quarters, in the tenth month (the month of Tebeth) in the seventh year of his rule. (17) And the

king loved Esther more than all the other women, and she gained his favor and kindness more than all the other virgins, and he placed the royal crown on her head and set her to reign in place of Vashti.
(18) Then the king gave a great feast—the feast of Esther—for all his princes and servants, and he declared a remission of taxes to the provinces, and he gave out gifts with royal bounty.
(19) And at the time when virgins were brought back again, while Mordecai was sitting in the King's Gate, (20) Esther still did not reveal her kindred and her people, just as Mordecai had commanded her, for Esther obeyed the word of Mordecai just as when she was his ward.

Esther is chosen queen.
Date: ?.x.7

(**2:15**) Esther does not take advantage of the chance to bring anything with her. She does not push matters, but, as always, is compliant and receptive. Perhaps this shows a certain indifference to the outcome. She does not reveal any special eagerness for the queenship. (Similarly, Mordecai will reveal no special eagerness for honor or for the viziership.) But this detail mainly emphasizes her pliancy, which makes everyone who knows her like her.

The motif of the refusal of proffered luxuries in the heathen court appears in Dan 1:8 and Tob 1:10–11 and may be a convention: the rejection of a luxury that is supposed to enhance beauty produces even greater beauty (Gerleman). But the motif is used somewhat differently in the Scroll, for Esther does not reject all beauty aids, but only avoids asking for more than she is offered. Her virtue is not abstinence from heathen luxuries but self-effacing receptivity and passivity.

(**2:16**) Almost every word stresses Esther's passivity in all this. She is "gathered" and "taken" to the seraglio, then "taken" to the strange man in the palace, who, when she pleases him sexually, makes her queen.

(**2:17**) Whereas a girl whom the king "likes" (*ḥapeṣ*) may be summoned for sex, in Esther's case the king fell in "love" (*wayyeʾĕhab*) with her—a stage beyond liking. This "love" can only mean that he enjoyed the night with her, but that is apparently enough for him, and he makes her queen. The Hebrew word for love, *ʾahab*, usually implies a significant emotional bond, but it is sometimes used of feelings far more superficial—Amnon's crude lust for Tamar, for example (2 Sam 13:1). Xerxes' feelings for both Vashti and Esther

37

could hardly amount to more than pride of possession plus sexual arousal.

(2:18) Xerxes holds a feast in Esther's honor. "The feast of Esther," in apposition to the first "feast" in the sentence, seems to be a name given this banquet, which is actually a feast *for* Esther. Again the king shows his generous impulses, granting tax relief (or a relief from forced labor, which amounted to a tax). The author is hinting that when things go well with the Jews, others benefit too.

(2:19) This is a difficult sentence. No explanation is given for a second gathering of maidens (if the sentence is to be understood thus), nor is there any apparent connection between that gathering and Mordecai's "sitting in the King's gate" or his charge to Esther to keep her origins secret. Various explanations have been offered to explain a second gathering (they are summarized by Paton): (1) The king wanted a fresh supply of concubines. (But that would be irrelevant.) (2) The courtiers were jealous of Esther's influence and wanted to find another favorite for the king. (But Esther has no influence at this time—see 4:11). (3) The remark is parenthetical and refers to a time prior to Esther's marriage. (But that too would be irrelevant; moreover, v. 20b shows that Esther was married at the time to which this sentence refers.) (4) "Second" refers to a gathering into the second harem. This is the best explanation. The phrase seems to refer to the stage in the process when the women were moved to the second harem. We should note that whether "second" in verse 14 refers to "women's house" or is adverbial ("a second time"), there *is* a second harem or a second division of the harem, for the women now have a different keeper. In other words: when Esther moved into Shaashgaz's harem, Mordecai being that time in government service . . . (for further discussion see the Appendix on 2:19). To be sure, the women brought back to the harem are no longer virgins, but the application of the term is a minor slip, for the young women as a group are called "virgins," including those who have already slept with the king, as in verse 17, where Esther is compared to "virgins" past as well as present.

When the women return to the harem they are under the supervision of a different eunuch, Shaashgaz, for they are now officially "concubines," having slept with the king.

"Sitting in the King's Gate" means holding a government office in the palace compound (Wehr 1964); the "Gate" refers to the royal court in its entirety (Rüger 1969). As Horowitz observes (1882:62), the fact that the "king's servants" are in "the King's Gate" (3:2), probably indicates that Mordecai is one of them.[22] (The "king's servants" are high officials, included among the nobility at the king's first banquet; see 1:3.) The "King's Gate" refers to the entire palace administrative complex. Mordecai's constant presence in the palace gives him the opportunity to communicate with Esther and to uncover the assassination plot.

(2:20) The fact that Esther kept her origin secret is repeated because her rise to prominence could so easily have given it away.

In scene v, much more time is devoted to describing the process of selection than to Esther's selection and crowning. This takes place some four years after Vashti was deposed, in other words, some one thousand women later. There is a vast crowd in the competition, and Esther could easily have gotten lost in it.

vi

(2:21) In those days, when Mordecai was sitting in the King's Gate, Bigthan and Teresh, two of the King's Eunuchs from the Threshold Guards, became angry at the king and sought to strike out at King Xerxes. (22) But the matter became known to Mordecai, and he informed Queen Esther, and Esther informed the king in Mordecai's name. (23) The matter was investigated and found to be true, and the two [eunuchs] were impaled on stakes.
And this was recorded in the book of the chronicles in the king's presence.

Mordecai discovers a conspiracy
Date: Vague; approximately year 7[23]

(2:22–23) The conflicts of the Persian court have a dark side as well as a funny one, for they may issue in murderous conspiracies. Mordecai learns of one such intrigue and has Esther report it to Xerxes. The verb chosen to refer to the discovery, *wayyiwwada᷃*, "became known," suggests that Mordecai did not simply overhear the conspirators speaking (as LXX [A 12–13] assumes), but somehow learned of it from an unnamed source. Mordecai is alert and knows how to handle himself in his tangled surroundings; he has

---

22. Paton reveals both hostility and ignorance in calling Mordecai "an idler in the King's gate" (p. 188).
23. The discovery of the conspiracy takes place some time shortly after Esther's rise to queenship. The event is well in the past when Xerxes is reminded of it in year 12 (6:2).

connections that allow him to communicate with the queen and to discover secrets. All this is quite mysterious.

Why does Mordecai have Esther rather than a messenger transmit the message to the king? Did he distrust other palace officials, not knowing who was allied with the conspirators? Perhaps he wished to promote her importance in the court. In any case, the procedure shows that Esther is still obedient to her cousin (v. 20). It also suggests a slight shift in their relationship. They are now working together; Mordecai needs her assistance.

Mordecai could easily have informed the authorities about the conspiracy himself. Having Esther relay the information might alert the king to their relationship, though in fact it did not. This may be a slight slip in narrative logic. On the other hand, Esther could pass a message on to the king without tipping him off about her relation to Mordecai. A queen might have various mediated contacts with people besides her relatives. Herodotus' stories of Persia do not depict an absolute sequestration of the royal women.

(2:23) That the matter was recorded "in the king's presence" shows that he was fully aware of it; all the more negligent, then, was his failure to reward Mordecai. Herodotus depicts Persian kings as diligent and generous in rewarding beneficial acts (III 139–41, 153; V 11; IX 107). In fact, he knows of an official list of the "King's Benefactors" in the royal archives (III 140) and reports that these benefactors were called "Orosangs" in Persian (VIII 85). Thucydides, too, testifies to the practice (I 129).

This incident, missing in the proto-AT and probably added by the author of MT-Esther, establishes Mordecai's loyalty before it can be called into question by his violation of the royal decree in 3:3 (Clines 1984:105). As with Joseph, the reward for Mordecai's virtue is delayed, and neither complains. Mordecai does not remind the king of his deed (as he could easily have done through Esther), not even when he might call upon the moral debt to counteract Haman's plot. He is certainly not pushing for personal advancement. He waits, and that silent waiting is itself a statement of faith.

Act II (= chap. 2) is divided into five scenes:

(i) the king decides to seek a new queen

(ii) Mordecai and Esther are introduced

(iii) the maidens are gathered

(iv) the beauty treatment

(v)　Esther is chosen queen

(vi)　Mordecai discovers a conspiracy

These scenes are distinguishable because they take place in different times and places, but in function they constitute a single literary unit whose purpose is to introduce the principals and describe Esther's rise to queenship. The events extend over more than a year—from the decision to choose a new queen, through Esther's twelve-month beauty treatment, to her coronation in x.7, some four years after the banquets of chapter 1.

The overall structure of this act is simple: it moves from the search for Vashti's replacement to the selection of a new queen, then reports a service that Mordecai performed for the king. On a smaller scale, the structure is more convoluted, zigzagging between the story line and various background statements (vv. 5–7, 10, 20, 21–23). The author delays giving background information. He introduces the protagonists only at the moment when Esther is taken to the palace, apparently wishing to bring them into a setting that is already fully developed, rather than having their external setting develop from them outward. In other words, if they had been introduced before the events of chapter 1, we would be waiting for the world to move toward the situation where it needs them. As it stands, the world proceeds by its own principles, and two Jews appear in it suddenly and rather late. We are thus reminded that in the larger scheme of things, they play a modest, instrumental role.

Act III. 3:1–15. Haman's Scheme. i = 3:1–6; ii = 3:7–11; iii = 3:12–15

i

(3:1) Sometime later, King Xerxes promoted Haman son of Hammedatha the Agagite, and advanced him and set his chair above those of all the other princes who were with him. (2) And all the king's servants who were in the King's Gate would bow and prostrate themselves to Haman, for thus the king had commanded on his behalf. Mordecai, however, would neither bow nor prostrate himself.
(3) The king's servants who were in the King's Gate asked Mordecai, "Why do you transgress the king's command?" (4) And as they said this to him day by day, and he would not listen to them, they informed Haman, to see if Mordecai's claims would prevail, for he had informed them that he was a Jew.

41

(5) When Haman saw that Mordecai would not bow down or prostrate himself to him, he was filled with wrath. (6) But he thought it beneath himself to strike out at Mordecai alone, for he had been informed who Mordecai's people were. So Haman sought to destroy all the Jews, Mordecai's people, who were in Xerxes' entire kingdom.

Haman's wrath is aroused.
Date: near the end of year 11[23a]

(3:1) For unstated reasons, Xerxes makes Haman vizier. Haman is a son of Hammedatha (apparently a Persian name) and an Agagite. Agag was king of Amalek in the time of Saul and scion of Israel's bitter enemy, the Amalekites. They had attacked Israel during the desert wandering when the nation was at its weakest, and Amalek was therefore cursed to oblivion (Exod 17:8-16; Num 24:7; Deut 25:17-19). Saul fought Agag but, contrary to the rules of the ban, failed to kill him, whereupon Samuel repudiated Saul and carried out the execution himself (1 Sam 15:8). 1 Chr 4:42-43 states that the last of the Amalekites were killed off in the days of Hezekiah, and they may indeed have disappeared as a nation at about that time. But we do not know the canonical status of Chronicles at the time Esther was written, and it would appear that the author of Esther did not know of that statement or did not apply it to the Esther story. Moreover, 1 Chr 4:43 does not deny the existence of an Amalekite diaspora. For the purposes of the Esther story, the main point is that Haman is an enemy of the Jews by birth, and the enmity between Mordecai and Haman is tribal as well as personal.

(3:2-3) Mordecai is among the king's "servants," that is, the palace officials. The fact that his refusal to bow could at first go unnoticed suggests that he was not in the highest echelons, where he would not escape Haman's attention. The exchange between Mordecai and the other officials has the tone of an argument of equals.

An enmity develops between Mordecai and his superior, Haman, without their exchanging words. All the other officials prostrate themselves to the vizier, but Mordecai will not. Why won't Mordecai bow down to Haman? His motive is not stated. The

---

23a. Mordecai's refusal to bow must have begun with Haman's promotion. It continued "day by day," but not many months could have passed before his fellow officials informed Haman. Haman, for his part, was filled with wrath and would not have waited long before undertaking his scheme in 12.i.12.

author chooses not to give the expected data, as if Mordecai's behavior needs no explanation or excuse. Nevertheless, it is, I believe, possible to fathom his reasons. Several explanations for Mordecai's action have been suggested:

(a) Arrogance. Paton sees Mordecai's refusal to bow as "inexplicable" and "unreasonable" (p. 197); indeed, the genocidal plot was "the consequence of his [Mordecai's] arrogant refusal to bow down to Haman" (p. 213). This possibility is mentioned and rejected by Septuagintal Addition C, which has Mordecai say to God:

> (5) You know all. You know, O Lord, that not in arrogance or in haughtiness or in love of glory did I refrain from prostrating myself to the haughty Haman, (6) for I would have agreed to kiss the soles of his feet for the sake of the safety of Israel. (C 5–6)

Attributing Mordecai's refusal to arrogance is a misreading. It contradicts the book's image of Mordecai as wise, provident, unassuming, and never pursuing personal honor.[24] In any case, whatever distaste Paton (and many other commentators of his ilk) may feel for the Jewish protagonists of the book, the view of Mordecai as arrogant could hardly be the *author's* attitude. Bickerman, too, ascribes the refusal to personal pettiness: after discovering the eunuchs' conspiracy, Mordecai should have been made vizier, and when he was not, he fought for his honor by refusing to recognize Haman's rank (1967:179–80). But there is no reason for Mordecai to expect the viziership as a reward for his deed, and in any case the king's oversight had nothing to do with Mordecai's being Jewish, whereas his Jewishness is apparently his explanation for his refusal to bow (3:4b).

(b) Monotheism. According to Targum Sheni, Rashi, and others, Haman demanded divine homage, which of course Mordecai could not grant. But this is an ad hoc explanation; and it is in any case not credible that a vizier would claim divinity when the king himself did not. Had the king done so, Mordecai would have had to refuse to bow to him too when he became vizier, and we can hardly imagine the king passing over such a refusal. A similar ad hoc explanation is that of Targum Rishon, Midrash Esther Rabba, Ibn Ezra, and others, who imagine that Haman had set up an idol or had one embroidered on his robe. Josephus rather lamely as-

---

24. It would, for that matter, also contradict Paton's (mistaken) perception of Mordecai as an ambitious, opportunistic official eager for advancement.

cribes the refusal to Mordecai's "wisdom and his native law" but does not identify the law.

Mordecai's refusal has been compared with the Greeks' denial of proskynesis to any man, even the Great King of Persia.[25] For the Greeks, proskynesis was a sacral gesture, and they assumed, probably incorrectly, that the Persian king was claiming divinity.[26] But whatever the status of the king (in reality or in the Greek imagination), he would not have bestowed divine status on his vizier.

(c) God's dignity. Even if no violation of monotheism is envisaged, bowing to mortals might be in some cases a slight to God. This seems to be the viewpoint of LXX Addition C, where Mordecai explains (in the continuation of the passage quoted above):

> Rather, I did this so as not to set the honor of man above the honor of God, and I will not prostrate myself to anyone other than you, my Lord, nor will I do this [refraining from prostration to man] in haughtiness (C 7).

But nothing forbids a Jew to bow down to a mortal. Esther prostrates herself to Xerxes in 8:3 (a different verb is used, but the act can hardly be distinguished from prostration). Mordecai was an official ("sitting in the King's Gate") for some time before Haman was promoted, and if he had all along been declining on principle to bow to all humans, his fellow officials would have noticed long ago. And as vizier, Mordecai could hardly avoid bowing to his king.

Not only does Mordecai refuse to prostrate himself, a gesture that might be taken as an expression of personal or religious obeisance. As the tension grows, he will not even rise or tremble before Haman (5:9). Thus it was not the gesture of bowing in itself to which Mordecai objected, but rather something peculiar to the relationship between the two men. After all, we cannot imagine Mordecai scrupling to *rise* before anyone; he could not have always remained seated in everyone's presence. This consideration rules out explanations (b) and (c), while (a) runs contrary to the portrayal of the hero.

(d) Tribal enmity. Mordecai refuses to bow because he will not humble himself before a scion of Israel's archetypal enemy (Ehrlich, Moore, Meinhold, Bardtke). This, I think, is the right explanation.

---

25. Bickerman 1967:220–21; Sachsen-Meiningen 1960:145–47.
26. Sachsen-Meiningen 1960:150–51.

Tribal enmity also explains why Mordecai points out to the other officials that he is a Jew.

(3:3–4) Mordecai is adamant; he maintains his behavior day after day. The other officials are naturally puzzled and perhaps annoyed at Mordecai's peculiar disobedience of the king's command.

The fact that the officials must inform Haman is, as Bardtke notes, a fine narrative touch suggesting Haman's haughtiness. We are to picture him wafting through the crowd seeing only the adulation he is receiving, noticing no one individually, not even the one person who—as everyone else sees—remains unbowed and thus most conspicuous. And we can be assured that Haman does not see this, or he would become obsessed with the slight to his honor and see nothing else (cf. 5:13).

The officials inform Haman to see whether Mordecai's claims (lit., "words") would "prevail" (lit., "stand" or "stand up"). For one's words to "stand" means that they prove valid. Mordecai has been making claims that can be tested. There has been some discussion going on between Mordecai and the other officials, for he has made statements that they want to see tested, and he has also told them that he is Jewish. Thus he is not so arrogant as to place himself above explanation.

It is not immediately apparent how the motive clause "for he had informed them that he was a Jew" gives the reason why "they informed Haman, to see if Mordecai's claims would prevail." It is worthwhile examining this relationship for the light it may throw on the type of argumentation considered valid in this setting and the assumptions underlying that argumentation.

The motive clause might be thought to give the reason why "they informed Haman." However, if that were the intention, we would expect the formulation of the reason to be "for he was a Jew," not "for he had informed them that he was a Jew." Moreover, this interpretation implies that they would not have informed Haman about similar behavior on the part of a non-Jew, but they are bothered by the transgression of the king's command in itself, even before they know the nationality of the violator. Finally, this interpretation implies an antisemitic maliciousness on their part, whereas the officials are not basically hostile to Mordecai or they would have exploited his act immediately in order to bring down upon him the wrath of Haman and the law. Instead, they argue with him "day by day."

More likely, the clause "he had informed them that he was a

45

Jew" gives the reason for the preceding infinitive; in other words, it explains what lay behind their desire "to see if Mordecai's claims would prevail." In that case, Mordecai's declaration of Jewishness was part of the argument he offered to explain and justify his refusal to obey the royal command, and that argument must have been sufficiently plausible that the officials wanted to test it out. The background reasoning must have gone something like this: "I cannot bow to Haman because I am a Jew and he is my ancestral enemy. I must not be forced to violate my ethnic sensibility." The officials assume that it is at least conceivable that an argument from ethnic particularity will prove acceptable, that Mordecai's words *might* "stand" in such a matter. Mordecai, too, expects the fact of his Jewishness to be taken as a comprehensible reason for his refusal to bow to the Agagite. The Persian empire is elsewhere pictured as respecting ethnic diversity (see especially 1:22), so it was not *a priori* impossible for such an argument to have weight. It does not, of course, have weight with Haman. Nevertheless, in the long run, Mordecai's words do prove valid, and he never is forced to violate his Jewish sensibilities by bowing to Haman.

(3:5–6) Now Haman notices that Mordecai is not bowing to him, and he is enraged. His motive is simple and petty: revenge for a personal insult. Haman excels only in the magnitude of his drives. In his arrogance he must do things, however petty, in a grand way, so he decides to exterminate *all* of Mordecai's people in Xerxes' *entire* kingdom. He could not reach beyond the kingdom, which is virtually the world in the purview of the story.

ii

(3:7) In the first month, the month of Nisan, in the twelfth year of King Xerxes, the *pur* (meaning "the lot") was cast in Haman's presence for each day in succession, and for each month, [to annihilate the people of Mordecai in one day. And it fell on the thirteenth day of the month,][27] on the twelfth month, the month of Adar. (8) And Haman said to King Xerxes: "There is a certain people scattered and unassimilated among the peoples in all the provinces of your kingdom whose laws are different from those of every other people and who do not obey the laws of the king. It is not worthwhile for the king to leave them alone. (9) Should it so please the king, let it be written to have them destroyed, and I will pay out 10,000 talents of silver to the executive officers to put in the royal treasuries." (10) Thereupon the king took his signet ring off his finger and gave it to

---

27. This clause, required by the context, is based on the LXX; see the Appendix.

Haman son of Hammedatha the Agagite, persecutor of the Jews. (11) And the king said to Haman, "The silver I grant you,[28] as well as the people, to do with as you please."

Haman gets permission to exterminate the Jews.
Date: ?.i.12

(3:7) At the beginning of year 12, Haman has the lot cast before him. The impersonal construction indicates that others did the casting "before Haman." Haman already has others involved in his plot; these are probably professional diviners.

The MT does not say what he was trying to ascertain; the LXX says that he cast the lot to determine the day to destroy the Jews. This information may have been in the Hebrew as well, for the verse is scarcely meaningful without it. Paton believes that the lot was cast to select the right day for Haman to present his petition to the king. That would, however, set the fatal day itself almost two years in the future, and it is hard to imagine that the man who rushed to the palace in the middle of the night to ask the king to impale Mordecai (6:4) would have the patience to wait that long for revenge. Moreover, if the decree were put in writing one year after the lot casting, the year of the writing would have to be noted in 3:12, but it is not. The awkwardness of the text of 3:7 suggests that originally the day was specified but fell out through copyist error (see the Appendix).

The lot is called *pur*, which is derived from Old Babylonian *pūru*, meaning "lot," hence "fate" (Lewy 1939a:144; 1939b, passim). The author might have thought the word to be Persian or have known it as a loan word in Persian. The festival name Purim is a Hebraized plural of that word. The lot falls on the twelfth month; the decree later composed specifies the thirteenth day (3:13).

The artificiality of the connection between this verse and its context is manifest. The verse prepares the way for the explanation of the name of Purim (9:26) but has no other bearing on the story. It would seem that the name of Purim alone, which may indeed mean "lots," evoked the remark about the (supposedly) Persian name of the lots Haman cast.

(3:8) Haman approaches the king and produces an epitome of antisemitic rhetoric. As Rava says (b. Meg. 13b), "there was never another slanderer so skilled as Haman." He begins with a truth

---

28. Lit., "The silver is given to you."

stated in a way that makes the facts sound sinister, then slides into a half-lie, then into full lies.

Haman speaks of ʿam ʾeḥad, "a certain people." The name of the people is not, contrary to Dommershausen, unimportant and omitted only for "technical reasons of composition." The identification of the people to be destroyed is actually quite important and its repression is significant. Haman omits the name in order to keep the king from thinking in terms of specific persons, such as Mordecai the Jew, lest he recoil from killing known individuals. Haman alludes to the Jews in vague terms, making them anonymous, indefinite, and depersonalized. It is easier to kill an abstraction than a person. Dommershausen also believes that the Jews are so unequivocally characterized that the king must immediately have recognized whom Haman is speaking about. But that is so only if one assumes the accuracy of Haman's description of that "certain people."

ʿam ʾeḥad can also be translated "one people." Haman chooses phraseology that insinuates: Your empire embraces many peoples. One of them (just one; no big deal) is peculiar and dangerous.

They are scattered [mᵉpuzzar] *among the peoples.*[29] This is true and does that people no discredit. The Jews were not the only exiled people dispersed in the former Babylonian empire. But in the context of the accusation, "scattered" insinuates moral disintegration and lack of substance, as well as an insidious ubiquity: this unnamed people is all around you. "Cosmopolitan" is used in a similar double-edged way today, and has often been applied to the Jews in particular, with similarly disparaging connotations.

These people are "unassimilated," "separated" or "segregated" [mᵉporad], *among the peoples,* which is to say that they are kept apart from them socially.[30] This is true insofar as their religion prevents their joining in the gentile religious life and their dietary laws hinder

---

29. On the distinction between *mᵉpuzzar* and *mᵉporad*, see the Appendix.
30. The charge of Jewish *amixia*, "non-mingling," was commonly used by Greco-Roman antisemitic writers. For example, according to Diodorus, Posidonius said that the Jews had made their hatred of humanity into a tradition and had introduced outlandish laws to keep themselves separate from other nations. Pompeius Trogus claimed that the Jews avoided all contact with aliens. Philostratus wrote: "The Jews have long been in revolt not only against the Romans, but against humanity; and a race that has made its own a life apart and irreconcilable, that cannot share with the rest of mankind in the pleasures of the table nor join in their libations of prayers or sacrifices, are separated from ourselves by a greater gulf than divides us from Susa or Bactra in the most distant Indies" (Sevenster 1975:92; see 89–93 and chap. 3, passim).

some forms of social intercourse. But Haman's unqualified statement is a distortion, for the Jews are not thereby isolated. Mordecai's Jewishness does not prevent him from working, and perhaps living, in the palace compound. In fact, his Jewishness is so little an issue that his fellow officials are aware of it only because he informs them.

Rab heard a further insinuation here, perhaps correctly: being dispersed and isolated, the Jews are of little profit to the king (b. Meg. 13b).

This people's laws are different from those of every other people. This is true if "their laws" is understood as designating exclusively Jewish ones. But they do not live by those laws alone. As Persian subjects, "their laws" include those of the state they live in.

Haman insinuates that ethnic diversity is in itself culpable in a multinational empire. This was not the official attitude of the Persian empire, neither in history nor in the book of Esther. Herodotus (I 135) says that the Persians welcomed foreign customs more than any other people. The book of Esther (as well as Nehemiah) shows the empire respecting ethnic diversity. Haman's view is closer to an attitude common in the Hellenistic period, when cultural uniformity became a ruling ideal and occasionally a demand. Antiochus IV, according to 1 Maccabees, forbade all peoples in his realm their ancestral practices and laws on the grounds that "all should become one people, and everyone should give up his particular customs" (1 Mac 1:41). Haman's attitude is similar to one expressed in Hellenistic antisemitic tracts, which continually harp on Jewish distinctiveness as a great evil and an offense to the religious-political unity of the polis.[31]

The Persians were not xenophobic either in history or in the book of Esther, so Haman is not appealing to an established prejudice. Rather, by insinuating that the Jews' distinctiveness is inherently reprehensible and dangerous, he is trying to create a prejudice in the very moment he appeals to it.

Josephus casts Haman's charges in the terminology of Hellenistic antisemitism by having him accuse the Jewish nation of being *amikton* and *asumphulon* ("unsociable," "incompatible").

Jews, too, recognized that their laws distinguished them and caused a certain separation. Josephus (*War* II 488) explains that the Jews clustered in one section of Alexandria "in order that, through mixing less with aliens, they might be free to observe their rules more strictly." Jews believed that their separateness was motivated by their desire to keep the Torah, while antisemites believed it was engendered by hatred for others.

31. See Sevenster 1975, chap. 3.

They do not obey the laws of the king. A shred of truth stands behind this falsehood. If pressed for evidence, Haman could point to Mordecai's refusal to bow to him in accordance with the king's command. (*Dat*, the word translated "law" throughout, can apply even to incidental orders [1:8]; so Mordecai was indeed violating a "law"). It is also true that the Jews will place religious law above royal law when the two clash (this is the theme of the first part of Daniel). But as a generality—as it is meant—Haman's statement is a bald lie. Not every person of every people keeps every law and decree. We have already learned of two violations of "law" much closer to the king—Vashti's and the guards'—and these are by non-Jews. So it is an extreme distortion to single out the Jews as not keeping the king's laws.

In view of these national traits, Haman claims, "it is not worthwhile for the king to let them alone." Not: it will harm you to let them live; but rather: it is not worthwhile to let them be—as if there had to be a particular benefit for the king in a people's existence in order to justify their being *left alone*. The sentence has a peculiar ring. Given Haman's premises, he might logically (though deceitfully) claim that it is harmful to the king to leave them alone, or that it is not worthwhile for the king to give them special benefits. But to assert "it is not worthwhile . . . to leave them alone" is absurd. Yet rhetorically this is more effective than a straightforward exaggeration such as "They are destroying law and order in the empire and undermining the welfare of the peoples," for then Xerxes might start to wonder if that truly is what is going on. (Such gross lies have at times been accepted, but usually they require more preparation than Haman has invested). Haman's statement clouds the lack of true danger in the present situation and the brutal violence of the planned "remedy" with a low-key but twisted locution that would take energy to straighten out, and Xerxes is certainly not about to exert any of that.

Like Memuchan, Haman uses a "reasonable" rhetoric, building a case by a series of arguments that appeal to imperial interests and create an aura of far-reaching danger. In both cases, the speaker plays to the king's laziness by quickly proposing a "solution" (in both cases a written decree), thus relieving the king of the duty to think through issues of consequence (namely, who the queen will be and whether one of his peoples shall exist). The danger Memuchan warned against was a silly thing to worry about, but at least it was an actuality: women *will* disobey their husbands. Haman proceeds with a series of indictments, but he cannot add them up to a substantive danger.

Haman accidentally reveals what the current—and desirable—situation is: being left alone, simply being allowed to be. An aural and visual play on words alludes to the situation to which the Jews will return at the end of the crisis. "To leave alone," להניח (l⁺hanniaḥ), is identical graphically (in the original consonantal script) to the word להניח (l⁺hāniaḥ), "to give rest" or "give respite," and nearly indistinguishable from it in sound. "Respite" is what the Jews gain by battle and what they will celebrate in the festival of Purim (9:17, 18, 22).

(3:9) Only one word in Hebrew—l⁺abbᵉdam, "to have them destroyed"—states the substance of the scheme. Haman slips it in offhandedly, then hurries on to the monetary inducement. He also obscures Xerxes' role with a passive verb in language redolent of bureaucracy: "let it be written to . . . ." Haman does not rely on Xerxes being so actively brutal as to destroy a people in full consciousness of what he is doing. Haman counts rather on the king's laziness and cupidity and allows him to feel that he is not a full accomplice. He need only "let it be written"; Haman will take care of the details.

Haman offers to transmit to the executive officers (perhaps revenue officials) ten thousand talents for deposit in the royal treasury. The bribe reveals—though Xerxes does not see this—that Haman is pushing his own interests, not, as he pretends, the king's. It is possible that the payment was to be understood as compensation for loss of revenue from taxes paid by the Jews or as the equivalent of what the king could have received by selling them into slavery, but there is no indication that Haman had anything so specific in mind. It is probably a simple bribe to tempt the king's greed.

It is hard to translate such sums into modern currencies, but we may gauge its magnitude relative to the state's revenue. According to Herodotus (III 95), the total revenue of the Persian Empire was 14,560 Euboeic talents or nearly 17,000 Babylonian talents (we do not know which measure would apply in our verse).[32] In these

---

32. In Xerxes' time, the huge satrapy of Media was assessed a tribute of 450 talents plus 100,000 sheep and pasturage for 50,000 horses. Other satrapies paid about 200–400 talents annually. The highest payment in the empire was 1,000 from Babylon (Olmstead 1948:291–93). Thus the sum in Haman's offer is fantastic.

terms, Haman's bribe amounted to 58%-68% of the annual revenue of the empire. However reckoned, the vast size of Haman's offer is legendary hyperbole, rather than (as Bardtke thinks) an indicator of Jewish economic prominence.

(3:10) The king gives Haman his ring, thereby granting him full power to issue decrees in this matter. The ring was used in sealing official documents; this Haman may now do on his own. This does not bestow upon him absolute authority in all matters (he must get special permission to kill Mordecai before the pogrom; 6:4).

The phraseology of this verse is taken from Gen 41:42, where the king of Egypt gives his ring to a Hebrew, who will use it to keep people alive. Now, in contrast, a king transfers power to an Agagite, the persecutor of the Jews, who will use it in an attempt to destroy a nation.

"Persecutor of the Jews" is now Haman's title, marking his recognized position in the story; he will be called this again in 8:1; 9:10, and 9:24. The epithet "persecutor of the Jews" may be based on the phrase "persecutors [or adversaries] of Judah" in Isa 11:13.

(3:11) The king first says (literally), "the silver is given to you." He speaks as if he is accepting the money (by right), then magnanimously returning it to Haman. This does not mean that Xerxes really refused the offer. In 4:7 Mordecai mentions "the exact sum of silver" that Haman said he would pay the king, a detail that would have no purpose if the king had refused the offer. Also, in 7:4 Esther says that she and her people were *sold* to destruction. Many commentators have aptly compared Xerxes' refusal to the polite dickering that goes on in Gen 23, where Abraham asks to buy a field and Ephron answers, "I give you the field, and the cave within it I give you" (v. 11), then, after a few more polite exchanges, sets a high price. The technique of polite refusals is standard practice in Middle Eastern markets even today.

Xerxes makes the gesture of turning down the offer. Although the gesture is understood to be false, it is in line with his self-image as munificent (see, for example, 1:7–8; 5:6; 9:12). His generosity is largely a pose, for all his decisions are governed by his concern for his ego.

Xerxes rolls the responsibility entirely on to Haman. Haman must be the doer and decision maker. Xerxes gives him the people to do with them as he, Haman, pleases, then seems to forget about the project, for, although the edict is published in the entire empire, he does not realize what Esther is talking about when she says that she and her people have been given over to destruction (7:5). (To be sure, at that point it has not yet dawned on him that Esther is Jewish, but how common were schemes of genocide in his empire that he need to cast about to identify the perpetrator of such an act?)

Haman presents himself as punctilious in law and procedure; Xerxes has already demonstrated his concern for such matters (1:15). The unnamed nation is to be destroyed for having different laws and for disobeying the king's laws. But he does not discuss punishment for specific violations and is thus himself overriding the rule of law, which must deal with specifics.

In scene ii, Haman builds an argument that proceeds by a series of lies derived from truths. Each statement could be defended, should the king challenge him. Each statement moves further from validity. It is indisputably true that there is one people spread out among the others. It is true that they are separate, but only in some ways, and none of these dangerous to the general welfare. It is true that they have their own laws, or, rather, that they have a set of laws of their own; but these are not *all* the laws they follow. It may be granted that "they"—some of them, or at least one of them—do not obey the king's laws—some of his laws, or at least one of them, at least in certain limited circumstances. Having taken the king step by step up an ever shakier structure, Haman comes to a conclusion that has the tone of restraint but is actually meaningless: it is not "worthwhile for the king to leave them alone." Before the king can ask himself, "Well, what *is* it costing me to leave them alone?," Haman glides into a more convincing argument: a huge sum of money. His murky reasoning need not truly convince the king. It need only allow the king to feel that he has heard arguments that justify taking the bribe.

iii

(3:12) So on the thirteenth day of the first month, the royal scribes were summoned, and it was written in accordance with all that Haman had commanded the king's satraps and the governors who were over each and every province, and the princes of each and every people—to each and every province in its own script and each and every people in its own language. In King Xerxes' name it was written, and it was sealed with the king's signet ring. (13) And letters were sent by means of couriers to all the king's provinces
>to slaughter, slay, and destroy all the Jews, young and old, together with children and women,

on a single day, the thirteenth day of the twelfth month, the month of Adar, with their property as spoil, (14)
with a copy of the edict to be issued as law in each and every province, made public to all the peoples, that they be ready for that day.
(15a) The couriers went forth urgently at the king's command, while the law was also issued in the Fortress of Susa.
(15b) And the king and Haman sat down to feast, while the city of Susa was thrown into dismay.

Haman's decree is issued.
Date: 13.i.12

(**3:12**) Thirteen days after Haman cast lots, he summons the scribes to write out the edict. Though this is not stated, the machinery of annihilation gets under way the day before Passover, the commemoration of the liberation from Egypt. The scribes "were summoned," the edict "was written," the letters "were sent," and so forth. The series of passives gives the impression of an impersonal fate working itself out with a certain mysterious precision (Bardtke).

The edict is "in accordance with all that Haman had commanded"—for now *he* is in charge, and he is issuing the orders. The letter is, strictly speaking, not itself a law, but a record of the command to the regional officials, who are to inform the populace of its contents. Like all Persian laws, this edict is directed to the native princes as well as the imperial officials, and it is issued to all the peoples, in the script and language of each. An empire that tolerates variety and respects the individuality of its subject peoples (and this was indeed a virtue of the historical Persian empire) is about to destroy one of those peoples because of its distinctiveness.

(**3:13**) The tremendous administrative and communicational apparatus of the empire goes into action to spread the edict throughout the 127 provinces. The vehemence of Haman's hatred, controlled during his petition to Xerxes, comes to expression in the series of synonyms—slaughter, slay, destroy—and in the horrifying globality of the list of victims—all the Jews, young and old, children and women. Those gentiles who are inadequately motivated by hatred may be tempted by the final license, to take the Jews' property as spoil.

(**3:15**) The couriers go forth in haste, although Adar is eleven months off. Their speed is in accordance with the practice of the renowned Persian courier system, but it also suggests Haman's eagerness to maintain the momentum of his scheme, now going so well.

54

As the state bureaucracy goes into urgent activity, Haman and Xerxes coolly and callously sit down to feast. For Haman, it is all over but the killing, and he may relax and enjoy his victory. Xerxes, having turned the whole matter over to the vizier, is simply enjoying one of his regular dinners.

The inhabitants of the city of Susa, however, are in dismay. "The city of Susa" is distinct from the Fortress of Susa, the seat of officialdom. We are not told that the fortress was in dismay, and that silence sets it in contrast to the city. This distinction is maintained in chapter 9, where the Jews kill five hundred enemies in the Fortress of Susa (9:6) but only three hundred in the city (9:15), even though the latter must be much larger.

The term "city of Susa" must include the gentiles, and not only the Jewish inhabitants. Thus the world is not overwhelmingly anti-semitic. On the contrary, the generalization in this sentence must mean that the great majority of the inhabitants are genuinely concerned for the fate of the Jews. Paton believes that the inhabitants of Susa would not be much grieved by the destruction of the Jews and hence that the author is ascribing his own emotions to them. We cannot, of course, know what the actual Susans would feel; nor could the author. What is significant is that the author does indeed "ascribe his own emotions" to the gentiles, believing them essentially sympathetic and, moreover, assuming that his readers would find gentile sympathy credible.

Haman's edict in scene iii presumes that a great many people are waiting for the opportunity to destroy the Jews and need only be unleashed. The edict need not convince them to set to the task or explain why the Jews should be destroyed. In this we have hint that the conflict is not between two men alone, or even between two peoples within the empire, but between the Jews and masses of people throughout the empire. Danger on a mass scale is always a reality for the Jews, but until a demagogue gives the hostility free rein, it stays fairly well in the background.

Act III (= chap. 3) is Haman's hour of glory, and that focus determines the structure of the chapter. Seen from Haman's standpoint, the act begins with the king exalting Haman to great honor. It proceeds with a challenge to that honor (one that violates the king's command), continues with the response—a massive, crushing one—to that challenge, and ends with the confirmation of Haman's honor by a congenial dinner with the king.

In Act III, as in Act I (chap. 1), a personal conflict burgeons into an imperial crisis; but while the first crisis was treated as burlesque, the second is treated as danger and potential tragedy. In Act I, an independent-minded woman defies the king and fills him with wrath (1:12). In Act III, an independent-minded Jew defies Haman and fills *him* with wrath (3:5). Within Act III, the focus moves from Mordecai (scene i), to Haman and, secondarily, Xerxes (scene ii), to the entire empire (scene iii).

Act I was the moment of Xerxes' "greatness": he got to display "the splendid honor of his greatness" to his subjects, and he later "proves" his greatness by a victory (as his advisers present it) over his wife. Act II scene v (2:15–20) was Esther's moment of "greatness." She rose from being one of a bevy of beauties to the queenship of the greatest of empires, for the king loved her more than "all the other women" (2:17). Act III scene i (3:1–6) is Haman's moment of "greatness": the king "promotes" him above all the other officials ("promotes" and "greatness" are derived from the same root in Hebrew, *GDL*, "be great," etc.). Haman's greatness seems to be confirmed by his apparent victory and capped off by his banquet with the king himself. In all three cases the greatness is only apparent. In chapter 1, Xerxes proves to be putty in the hands of his advisers and ends up issuing a meaningless decree. In chapter 2, Esther gains a desired position, but it is a rank without substance. For all her favor with the king, she will spend most of her time ignored in the harem. Haman's greatness, attained in chapter 3, will soon turn to dust.

A tremendous, unwieldy, deadly machine has been set in motion, proceeding ineluctably, it would seem, toward disaster. A lone Jewish official, who is the open enemy of his chief (and can thus expect no help from other officials), along with his young cousin, who is sequestered in the harem and largely ignored by her husband, must bring it to a halt.

Act IV.   4:1–17. Esther's Mission. i = 4:1–3; ii = 4:4–9; iii = 4:10–17

i

(4:1) When Mordecai found out all that had happened, he tore his garments and put on sackcloth and ashes. And he went out into the midst of the city and cried out, loud and bitterly. (2) And he came up to the King's Gate but no farther, for it is forbidden to enter within the King's Gate dressed in sackcloth.

(3) And in each and every province, wherever the king's word and his law reached, there was severe grief among the Jews, with fasting and weeping and lamenting, with sackcloth and ashes being spread out for the masses.

Mordecai reacts to the decree.
Date: approximately 13.i.12[33]

(4:1–2) Mordecai learns of all that has happened (the edict had been published in Susa), but he knows much more than that, including details of the private deal between Haman and the king. The author does not say how he discovered these matters. Mordecai has his sources; he seems to be always present, listening and observing. He immediately takes control of matters by going into demonstrative lamentation, wailing, wearing sackcloth, and throwing ashes on himself.

Some commentators have found it necessary to search for the reasons for Mordecai's outburst, and a variety of motives have been put forward (see Moore, p. 47, for a summary). Wildeboer, for example, thinks that Mordecai is reproaching himself for having provoked Haman. But the author never blames Mordecai; nor should the victim feel responsibility for the crime. Ringgren, Haller, and Anderson believe that the lamentation is a way of getting Esther's attention; but Mordecai has no difficulty contacting her and would not need a public display to do so. Gerleman explains Mordecai's act as a legal usage, the presentation of a formal legal complaint (*Klageerhebung*) to demand the intercession of the competent legal authority. But Mordecai does not direct his lament to the king, nor does it get any attention as a legal matter.

Genuine grief and agitation are natural reactions in a man whose people has been threatened with annihilation. It is, after all, the reaction of Jews throughout the empire. At the same time, Mordecai's behavior may have an additional purpose, namely to shock Esther into action. That would explain why he comes to the palace gate to lament, for he expects the message to be carried to Esther, and it would clarify why, as soon as Esther is persuaded to take matters into her own hands, he ends his mourning and returns to

---

33. Mordecai would have learned of the widely publicized decree upon its issuance in Susa (13.i.12) and reacted immediately.

his seat in the King's Gate—an act requiring removal of mourning garments.[34]

(4:3) As the news spreads throughout the empire, Jews everywhere fast and bewail their fate. Fasting is a religious act designed to influence God's will; it is also perceived as a form of prayer (see 2 Sam 12:22). The absence of any reference to a religious motive is curious, as if the outburst of the Jews were a spontaneous overflow of emotion not intended to influence God or to achieve anything. Clearly the absence is deliberate, but what it means is not evident.

In discussing what I have designated as scene i, some commentators (Haller, Ringgren, and Ehrlich, among others) suggest that 4:3 has been dislocated and should be placed after 3:15 (that is where the OL has the substance of 4:3). They consider it more logical for the people as a whole to react first, with Mordecai's response mentioned afterwards as one instance of that reaction. In my view, however, the placement is original and deliberate. Susa receives the edict (3:15), and Mordecai reacts at once (4:1). But communications are not instantaneous, and Jews elsewhere can respond only as the messengers spread the message throughout the empire.

While Mordecai is displaying his grief in one of the most visible spots in the kingdom, and Jews throughout the kingdom are fasting and lamenting, Esther, cloistered in luxury, remains oblivious to the uproar.

ii

(4:4) Esther's maids and eunuchs came and informed her of this, and the queen was deeply shaken. She sent garments to clothe Mordecai and to

---

34. Professor Danna Nolan Fewell, in a private communication, suggests an interesting alternative understanding of Mordecai's action. She says that this scene holds a generally unrecognized element of ambiguity. Mordecai could be going to the gate in sackcloth precisely *because* this is not allowed, in order to make a symbolic statement. If he has not yet gone into the gate, he is threatening to do so. This could easily be interpreted as an act of rebellion, hence the scuttlebutt brings the situation to Esther's attention. She sends Mordecai clothes not merely to improve appearances, but to save his life by keeping him from getting into trouble with the king. This reading, of course, casts more ambiguity on Mordecai while putting Esther's values in a more positive light, suggesting that even at this stage she is not concerned with superficials but is trying to save her cousin's life. It seems to me, however, that the contrast between ʿad lipney, "up to," and ʾel, "into," indicates that the sentence explains why he stopped short of entering the gate, not why he came up to it.

take his sackcloth away from him, but he would not accept them. (5) So Esther summoned Hatach, one of the King's Eunuchs, whom he had put into her service, and commanded him to go to Mordecai in the city square in front of the King's Gate, to find out the what and the wherefore of the matter. (6) And Hatach went to Mordecai at the city square before the King's Gate. (7) And Mordecai informed him of all that had happened to him and of the exact sum of silver that Haman said he would pay into the treasuries of the king for the destruction of the Jews. (8) He also gave him a written copy of the law decreeing their destruction, which had been published in Susa, that he might show it to Esther and inform her of the affair, and also to command her to go to the king and to implore and beseech him on behalf of her people. (9) So Hatach went and told Esther what Mordecai had said.

Mordecai informs Esther of the decree.
Date: approximately 13–14.i.12.

(4:4) A whole delegation of maids and eunuchs come to tell Esther what Mordecai is doing. Since they know that she is Mordecai's relation, they should be aware that she is Jewish (though the author may not have noticed this point). But palace underlings may be privy to much that the king and princes are not.

(4:5) When a simple gift of garments does not suffice, Esther, somewhat belatedly, sends a eunuch to ask Mordecai what he is doing and for what purpose he is doing it. Previously the meaning and cause of Mordecai's behavior does not seem to have mattered to her. If she could have gotten rid of the unpleasantness, that would have been enough. Now she seeks to discover the meaning of certain events. Concurrent with this step, she "commands" Hatach to go to Mordecai. When she sent her servants to Mordecai earlier she must have "commanded" them, but only now is this keyword used in connection with her.

(4:6) The author is careful to keep the spatial relationships clear and near the foreground. Mentioning Hatach's passage to the city square gives us a sense of the spatial separation that both signifies and exacerbates the personal gap that Mordecai and Esther must overcome in establishing communication.

(4:7–8) Mordecai gives Hatach the facts to bring to Esther and gives him a copy of the written decree to show her. Mordecai tells Hatach to go to Esther and command her to approach the king and entreat him for the life of her people. This is the last time that Mordecai will give a command to Esther. But even now he is not merely giving Esther orders; he is using argumentation as well. He sends her the details of events, including the exact amount of Haman's bribe. (Mordecai once again has access to information on the secret affairs of the palace.) He also sends her a copy of the written decree so that she may see for herself just what is happening.

At this point, if not earlier, Hatach must realize that Esther is Jewish. Mordecai and Esther apparently feel that they can rely on him and the other servants to keep the secret and to carry the communication faithfully. Or putting it another way, the author tends to view eunuchs and other palace servitors as friendly: Hegai likes Esther and furthers her chances, Hatach preserves her secret and aids her in communicating with her uncle, and at a crucial moment Harbona comes up with a device for punishing Haman (7:9).

Verse 8 seems to presume that Esther is literate; if she were not, there would be no point in Hatach "showing" her the document (contrast the passive construction in 6:1 meaning "to be read to"). In other words, the author takes it for granted that the reader will assume that a woman could be literate. Whatever the likelihood of this happening in Achemenid Persia, literate women were not uncommon in the Hellenistic world, and that is probably the background for the author's assumptions (see chap. III §2).

Scene ii is narrated from Esther's, not Mordecai's, point of view. The maids *come to* her, and she *sends* garments *to* Mordecai, and Hatach *goes out* to Mordecai. We are, as it were, stationed in the palace with Esther, and go back and forth with *her* servants to learn Mordecai's communications. Esther is moving to center stage.

Esther is dismayed upon learning of Mordecai's acts of mourning. She sends him clothes to replace his mourning garments, as if his outer appearance were the problem. But whatever Mordecai's problem, it does not lie in the way he appears to others and cannot be changed by changing his clothes. Esther should at least inquire about what is wrong. Her attention to superficials exposes her own superficiality.

iii

(10) And Esther spoke to Hatach and commanded him to go to Mordecai [and say]: (11) "All the king's servants and the people of the king's provinces know that for every man or woman who comes unsummoned to the king in the inner court there is but one law—to be put to death—unless

the king extend to him the gold scepter, in which case he may live. But *I* have not been summoned to go to the king these thirty days." (12) And they told Mordecai what Esther had said.

(13) Then Mordecai said to bring Esther this reply: "Do not imagine that you alone of all the Jews will escape in the king's palace. (14) For if you are silent at this time, relief and deliverance will arise for the Jews from another source, but you and your father's house will perish. And who knows if it was not just for a time like this that you reached royal station?"

(15) And Esther said to bring Mordecai this reply: (16) "Go, gather all the Jews who are in Susa, and fast for me. Do not eat or drink for three days, night and day, and I too, with my maids, will fast in this way. And in this condition I will go to the king, contrary to law, and if I perish, I perish." (17) And Mordecai crossed over and did all that Esther had commanded him.

Esther resolves to approach the king.
Date: approximately 14–15.i.12[35]

(**4:11**) Esther does not directly disobey Mordecai, but she does argue the impossibility of compliance (Berg, p. 76). She assumes that the danger to her life is a sufficient argument—sufficient for Mordecai as well as for her—to avoid approaching the king. Her vision is still self-centered, although she has been informed of the massive danger facing the people.

She tells Mordecai that to approach the king unsummoned probably means death. There is a touch of reproach in her words: *everybody* knows this. Certainly the palace employees ("the king's servants") know it, and even the ordinary people of the provinces, who could be least expected to know the rules of the court, are aware of it. She may be peeved at Mordecai for apparent ignorance of what is common knowledge in Susa (as Meinhold suggests). Or she may assume that he shares this common knowledge (he is, after all, an official in the King's Gate) yet perplexingly neglects to take it into consideration when making such a dangerous request.

Gerleman sees Esther's hesitancy as an echo of Moses' demurral in accepting the task God lays on him (Exod 3:11; 4:10, 13; 6:12, 30). This comparison is, however, instructive rather for the contrast it offers: Moses—like Gideon (Judg 6:15), Saul (1 Sam

35. This date assumes that Esther learned of Mordecai's mourning within a day or two. Slower communication than that seems unlikely, especially since no remark is made on the passage of time. All this could have taken place several days later, of course. The 14th is chosen for convenience, to give a sense of the pacing of the narrative for the next four days.

9:21), and Jeremiah (Jer 1:6)—hesitates out of feelings of personal unworthiness, whereas Esther is simply concerned for her personal safety.

To emphasize the danger she would face, Esther comments that she has not been called to the king for a month. In spite of his swell of enthusiasm five years previously, the king does not seem overwhelmed by love now. His apparent absence of ardor for Esther makes it less likely that he will hold out the scepter to her.

Herodotus testifies to a law set down by Dioces the Mede (I 99) and enforced by the Persian monarchs (III 72, 77, 84, 118, 140) forbidding the approach to the king without a summons. It was, however, possible to request an audience. But even if the historical Persian law allowed for this possibility, the Persian law in the book of Esther does not.

(4:13–14) Mordecai replies with a stern description of the alternative: do not imagine that you will escape just because you live in the palace. She might have imagined she could do so because her identity might remain hidden, at least until after 13 Adar. She might also think to escape through the personal protection of the king. After all, the edict did not say that all Jews *must* die, but rather that everyone had the right to kill the Jews, and Esther would hardly have been exposed to the mob. But Mordecai insists that if she avoids approaching the king, she will still be in jeopardy. It is dangerous for her to stay out of the king's presence as well as to enter into it, as Vashti discovered when she was called to him (Clines, p. 35). Esther, however, would be hazarding death, not banishment.

The danger on one side clearly comes from the king, but what is the danger if she chooses silence? Perhaps it is the anger of the providence that set her on the Persian throne for "such a time like this" (Clines, p. 36); perhaps it is the wrath of her kinsmen; or perhaps it is the vindictiveness of Haman, who will continue his campaign beyond 13 Adar if necessary. Mordecai does not state the nature of the danger, and his warning is all the more unsettling for what it hides.

Mordecai calls Esther's family her "father's house," a somewhat strange designation, since her family seems to consist of herself and Mordecai. (We do not know that there were no other family members, but none come into the purview of the story). The phrase may have been chosen as an echo of the narratives in which God punishes an individual by destroying his family along with him (Achan and Korah). Nevertheless, the vagueness of the threat does not in itself constitute a theological statement.

If Esther chooses silence, salvation will come from "another source," lit. "place" (*maqom 'aḥer*). "Another place" does not, contrary to one ancient interpretation, refer to God. The use of *ham-maqom*, "the Place" in rabbinic Hebrew as a designation of God is not comparable. In rabbinic Hebrew, God is called "the Place" because (according to the most likely explanation) he is the place in which the world exists (Genesis Rabba §68). God is the Place par excellence, and it would make no sense to call him "another place." (Even when the term appears without the article, it is a specific epithet and thus semantically definite.) In any case, if God is *another* place, then Esther is herself "a place," meaning that they are on the same plane—two distinct loci of salvation—and that is not conceivable. "Another place" must be simply another human as a source of deliverance.[36]

Mordecai's argument is twofold: a warning—there is no escape in inaction—and an appeal to duty—her surprising good fortune may signal that she has been designated for a special mission.

(**4:16**) Esther accepts the charge laid upon her. But she has not merely been cowed into obedience by Mordecai's authority or threats. She immediately issues commands—to Mordecai in the second person singular, then to the community, through Mordecai, in the second plural. She now behaves as Mordecai's equal and as a leader of the community.

The Jews are to fast three days and nights, and Esther and her maids will do likewise. "Three days, night and day" includes the present day and the day of her visit to the king (5:1), but it is still a harsh fast. It could in fact harm the beauty she will have to utilize; but, like Daniel and his colleagues (Dan 1), Esther puts her trust elsewhere. The text avoids saying where.

This fast stands in contrast to the banquets described throughout the book. It is bracketed by gentile banquets (the royal celebrations in chapter 1 and Haman's premature celebration in 3:15) and Jewish banquets (Esther's dinners in chapters 5 and 7 and the Jews' celebrations in chapter 9).

Esther will go to the king *illegally*, violating the law as Mordecai

---

36. It is noteworthy that the LXX, in spite of its introduction of religious statements, does not turn this phrase into an explicit reference to God, but simply translates "help and shelter will be for the Jews from another place [*allothen*]."

did earlier. She recognizes a higher law, her duty to the community and, possibly, to God.

"And if I perish, I perish," Esther says, echoing the verbal pattern of Jacob's resignation to his fate: "and if I am bereaved, I am bereaved"; Gen 43:14. What is it that finally sways her? Paton believes that Esther "goes, as one would submit to an operation, because there is a chance of escaping death in that way" (p. 226). But does she really believe that death is certain if she refuses to confront the immediate danger? After all, Mordecai's vague warning is no more alarming than the concrete danger from the king's anger.

Mordecai does not merely intimidate Esther. Rather, he reminds her that there is risk in both pans of the balance (Clines, p. 35). She must choose the one that offers a possible benefit. "If I perish, I perish" does not suggest a person seeking an escape route, but (like Jacob) one facing and coming to grips with a danger. The statement recognizes the possibility of failure, yet also expresses the hope—though not certainty—of success.

(4:17) Mordecai, who came to make demands upon Esther, now does as Esther commands—again the keyword "command." Her command corresponds to his own will, but it *is* her order. Their communication has issued in harmony but also in enhanced stature for Esther, who has, without preparation, accepted massive responsibility. Now Mordecai will wait while she alone carries on the mission.

"Crossed over": This seems to mean that Mordecai crossed a river, as suggested by R. Samuel in b. Meg. 15a ('*BR* with no direct object is used of crossing a river in Josh 2:23). The Ab-Kharkha River separated Susa from the fortress. This detail points to a Susan provenience, for the author takes it for granted that the reader will understand what is being crossed.

Act IV might be viewed as a single scene, for it consists of a set of communications between Mordecai and Esther in the same location, with Esther in the seraglio and Mordecai in the square before the palace compound. But a subdivision is justified by the structure of the dialogue between Mordecai and Esther: first, Mordecai's and the Jews' shock (vv. 1–3); second, Mordecai's information and charge to Esther (vv. 4–9); third, Esther's resolution (vv. 10–17).

Clines assigns the objects of communication—the news and written document that Mordecai sends into the palace—a special structural function: they are the physical counterpart of the clothes Esther sent him. But they also stand in contrast to the clothes insofar as the edict cannot be refused—as yet—whereas with the clothes there is a choice (pp. 34–35). I agree that there is an opposition between what Mordecai sends and what Esther sends, but not with respect to freedom of choice. Esther does have a choice, not between edict and counter-edict, but between action and inaction. Esther, whose life so far has been governed by concern for appearances, and who has in fact lived a life of concealment, sends out items that will improve appearances. Mordecai counters by sending in items that give Esther information, appealing to her mind and conscience, and revealing facts that concern her as one of the nation.

Not only are the objects of sending significant; so is the act of sending in itself. The act of sending messages via intermediaries is given more attention than required for simple exchange. Intermediaries were, of course, necessary, but the presence of intermediaries could adequately be implied by short statements such as "and Esther sent to Mordecai" or the like.[37] Instead, the presence of intermediaries is underscored at every step, with sometimes one or even two whole verses devoted to description of the procedure (4:5–6, 10). At each stage the presence of intermediaries is spelled out in detail:

4   Esther's maids and eunuchs come and inform her of Mordecai's behavior.
    She sends garments.
5–6 Esther summons Hatach, one of the King's Eunuchs, whom the king had put into her service, and commands him to go to Mordecai, at the city square in front of the King's Gate, to find out the reason for his behavior. Hatach goes to Mordecai at the city square before the King's Gate.
7   Mordecai informs Hatach . . .
8   and also gives him a written copy of the law to show . . . and inform . . . and command . . .
9   Hatach goes and tells Esther what Mordecai has said

---

37. This is the way the narrative is handled in the AT (v 3–12), in what is probably an earlier version of events. In describing a similar exchange of messages (see below), Herodotus simply says that Otanes "sent a message," "sent a second time," "sent a third time" (III 68–69).

10 Esther speaks to Hatach and commands him to go to Mordecai.

12 They [unnamed servants] tell Mordecai what Esther has said.

13 Mordecai says to bring this reply to Esther . . .

15 Esther says to bring this reply to Mordecai . . .

Such an amassing of circumstantial data (note especially vv. 5–6), which are not essential to the progress of the plot, probably has a scenic or psychological function. First of all, the details point to the cumbersome mechanics of the cousins' communication. As time moves on toward disaster, Mordecai must wait before every sending and receiving while educating his sheltered ex-ward in her higher duties and convincing her to transgress a law at risk to her life. He must do this at a distance, through messages conveyed by a man with no personal stake in the crisis. The emphasis on messengers also conveys a sense of Esther's dependency. Virtually a prisoner in the harem, she can speak only through the good offices of servants.[38]

4:13–17 is the turning point in Esther's development. She moves from being a dependent of others (all of them men) to an independent operator who, whatever the objective restrictions on her freedom, will work out her own plans and execute them in order to manipulate one man and break another. These verses are not, however, the turning point of the book (contrary to Berg, p. 110). The crisis lies ahead, tension is still building, and Esther may yet fail. There has been no clear sign presaging Haman's

---

38. Herodotus (III 68–69) has a strikingly similar scene of communication between a man and his daughter in the harem. One Otanes, a Persian nobleman, communicates with his daughter Phaidime by messages to and from her. He is trying to persuade her to find out if the reigning king is an impostor, though to do so would endanger her life. After three exchanges of messages Otanes succeeds in getting her to agree to his request: "Phaidime answered that it would be an extremely risky thing to do; for if her husband proved to have no ears [and was thus the impostor], and she were caught feeling for them, he would be certain to kill her. Nevertheless she was willing to take the risk" (III 69). Note that Otanes does not seem concerned that this type of communication will compromise his secrecy, which he requires even more than Mordecai does. (Another point of resemblance between this scene and the book of Esther is that in I 69 Herodotus notes that in Persia a man's wives sleep with him "in turns" and also says that when Phaidime's "turn" came she "was taken" to the royal bed.)

The scene in Herodotus is probably fictional; its relevance lies in showing what behavior a contemporary writer would consider likely to have occurred in the Persian palace.

downfall. Now hope has emerged. Yet it resides, rather uncertainly, in a young lady whose life has hitherto been devoted to beauty treatments and the royal bed.

Act V. 5:1–8. Esther Goes to the King.

(5:1) On the third day, Esther put on royal garments and stood in the inner courtyard of the palace, in front of the king's quarters, while the king was sitting on his royal throne in the royal quarters opposite the door of the building. (2) As soon as the king saw Queen Esther standing in the court, she gained his favor, and the king extended to Esther the gold scepter he was holding, and Esther approached and touched the end of the scepter.
(3) The king said to her, "What troubles you, Queen Esther, and what is your request? Be it as great as half the kingdom, it shall be granted you."
(4) And Esther said, "Should it so please the king, let the king and Haman come today to the feast which I have prepared for him." (5) And the king said, "Bring Haman quickly to do what Esther has said." So the king and Haman came to the feast Esther had prepared.
(6) At the wine course [39] the king said to Esther: "What is your wish? It shall be granted you! And what is your request? Be it as great as half the kingdom, it shall be fulfilled!" (7) And Esther replied: "My wish and my request . . . [40]
(8) If I have found favor in the king's eyes, and should it please the king to grant my wish and to fulfill my request, let the king and Haman come to the feast I shall prepare for them, and tomorrow I will do as the king has said."

Esther's first audience with the king.
Date: approximately 17.i.12.[41]

(**5:1**) When the time comes to approach the king, Esther arrays herself in *malkut*—regal apparel, not merely attractive clothes. Perhaps she wishes to remind Xerxes of the royal dignity he conferred upon her, for an affront to her royalty is an insult to his. But additionally, these clothes are appropriate to the stature, and not merely the station, she is gaining. The word translated "royal garments," *malkut*, literally means "royalty"—Esther puts on "royalty." Though

---

39. Lit., "the feast of wine," apparently a special course at the end of the meal when wine was served.
40. The ellipsis is intended to suggest hesitation, which is conveyed by the incomplete sentence (Haupt 1908:140). Esther begins to state her request, then, it appears, falters or pauses.
41. This assumes that Esther was commissioned on 14.i.

"garments" is implied by the verb "to clothe oneself," the choice of the word *malkut* without a qualifier hints at a comparison of her royal status to Xerxes' (Berg, p. 70). Moreover, this is the word Mordecai uses in 4:14 (there translated "royal station") to describe Esther's queenship. Esther's assumption of *malkut* may be her response to Mordecai's challenge (Berg, p. 70.). The royalty is now not only a station but a personal quality.

Esther *stands* before the king, rather than falling down in supplication. Her stance in itself reminds the king, and the reader, of her royal status. She is approaching him as queen of Persia.

(5:2) When the narrator is speaking, Esther's attainment of favor is always described by the idiom "she gained [*naśa'*] favor" (2:9, 15, 17; 5:2). When Esther speaks of herself, she uses the idiom "finding [*maṣa'*] favor" (5:8; 7:3; 8:5). The verb *maṣa'* ("find") in this idiom suggests a less active participation in attainment of favor than does the verb *naśa'* ("take" or "gain"); see the comment on 2:15. When Esther speaks of herself as having "found favor" with the king, she is downplaying her influence by implying greater passivity on her part and more initiative on the king's.

(5:3) The king asks Esther what troubles her. This is the nuance of the idiom he uses, which is, more literally, "What's with you?" (*mah lak*). He realizes that something urgent and troublesome has brought her here at peril to her life.

By calling Esther by her title, "Queen Esther," the king recognizes her royal station. He asks her what she wants and extends a vast, unconditional promise in advance of her answer. So excessive is his offer that he must not actually be expecting an unusual request. There is a parallel to this offer in Xerxes' behavior as reported by Herodotus. Xerxes offered to give his son's wife Artaynte, with whom Xerxes had become infatuated, whatever she wished ("He told her to ask for anything she fancied as a reward for her favours, and he would assuredly grant it"). Xerxes was distressed when Artaynte took him at his word—not because he did not expect his offer to be taken seriously, but because the particular request would get him in trouble with his wife. This intemperate gesture does not represent a general Persian custom, but a one-time promise made by Xerxes.[42] Herod made a similar offer to

---

42. Herodotus also mentions Amestris's request, on Xerxes' birthday, that he give into her power a woman who had aroused her anger (IX 111). This story is sometimes considered a parallel to the Esther story, but it only shows a king giving in to his wife's nagging, not a custom that would require the king to grant whatever was asked of him on certain occasions.

Salome and was likewise forced into an action he disliked (Mark 6:23). In contrast to these parallels, which are often noted in the commentaries, Esther does not come up with a difficult request, nor does she take Xerxes at his word and rely on his promise as an adequate guarantee. Instead, she proceeds to create a situation that will secure her goal independently of this promise.

(**5:4**) Esther responds by a preliminary request, asking the king and Haman to a banquet that very day. This is not the request that the king had invited; nor does that come in v. 7. When Esther finally does answer the king's query (in 7:3), she will identify her "wish" and "request" in those very terms.

She speaks of the banquet she has prepared "for him." The pronoun allows some ambiguity, but logically "him" refers to the king, who is receiving the invitation and who would be the main personage present.

(**5:5**) Xerxes responds with such alacrity that he does not even pause to say yes. He just orders Haman brought quickly so as to do what Esther said. "Esther's word" (*dᵉbar ᵓester*) begins to gain authority.

The author plays on the question of who comes to whom, a theme introduced when Vashti refused to come to the king and was consequently forbidden ever to come to him in the future. Now it is the king who comes to the queen's banquet.

(**5:6**) When it is time to drink wine, Xerxes renews his question and offer. He realizes that Esther's earlier invitation (5:4) was not her real request.

(**5:7–8**) In reply, Esther invites Xerxes and Haman to *another* banquet; *then* she will reveal her request, as the king wants. She says that if she has "found" favor with him and if it pleases the king to grant her wish and to fulfill her request, he should come to dinner with Haman tomorrow as well. (Again, the idiom "finding favor," as opposed to "gaining it," is a touch of humility.) The request she now makes hardly seems to call for such an elaborate, ingratiating buildup. Compared to the introduction she prefixes to this invitation, the introduction to her first invitation, "should it so please the king" (5:4), seems rather offhand. The greater importunity and humility in the request suggest that she is worried about testing the king's patience by postponing her real petition once again (Dommershausen).

Act V is structured in a double tripartite pattern: (a) request, (b) grant of request, (c) offer:

(a) Esther, by her presence, requests an audience and clemency for herself.

(b) Xerxes, by gesture, grants both.

(c) Xerxes offers her whatever she wants.

(a) Esther requests that Xerxes and Haman come to her banquet.

(b) Xerxes grants that request.

(c) Xerxes offers her whatever she wants.

(a) Esther requests that Xerxes and Haman come to another banquet.

This pattern might be expected to lead to a satisfactory completion, for every request is accepted and followed by an offer that goes beyond it. But the expectation is frustrated, for Esther does not divulge her real wish, but only presents interim requests. The tension between form (i.e., the pattern of their discourse) and content (the substance of what Esther actually asks for) keeps the reader in suspense, waiting uneasily for the pattern to resolve itself in the true request and its acceptance.

Esther had been charged to entreat the king to spare her people, but she has not yet done so. Twice it seems she is about to have her wish granted without even having to beg for it, because the king has promised to fulfill her desire even before she has stated it. Instead, Esther twice passes up the opportunity to present her petition. Why does she not come out and say what she wants? The delays, after all, risk spoiling the king's magnanimous mood and increase the danger that Haman will discover Esther's Jewishness and take countermeasures. Especially when Haman hears the queen postpone her request he may well begin to wonder at her strange demeanor.

According to Cazelles (1961:27), the two banquets derive from two different sources. This is dubious, because if each conjectural source had its own Esther-banquet, the denunciation of Haman must have appeared in each, and the two episodes would have appeared to the editor to be versions of the same banquet, so that it would have been most natural to conflate them. Even if there were two such sources,[43] the author (or editor) chose not to do so. Hence he had some reason to report two separate banquets, and we must account for this choice without appeal to hypotheses about the text's origins.

---

43. I argue against this and similar hypotheses in Fox 1991: chap. II, §2.

Esther's puzzling behavior cannot be explained merely by appeal to the author's literary needs. We gain no insight into her actions by claiming that the author needed time to work out Mordecai's victory over Haman and also wanted to magnify the suspense (thus Paton, Dommershausen, Bardtke, Moore, and many others). There would have been ample time for Haman's humiliation before the first banquet, if it had been set on the following day.[44] Nor is the desire for suspense an adequate explanation, for although suspense is undoubtedly created, it could have been produced in countless other ways, some more easily understandable than this; the king, for example, could have been made less accommodating. So we must still ask why *this* way of heightening suspense was chosen. Gerleman, too, explains Esther's procrastination by external factors, explaining it as a reflex of the retarding factors in the Exodus story, where Moses must appear repeatedly before the king. But Moses does not draw matters out on his own initiative, nor is he dilatory in presenting his demands. More fundamentally, whatever the author's literary needs and sources, Esther herself has no interest in plot retardation or creation of suspense in the reader, nor is *she* concerned with modeling her behavior on that of a figure in another story.

We must account for Esther's behavior in terms of *her* world. The author has a notion of what Esther is doing and why and has transformed this notion into the substance of the literary character. Is Esther simply being indecisive or fearful? (This opinion is shared by Gunkel [p. 28], who believes it a "truly female" quality of Esther to delay the decisive moment, and Ibn Ezra, who thinks that she was hesitant until seeing Mordecai's honors, which emboldened her because she took them as a sign of divine favor.) But, as Bardtke observes, if she were merely nervous and wanted to make it easier on herself, she would not have invited Haman to the banquet, thereby forcing a direct confrontation with her enemy.

Esther is planning and maneuvering, and doing so on her own initiative. She does not follow Mordecai's instructions precisely, for he told her simply to go to the king and entreat him on behalf of her people (4:8). As always, her motives must be extracted from her actions. We may first of all conclude that she does not entirely rely on Xerxes' offer. If she had, she would have seized the opportunity to make her appeal. Rather, she treats the offer as a grand

---

44. As it is in the present AT (vi 14). In the AT, this verse is directly borrowed from the LXX (5:4), with a change of "today" to "tomorrow."

gesture that must be converted to action. In the past, Xerxes has shown himself both mercurial and malleable. Once Esther's request is out in the open, Haman and possibly other advisers can be expected to go to work on him, and they might well succeed in making him retract the offer. Their argument would be simple: the laws of the Medes and the Persians cannot be rescinded. This is the rule they are used to playing by, and their interests demand its continued enforcement.

Esther chooses to clash with Haman head-on. Her inclusion of him in the invitation is far from being "psychologically most improbable," as Paton (p. 234) thinks , though it does run counter to the expected impulse, namely the desire to keep one's enemy at a distance when attempting to undermine his position. The rabbis (b. Meg. 15b) recognized the problem and offered numerous solutions, including the suggestions that Esther was giving her enemy bread in accordance with Prov 25:21 (R. Joshua); that her willingness to eat with Haman helped keep her Jewishness secret (R. Judah); and that she wished to make the king and other princes jealous of Haman (R. Eliezer of Modi'in). The best explanations in this discussion are that she was setting a trap for Haman (R. Eleazar); that she wanted him to be at hand for an accusation (R. Jose); that she did not want to give him the opportunity to form a conspiracy (R. Meir); and that Xerxes was an erratic king (R. Gamaliel).[45]

Esther's deliberate inclusion of Haman shows that she has a well-designed plan. She realizes that she must defeat him quickly and must certainly prevent him from parleying with the king (and others) behind her back. She must get events moving so quickly that the momentum will sweep the wishy-washy monarch into action. She may also be seeking to arouse in Xerxes the suspense that the commentators see created in the reader. If the king's curiosity and suspense are tweaked he might be pushed into irreversible action in accordance with Esther's designs. She cannot assume that her husband's impulsiveness alone will result in quick action. He did not, after all, repudiate Vashti in his fit of pique, but rather turned to his advisers and took action only upon hearing their counsel; and such hesitancy could be disastrous in the present case. Esther can, however, steer that impulsiveness in the right direction.

---

45. The discussion ends with the report that Rabbah b. Abbuha later met Elijah, who validated all the reasons given. This conclusion recognizes the complexity of Esther's motives and shows that the rabbis respected her as a planner and tactician, not merely as a tool of Mordecai or an attractive charmer.

To better control the situation, Esther must have both principals before her, so she invites them to a banquet, the setting of so much activity in the Persian court. At this first banquet, she still does not reveal her wish, even though she thereby disobeys the command implicit in the king's renewed query. Her next maneuver is brilliant. She starts to answer—"my wish and my request"—but breaks off and comes out with something other than what the occasion calls for. She delivers this lesser, diversionary request with great flourish ("If I have found favor in the king's eyes, and should it please the king to grant my wish and to fulfill my request . . ."), then concludes with nothing more than an invitation to another dinner (5:8). The king's curiosity must have been piqued by the near-revelation of Esther's request, and he is certainly not going to refuse the invitation. Moreover, as Clines observes (p. 37), by phrasing her invitation as a conditional sentence, Esther is making the king virtually commit himself in advance, signifying by his presence at the second banquet that he has already granted her wish. Yet even while manipulating the king into committing himself to an unstated request, Esther is able to represent her program as a way of doing what the king commanded: "and tomorrow I will do as the king has said" (5:8). The king, Haman, and the reader wait for her to do so.

Act VI.   5:9–6:14. Haman's Humiliation; Mordecai's Exaltation. i = 5:9–14; ii = 6:1–11; iii = 6:12–14

i

(5:9) So Haman went out that day merry and lighthearted. But when he saw Mordecai in the King's Gate, and Mordecai did not rise nor quake because of him, Haman was filled with wrath against Mordecai. (10) But Haman controlled himself, went home, and called for his friends and his wife Zeresh.
(11) And Haman described to them his opulent wealth and his numerous sons, and all the ways in which the king had promoted him and advanced him above all the other princes and servants of the king. (12) "Moreover," Haman said, "Queen Esther invited no one but me, together with the king, to the feast which she prepared, and for tomorrow too I am summoned to her with the king. (13) Yet all this is worthless to me so long as I must see Mordecai the Jew sitting in the gate of the king."
(14) And his wife Zeresh and all his friends said to him, "Have a stake made fifty cubits high and in the morning tell the king to have Mordecai impaled

on it. Then come merry with the king to the feast." The idea pleased Haman, and he prepared the stake.

Haman takes counsel with his wife and friends.
Date: 17.i.12, in the evening or late afternoon

Scene i is framed by Haman's leaving a feast "merrily" at the beginning of the scene and his going to a feast "merrily" at its end.

(5:9) Haman leaves the palace swelled with pride by his invitation to two private banquets with the king and queen. His smug pride soon clashes with pride of another sort—Mordecai's sense of dignity (v. 9). Nevertheless, Haman restrains himself and hides his chagrin (v. 10a).

Not only does Mordecai refuse to bow to Haman, he shows no lesser sign of fear or awe, such as quaking or rising. For the author, Mordecai's refusal to show respect is not (as some commentators feel) stubborn and foolhardy, but a heroic trait, a refusal to accord the wicked man the fear he wants to inspire. Of course, this time Mordecai is endangering only himself if he enrages Haman further, and that danger is rendered insignificant by the doom awaiting him along with the other Jews.

To his wife and advisers, Haman boasts of his numerous sons. Though pride in numerous sons was probably universal in the ancient (as in the modern) Orient, Herodotus (I 136) notes this as a special Persian trait.

It is not only Mordecai's presence that infuriates Haman, but the fact that the Jew is still in the King's Gate, that is, serving among the palace officialdom (Ibn Ezra).

(5:14) Haman's wife and friends advise him to prepare an enormous stake and to get permission for Mordecai's immediate execution. Such speedy vengeance would ease Haman's frustration. It would also advertise his power—displaying the Jew's corpse at a height of some twenty meters—and bolster his wounded pride. This plan would also correct a deficiency in Haman's first scheme, which was that his personal revenge upon Mordecai would be submerged in the global destruction of the Jews.

Haman readily accepts advice formulated in the imperative from his wife as well as from his counselors, reminding us of the ironic but inevitable thwarting of the king's decree that every man shall rule in his own house (1:22).

Note the sequence of events in the advice that Haman's associates give him: Haman should first erect the stake and only afterward tell the king to have Mordecai impaled. They know that Xerxes can be pushed into a hasty decision, and if the stake is in place, Mordecai can be killed before the king has second thoughts.

ii

(6:1) That night the king's sleep forsook him, so he sent for the book of chronicles, the annals. And as they were being read aloud to the king, (2) it was found written that Mordecai had informed on Bigthan and Teresh, two of the King's Eunuchs from the Threshold Guards, who had sought to strike out at King Xerxes. (3) The king asked, "What was done for Mordecai for this by way of honor or promotion?" And the young attendants who served the king answered, "Nothing at all was done for him."
(4) Then the king asked, "Who is in the courtyard?" (Now Haman had come into the outer courtyard of the palace to tell the king to impale Mordecai on the stake he had readied for him.) (5) And the king's attendants answered him, "It is Haman standing in the courtyard," and the king said, "Let him enter."
(6) When Haman entered, the king asked him, "What should be done for the man whom the king desires to honor?" And Haman thought to himself, "Now whom could the king desire to honor more than me?" (7) So Haman answered the king, "The man whom the king desires to honor . . ."[46]
(8) Let royal garments be brought—ones the king has worn—and a horse upon which the king has ridden, and upon whose head the royal crown has been placed. (9) And let the garments and the horse be given to one of the king's princes of the *ancienne noblesse* itself. Have them put the garments on the man the king desires to honor, and have them set him on the horse in the city square and cry out before him: 'Thus shall be done for the man whom the king desires to honor!' "
(10) And the king said to Haman, "Quick! Take the garments and the horse, just as you said, and do this for Mordecai the Jew who sits in the King's Gate. Don't neglect a word of all you have said." (11) So Haman took the garments and the horse and clothed Mordecai and set him on the horse in the city square and cried out before him, "Thus shall be done for the man whom the king desires to honor."

Haman traps himself into honoring Mordecai.
Date: 18.i.12, in early morning[47]

(6:1–2) By coincidence the king could not sleep that night, by coincidence he whiled away the time listening to a reading of the

---

46. The ellipsis is meant to represent the broken syntax in the Hebrew, which suggests a pause in which Haman hastily cogitates on how he should exploit his unexpected opportunity.
47. See 5:14a.

royal annals, and by coincidence the reader hit upon the mention of Mordecai's discovery of the assassination plot. The nearly exact repetition of 2:21 conveys a sense of the reading aloud of the annals (Dommershausen).

(**6:3**) The phrase "the man whom the king desires to honor" is the leitmotif of this scene. The phrase presages not only the honor that Mordecai receives in this chapter but also the status he will attain by the end of the book.

(**6:4**) Xerxes' question, "Who is in the courtyard?," presumes that some highly placed adviser is likely to be around; hence Haman has not appeared before working hours.

(**6:5**) Haman, like Esther (5:1), stands in the inner palace court waiting for an audience with the king.

(**6:6**) Haman (his thoughts again transparent) assumes that he himself must be the man the king wishes to honor. It is, of course, blind pride that leads him to this assumption, but he may also be inspired by what must seem like a fortuitous invitation into the king's chamber in the early morning, at the very moment he was so eager for an audience.

(**6:7**) Haman, answering the king's question, begins a sentence and breaks off, as Esther does in 5:7. Here, however, the anacoluthon conveys not hesitation but eagerness. Haman is fascinated by the phrase, "the man whom the king desires to honor." The break in the syntax suggests that Haman is pausing to savor the phrase, which he applies to himself. In his eagerness, he begins his reply with this phrase rather than with a courtesy formula such as "if it please the king" (Schötz 1933:276). Haman rolls the phrase "the man whom the king desires to honor" around in his mouth four times, beginning and ending his little speech with it. But in the end he will have to use it of Mordecai, and do so loudly and repeatedly (though that use is quoted just once, in v. 11b), and in the city square no less. It is easy to imagine how the words Haman once savored will then fill his mouth with gall.

(**6:8–9**) Haman describes a ceremony that will lavish near-royal dignity on the honoree in the most public of settings. He does not mention wealth or power; those he has already. He craves honor and recognition; those he has too, but his appetite for them is insatiable.

The author clearly models the forms of royal honor on those accorded Joseph (Gen 41:42–43), but the dignities Haman desires are more lavish: instead of Joseph's linen garment and gold

76

necklace, Haman prescribes a garment the king has worn (Joseph also gets the royal signet, but Haman already has this). Instead of Joseph's ride in the viceroy's chariot, Haman wants a ride on the king's horse, with the horse itself bedecked in splendor. Instead of the simple call, "*abrekh*" (an exclamation of obscure derivation), Haman would have himself acclaimed by the cry, "Thus shall be done for the man whom the king desires to honor!" On top of all this, Haman specifies that the man leading the horse be a nobleman— unwittingly making his own rank a qualification for the role that will humiliate him.

Asking for a garment the king has worn may be a genuine Persian touch. According to later Greek historians, the Persian royal robe was thought to possess magical power, in some way conferring royalty on its wearers (Eddy 1961:46–47[48]). Plutarch (*Artaxerxes* 5) reports that one of Artaxerxes' subjects asked for the royal robe; he received it but was allowed only to touch it. Rich apparel was given as a mark of royal favor and special rank among both the Persians (Her. III 84; Xenophon, *Cyropaedia* VIII 2, 8) and the Seleucids (1 Mac 10:20, 62, 89; 11:58).

Some commentators have considered it outlandish for the horse to wear a crown. Others observe that Assyrian reliefs show the king's horses wearing tall, pointed head ornaments. Whether or not this custom actually pertained in Persia, these reliefs show that the notion of a crowned horse is not out of the question. Haman wants each detail of his honoring to bespeak royalty.

(**6:10**) The king now identifies the recipient of honor, calling him "Mordecai the Jew." He does not connect Mordecai's Jewishness with the decree of destruction he authorized. The king had not bothered to find out which people he was consigning to destruction, and in any case he does not seem to recall the incident, as 7:5 implies. His memory is short, as his failure to remember Mordecai's service has already shown.

Xerxes delays mention of Mordecai until after he gives the

---

48. Eddy adduces the Artaynte story (Her. IX 110–111) as evidence that extraordinary powers were invested in the royal robe; but it does not really prove his point. Other cases he mentions are more decisive. In particular Ktesias refers to a vermilion garment that struck an almost religious awe in the Persians. Alexander wore "Median dress" to prove his inherent royalty. The royal robe continued to have some significance for the Seleucid monarchs (1961: 45–46). A "suit of Median clothes" was among the gifts awarded Otanes and his descendants as a sign of their special status (Her. III 84).

orders. He accidentally exacerbates Haman's discomfort by reminding him—twice—that he himself prescribed the forms of honor.

(**6:11**) All the elements of Haman's fantasy except for the horse's crown are repeated in the description of the honoring of Mordecai. The author rubs it in, as it were, savoring Haman's humiliation and Mordecai's reception of royal symbols.

Anderson (p. 860) argues that there is no dialogue between Mordecai and Haman during the ride because the author's interest "centers in plot rather than character." But the silence itself speaks, leaving the impression that nothing was said. Haman gritted his teeth and did what he had to, while Mordecai taciturnly accepted the honor.

The king, in scene ii, intended neither the unusually high honoring of Mordecai nor the humiliation of Haman. Haman's blundering pride brings about both, but they are made possible by the multiple silences in the king and Haman's dialogue. The motif of multiple silence is, as Dommershausen observes, the formative device of this scene's dramatic tension. The name of the honoree is not mentioned until after Haman describes the honors; the fact that the honoree is Haman's enemy and the king's benefactor is unknown to Haman; the conflict between Haman and Mordecai is unknown to Xerxes; and Haman maintains silence about his personal enmity toward Mordecai (Dommershausen, p. 86). Moreover, the farcical quality of the scene derives from these disjointed silences and misapprehensions, with each party speaking out of a conflicting set of assumptions and at cross-purposes. It all resembles the delightfully tangled confusions of Restoration comedy.

iii

(6:12) Then Mordecai returned to the King's Gate, and Haman hastened home in grief, his head covered. (13) And Haman described to his wife Zeresh and all his friends everything that had happened to him. And his advisers[49] and his wife Zeresh said to him, "If Mordecai, before whom you have begun to fall, really is of the Jewish race, you will not overcome him, but will undoubtedly fall before him."

---

49. Lit., "wise men," elsewhere called his "friends."

(14) While they were still speaking with him, the King's Eunuchs arrived and hastened Haman to the feast that Esther had prepared.

Haman takes counsel with his wife and friends.
Date: approximately 18.i.12, in the afternoon

(**6:12**) Nothing is said about Mordecai's reaction to the honors. The sparseness of the description suggests that there was no particular effect. Mordecai simply returns to the King's Gate, which is to say, to his work in the middle echelons of the palace bureaucracy (see comment on 3:2—3).

Haman, in contrast, hurries home, even more despondent than the last time he went home from the palace. He is in mourning (again we are shown Haman's feelings), with his head covered as a sign of misery (see 2 Sam 15:30; Jer 14:3—4). Covering the head was a sign of mourning among the Persians (Curtius IV 10.34; X 5.24). While the signs of mourning do not necessarily indicate mourning for the dead, they do mark the sorts of emotions associated with that situation. Haman is bewailing the death of his honor. All this augurs hope for the Jews, for now their enemy is as wretched as they were earlier (4:3).

(**6:13**) Haman returns home and tells his wife and friends all that happened, hoping, perhaps, for consolation. Haman's advisers, called his "friends" when he addresses them (v. 13a), are called "his wise men" (i.e., his expert advisers) when they address him. They have no more words of friendship, consolation, or advice, but they do offer a wise observation. They and Zeresh tell him that if Mordecai is indeed a Jew, there is no staying his own fall, for Mordecai will prevail. (The "if" of their statement is not a true conditional, as if Mordecai might or might not be Jewish—they know he is [5:13]. Rather it is a rhetorical conditional, whose sense is: "if, as is indeed the case . . . . ")

Elsewhere in the Bible and Apocrypha, wisdom is placed in the mouth of gentiles to show that the truth about Israel and its God is so certain and obvious that even neutral or hostile people recognize it (cf. Num 22—24; Dan 2:46—47; 3:28—33; 4:34; Judt 5:5—21; 2 Mac 9:12—27; 3 Mac 5:31; 6:25—28; 7:6—7).

Even Haman's associates see Jewish victory as a principle of history. Perhaps they are supposed to be aware of oracles prophesying Amalek's defeat by Israel (Exod 17:16; Num 24:20; Deut

25:17−19; 1 Sam 15). This knowledge was not thought to be confined to Jews; it is, after all, included in an oracle of Balaam (Num 24:20). The Targumim expand the gentiles' speech, having them quote Scripture and mention other acts of God in history.

"Falling," as Haman's associates see it, is not the outcome of causally linked events. They do not present Haman's humiliation as the cause of his further decline. It is Mordecai's identity, his Jewishness, that they see as guaranteeing Haman's defeat. "Falling" is a movement with its own dynamic, a trajectory propelled by a force they do not identify.

(6:14) While they are still speaking (their conversation must have been longer than the single sentence quoted in v. 13b), the king's servants come to hurry Haman to the banquet. The verb used here for "hasten," *hibhil*, connotes excitement or agitation. The motif of hurrying runs through Acts V and VI. Haman hurries to the banquet (5:5a), then hurries to honor Mordecai (6:10), then hurries home in misery (6:12) (noted by Gerleman). Only Haman is said to hurry. His hurrying evinces lack of inner certitude and self-assurance. A wise man, such as Mordecai, understands that events must move at their proper speed.

Act VI comprises three scenes:

(i)   5:9−14, the pride that precedes a fall;

(ii) 6:1−11, the fall itself;

(iii) 6:12−14, the interpretation of Haman's fall (v. 14 is transitional).

The core of Act VI is scene ii, in which Haman, befuddled by pride and spleen, brings about his own humiliation. This is framed by two identically structured scenes in which Haman comes home in misery, complains to his wife and friends, and hears their statement. Haman's movements to and from the palace punctuate the act, as do his swings of mood.

The action develops from Haman's perspective. He

(i)   leaves the palace happy,
      goes home miserable,
      speaks with his associates, with an encouraging outcome,

(ii) goes back to the palace hopeful,
      speaks with the king and blunders into humiliation,

80

(iii)   goes home miserable,
        speaks with his associates, with a discouraging outcome,
        and
        is brought back to the palace.

The passivity of the last step—the eunuchs "hastened Haman to the feast Esther had prepared"—is significant. Haman, the skilled manipulator of the king's will and (he hopes) a people's destiny, is no longer in control of of his own life. He is rushed out and taken to a situation that *Esther* has prepared. He has been brought to *her* territory, and the initiative is now with her.

Various commentators apply the proverb about a man falling into the pit he dug for another (Prov 26:27, e.g.). The saying is apt, insofar as Haman does die by the instrument he prepared, but the process the proverb envisages is not precisely what happens in this story, for neither Haman's humiliation in the next chapter nor his death on the stake he prepared for Mordecai was *caused* by the preparation of the stake. It is not a strict causal mechanism, the "deed-result nexus" characteristic of Wisdom thought, that leads to Haman's fall.[50] Chance plays an important role in his humiliation in chapter 6, and human effort brings about his downfall in chapter 7.

Haman is not acting the role of the typical fool of Wisdom Literature (contrary to Talmon [1963:443–47], Gerleman [p. 116] and Dommershausen [pp. 83, 91]. On the image of the fool in Wisdom Literature see von Rad 1972:64–65. See further the discussion below, chap. VIII §3). Dommershausen, for example, says that one of the genre-qualities of 5:9–14 is Wisdom, and that its topic is Haman's pride, or pride itself (p. 83). But the fool's pride is not the center of focus here. Haman is not merely gloating for the sake of feeding his pride, nor is he simply basking in the prideful illusion of security that marks the fool in Wisdom Literature. Haman's boast

---

50. In an influential article, K. Koch (1972 [1955]) argued that there is no concept of retribution ("Vergeltung") in the Hebrew Bible, in the sense of a judicial decision based on predefined norms. Rather, reward and punishment are natural consequences of behavior and inseparable from it (p. 133). The connection between deed and reward or punishment he called the "act-consequence connection" ("Tat-Ergehen-Zusammenhang"). While I do not agree that the "act-consequence connection" is the dominant, let alone exclusive, mechanism of justice in the Hebrew Bible, it is true that many passages, especially in Wisdom Literature, formulate reward and punishment in terms of natural causality. This type of causality operates only occasionally in the events of the Scroll.

is actually part of a doleful self-observation. His point is that however great his wealth, honor, and other possessions may be, his chagrin at seeing Mordecai sitting in the King's Gate ruins his pleasure in his good fortune. It is not just Mordecai's refusal to *show* respect that irks him, but the Jew's very presence in the gate. His withholding the usual signs of respect rubs this in.

Act VI is an episode without practical effect on the progress of events. Haman remains vizier and Mordecai returns to the gate. The significance of this episode is structural: it holds the book's turning point and sets Haman on the way to his destruction. Haman, as his associates recognize, has now *begun* to fall. He is deprived of the royal insignia he had hoped for, and they are given to Mordecai instead. This foreshadows the transfer of vizierial power, which is a derivative of royal power and well symbolized by the wearing of the king's garments. The forward momentum of Haman's scheme has been broken. He is on the way down, Mordecai on the way up.

Act VII. 7:1–10. Esther Defeats Haman.

(7:1) So the king and Haman came to feast with Queen Esther. (2) On the second day too, during the wine course, the king said to Esther: "What is your wish, Queen Esther? It shall be granted you! And what is your request? Be it as great as half the kingdom, it shall be fulfilled!"
(3) Queen Esther replied: "If I have found favor in your eyes, O king, and should it so please the king: as my wish, may I be granted my life; and as my request—my people. (4) For we are sold, I and my people, to be slaughtered, slain, and destroyed. But had we just been sold to be slaves and maidservants, I would have kept silence, for then the adversity would not have justified causing loss to the king."
(5) Then King Xerxes spoke to Queen Esther and said, "Who is the one and where is he, who had the audacity to do this?" (6) And Esther replied, "A man hateful and hostile—this evil Haman here!" And Haman shook in terror before the king and the queen.
(7) And the king arose in his wrath from the wine course and went out to the pavilion garden, while Haman stood to beseech Queen Esther for his life, for he saw that the king was bent on his ruin. (8) When the king returned from the pavilion garden to the hall of the wine feast,[51] Haman had fallen across the couch on which Esther was reclining. And the king said,

---

51. Lit., "the house of the feast of wine," the same structure as the pavilion; cf. 1:5.

"What, would you even ravish the queen right here in the house with me
at home?" At this word from the king's mouth, Haman was humiliated.
(9) Then Harbona, one of the eunuchs, said to the king, "What's more, a
stake is standing at Haman's house—fifty cubits high—which he prepared
for Mordecai, whose word saved the king." And the king said, "Impale him
on it!" (10) So they impaled Haman on the stake that he had prepared for
Mordecai, and the king's wrath subsided.

Haman is undone.
Date: approximately 18.i.12, in the late afternoon or evening

(7:2) For the third time Xerxes repeats his offer, which by
now has become ritualized, making Esther's response all the more
shocking.

(7:3) Again Esther opens with a courtly introduction, one
identical to the beginning of 5:8, but she now puts one phrase, "in
your eyes," in the second person, a formulation suggestive of
greater intimacy.

Finally, Esther comes to the point: she asks for her life and for
her people, that is to say, for her and her people's life. She repeats
the main terms of the king's offer—"grant," "wish," "request"—as
well as its bimembrality ("wish" = "my life"; "request" = "my
people") and formulates her petition to match the two parts of the
offer: "wish" and "request" (Dommershausen).

Her imitation of the structure of Xerxes' offer hints at an equation: since "request" is the same as "wish," "my people" is equivalent to "my life" (*napši* means "myself" as well as "my life"). Esther
equates herself with her people, realizing (as proves to be the case)
that the king will be ready to save his wife but will show less vigor
in acting on behalf of her people. She intimates that the two are
one, and to kill her people is to kill her.

The decree has, of course, identified the victims as the Jews,
but the king fails to connect Esther to them, apparently still unaware that she is Jewish. Mordecai's insistence on Esther's conceal-
ing her Jewishness serves the narrative only if the secret has been
maintained up to now.[52] Furthermore, 8:1b shows that the king is
unaware that Esther is related to Mordecai the Jew. Moreover, if

---

52. Some people, of course, do know Esther's identity, since they carried messages
    between her and Mordecai in chapter 4. But the harem servants who know
    her like her and may be presumed loyal (2:15).

Haman were aware that Esther was Jewish, he would have been more chary about the banquets with her, and if he is ignorant of this, the king, in his greater isolation, must be no less in the dark.

(**7:4a**) Esther does not mention the Jews yet, for she does not want Xerxes to link himself with the deed. Let the guilt fall entirely on someone else: someone, unbeknownst to the king, had tried to kill his queen and (incidentally, as far as Xerxes is concerned) her people. She underscores the danger to her own life, which is not actually in immediate peril, in order to make the king feel personal injury. She stokes his indignation by saying she has been "sold"—a disgraceful fate that shames her husband no less. The use of the passive "are sold" is important, for Esther does not want to put Xerxes on the defensive, as would of course happen if she had said who had done the selling. She knows she must direct the king's anger outward.

Esther does not name Haman yet, for she seeks to point the king's anger at a nameless perpetrator, before the king starts fretting about harming his vizier and favorite, and before he recalls how the "sale" came about. Once his ire is provoked, Esther will give it a target. After Xerxes' accusatory question in verse 5, there is little he can do but punish Haman, for he himself has defined the deed as an arrogant crime.

Esther cites words from Haman's edict (3:13) to describe the fate in store for her people. The decree was published throughout the kingdom, first of all in Susa, yet even now Xerxes fails to realize just what she is talking about. His surrender of the Jews to Haman was so offhand that an allusion to the edict does not make him think of the act.

(**7:4b**) Instead of going into detail, Esther balances her boldness by a humble demurrer. She lets the king absorb her meaning and stew a moment in uncertainty. She asserts that she would not have complained if she and her people had merely been sold into slavery. In this way she reminds the king that being sold to destruction is worse than being sold into slavery, so that he should feel as degraded by the sale as if his wife had been sold into bondage. But if they had been sold into slavery, she says, she would not have complained, because "then the adversity would not have justified causing loss to the king." The "loss" or "damage" (*nezek*), as I understand it, refers to the financial loss that cancelling the sale would cause to the seller. (Others have understood "loss," usually trans-

84

lated "damage," as referring to the unpleasantness she is causing the king by raising the matter; see the remarks in the Appendix.)

We may paraphrase v. 4b thus: "Please understand that if we had merely been sold into slavery, I would not have asked for a cancellation of the sale, for the misery we would suffer thereby would not have been severe enough to justify causing the king to forfeit the money the sale was supposed to bring him." She thus hints, obliquely, that Xerxes is involved in the deed. While he will not have to confront his guilt, the hint may make him somewhat uneasy and all the more eager to demonstrate his innocence.

In conceding that if slavery were the threatened outcome, "then the adversity would not have justified causing loss to the king," Esther appears to grant that usefulness to the king is a serious consideration that only the weightiest concerns can override. Esther uses the same word as Haman did in speaking of what was "worthwhile" to the monarch in 3:8: šoweh, whose root meaning is "equal." "Commensurate with" might represent the sense common to both verses. Both she and Haman recognize that the king's convenience is the primary factor in his decisions. Esther, unfortunately, cannot appeal to this as easily as Haman could, for the decision she requires is not at all convenient.

On the face of it, Esther's diffidence seems almost craven. Would she really have refrained from speaking out if Haman's scheme had only entailed bondage? Certainly not, for the moral imperative Mordecai taught her would apply in that situation too. Esther's meekness and caution in this passage are tactical, not integral to her personality. She may be forestalling an argument that Haman could raise, namely that the king should consider the "loss" to the royal treasury. At the same time, she is displaying apparent solicitude for a matter very dear to her husband's heart—his wealth. Perhaps most important, she is toning down the assertiveness of her previous sentence by a humble recognition of her own (and, of course, her people's) insignificance in the king's scale of values.

(7:5) King Xerxes speaks to Queen Esther—the use of the title plus the name for both persons reminds the reader that this is a dialogue of "majesties" and that the fancied greatness of the minion Haman is only dumb vanity (Dommershausen).

Xerxes inquires *who* has dared to do such a thing. As a response to 7:4a, his question asks who has done the "selling." Esther will not, of course, answer on those grounds, for the "seller" is Xerxes himself. Rather, she will point to the initiator of the scheme. The king also asks *where* the guilty party is, ironically unaware that he is sitting in the same room.

The king does not ask Esther for details about what happened, though her cryptic statement about being "sold" does not really explain what is going on. Rather, he at once fixes his mind on discovering the guilty party. Xerxes' concern is not for the endangered people, and not even primarily for Esther's safety, but for the royal honor. This has somehow (it does not matter exactly how) been offended, and he wants to know who is to blame. Likewise the king does not ask, now or in the future, *which people* has been consigned to destruction. He may know that from the decree, or he may simply be uninterested in them. Esther will volunteer that information by informing the king of her relation to Mordecai (8:1).

(**7:6**) Against the background of her flowery preamble and meek apology, Esther's denunciation of Haman cracks out in angry staccato:

'ISH TSAR wᵉ'oyEV   a MAN HATEful and HOStile—
haMAN haRAᶜ hazZEH.   THIS WICKed HAMan.

The accusation is built of two phrases of three beats each, with the second phrase punctuated by identical opening syllables. Each word is a blow. We picture Esther pointing an accusing finger at a shocked Haman, who quakes in terror "before the king *and the queen*." She too is dangerous.

(**7:7a**) The king gets up in his wrath and goes out to the garden. We are not told why he does so, but we can grasp the quandary he faces. Can he punish Haman for a plot he himself approved? If he does so, won't he have to admit his own role in the fiasco? Moreover, he has issued an irrevocable law; how then can he rescind it? Clines (p. 15) observes that the king's first instinct is to escape the revelation Esther is forcing upon him. Never very decisive, the king certainly cannot handle this predicament on the spot.

The clause translated "the king was bent on his ruin" is actually passive; literally, "the evil was completed for him from the king" (cf. 1 Sam 20:7, 9; 25:27). This formulation suggests an impersonal working-out of Haman's fate, with the king as the device of this process.

(**7:7b**) Now Haman faces Esther alone. He stands up to beg for his life from Esther, then falls on her couch. Fool that he is, Haman has not only come too near the queen's person, he has also thrown himself *on* her couch. It is a satisfying irony that the proud Agagite, obsessed with a Jew's refusal to bow, now falls groveling before a Jew to plead for his life. The same word for "fall" is used of his predicted downfall before Mordecai in 6:13.

Like Mordecai, Esther ignores her enemy. Some commentators have seen her behavior as cruel. Paton says, "it must be admitted that her character would have been more attractive if she had shown pity toward a fallen foe. . . . Here, as everywhere, [the author] gloats over the destruction of the heathen" (p. 264). Whether or not such pity would indeed be attractive (Haman is hardly contrite), the conflict is not between Haman and Esther, but between Haman and the Jewish people, and mercy is not Esther's to offer. As Moore observes, Haman was a falling, not a fallen, enemy. The archfoe cannot be let off the hook with the battle still ahead.[53]

(7:8) When he returns from the garden, Xerxes sees Haman on the couch and accuses him of attempting to rape his wife, with her husband in the house no less—a double insolence! The personal insult is what enrages Xerxes; he does not deal with the impending genocide. His misunderstanding may be feigned. It is hard to imagine that even one as thickheaded as Xerxes could really think that Haman would choose this time and place for a sexual assault on the queen. Xerxes was just looking for an excuse to eliminate the troublemaker; now he has a way of doing so with no further explanations.

Xerxes' reaction is an exclamation, literally: "Also to ravish the queen with me here in the house?" The fragmented sentence may mean to convey the king's haste and agitation.

The difficult idiom *up^{e}ney Haman ḥapu*, lit. "Haman's face was covered," should probably be emended (reading *ḥapru* for *ḥapu*) and translated "Haman was humiliated" (see the Appendix). The clause describes Haman's reaction to the accusation. It might also imply a loss of official standing, a fall into disgrace. Haman first loses his honor, then his life and his position, then his property and sons.

(7:9) Even though the king's accusation is tantamount to a death sentence for Haman, Xerxes still needs guidance. Harbona

---

53. Paton is wrong in thinking that the author is gloating over the destruction of the heathen. Haman's crime in no way lies in his belonging to a certain religious or ethnic group. His being an Agagite motivates his crime, not his punishment.

steps forward and gives direction to Xerxes' confused fury. (Compare the way his servants manipulate him in 2:2.) Harbona's intervention is another sign of the palace staff's favor toward Esther. According to Herodotus (I 137), the Persian king could not execute a man for a single offense. Harbona supplies the second grounds for execution, for an attack on a benefactor of the king is an offense to the king himself. This too is something Xerxes can easily grasp. Harbona does not exactly tell Xerxes what to do, but a suggestion, which he quickly grasps, is implicit in the eunuch's observation. In the entire scene, Xerxes has made no independent decision.

(7:10) The concept of a man suffering the fate he had planned for another is encapsulated in the popular Wisdom saying "He who digs a pit will fall in it" (Prov 26:27; Ps 7:16, cf. 15 and 17; Qoh 10:8; Sira 27:25–27), but it is not a specifically sapiential notion. It also, for example, underlies the sentence for false witnesses (Deut 19:18–19).

Haman gets the punishment he deserves but is punished, in part, for a crime he did not commit. Haman did not try to rape Esther, and he did not try to kill the queen as such, for he did not know that the queen was Jewish. Once again, ignorance, misapprehension, and bungling move events forward in the right direction.

Now the king's anger is assuaged. Xerxes can think only in terms of the immediate crisis: someone was threatening his queen and his honor. When the target of his anger is eliminated, the king's wrath is assuaged—prematurely, as far as Esther is concerned, for the danger lives on.

Act VII is articulated by the king's departure in verse 7 into three parts of unequal length.

(a) The accusation (1–6)
    Esther asks for her life

(b) The "deliberation" (7)
    Haman asks for his life

(c) The sentencing (8–10)
    Haman loses his life

The events take place in the same setting and proceed with such momentum that the chapter in its entirety constitutes a single unbroken scene.

This is the moment Esther has built toward, the confrontation with Haman. She is now on her own, faced with a self-centered, fickle man she must manipulate and an evil, clever, and determined man she must overcome. Her wit and charms alone must suffice for the task. Her wit guides her steps, but her charms too are essential, for nothing would avail if she lacked the power of erotic attraction.

Xerxes' bewilderment when the offender is exposed shows that Esther did indeed have to approach the subject with extreme circumspection. She was forcing the king to "choose between his prime minister, whom he himself has publicly promoted (3:1), and his queen, a girl of uncertain ancestry who has nothing much to recommend her except her good looks and her cookery" (Clines p. 15)—and, we might add, her sexual talents. When Haman is finally exposed, we are still in suspense about the king's response: Are not wives easier to come by than good viziers? Will the king reverse the favor he has publicly shown Haman?

Even when this dilemma is resolved and Haman is gone from the scene, the murderous edict is still operative. Nevertheless, Esther does not immediately pursue the matter. She first gets Mordecai situated in a better position from which to continue the struggle.

Act VIII. 8:1−8. The Grant of Authority. i = 8:1−2; ii = 8:3−8

i

(8:1) That day King Xerxes gave Queen Esther the estate of Haman, persecutor of the Jews, and Mordecai came into the king's presence, for Esther revealed how he was related to her. (2) And the king took off his signet ring, which he had taken away from Haman, and gave it to Mordecai, and Esther set Mordecai over Haman's estate.

Mordecai is appointed to replace Haman.
Date: 18.i.12, at night

Since 8:1−2 is separated from the preceding by the strong closure of 7:10, I have taken it as the start of a new act. Nevertheless, the events it records take place during the same action-packed day as those of chapters 6−7, presumably at night.

(8:1) As the continuation shows, Xerxes is still anxious to please Esther, and so gives her Haman's vast wealth. She alone is the recipient because the king views her (rather than Mordecai or the Jews generally) as the party wronged by Haman; indeed, her rhetorical strategy exploited and promoted that view.

Only now does Esther reveal that she is related to Mordecai, who is thereupon invited to the palace. It is significant that Mordecai is summoned not because of his own services, but because of his relationship to Esther. She is made the cause and agent of the rewards Mordecai receives.

(8:2) Xerxes, reversing his action of 3:10, transfers the royal signet to Mordecai. (The grant of the ring as a token of bestowal of power is based on Gen 41:42a.) It is not stated that Mordecai is made vizier, but he does come into Haman's place and receive the symbol of power held by Haman. In fact, the grant of the ring goes beyond appointment as vizier, for Haman received the signet ring some time *after* his appointment.

Esther puts Mordecai in charge of Haman's estate ("house"). The author had the option of making Mordecai the immediate recipient, which would be logical because he is Haman's counterpart and replacement, and Haman had schemed against him personally. In fact, this is the way it happens in the proto-AT (viii 14–15.[54]), which in this passage is probably close to the form of the earlier story that the MT-author received and adapted. The MT deliberately makes Esther pivotal in the transfer of Haman's property to Mordecai.

Clines believes that the statement in 8:2b is gratuitous, because nothing comes of it and because the king still thinks he gave the estate to Esther (v. 7). Clines (p. 104) considers the sentence explicable only as a development from an earlier version of the story. However, this sentence is not a mechanical transfer from the version represented in the AT, which says that the king "bestowed upon him [Mordecai] all that was Haman's" (viii 15). The difference between the two versions indicates the special intention of the MT-author in this verse. Whereas Xerxes "gave" (*natan*) the estate to Esther, she does not "give" it to Mordecai, but rather "sets him over" it (*wattaśem . . . ʿal*). Thus she retains legal possession of her enemy's vast wealth while placing her former guardian in control of it.

---

54. "And the king said to Esther, 'Did he determine to hang Mordecai too, who saved me from the hand of the eunuchs? Did he not know that Esther is of his familial race?' And the king called Mordecai and bestowed upon him all that was Haman's."

Esther acts freely. She could have retained control of Haman's estate for herself, for a Persian woman could hold wealth in her own right. Herodotus (IX 109) reports that Xerxes offered to give Princess Artaynte cities, gold, and an army under her sole command. Hence Esther does not require a trustee. Her motive for transferring control to Mordecai is not stated. She may be acting as a dutiful foster daughter or as a queen conferring a benefit on a capable minister. In either case, Esther is now a source of power and vast wealth.

While the king has reallocated influence and favor, the real problem is still unresolved—as far as Mordecai and Esther are concerned, though not in Xerxes' mind, for once he has rewarded and punished individuals, he shows no further interest in undoing the mortal peril in which he has placed the Jews.

ii

(3) Then once again Esther spoke unto the king. Falling before his feet, she wept and implored him to do away with the evil of Haman the Agagite and the plan he had devised against the Jews. (4) The king extended the golden scepter to Esther, and Esther arose and stood before the king (5) and said: "Should it so please the king, and if I have found favor with him, and if the idea seem proper to the king, and if I am pleasing to him, let it be written to revoke the letters—the plan of Haman the son of Hammedatha the Agagite, which he wrote with the intent of destroying the Jews in all the king's provinces. (6) For how can I bear to see the evil that will befall my people, and how can I bear to see the destruction of my kindred?"
(7) And King Xerxes said to Queen Esther and to Mordecai the Jew: "See, I have given Haman's estate to Esther, and him they have impaled on the stake, because he struck out at the Jews. (8) Now as for you [two], write in the king's name as you please concerning the Jews and seal it with the king's signet ring.[55] For a document written in the king's name and sealed with the king's signet ring can not be revoked."

Xerxes gives Mordecai and Esther the right to issue an edict.
Date: 18.i.12, at night

Since the author is elsewhere careful to note the progression of days (although not always giving dates), in the absence of a new

---

55. The pronoun and imperatives in this sentence are plural.

time indicator it is natural to read this scene as a continuation of the previous one. This is not a new audience with the king, for Esther is said to "speak" again rather than to "come" again. There is no time indicator in verse 3.

(8:3) Esther "implores" the king on behalf of her people, as Mordecai (using the same verb, *hiṯḥannen*) had told her to do in 4:8. Xerxes seems to need further urging before fulfilling Esther's request—made in 7:3 but not yet granted—to save her people. We can understand his hesitancy, because he is being asked to annul his earlier command, in violation of Persian law and possibly the integrity of his own authority. Such a request calls for a more intense entreaty. Esther falls before his feet and weeps—neither of which she had done previously—and "implores" him—the verb connotes intensity and importunity.[56]

Esther begs the king to do away with Haman's evil and his plot. The words "evil" and "plot," though not conjoined, function as a hendiadys meaning "evil plot." The term she uses, *lᵉha'ᵃḇir*, "remove" (lit., "make pass away," from the root 'BR, "pass away"), reveals the nature of the dilemma, for Persian law, we have been told (1:19), does not "pass away" (*ya'ᵃḇor*, from the same root). *Lᵉha'ᵃḇir* was also used of the removal of the signet ring from Haman in 8:2.

(8:4) The king indicates his favor by stretching out his scepter, as at Esther's first audience (5:2). On that occasion the gesture showed his willingness to accept her approach. Now it apparently signals general good will and allows her to make a specific request.

(8:5) Esther begins with the longest preamble of all her petitions, again showing that she is unsure of its reception. In 5:4 she used one formula, in 5:8 two, and in 7:3 two (but strengthened by the second-singular address); in 9:13 one formula will suffice. Here she introduces her supplication with four formulas. When the issue was the queen's life, Xerxes' own honor and feelings were at stake. Now the crisis touches him less directly. (Apparently she is not at personal risk, for if the decree is carried out she will be there

---

56. *Hiṯḥannen* is commonly used of supplicating God (Deut 3:23; 1 Kgs 8:33; Ps 30:9; etc.). It is typically used of the entreaties of people in desperate straits, such as Joseph in the pit (Gen 42:21), the Israelites in captivity (1 Kgs 8:47; 2 Chr 6:37), and Job in his suffering (8:5; 9:15). The verb refers to an act accompanying weeping in Hos 12:5 as well as in Est 8:3.

to "see" her people's misfortune [8:6].) Hence her pleading must wax more intense and personal. Moreover, this time Esther is not going against a man only, but also against the administrative apparatus, the legal axioms, and the organization of the kingdom itself, and she is forcing the question of how far the king himself is bound by his laws. The third clause in her preamble, "if the idea seem proper [kašer] to the king," shows that she realizes the impropriety of her suggestion that a royally authorized decree should be abrogated (Clines, p. 101).

Her preamble reminds Xerxes that he still has to "prove" his love: "Should it so please the king, and if I have found favor with him, and if the idea seem proper to the king, and if I am pleasing to him." The last condition in particular is cajolery, making the king prove that he finds her pleasing or "good." She bundles two attitudes together: the king's love for her and his approval of her plan. He would have to pause and think in order to separate the two and say: "You have indeed found favor with me, you please me greatly, but I cannot agree to this breach of Persian constitutional law." But Xerxes is hardly capable of such analysis.

Esther must now ask to have Haman's edict repealed. Although the edict was signed and sealed in the king's name, making it his own decree, Esther emphasizes that the edict was actually Haman's device by defining "the letters" with an appositional phrase which calls attention to itself by its length and awkwardness: "the plan of Haman the son of Hammedatha the Agagite, which he wrote with the intent of destroying the Jews in all the king's provinces." Not only does she avoid recalling the king's complicity, she also stresses that the decree was an *individual's* scheme. Perhaps if it can be seen as merely an individual administrative order, it can be annulled. As Clines (p. 102) observes, Esther's careful phrasing allows her to tell the truth but not the whole truth.

(8:6) Esther reinforces her behest with an appeal to the king's solicitude, reminding him how severely her people's destruction would pain *her*. This is not selfishness on her part; she appeals to the king on the grounds he will best understand: think of what it will do to *me*, your queen. Of course, this appeal is not only tactical. She is truly and deeply concerned for her people's fate.

She does not beg for her own life; on the contrary, she speaks as if she would be alive to see her kinsmen's destruction, apparently assuming that she herself would escape. Mordecai mentioned this possibility in 4:13 as something Esther might be thinking of, and he did not deny that it was possible, at least in the short run. He did not say that she would die in a national holocaust (which would, he believed, be averted anyway), but that she would be overtaken by retribution from an unnamed source. Thus the concern Esther showed for her own life in 7:3–4 was tactical; she was not herself in danger from the edict. But it would be a mistake to use that tactic again, since the king, his anger cooled down and his mind somewhat cleared by the need to extricate himself from a dilemma, might merely guarantee her personal safety.

(8:7) Xerxes speaks to "Mordecai the Jew" and "Esther the queen." He addresses them both, using the second plural in this verse and the next, where he bestows authority on them jointly. "The Jew" is Mordecai's fixed title now. Whereas previously it was used by people within the story as an epithet for greater specificity (as in 5:13 and 6:10), it is now used by the narrator as a component of Mordecai's title (similarly in 9:29, 31; 10:3), just as "the queen" is a component of Esther's. Esther is always called (translating literally) "Esther the Queen," whereas Xerxes is called "the King Xerxes," which is the usual word order in royal titles in late biblical Hebrew. The form of Esther's title corresponds to Mordecai's title, "Mordecai the Jew." The use of "the Jew" as Mordecai's epithet, together with its pairing with Esther's title in the particular form chosen for it, suggests that "the Jew," like "the queen," is an epithet of high dignity.

Xerxes reminds the cousins that he gave Haman's estate to Esther (as if wealth were one of her concerns) and that he had Haman executed for attacking the Jews. Does he speak in simple friendliness (Gunkel), or rather with a bit of annoyance, as if to say: "I've already done a lot for you; why must you bother me for more?" His eagerness to get the whole messy business off his hands makes the latter attitude seem the more likely.

The reason Xerxes offers for punishing Haman and turning his wealth over to Esther is simply not true; he did not punish Haman for attacking the Jews. There is no mention of the Jews in chapter 7. But, ever eager for gratitude, Xerxes plays up to Esther's and Mordecai's concern for their kinsmen to show that he has not been slack in that regard either. He has swallowed Esther's formulation of the edict as Haman's solo machination, and he now presents himself, and perhaps sees himself, as the protector of the Jews. That is, of course, all to the good.

Now *you* [plural], the king says, write whatever you wish in my name. The "you" before the imperative is very emphatic, suggesting a contrast: *I* have done my part, now *you* go finish the job. Xerxes has had enough bother for now.

Moore says that 8:8b, "For a document written in the king's name and sealed with the king's signet ring can not be revoked," is a gloss or a remark of the narrator. In fact, it belongs to the interplay between Xerxes and the two Jews. By this explanation, the king excuses himself for not simply granting Esther's request to "revoke" the documents—it is not in his power to do so—at the same time underscoring the significance of the boon he is about to offer (in 8:8a): their own edicts, too, will be irrevocable.

The theme of Act VIII is the bestowal of authority on Mordecai and Esther. It begins with Mordecai's appearance at the palace, where he receives control of the signet ring and the wealth taken from his enemy, and proceeds to the authorization to him and Esther to issue their own decrees, with a reminder of the unconditional power invested in the signet.

Mordecai and Esther have not sought the authority they receive. Mordecai, as is his custom (outside chap. 4), remains silent, waiting for matters to develop to his advantage. Esther, as in the past, asks for the king's aid. She uses smooth and clever rhetoric (insightfully analyzed by Clines, pp. 101–2, to which the above analysis is indebted). This time, however, Xerxes does not grant her particular request, for that is not within his power, but her entreaty does have the desired emotional impact. The king wants to say yes but cannot, so he gives her the means of pursuing her cause. The result is a great and unsought increment in the two Jews' power. They now have the means to bind the monarch himself.

Excursus: The Two Days of Acts V-VIII

The events of the book of Esther extend over some ten years—3 to 12 (inclusive)—of Xerxes' reign. Within this period there are long gaps, some of them in places where we would expect swift action, such as the eleven months between Haman's decree and the scheduled date of execution, or the two months between the permission to write a counter-decree and its issuance.

The leisurely pace of the opening shifts into a desperate rush when the moment of crisis arrives. That moment is not the day slated for the pogrom, 13 Adar (as shown by the change of pace itself, as well as the relieved rejoicing in 8:15–17). Rather, the crisis is reached at the time when Esther must act to defeat Haman and gain the power necessary to neutralize his scheme. These crucial events are compressed into two days, approximately the 17th and 18th of the first month (Nisan), a few days after Haman issues his decree. (The exact date of the crisis is not specified. The dating on 17–18.i is an approximation I use for convenience, as a reflection of the flow of events implicit in the narrative. The crisis takes place no earlier than the 15th-16th and not much later.[57]) These events are:

17.i.12 Esther goes to the king and invites him and Haman to a banquet.

Esther holds her first banquet and invites Haman and the king to a second.

Haman goes home in a mixture of glee and irritation, speaks with his friends, and prepares the stake.

18.i.12 Xerxes has insomnia, has the annals read to him, and is reminded of Mordecai's service.

Haman goes to the palace early in the morning and advises the king on forms of honor.

Mordecai receives those honors and returns to the gate.

Haman goes home in shame, complains to his friends, and then is hurried to the palace.

Esther holds her second banquet, in which Haman is undone.

Haman is executed.

Mordecai is brought to the palace and made vizier.

Esther receives Haman's wealth and puts Mordecai in charge of it.

Esther appeals to the king again, and she and Mordecai are given permission to write their own decrees.

It would not be impossible for this much activity to be squeezed into two days, especially since some of the events, such as Haman's

---

57. The Midrash (Est. Rab. IX 2) places the first banquet on 15 Adar. In this view, Mordecai goes into mourning on 13.i, Esther contacts him and is sent on her mission on the same day (chap. iv). She fasts on the 13th, 14th, and 15th, and on the third day of the fast approaches the king. The Midrash may be correct in allowing for no extra days in the rush of events at this time.

execution and Mordecai's summons, can be simultaneous. But the period is packed to the full, and activity proceeds at a furious pace, whose rapidity is underscored by the subsequent puzzling delay between the permission to write a decree (8:8), and the writing of the decree (8:9–14) over two months later.

The date designated for the massacre is 13.xii.12, eleven months after the edict is published. The delay is puzzling. Since the massacre is an unorganized pogrom rather than an action undertaken by the imperial army, little time for preparation should be needed. The eleven-month delay could give Jews time to seek to cancel the decree and to prepare resistance. Paton thinks that the author wished to put the massacre on the unlucky 13th of Adar in the unlucky 13th year. But if the number of the year were significant the author would have mentioned it. Moreover, if (as Paton assumes) the author was free to choose the dates, the casting of lots could have been placed closer to the day of execution. It is no explanation to say that the reason is "literary," meaning that the author wanted to give time for the dénouement (Paton) or for the counteraction of Haman's decree. If the characters did not need the time, the author did not need it, and it is hard to see why the characters needed it. Esther and Mordecai counteract Haman's decree much more quickly, publishing their own edict on 23.iii.12, only two months and ten days later, but even that is strangely delayed, since Esther and Mordecai received permission to issue their decree just a few days after Haman's went forth. If anything, the eleven-month hiatus runs counter to literary considerations by reducing the urgency of the countermeasures. Meinhold says that the delay underscores the responsibility of the Jews' enemies for their own downfall. But there is no hint that they might have used the interim for coming to their senses, and they would hardly be less responsible for their fate if the decree had been in the fourth month, for example. It is also puzzling that both messages go forth "urgently" (3:15; 8:14) when there is so much time left for preparations. I have no solution to these difficulties.

In any case, if we wish to explain the chronology from the standpoint of the author's needs, the inexplicable date is the day Haman issued the edict (13.i) rather than the day for the fulfillment of the decree. The latter was determined by the date of the celebration of Purim, which was a given for the author. We may note that Haman issues his decree one day before Passover, while the date of the pogrom is one day before Purim. The factors underlying the choice of dates may lie in the realm of calendar or astrology, but they are at present unknown.

Act IX. 8:9–17. The Counter-decree. i = 8:9–14; ii = 8:15–17

i

(8:9) The royal scribes were summoned at that time, on the twenty-third day of the third month, the month of Sivan, and it was written in accordance with all that Mordecai had commanded the Jews and the satraps and the governors and the princes of the provinces from India to Nubia, 127 provinces, to each and every province in its own script and to each and every people in its own language, and to the Jews in their script and their language. (10) He wrote this in King Xerxes' name, sealed it with the king's signet ring, and sent letters by the hand of couriers on horseback—riders of swift horses, steeds *pur sang*—(11) to the effect that

the king has permitted the Jews in each and every city to gather and to make a stand for their lives:

to slaughter, slay, and destroy the forces of every people and province who afflict them, together with children and women, with their property as spoil, (12)

on a single day, in all the provinces of King Xerxes, on the thirteenth day of the twelfth month, the month of Adar, (13)

with a copy of the edict to be issued as law in each and every province, made public to all the peoples, that the Jews be ready for that day to take vengeance on their enemies.

(14) The couriers, riders of swift horses, steeds *pur sang*, went out urgently and hastily at the king's command, and the law was (also) issued in the Fortress of Susa.

The counter-decree is published.
Date: 23.iii.12

(8:9) The counter-decree is issued two months and ten days after Haman's decree. The gap is puzzling. Why deprive the Jews of seventy days of preparation? It could not have taken Mordecai that long to devise his counter-measure. The LXX eliminates the problem by changing the date to the 23rd of *Nisan*, some five days after permission was granted to write the letter. It is hard to find a literary function for the gap the MT leaves. It is premature for the movement of events to slow down this much; though the height of the crisis has passed, the danger still stands. Only when the messengers will go forth "urgently and hastily" with the edict (8:14) can the pace ease up.

Mordecai composes and sends the edict. Although Esther received authority to issue decrees, this one is Mordecai's, for Haman's decree was written in reaction to *him*. Since Haman's edict was a royal decree issued by the vizier, so must it be countermanded by a royal decree issued by the vizier.

To the wording of 3:12 this verse adds "and to the Jews in their script and their language," a phrase irrelevant to Haman's decree. But beyond meeting the obvious need for the Jews to receive this edict (they would have been included among "each and every people"), this phrase reminds us that the Jews are no longer passive objects of administrative operations. They stand alongside the other peoples as a recognized national group that must be informed of royal law. What is more, the Jews receive this communication along with the empire's rulers (in v. 9a) as well as alongside the other peoples (in v. 9b); indeed, they head the list of addressees. The decree might have been addressed to the officials alone, ordering them to aid the Jews or to allow the Jews to defend themselves. The decree that Mordecai formulates emphasizes that the Jews are actors, leading actors, in the events to follow, not merely recipients of beneficence.

What was the Jews' language? Although the Jews throughout the Persian empire probably spoke Aramaic, the lingua franca of the Near East, and the Jews in Persia proper would have spoken Persian, it is doubtful that the author would think of either as the distinctive language of the Jews. To a Jew of the Hellenistic period looking back, the language of the Jews in the Achemenid Empire probably would have been Hebrew.

(8:10) Mordecai "wrote [the edict] in King Xerxes' own name," meaning that it was issued as a royal decree, not as an administrative order from the vizier.

(8:11) Mordecai opens his decree with a reminder of royal authorization not found in Haman's: "that the king has permitted." Both edicts had royal authority, but the narrator wishes to emphasize the royal backing of the second (Meinhold).

Unlike its parallel in 3:12, the counter-decree does not say "from old to young," but it does imitate Haman's in specifying "children and women" among the victims, showing that the slaughter of the Jews' enemies is to be total, embracing their families as well.

Gordis (1976:49–53) makes a valiant effort to eliminate the

moral difficulty by reading "children" and "wives" as direct objects of "attacking," thus: "and wipe out every armed force of a people or a province attacking them, their children, and their wives." But this rendering does not (regrettably) accord with the Hebrew, which lacks "their" before "children" and "wives," (see the Appendix). It is true that the later report of the encounters refers only to the killing of men (9:12, 15). But even if the Jews did not carry out this aspect of Mordecai's decree, the decree does allow it. Moreover, the report in chapter 9 does not explicitly deny the killing of women and children as it does the taking of booty, which the author apparently did see as a moral issue.

Why does Mordecai permit the Jews to take booty? The tit-for-tat principle plays a part; still, Mordecai's edict is not so closely bound to the wording of Haman's that this phrase could not have been omitted. The permission to take spoil allows the Jews to *refuse* to do so. The call for the annihilation of the Jews' enemies is derived from the rules of war that pertained to the Israelite conquest of Canaan and some of the wars at the time of the Judges and early monarchy. These rules prescribed the ban (*ḥerem*) for Israel's enemies. According to the Deuteronomic formulation, when nations outside the Promised Land offer resistance, the males are to be slain, but women, children, cattle, and other property may be taken as booty (Deut 20:13–15; cf. Deut 2:34–35; 3:6–7; Josh 8:2, 26). Against the peoples of Canaan, however, a more severe rule is to apply: all humans, livestock, and property that cannot be purified by fire are to be devoted to God, which is to say, destroyed (Deut 20:16–17; Josh 6:17–24). The strict form of the ban was also (at least according to Samuel's understanding) to pertain in the war against Amalek, Haman's ancestral tribe, though Amalek's land was outside the area of the Promise (1 Sam 15).

(**8:13**) A copy of the decree is to be published to *everyone* (it is emphasized), so that the Jews may be ready to "take vengeance" (*NQM*) on their enemies. Contrary to Meinhold, the term *NQM* is not from the judicial realm, but refers to the legitimate exercise of power outside a judicial context. According to Mendenhall: "all evidence points to the fact that the root *NQM* is used in situations calling for the exercise of force in contexts that the normal legal institutions of society cannot handle. It refers to executive rather than judicial action, but it is always either clearly based upon some sense of legitimacy or is actually the prerogative of the divine world which of course normally is delegated to the political institution" (1973:76—77).[58] Mendenhall glosses *NQM* as "vindicate" and translates the phrase in this verse "to deliver themselves from their enemies" (ibid.). However, *NQM* never refers to a simple defense or rescue, but everywhere designates a punitive action and presupposes a prior wrong, that is, some offense to which the avenging party is responding. Thus "vengeance" (understood with the above qualifications) is a more appropriate rendering. A call for vengeance makes sense only if there is a claim of an unpunished offense. (Haman's edict did not call for vengeance because he could not claim that the Jews had wronged his followers.) It is not stated just what offense Est 8:13 has in view, but its general nature can be inferred from the word *haṣṣarim*, "those who afflict." This affliction could take the form of prior oppression, or it might be the attack that took place this day. In the latter case, the aggression, though unsuccessful, was the offense deserving of vengeance. Nevertheless, in the battle to follow, the Jews do not actually execute blood vengeance, but rather exercise force, whose legitimacy derives from the king.

(**8:14**) Mordecai's edict, like Haman's (3:14a), is promulgated speedily—even more so, for whereas Haman's went forth "urgently," Mordecai's, having to counteract the earlier one, goes forth "urgently and hastily." The haste does not seem required by military needs, since nearly eleven months remain till the scheduled clash, and while the Jews are to "be ready," which might imply the necessity for some military preparations, the time frame does not seem to require true urgency. But if there really was urgency, it is all the more perplexing that Mordecai delayed two months before issuing his decree.

In scene i, Mordecai reverses Haman's edict using its wording to the opposite effect. The following alignment shows the differences between them. The most important are those bearing upon the position of the Jews. Points of difference in the wording (not

---

58. Contrary to Mendenhall (p. 100), Mordecai's decree did not give the Jews political sovereignty—there is no sign of greater political independence for the Jews following the edict and certainly no hint of sovereignty. Rather, it granted them the right to exercise force. A fundamental assumption of the author is that the right to exercise force in the realm, including defensive force, derives from the king and must be authorized by royal grant.

order) of Mordecai's decree are underlined. Some inconsequential differences are not noted.

HAMAN'S EDICT:	MORDECAI'S EDICT:
(3:13) And letters were sent . . .	letters . . . saying that
	<u>the king has permitted the Jews in each and every city to gather and to make a stand for their lives:</u>
to slaughter, slay, and destroy all the Jews, young and old,	to slaughter, slay, and destroy <u>the forces of every people and province who afflict them,</u>
together with children and women,	together with children and women, with their property as spoil, (12)
on a single day,	on a single day, <u>in all the provinces of King Xerxes,</u>
the thirteenth day of the twelfth month, the month of Adar, with their property as spoil, (14) with a copy of the edict to be issued as law in each and every province, made public to all the peoples, that they be ready for that day.	on the thirteenth day of the twelfth month, the month of Adar, (13) with a copy of the edict to be issued as law in each and every province, made public to all the peoples, that <u>the Jews</u> be ready for that <u>day to take vengeance on their enemies.</u>

Mordecai's edict incorporates most of the wording of Haman's. Both announce the king's will to the imperial officials, who in turn are to promulgate the ordinance to the public. The structure of the edicts is as follows:

(a) The command; the substance of the edict: 3:13a$\alpha\beta$ ("to slaughter . . . women") // 8:11

(b) Date (and place) of the event: 3:13aγ ("on a single day . . . Adar") // 8:12

(c) Form of promulgation of the law (including the reason for the promulgation): 3:14 // 8:13.

The remark "with their property as spoil" (3:13b and 8:11b) comes earlier in Haman's edict than in Mordecai's. Its placement in Mordecai's seems more appropriate. It may be that by its post-poned placement in Haman's decree, the remark draws attention to itself. In Haman's decree, the promise of spoil is the inducement to act upon the decree. Mordecai's decree, of course, requires no inducement.

The essence of Mordecai's edict is that the Jews are *allowed* to defend themselves; that is all. The aid the Jews will receive from various officials (9:3) is not commanded (though Mordecai, as vizier, presumably could have required it), but rather will result from Mordecai's personal influence. The scope of this edict implies that the Jews would otherwise be forbidden to defend themselves. Without Mordecai's edict, the army would have prevented effective Jewish resistance, since Haman's edict made the massacre of Jews legal. Now that the Jews are guaranteed the right to defend them-selves, the army can, and indeed must, stand aside.

ii

(8:15) Then Mordecai went out from the king's presence in royal clothing of violet and white, in a large golden turban and a cloak of linen and purple. And the city of Susa rejoiced and was merry. (16) And the Jews had light and merriment and joy and honor. (17) And in each and every province and in each and every city, wherever the king's word and law reached, there was merriment and joy for the Jews, feasting and holiday. And many from among the peoples of the land became Jews, for the fear of the Jews had fallen upon them.

Mordecai appears in glory, and all celebrate.
Date: 23.iii.12

This scene apparently brings to a conclusion the day in which the counter-edict was issued. We would expect the author to note the passing of time if much time had ensued since the decree, whereas there is no need for a time indicator if the sequence of events is unbroken. This dating is reinforced by the parallel in 3:12—15: just as Haman's celebration (3:15b) certainly followed immediately upon the issuance of his decree (3:12—15a), so the Jews' celebration would come in the wake of Mordecai's decree.

(**8:15a**) Mordecai's garments signify the highest royal recognition. The materials are royal; they are all mentioned in 1:6 among the opulent appurtenances of Xerxes' feast. In particular, purple cloth was deemed royal in character. In a story reported by Herodotus, Xerxes granted a commoner a gold crown to honor him (VIII 118). The conspirator Otanes was granted a "suit of Median clothes" (among other gifts) for himself and his descendants as a sign of their special status vis-à-vis the kingship (Her. III 84). Haman himself, a connoisseur of honors, listed royal clothing among the ways the king could express esteem. The practice continued in the Seleucid empire. According to 1 Mac (10:20, 62), Alexander granted Jonathan a purple robe and gold crown, in admiration for his prowess. Dan 5:7, 29, probably reflecting Seleucid practice, tells that Belshazzar, king of Babylon, offered a garment of purple and a gold necklace as the highest royal honors. Among both the Persians and the Seleucids, the highest nobility, called the "Friends" of the king, were distinguished by purple garments (Bevan 1902: II, 280).

(**8:15b**) As in 3:15b, the population of Susa generally—though certainly not entirely—shares the emotions of the Jews: then misery, now joy.

(**8:16**) The Jews now have light and joy and *honor*—their honor a reflection of Mordecai's. Light signifies joy (e.g., Ps 97:11; 112:4; Job 12:25). In accordance with the distinction between Susan and provincial Jews maintained throughout the book, we are told (in two four-element phrases) that the Jews of Susa had light, happiness, joy, and honor, and that the provincial Jews experienced joy, happiness, festivities, and a festival day.

(**8:17**) Wherever the new edict (which is "the king's law") reaches, the Jews rejoice and celebrate. This celebration may seem rather premature, since they still face massive battles against numerous enemies. But the crisis has passed. Its resolution is not in the military victory itself but in the decree allowing self-defense. The Jews, and behind them the narrator, seem to take military success for granted. They assume the principle that Haman's associates enunciated in 6:13b, which may be formulated positively: the beginning of a Jewish victory—such as the Jews now see embodied in Mordecai's glory—is an infallible sign that the Jews will eventually triumph conclusively.

Seeing the rising tide of Jewish success, many of the heathen (as "peoples of the land" means here) *mityahădim*. This verb (derived from the noun *yᵉhudi*, "Jew") may mean either "became Jewish" or, as Ehrlich proposes, "gave themselves out to be Jewish" (the *hitpael* conjugation often has the sense of "present oneself as," "pretend to be"). Ehrlich argues that conversion motivated by fear of death would contradict the principles of Judaism. But people ready to convert out of fear of death would not scruple to violate the principle—in another religion!—that conversion be uncoerced. One case of conversion to Judaism by force of arms is known to history: Alexander Jannaeus' conversion of the Idumeans in ca. 80 B.C.E. In any case, what could it mean that many of the peoples of the land "gave themselves out to be Jews" ("gaben sich aus für Juden") in Ehrlich's translation, p. 122? There was no distinctive Jewish dress they could wear as a disguise (if there were, Mordecai's fellow officials would have known he was Jewish without his telling them; 3:4). The judaizing gentiles might have declared that they were Jewish, but (as Bardtke points out) Jews from the same town would have known that they were lying. Hence the action of the gentiles is to be understood as joining the Jewish people. Neh 10:29 refers to "everyone who separated himself from the peoples of the land [to follow] the law of God" (using the same term for the heathen, "peoples of the land," as is employed here).

But conversion need not be motivated by religious awe, especially when the change is ethnic (becoming a Jew) more than religious (cleaving to God's law). In the book of Esther, it is the "fear of the Jews" that inspires these people to become Jewish. Clines contends that this fear was religious awe and had nothing to do with any perceived military prowess of the Jews. It was, he believes, motivated by the sensitivity of proselytes to the religious significance of the events they beheld (p. 41). Similarly, Dommershausen regards the emotion as awe before the God who protects this people so wondrously (p. 110). But the word for "fear"—*pahad*—does not refer only to fear of God or religious awe (cf., for example, Ps 27:1; 78:53 [verb]; Ps 31:12; Job 21:9; Est 9:2 [noun]). "Fear of the Jews" is not religious awe any more than is the "fear of the Jews" in 9:2 or the "fear of Mordecai" in 9:3, which the officials feel because Mordecai is "important" or "great," as Haman once was (*GDL* is used of Haman's promotion in 3:1 and of Mordecai's current growing importance). Of course, the enemies might be aware that an unnamed power is on the Jews' side. Haman's advisers and wife reveal such a fear in 6:13 (though the term *pahad* is not used there). Their feeling may recognize divine power somewhere in the background, but it is hardly a matter of "enlightenment" or sensitivity to the numinous, and it is not distinguishable from dread of a superior military power. To the extent that some awareness of the power supporting the Jews is intended in 8:17, it may be intended in 9:2−3 as well, but even so it is not really fear of that power, but fear of the Jews themselves, that shakes up the gentiles. Danger, and not only "enlightenment," can bring about proselytism—as it did in the time of Alexander Jannaeus and as it has done often enough in the history of Christianity and Islam.

In fact, the heathen mentioned in this verse did not have to convert to save their lives; they merely had to refrain from assaulting the Jews, for the royal edict only allowed the Jews to kill those who attacked them. But a widespread fear of growing Jewish power could make many people deem it worthwhile to become Jewish, just as Mordecai's growing power made it seem prudent to the Persian bureaucrats to support his people.

Scene ii (8:15−17) links up with 8:1−2, when Mordecai *came into the king's presence* and received the signet ring. Now he *goes out from the king's presence* adorned with signs of royal honor. These actions frame chapter 8, which tells about the authorization and issuance of the counter-decree; but the chapter does not constitute a single scene or act, since it encompasses events on days about two months apart.

The current rejoicing is profound and widespread, embracing all the Jews and many non-Jewish Susans as well. Mordecai's honor counterbalances and reverses his moment of mourning, in 4:2, when he went into the city square dressed in sackcloth and ashes. That action is followed in the narrative (if not in the sequence of events) by Jewish fasting and mourning (4:3). His present appearance is correspondingly followed by Jewish feasting and rejoicing.

Upon completion of the administrative action that enables the Jews to save themselves, Mordecai enjoys his triumph. It is not a personal victory alone, but rather a sign to the Jews that they have a protector who can lead them to safety. It is the triumph of all Jews and is celebrated as such.

Earlier Mordecai was been honored for saving the king's life (6:1−11). The reason for the present honor is not stated, but since it follows upon an action that rescues the Jews and inspires general Jewish rejoicing, the reader will perceive this glory as a reward for his brave intervention on behalf of Jewry (Bardtke). Mordecai's ear-

106

lier honor was episodic. Now honor is his permanent state. And, following upon the efforts described in the preceding verses, Mordecai appears in his glory not merely as a recipient of royal favors, but as one who has demonstrably earned his glory.

Mordecai's rise to the viziership (8:2) and glory (8:15) is not a necessary prerequisite for the salvation of the Jews. Esther could have issued the decree herself, independently or at her cousin's behest,[59] or she could have convinced the king to sign an edict that she and Mordecai had drafted. But even if the surface of the plot does not require Mordecai's promotion, there is a significant thematic connection between it and the Jews' salvation: the Jews see their salvation entailed by their leader's success. The concept of leadership underlying this idea will be discussed in the context of the author's ideal of community, in chap. XI §2c.

Clines (chap. 5) has shown how 8:15–17 draws together the principal threads of the plot: the threat to Mordecai and the threat to the Jewish people have been abrogated. Mordecai is publicly honored and the Jews are secure. Various conflicts have been resolved; racial identity is now a source of gratification rather than tension; the "public relations" image of the king is clean again; law is not undermined but is rather "demoted to the infrastructure of the good life" (p. 67); irreversible laws still stand but may be counteracted.

It is true that the story has reached its climax, but it has not reached its end. The Jews have received the power to save themselves but have not yet done so; the actual victory must be reported. But the dramatic tension is released and little suspense remains; the victory is secured. The fighting in Adar will merely work out a process set in motion.

Act X. 9:1–19. The Battles of Adar. i = 9:1–5; ii 9:6–10; iii = 9:11–15; iv = 9:16–19

i

(9:1) Now on the thirteenth day of the twelfth month, the month of Adar, when the king's word and his law were due to be carried out—on the very day when the enemies of the Jews had expected to gain control over them, whereas things would be turned about, in that the Jews would gain control

---

59. Since Esther receives the permission to issue and seal edicts along with Mordecai (8:8; the imperatives are plural), she presumably could have received permission to do so on her own, had her cousin not been at her side.

over their adversaries—(2) the Jews gathered in their cities in all the provinces of King Xerxes to strike out at those who sought to harm them, and no one could stand up against them, because fear of them had fallen upon all the peoples.

(3) Now all the princes of the provinces and the satraps and the governors and the king's executive officers were promoting the Jews, because the fear of Mordecai had fallen upon them. (4) For Mordecai was important in the palace and his reputation was spreading throughout all the provinces, since the man Mordecai was growing increasingly important.

(5) And the Jews slaughtered all their enemies by the sword, slaying and destroying, and so wreaked their will on their enemies.

The battles, first day
Date: 13.xii.12

(**9:1**) The events of the day are summarized in a single, long, complex sentence, 9:1–2. Within this sentence, the victory of the Jews—in fact, the entirety of the story—is encapsulated in a clause embedded in a parenthesis: "things would be turned about, in that the Jews gained control over their adversaries." (The translation uses "would" to reflect past-future, i.e., the future from the standpoint of the earlier expectation; the Hebrew employs verb forms commonly used for past tense.) By stating the scene's outcome at its beginning and submerging the high point in a parenthesis, the author eliminates suspense.

The 13th of Adar was the day scheduled for the fulfillment of the "king's word and his law." This phrase could apply to either decree or both. The king's "law" encompasses two contrary measures. The resolution of this conflict is about to be paid for in blood.

The Jews gain "control" (*yišlᵉṭu*) over their enemies. The issue of control, of doing one's will with others, however this power may be exercised, is one of the book's central themes. It appears in the clash of wills between Xerxes and Vashti, in the description of Esther's malleability and obedience, in Mordecai's refusal to bend to Haman's will and the latter's splenetic attempt to control his enemies by eradicating them, and in other interactions as well. Now, at their moment of triumph, the Jews' not only escape their enemies' power but also impose their own will on *them* (9:5). Bardtke explains "control" in this context as the power to do whatever one wishes with one's enemies, such as enslaving them. But since the only hostile action mentioned here is killing, the Jews' "control" means killing their assailants.

(9:2) Although the Jews are a danger only to those who seek their harm, "all the peoples" are terrified of them. This does not mean that the Jews are hostile to all gentiles, but that a widespread terror has arisen among the peoples that affects them variously: it incapacitates enemies in battle, causes other gentiles to join the Jewish people, and leads the officials to support the Jewish cause.

(9:3) The officials are swayed particularly by the fear of Mordecai, their superior in the imperial service. Motivated by this fear (and not by an order from the king or from Mordecai himself), they aid the Jews in the cause. We are not told exactly how the officials contributed; perhaps they provided them with arms.

(9:4) The officials fear Mordecai because he is powerful and famous and growing increasingly so. This sentence seems to be based on Exod 11:3, "the man Moses was very great" (*weha'iš mošeh gadol me'od*) (Gerleman). (*Gadol*, translated here as "important," means more generally "great." The particular sense of this word depends on context, which here refers to political power.) The idiom "the man Mordecai" itself implies his importance (Dommershausen).

The growth of Mordecai's power might require the extended period provided by the nine-month interim. Hence the narrator is not entirely neglecting the time frame, though nothing is said about preparations during that period.

(9:5) The Jews kill their enemies and do their will on them. On the "power/will" motif see the comment on 9:1. Slight variants of the phrase "wreaked their will on [their enemies]" (*wayya'ašu ... kirṣonam*) are used of conquests by irresistible military forces in Neh 9:24 and Dan 11:16 (which adds the phrase "and none could stand before him," found in Est 9:2).

In Scene i, the Jews seal their deliverance by force of arms, a victory achieved, in essence, nine months earlier. There is no suspense; the results are given at the start. More than recounting events, this scene, like Act X as a whole, analyzes them.

ii

(9:6) In the Fortress of Susa the Jews slew and destroyed 500 men, (7) slaying

Parshandatha	and
Dalphon	and
Aspatha	(8) and

Poratha	and
Adalia	and
Adiratha	(9) and
Parmashta	and
Arisai	and
Aridai	and

Vaizatha, (10) the ten sons of Haman son of Hammedatha, persecutor of the Jews. But upon spoil they laid not a hand.[60]

The fighting in the Fortress of Susa, first day
Date: 13.xii.12

(9:6–10) In the Fortress of Susa alone the Jews kill five hundred men, including the ten sons of Haman. Five hundred enemies would be a large part of the male population of the fortress. The figure is hyperbolic, reflecting an assumption that there was much hostility toward Jews at the very center of the empire.

The sons of Haman, in the schematic moral order of this book, are to be thought of as belonging to the active enemies of the Jews, rather than as merely appendages of their father, like the children mentioned in 8:11. We may imagine them actively organizing hostilities during the months since the decree was issued. Their death completes Haman's downfall: not only is he killed, but his honor, his position, his wealth, and now his sons—all his boasts from his days of glory (5:11)—are stripped away.

Scene ii does not describe battle; it reports victory. Jewish losses are not mentioned. The panic of the foes and the almost effortless victory of the Jews are, as Gerleman observes, characteristics of battle reports in Chronicles (e.g., 2 Chr 20) and Exodus (e.g., 14:24–25; 15:16). The difference—no minor one—is that in those books victory is ascribed to the Lord. The effortlessness of

---

60. In the Massoretic text, the names of Haman's sons are written in one column on the right side of the page and the word w'et ("and" plus the direct-object marker) on the left. A similar arrangement is used in the list of the kings of Canaan, Josh 12:9. The reasons behind the arrangement are not clear. According to one midrashic explanation, the columns represent the gallows; according to another, they are stacked directly atop one another like an unstable row of bricks, rather than being securely staggered (j. Meg. 3:7; b. Meg. 16b). More likely, this is simply a logical arrangement for a repetitive list. It also has the effect of keeping the names distinct and thus emphasizing the number of the executed enemy, rather than letting the names be run together and de-emphasized as they would be if written continuously on the horizontal.

the Jews' victory in Esther works against one of the book's themes—the necessity of Jewish courage and initiative, while promoting another—the durability of the Jewish people.

The Jews gather on the appointed day and fighting erupts as expected. The narrator has a somewhat strange concept of a society where people wait in an orderly fashion before rioting, while their intended victims wait before taking defensive action. This notion is not realistic in the sense of representing the natural course of ethnic conflicts. Rather it is ideological, showing a profound respect for government in and of itself as the source of order, but also, by default, of disorder.

We never learn why the enemies are so hostile to the Jews—so much so that they are ready to endanger their own lives to carry out their malicious plans. Though living in the Fortress and surely aware of the realignment of forces, they attack the Jews right under Mordecai's nose at the king's doorstep. They do so in the face of Mordecai's power, the king's current and manifest support of the Jews, the support of officialdom for the Jewish cause, the widespread fear of the Jews, and above all, the counter-edict itself (9:2). It seems that Haman's still-valid edict is a golden opportunity they must seize upon, whatever the peril to themselves. But, of course, the explanation for antisemitism resides within the antisemite's soul, and the narrator's refraining from giving further motivation for this irrational behavior is realistic.

iii

(9:11) On that day the number of the slain in the Fortress of Susa was reported to the king. (12) And the king said to Queen Esther, "If in the Fortress of Susa alone the Jews slew and destroyed 500 men, as well as the ten sons of Haman, what must they have done in the rest of the king's provinces! Now what is your wish? It shall be granted you. And what further request do you have? It shall be fulfilled."
(13) Esther replied, "Should it so please the king, let the Jews in Susa be allowed to act tomorrow as well in accordance with today's law, and let them impale Haman's ten sons on stakes." (14) So the king commanded this to be done, and the law was issued in Susa, and they impaled the ten sons of Haman. (15) Then the Jews in Susa gathered also on the fourteenth day of the month of Adar, and they slew 300 men in Susa. But upon spoil they laid not a hand.

Esther's request and the second day of fighting
Date: 13–14.xii.12

(**9:12**) Upon hearing the casualty figures, the king, apparently undisturbed by the combat and slaughter raging about his palace, reacts rather blithely, reminding his queen of how well things are going. He exclaims—admiration is the only possible tone here—upon the high number of dead in the Fortress and remarks upon how much greater the casualties elsewhere must be. He seems impressed, perhaps bemused, by the death toll more than by the Jews' deliverance.

(**9:13**) Esther asks that the Jews in Susa be allowed another day of fighting—she does not explain why—and that Haman's dead sons be impaled, in other words, that their corpses be exposed to the public to degrade them (cf. Josh 8:29; 1 Sam 31:10) and to make them a further source of the "fear of the Jews" that has already advanced the Jewish cause. Since everyone in the empire seems to operate in strict accordance with law, the Jews' enemies could not have attacked on the 14th of Adar as they did on the 13th and so do not present an immediate threat. Esther's action is now punitive and precautionary, eliminating opponents who might cause problems in the future.

(**9:14–15**) The king's grant enables the Jews to kill another three hundred enemies in the city of Susa as a whole (the earlier figure of five hundred applied only to the Fortress). The Jews' refusal to take spoil is again emphasized.

In scene iii, Xerxes, using the same demonstrative formula as earlier, asks Esther to make another request. His present offer is unexpected and unmotivated by the movement of the narrative. Previously he had made one offer, inspired to do so by her appearance as supplicant, and he had renewed it at the appropriate time. At present he has no reason to think that Esther has, or should have, any further requests. She has received what she had asked for and is obviously safe, as are the other Jews. Xerxes seems carried away by the momentum of offering and granting requests. He wants to maintain his role as generous donor and to further display his uxoriousness. Also, having willy-nilly taken sides, he has become a partisan of the Jews, and he wants to benefit his side further. By remarking, "see what the Jews have done," then immediately asking Esther what *more* she wants, he implies that the scope of the Jewish victory is his gift as well, though in fact he had merely told Esther and Mordecai to write whatever they wished.

In this little dialogue, as Dommershausen observes, the narrator shows no interest in causal, psychological, or even moral factors. Xerxes' offer, while not out of line with his character as portrayed earlier, is not well integrated in the narrative development. The author includes this scene only to prepare the way for the second day of fighting, which is introduced for etiological reasons, to justify the Susan practice of celebrating on the 15th of Adar. To explain this scene by considerations external to the requirements of the narrative—an approach I have not had to employ elsewhere—in effect asserts a literary flaw in the passage. There is little doubt that in literary terms, the drama has fizzled out and been replaced by somewhat tedious reportage and analysis.

iv

(9:16) Now the rest of the Jews in the king's provinces had gathered and made a stand for their lives, gaining relief from their enemies and slaying their adversaries, some 75,000 in all—but upon spoil they laid not a hand—(17) all on the thirteenth day of the month of Adar, so that on the fourteenth day they had respite and celebrated a day of feasting and merriment.
(18) The Jews in Susa had gathered on the thirteenth day and also on the fourteenth; thus it was on the fifteenth day that *they* had respite, making that their day of feasting and merriment.
(19) That is why village Jews, living in unwalled towns, celebrate the fourteenth day of the month of Adar, with happiness and feasting and holiday and the sending of portions to one another.

The rationale for the date of Purim in the villages
Date: 13–15.xii.12

(9:16) Xerxes' exclamatory question in 9:12a receives an answer: the Jews killed 75,000 in the provinces. Again they decline to take spoil.
(9:19) This verse shifts the focus to the narrator's—and the reader's—present, where the significance of the Esther story lies in the festal activities that events have given rise to.
The narrator resumes the issue of the provincial practice of celebrating Purim on the 14th of Adar. Although mention of the Susa Jews intervenes in verse 18, and the notice in verse 19 seems premature (the holiday is not yet established), this verse is not necessarily a misplaced gloss (contrary to Moore, Meinhold, and

many). The unit as a whole is outside the time sequence (14 Adar has already passed in v. 15.), because it is not another event in the story but an etiology for the later usage. Verse 19 is the heart of the etiology and could not appear earlier in the unit. To be sure, many commentators (e.g., Paton, Würthwein, Moore) hold that verse 19 contradicts verses 21–22, the former calling for two different days of celebration, the latter for a universal two-day celebration. But the wording of verses 21–22 (and 27) may equally well be understood to mean that the Jewish people is to commemorate two days only in the sense that every Jew celebrates the day appropriate to his or her[61] location (Bardtke). Certainly the battle reports strongly undergird a distinction. Moreover, the phrase "what [the Jews] began to do" in 9:23 can only refer to the practice of verses 17–19, where there are clearly two separate days of festivities. Even a later supplementer (if 9:20–32 is indeed to be attributed to one) would have realized that his own restatement of the celebration would be understood in the light of the distinction drawn in 9:1–19.

There is, however, a certain tension between the etiology in verse 19, which has the 14th celebrated by Jewish villagers living in unwalled towns, and the story itself, which draws a distinction between the Jews in Susa and all those living elsewhere, which would include those in walled cities. The reason for this unevenness might be that the MT-author cannot match the story precisely to the existing practice it is supposed to explain. As the text stands, Susa is taken as representative of others in its category, that is, walled cities.

Verse 19 is formulated as an explanation of why 14 Adar is celebrated by the provincials, as if the Susan celebration date is the one that can be taken for granted. This shows the narrator's point of view to be Susan.

Purim customs include the sending of portions of food to fellow Jews. Esther received "portions" from Hegai (2:9), anticipating Xerxes' favor and her coronation feast (2:18). So too the Jews' receipt of portions may symbolize the special status they achieve by the book's end (Berg, p. 45). Gerleman observes that the exchange of portions also characterizes the celebration in Neh 8:10–12.

---

61. In this case, "his or her" is not a nicety. The primary rabbinic requirement for the celebration of Purim is to hear the reading of the Scroll of Esther, and this, according to the Talmud, is encumbent upon women as well as men (b. Meg. 4a).

The purpose of scene iv is to give the reason for the celebration of Purim on two days, 14 Adar for the provincial Jews, 15 Adar for the Susans. More precisely, the scene is a rationale for the village celebration on 14 Adar written from a Susan perspective. The narrative itself, in 9:11–18, deliberately adds a second day of fighting, whose only function is to prepare for the institution of a two-day observance of Purim.

In spite of the martial fantasies that animate the author, the festival is not said to commemorate the victories but rather the respite that followed the victories. The Jews celebrate "not their victory but the absence of cause for blood or victory in the future" (Clines, pp. 161–62). Elsewhere it is God who is said to give the Jews' respite after victory (e.g., Deut 25:19; Josh 21:44; 2 Sam 7:11). Some passages (e.g., Deut 3:20, 12:9–10, Josh 1:13, 15) present the purpose of the conquest of Canaan as the "respite" that is to follow it (Clines, p. 162). But this does not mean (contrary to Dommershausen) that the mention of "respite" here hints at divine guidance. The non-mention of Yahweh in this connection could equally well signal a secularization of the concept of "respite."

The personality of Esther changes in Act X, as does the whole tenor of the tale. Esther seems harder, blunter, even crueler. She no longer shows uncertainty. She does not even bother to avail herself of entreaty and manipulation to get her way. She simply asserts her will and uses her power.

In accordance with Mordecai's decree, the Jews "made a stand for their lives," but they deny themselves personal gain from the battles. Earlier they gathered *lišloaḥ yad*, literally, to "send forth their hand"—to attack—their enemies (9:2); now they refrain from "sending forth their hand" to take booty. This refusal is a sort of free-will offering, by which the Jews wipe away the stain of the greed of the Israelites who defeated the Amalekites in Saul's time (1 Sam 15). Saul spared Agag; Mordecai and Esther destroy Haman the Agagite. Saul took booty and blamed the people (1 Sam 15:15); now the Jews surpass their leader's expectations by refusing to take booty. To be sure, the reversal is not perfect: the enemies are not Amalekites (as observed by LaCocque 1987:218), and the author does not say that the Jews *destroyed* the spoil (McKane 1961:260). But the contrast is enough to show that the Jews are undoing their ancestors failure: the ancestors took spoil, their descendants now refrain from it.

115

Act XI. 9:20–32. The Establishment of the Festival of Purim. i = 9:20–28; ii = 9:29–32

i

(9:20) Then Mordecai wrote these things down and sent letters to all the Jews in all the provinces of King Xerxes, near and far, (21) to confirm upon themselves the celebration of[62] the fourteenth day of the month of Adar and the fifteenth day thereof, each and every year, (22) to correspond to the days in which the Jews had respite from their enemies and the month that turned about for them—from misery to merriment and from mourning to holiday—to celebrate them as days of feasting and merriment and the sending of portions to one another and gifts to the poor.

(23) And the Jews committed themselves to continuing[63] what they had begun doing and what Mordecai had written to them. (24) For Haman son of Hammedatha the Agagite, persecutor of all the Jews, had plotted to destroy the Jews and had cast the *pur*—that is, the lot—to harry them and to destroy them. (25) But when the matter[64] came before the king he said, "With the promulgation of this letter, let the evil plan that he formed against the Jews recoil back upon his own head." And they impaled him and his sons on stakes. (26a) (That is why they named these days "Purim"—from the word *pur*.)

(26b) For this reason—because of all the words of this epistle, and because of what they had seen in this regard, and because of what had come upon them—(27) the Jews confirmed and took it upon themselves—so that it might never pass away—and upon their descendants and upon those who would join themselves to them, ever to observe these two days just as written, according to the time set for them, each and every year. (28) And so these days are celebrated as a memorial and observed in each and every generation, each and every family, each and every province, and each and every city. And these days of Purim shall not pass away from the Jews nor their remembrance disappear from their descendants.

The Jews institute the celebration of Purim.
Date: not long after the events of 13–15 Adar, year 12.

Apparently Mordecai issues his epistle before Adar of the following year, because he speaks only of their spontaneous merri-

---

62. Lit., "to confirm upon them to celebrate."
63. Lit., "And the Jews accepted what they had begun . . . ."
64. Possibly: "when she [Esther] came."

ment after the battle (in year 12) and seeks to make it a regular institution.

(9:20-21) Acting as a communal leader, Mordecai takes a bold, unprecedented step: to inaugurate a Jewish holiday. He calls upon Jews everywhere to obligate themselves to its celebration. As argued in the comment on 9:19, the intention in 9:21-22 and 27, as in 9:19, is that each locality should observe a single day, while the people as a whole is considered as celebrating both days.

Mordecai grounds his call in the recent experience by writing down "these things." This phrase was traditionally thought to indicate Mordecai's authorship of the entire book. Most modern commentators (e.g., Bardtke, Moore, Gerleman) take the phrase as applying to the events of 13-15 Adar only. I think the reader is to understand that Mordecai recorded not only a report of the battles, which everyone knew about anyway, but also—at a minimum—a report of the events leading up to the battles. In other words, the letter recounted the conflict with Haman. The call to inaugurate a new holiday requires more than just mention of a victory in battle. Mordecai would have to appeal to the entire tale of danger and salvation to convince the people that the recent events justify a perpetual holiday.

The phrase "these things" does not necessarily refer to the text of 1:1-9:19 as we have it (though that could be the case). The phrase does, however, imply at least a summary statement of the narrative beginning with Haman's decree. Such a summary occurs in verses 24-25, and I take that as giving the gist of the narrative portion of Mordecai's epistle. Those verses are not formulated as a direct quotation from Mordecai's letter, but they are presented as the reason for the Jews' acceptance of Mordecai's suggestion: the Jews agreed to Mordecai's suggestion (v. 23) *because of* the events surveyed in verses 24-25. In other words, the MT-author believes that it was the history of Haman's overthrow that convinced the Jews to accept the institution of Purim. Hence it stands to reason that Mordecai would (in that author's view) use just that motivation in his letter. The summary as it stands is, as Dommershausen says, "erlebte Rede," that is, thoughts indirectly attributed to Mordecai. What Mordecai actually wrote is, of course, a moot point; indeed, the notion of "actual" is probably meaningless for this story. The only question we can reasonably pose is what the author intends us to picture Mordecai writing. This, I believe, includes an appeal to recent history.

Mordecai writes in order to *qayyem* the celebration of Purim. The uses of *qayyem* elsewhere show that it means "validate" or "confirm," rather than "command, demand." Thus in Ruth 4:7 the ancient legal gesture of removing the sandal served "to validate [*qayyem*] any matter" *after* agreement was reached. This verb is used in Est 9:27 and 31 to report that the Jews made the Purim celebration binding upon themselves—clearly not a matter of commandment. In Ps 119:106 the verb is used of keeping a vow and in Ezek 13:6 of the fulfillment of a prophecy. In all cases, it refers not to the inception of a legal action or condition, but rather to the formalization or fulfillment of a decision or a previously declared intention. Nowhere does it mean the imposition of one person's will on another. Mordecai is not *demanding* obedience.

(**9:22**) The festival is to commemorate the respite the Jews enjoyed following the battles. Purim celebrates freedom from conflict and danger (Bardtke). It also celebrates "the month that turned about for them. . . . " That does not mean that the entire month is a celebration. This verse is structured in parallelism, and "days" requires a synonym to balance it, even one that does not fit the context precisely.[65]

Time here (as commonly in the Bible) is conceived of as equivalent to all that happens within it. Thus the author can speak of the month being "turned about" whereas we would usually speak of the time *in which* things turned about for them.

In addition to enjoying festivities, the Jews are to send portions to the poor. (Deuteronomy [e.g., 16:11] and Tobit [2:2] also speak of the practice of giving food to the poor on feast days.) The giving of *manot* becomes part of the Purim celebration (9:19, 22). Since portions are not only donated to the poor but are exchanged among Jews generally, the gift-giving must have a function beyond the charitable supplying of needs, namely the creation of a symbolic communal banquet to which everyone is invited.

(**9:23**) The Jews receive or take upon themselves *what they had begun to do* and what Mordecai wrote them. Specifically, this refers to the celebration of two days of Purim. The author insists that the form of this unsanctioned holiday did not arise from a unilateral decision by Mordecai but had its source in the people's spontaneous

---

65. This is the phenomenon of "poetic automatism," in which the meaning of a parallel word-pair is restricted to one of the words; see Haran 1972. In this case, we have a poetic feature embedded in a prose passage.

action, which was then reinforced and regularized by Mordecai's letter.

(**9:24–25**) 9:26a explains the meaning of the word "Purim" by reference to Haman's *pur* in verse 24. Thus 9:25, whether written by the author of this passage or a later scribe, is parenthetical.

The historical summary in Mordecai's epistle is often considered an addition to his epistle because it diverges in several details from the narrative it purports to encapsulate.[66] The discrepancies are:

(1) 9:24 says that Haman threw lots to "harry" or "confound" the Jews (*l⁽e⁾hummam*), which is only loosely true. The lots were actually intended to ascertain the best day to destroy the Jews, not to affect them emotionally.

(2) In chapter 7, Xerxes reacted not to Haman's plan but to a personal offense. The historical summary depicts the king as a clear-thinking, exemplary proponent of justice. The bumbling, puttylike Xerxes of the tale can scarcely be recognized in this picture.

(3) In the story, the king did not say what he said "in [?] writing" (*ʿim hasseper*—a difficult phrase).

(4) 9:25, as Clines observes (p. 165), minimizes the roles of Mordecai and Esther (the degree of minimization depends on who or what "came" before the king, Esther herself or "the matter"; *b⁽e⁾boʾah* can be taken either way).

(5) The summary invests the moment of salvation entirely in Haman's overthrow, ignoring the crucial counter-decree and the battles of Adar.

These considerations show that the historical summary is not simply abstracted from chapters 1–9:19. They do not, however,

---

66. Although Hoschander considers 9:24–25 "an almost literal quotation from the Letter of Mordecai," he also believes that the MT, since it contradicts the earlier tale at many points, could not have been handed down correctly, whereas the LXX, lacking those contradictions, preserves the correct version (1923:265–70). But it is far more likely that LXX's version resulted from harmonistic presuppositions similar to Hoschander's rather than that later scribes introduced contradictions into the MT. Paton (pp. 58–59) takes the differences as evidence that 9:20–32 as a unit was derived from a earlier source (specifically, the Chronicles of the Kings of Persia and Media). Bardtke argues that the differences are due to the summary character of 9:24–25. But the discrepancies do not seem to be by-products of condensation. In all cases the commentators assume that the summary in 9:24–25 should agree with the story proper and consequently either harmonize the two accounts or place the summary at a different stage of development.

prove that the summary is the work of a later, none too clever, scribe. As for *lᵉhummam*, although Haman's immediate purpose in casting lots may not have been to harry or confuse the Jews, that was an intended effect of his plot, and so could be described as the long-range purpose of the lots. Moreover, the verb *hamam* often implies *deadly* confusion (e.g., Exod 14:24; Josh 10:10; esp. Judg 4:15). In any case, the word *lᵉhummam* was probably chosen less for historical precision than for its value as a word-play with the name Haman, perhaps as a way of reinforcing the pun of "Purim" on *pur*.

The reason that the summary is not a precise reprise of events as related earlier is that it presents the story from a different perspective. As argued above, the passage is best understood as a paraphrastic extraction from Mordecai's epistle. The author is not retelling the tale but showing Mordecai at work as a skilled courtier and protector of the Jews.

Mordecai, as vizier, gives credit to his king, not to himself or his cousin. He transforms the king's outburst in 7:8 into a deliberate judgment on Haman for scheming against the Jews. The king had revealed his new self-image as protector of the Jews by declaring that Haman was hanged "because he struck out at the Jews" (8:7). Mordecai, with subtlety and tact, publicly sets the king in that role. He encourages the king to adopt attitudes beneficial to the Jews by flattering him for having these attitudes already. By depicting the Jews as more passive than in the earlier narrative, the summary reflects the way Jews must operate in the foreign court: they must make the ruler do their will by making him think it is his own. This is exactly what Mordecai and Esther have been doing since chapter 4. Moreover, 9:25 agrees with the narrative insofar as it locates the essential victory in the events of Nisan (in which it includes the edict issued in Sivan).

(9:26a) The narrator speaks from his own perspective, breaking the temporal sequence and looking back to explain the etymology of Purim. The casting of the lot (the *pur*), mentioned in verse 24, is understood as the reason the holiday is called Purim. *Pur* is undoubtedly the Old Babylonian word *pūru*, meaning "lot," "fate" (Lewy 1939b:123–24), but that does not explain why the new holiday is called "lots." The author's explanation is but the first in a series of speculations, continued by modern scholars, about the origin and significance of the holiday's name. None of the explanations, ancient or modern, are very persuasive. It does not seem likely that the Jews would actually have named their holiday after Haman's lot, which they would not have known about, or, if they had done so, that they would have used the plural, *purim*. The author seems to understand the plural as an allusion to the two days of the holiday, but that would be no reason to call it "lots." Clines sees in the plural a hint of two contradictory lots cast for the Jews, one by Haman, another by God (p. 164). But the book never even alludes to a second lot,[67] and this explanation is certainly not the author's. Gerleman explains the name of the holiday Purim as originally meaning "portions." (*Goral*, "lot," and *manah*, "portion," are used as synonyms, or at least as allied concepts, in Jer 13:15 and Ps 16:5, where they mean "lot" in the sense of "fate."). However, nothing in the book of Esther identifies the "portions" with the *pur* or views the sending of portions as expressive of the holiday's origins. The opacity of the name "Purim" suggests that the holiday and its name existed before the book of Esther was composed and that the author is making an effort to connect the two.

(**9:26b-27**) The Jews take the obligations of Purim upon themselves and their descendants for two reasons: Mordecai's epistle and their own awareness of recent events. The latter reason is highlighted by being formulated as if it were two: "what they had seen in this regard, and . . . what had come upon them." In this way, special importance is given to the collective experience of those who took part in the events. The Purim festival grows out of their suffering and their joy (Bardtke).

The days are to be observed "just as written," literally, "according to their writing." This can only refer to Mordecai's letter, since that is the only writing the Jews have received on the matter.

Of the various things "written," the time of the holiday is singled out for mention as an obligation the Jews took upon themselves. The duty of celebrating the holiday on two days is stated so emphatically as to sound polemic, as if a contrary view or practice is being repudiated. Since any locality would have held festivities on only one day (the 14th or the 15th), it is likely that many people insisted that the holiday be observed on the day that *they* held it on.

"Those who join themselves to [the Jews]" are bound by the same undertaking as the rest of the Jewish people. This remark reinforces the interpretation of *mityahădim* in 8:17 as converts

---

67. God's lots are first mentioned in the LXX, Add F (F 7–8), where it says that God cast one lot for the nations and one for Israel.

rather than pretenders. Although their original motivation was fear, their continued loyalty is taken for granted.

(**9:28**) The narrator speaks from the standpoint of his own generation, revealing, as in 1:1, that he is looking back from a distance. This revelation gives authority to his assertion that the Jews have followed this practice for many generations now. The Jews of Mordecai's day, we are told, succeeded in creating a holiday that lives on in full vitality—everywhere. Just as the laws of the Persian Empire were disseminated among all its subjects, the practice of Purim was diffused among all Jews in every place for all times—the text is most insistent on the universality of the practice in the author's own day. The continued universality of the practice is taken as further evidence for its validity.

Like the laws of the Persians and Medes, this practice (though not called a law), "shall not pass away." The days will be commemorated everywhere and forever.

Scene i, Mordecai's letter and its effect, has five components:

(a) 9:20–22. Mordecai's letter calling for the celebration of 14–15 Adar

(b) 9:23. The Jews' acceptance of Mordecai's call

(c) 9:24–25. The reason for this acceptance, in the form of a historical summary

(d) 9:26a. The explanation of the name "Purim"

(e) 9:26b-28. The Jews' acceptance of the observance in perpetuity.

This scene is notable for its discursive character, with its etiology, analysis of motives, and rendering of the process of legislation into components. The narrator is not merely reporting what occurred. The lengthy and somewhat convoluted argumentation is directed at convincing the reader of the historical grounding and legal validity of the new holiday.

Rather than saying that this passage institutionalizes the celebration of Purim, it would be more precise to say that it institutionalizes the celebration of two days of Purim. The emphasis on observing precisely these two days in this section as well as in 9:1–19 and 31 ("in their times"—plural) suggests that for the author it was not so much the propriety of the holiday at issue as the way it is to be observed. It seems that the author is writing at a time when the holiday was already a popular custom but was being held on different dates in different places. The author reconciles the difference by enshrining it in history and the national will.

ii

(9:29) And Queen Esther, daughter of Abihayil, and Mordecai the Jew[68] conveyed in writing[69] all the authority necessary to confirm this second[70] Purim epistle. (30) And he sent letters to all the Jews, to the 127 provinces of Xerxes' kingdom—words of greeting and faithfulness—(31) to confirm the observance of these days[71] of Purim in their set times, just as Mordecai the Jew and Queen Esther[72] had confirmed upon them, in the way that they confirm upon themselves and their descendants matters of fasting and the accompanying laments.[73] (32) And the declaration of Esther confirmed these matters concerning Purim, and it was written in a document.

EMENDED VERSION:
(29) And Queen Esther, daughter of Abihayil, conveyed in writing all the authority necessary to confirm this Purim epistle. (30) And letters were sent to all the Jews in the 127 provinces of Xerxes' kingdom—words of greeting and faithfulness—(31) to confirm the observance of these days of Purim in their set times, just as Mordecai the Jew had confirmed upon them, in the way that they confirm upon themselves and their descendants matters of fasting and the accompanying laments. (32) And the declaration of Esther confirmed these matters concerning Purim, and it was written in a document.

Esther adds her authority to the practice of Purim
Date: not long after Mordecai's epistle

(9:29–31) The Massoretic text in this passage presents several difficulties that have led to certain emendations widely accepted by modern commentators (e.g., Paton, Moore, Gerleman, Bardtke). We will consider these emendations later; but whatever their virtues, we should first try to understand the MT in its own terms. Since the difficulties do not seem to be simply errors of copying, we must ask just what the present text meant to whoever produced

---

68. MT's "and Mordecai the Jew" is probably a gloss; see comment.
69. "Conveyed in writing": lit., "wrote" (3 fem. sg.).
70. "Second" is probably a later addition; see comment.
71. Lit., "to confirm these days. . . ."
72. The phrase "and Queen Esther" is probably a secondary addition; see comment.
73. Lit., "matters of fasting and their outcry"; i.e., the lamentation accompanying the fasting. See comment.

it—whether this was the MT-author or a later scribe. The main problem is who (according to the MT of this passage) wrote letter #1 (9:20–25) and who wrote letter #2 (9:29–31).

According to the MT, letter #2 was written by both Esther and Mordecai (v. 29), who write to confirm "this second Purim epistle," that is, letter #2, which they are now writing. Letter #2, according to verse 31b, for its part confirms letter #1, the epistle whose authors were (according to verse 31b) both Mordecai and Esther (v. 31b). Finally, Esther's word—apparently distinct from letter #2—confirms "these matters of Purim" (v. 32), which seems to refer to letters #1 and #2 together.

This convoluted text may be interpreted, with some straining, as follows: In letter #2, Esther and Mordecai add their joint authority to their own epistle, letter #2. ("This second Purim epistle," which they are now confirming, must refer to letter #2, the one sent out in verse 30.) The gist of this reflexive confirmation may be imagined along these lines: "We, Mordecai the Jew and Queen Esther, hereby assert the following: 'We hereby confirm the validity by the practices previously confirmed by Mordecai the Jew and Queen Esther. . . .'" Their letter #2, the "second epistle," thus confirms both itself and letter #1, which validated the practice undertaken spontaneously by the Jews. Given the great emphasis the chapter places on confirmation and reconfirmation, it is not impossible that this additional validation—a complex self-confirmation—was indeed the author's intention.

The present text of letter #2 presents the two leaders as partners at each stage, both in the present proclamation *and* in the original epistle, letter #1. Authority is amassed by having both leaders write both letters. If this interpretation is correct, the purpose of letter #2 is simply emphasis, adding layer upon layer of confirmatory declarations. The "declaration of Esther" in verse 32 is an additional confirmation.

The above reading, though required by the text in its current state, does not really do away with the difficulties. These are listed below, along with the emendations that eliminate them:

DIFFICULTIES	EMENDATIONS
(1) Verse 29a is apparently contradicted by verse 32, according to which it is Esther's word alone at this stage that	Excise "and Mordecai the Jew" from verse 29, making letter #2 Esther's alone. Consequently, the verb "he sent" at

confirms the Purim practices (v. 32 is most naturally read as a reference to letter #2). And it does not make much sense for Esther and Mordecai to confirm their own confirmation.

the start of verse 30 must be modified to read "there were sent" (a relatively minor change in Hebrew) or "she sent" (see the Appendix).

(2) The MT of verse 31aα has Esther and Mordecai issuing letter #1, while according to verses 20–22, Mordecai did that alone.

Remove "and Queen Esther" from verse 31.

(3) There is little point in confirming a second letter *in* the second letter.

Omit "second" from the end of verse 29. "This epistle" then refers to the one previously mentioned (letter #1).

These are major emendations, all conjectural. The ancient versions (discussed in the Appendix) do not weigh for or against them, because they either lack the passage or differ too much to contribute to the reconstruction of the Hebrew text. The only argument on behalf of the emendations is that they produce a much neater text: Esther writes a letter (#2) to confirm by her authority the validity of Mordecai's epistle (#1).

The resulting text is coherent, but if we accept it we must explain how the present obscure one came about. In the case of "Queen Esther" in verse 31 and "Mordecai the Jew" in verse 29, we can surmise that a scribe wished to double the authority behind each letter. It is, however, hard to think of a reason for the addition of "second" in verse 29. Perhaps a later scribe did not know which letter was meant by "this epistle" and added "second" as an explanatory gloss, thinking to help the reader but actually injecting his own confusion into the text. Gerleman suggests that a scribe thought that "this letter" was the object of "wrote" rather than "confirm," and so believed that the addition of "second" made sense.

(**9:30**) The phrase "words of greeting and faithfulness" (thus Haupt 1908:173) is in apposition to "letters" (*sᵉparim*) and describes the character of their contents, but the purpose of this description is not evident.

(**9:31**) The phrase "matters of fasting and the accompanying laments"—literally, "matters of fasting and their outcry"—is usually understood as an additional regulation establishing a fast in conjunction with the holiday, to commemorate the Jews' earlier fast (4:3) or Esther's fast (4:16). It is often deemed a later addition; however, this phrase, whether original or additional, does not actually convey the notion that fasting is henceforth an obligation. To do that, the author (or glossator) would have to make Esther *call* for such a practice, rather than merely tacking it on to the end of a sentence as an incidental comparison. Moreover, by the usual interpretation, the end of the verse draws a comparison and must be rendered, "and just as [the Jews] had confirmed upon themselves and their descendants the matters of fasting and their outcry." But we were not informed earlier that the Jews had done this, so that there is nothing for the present act to be compared to. Finally, although this verse supposedly institutes a fast in conjunction with Purim, nothing is known of such a practice until several centuries later. The Talmudic tractate Megilla, which regulates Purim practices in detail, does not mention it.[74]

A better interpretation can be offered on the basis of Ibn Ezra's explanation, who writes: "The Jews confirmed for themselves to rejoice in the days of Purim just as they confirmed for themselves and their descendants to fast in the days of their mourning when the city [of Jerusalem] was broken open and the Temple was burnt, for the prophet did not command them to fast. . . . " Ibn Ezra is referring to Zech 8:19, which mentions fasts instituted in the fourth, fifth, seventh, and tenth months. Ibn Ezra recognizes that the comparison implied by the phrase in question only pertains to the *manner* of obligation. Fasts like those in the time of Zechariah were not commanded by the Torah or by a prophet, but were instead voluntary commitments on the part of the community. This explanation is followed by Schwarz 1923:196. Malbim further explains that one can legitimately undertake such obligations as a form of vow without ascribing their origin to the Torah. A further point of comparison, we might add, is that a vow cannot be imposed by religious authorities but must be freely undertaken by individuals or the community.

I would modify Ibn Ezra's interpretation only by suggesting that the phrase "fasts and their outcries" is too vague to point spe-

---

74. The post-Talmudic tractate Sopherim (21:1) mentions a three-day fast following Purim. A "Fast of Esther" on 13 Adar is first attested in the eighth century, in the *She'iltot* of R. Aḥa of Shabha. He derives the practice from 9:18, which refers to the Jews "gathering." Maimonides relates the practice to 9:31 (*Yad Haḥazaka* Ta'anit 5:5).

cifically to those mentioned in Zechariah. Instead, it refers generally to any communal fast that can be proclaimed following or preceding a disaster. Est 4:3 and 16 provide examples of communal fasts, and one might take this phrase as a specific allusion to one such event (thus Loewenstamm 1971:123). Those fasts, however, were one-time, spontaneous outbursts, which cannot be said to have been "confirmed," either for the community at that time or their descendants, whereas 9:31 speaks of the institution of permanent practices. Thus the comparison intended is probably more general: the voluntary institution of permanent fasts for whatever occasion might require them.

(9:32) Maintaining the MT would require us to distinguish the declaration mentioned in this verse from the "second epistle," whereas in the emended text the epistle of 9:29–31 *is* Esther's "declaration" (letter #2) confirming Mordecai's earlier letter.

By either text, it is Esther's statement that clinches the process, and her words are written down. It is not said in just what book her words were inscribed. This is not our book of Esther, for a self-reference would require "in this book," as often in Deuteronomy. In any case, 9:32b is not a bibliographic reference. It is the fact that her words were inscribed, not where they were inscribed, that is significant. By inscription her statement becomes a protocol—solid, permanent, important (cf. 1 Sam 10:25 and especially Exod 17:14, where the obligation to annihilate Amalek is to be written "as a reminder, in a document"). In Clines' words, "In Esther, reality tends toward inscripturation, and attains its true quality only when it is written down. What is written is valid and permanent; what happens merely happens and is thereupon cast to the winds—unless it is recorded" (p. 22). By inscripturation, words are also made available (in principle, at least) as evidence. Since the reader is not told where to find this evidence, 9:32 testifies to its existence rather than constituting evidence itself.

The significance of the second Purim epistle lies not in its difference from the first but in its identity to it: letter #2 seconds and undergirds the authority of letter #1, Mordecai's epistle. In the MT, the second epistle adds more of their joint authority to their first declaration. In the emended version, letter #2 supplements Mordecai's authority by Esther's royal stature.

Act XI is more interested in the process whereby current practices arose than in their historical causation. The propriety of the process is essential to validate the new practice. The events of year

12 do not directly engender the practices of Purim; rather they inspire and motivate the Jews' decision to celebrate the holiday in perpetuity and to call it Purim. The holiday is not divinely ordained, nor is it an inevitable outgrowth of historical processes. Though it is founded in spontaneous celebration, it became an institution through conscious exercise of leadership, persuasion, deliberation, communal decision, confirmation, and reconfirmation.

Gunkel (1916:44–45) says that between the lines we hear the opposition of pious Jews to celebrating a holiday not commanded by God; that is why the author has the protagonists create and validate the holiday. But the massing of authority does not necessarily indicate that anyone opposed the holiday, though that is a possibility. The non-Mosaic origin of the holiday would itself necessitate extensive formal validation to establish it as a legitimate and obligatory practice.

The holiday receives expression primarily in feasting because that is a concentrated form of rest or respite. The feasts of Purim annually bring to actuality the respite following the battles. They also point forward. By recalling and reenacting an historical experience of great "respite"—which is a return to a state of peace and harmony—they suggest that such a respite lies ahead.

In the final act, the protagonists' personalities have largely faded behind their functions, but there is no violation of continuity with the characters as presented earlier in the book. Xerxes is out of the picture in scenes i and ii, not only because he is no longer needed for the story, but also because he has, so far as it concerns the Jews, transferred his authority to his wife and his vizier. Mordecai continues unchanged—powerful, energetic, paternalistic, issuing public epistles, and exercising authority through his position as vizier and as recognized leader of the Jews. Esther has reached a pinnacle of power and authority.

Act XII.   10:1–3. Epilogue: Mordecai's Accomplishments.

(10:1) King Xerxes levied a tax on the land and the islands of the sea. (2) Now the entire story of his power and might, and the account of how the king had exalted Mordecai—these are all written in the book of the chronicles of the kings of Media and Persia. (3) For Mordecai the Jew was viceroy to King Xerxes and influential for the Jews and popular with his many brethren, seeking the betterment of his people and speaking on behalf of the welfare of all its descendants.

Mordecai's subsequent history
Date: indefinite

(**10:1**) Some time later Xerxes levies a *mas* on the empire and even on ʾiyyey hayyam, the "islands" or "coastlands," probably the Ionian lands, which were on the western extremity of the Persian empire. *Mas* means corvée elsewhere in biblical Hebrew; in rabbinic Hebrew it means tax. Either sense is possible here, but the latter is preferable because of the improbability that many forced laborers could be assembled from distant islands (though a hyperbolic statement is, of course, possible, as Meinhold points out). As for widespread taxation, we may compare Herodotus' statement about the revenue powers of Darius I: "but as time went on, more came in from the islands and from the peoples in Europe as far as Thessaly" (III 96).

Readers have wondered what relevance Xerxes' tax (or corvée) has to the story. Gunkel guesses that the tax served to rein in the king's subordinates, who had become too arrogant, thus teaching them to bear the common yoke and cease their quarreling (p. 47). But the Xerxes we have seen so far would show no such concern for self-discipline and ethical deportment. Nor is there anything to suggest that the nobles have become more arrogant than the author assumes nobles usually are. In any case, taxation might merely direct their hostility toward the king himself. Daube (1946) argues that the tax is a peaceful substitute for the revenues Xerxes would have gained by bribery and plunder had Haman's plot succeeded. But the text hints at no connection between the two acts, as if one were the reward for the other, and anyway Xerxes could have levied a tax in addition to taking Haman's bribe, had he so wished.

This tax may, however, be connected (by reversal) with an earlier act of Xerxes, his granting of "(tax) relief" (hănaḥah) in honor of Esther's coronation (2:18). No direct association is drawn, but levying a tax is the direct opposite of giving tax relief (Ehrlich). One message of 10:1, in the light of this connection, is that not only does Jewish success benefit other subjects of the realm (in this case, by a tax relief), it is good for the royal coffers. This is a message of Gen 47:13−26, in which Joseph delivers the Egyptians from starvation all the while bringing the entire land into the king's ownership and establishing a 20 percent income tax. Esther 10:1 may be a reflex of that passage, though different vocabulary is used and Mordecai is not said to have masterminded the taxation. (Perhaps the author is not eager to have a Jew blamed for taxation.)

Beyond suggesting that Jews benefit their royal employers, the verse emphasizes Xerxes' prosperity and the extent of his power, which reaches far to the west.

(**10:2**) An account of Mordecai's power and importance was recorded in the Persian annals. We might wonder why Esther's power and importance were not also mentioned, since these have by no means been neglected in the book so far. We are probably to understand that what was recorded in the annals was not Mordecai's deeds on behalf of the Jews (of less interest to the Persian annalists), but his power and importance in the service of the crown. The account in the annals is said to include Mordecai's promotion. Though a minor matter in the book of Esther, this would be significant to the official archives.

The reference to "how the king had exalted Mordecai" reminds us that Mordecai has replaced his enemy who, we were told in similar language, "King Xerxes had exalted" (or "promoted") (3:1).

(**10:3**) Mordecai was high in the favor of his fellow Jews and ever sought their welfare, advocating their cause like a Jewish *shtadlan* in the courts of Europe. Powerful protectors and advocates have always been important to minority groups with uncertain legal status.

At the close of the book of Esther, Mordecai's popularity among his fellow Jews is meant to demonstrate his virtue and success. A similar concern for popular attitudes permeates 9:20–32.

The book does not end with Esther; her role ended when she supports Mordecai's initiative. It is Mordecai's glory that interests the author in the epilogue, where he praises him for his personal glory and his unending concern for his people. Mordecai goes down in Persian history.

CHAPTER III

HISTORICITY AND DATING

1. Historicity

Did it really happen? The answer to this question bears on our understanding of character portrayal. To be sure, even if a book is historical in all details, we can speak about its characters in much the same way as we do fictional persons, since we learn about the two types of character in much the same way (see chap. I §2). But the greater the fictionality of a work, the greater the author's control over the characters, events, words, and omissions, so that every detail becomes potential evidence for a character trait. This is the case in Esther. Even if the story has, as some contend, a historical "core," the book in its present shape is certainly a fictional creation with strongly legendary features. Various legendary qualities as well as several inaccuracies and implausibilities immediately throw doubt on the book's historicity and give the impression of a writer recalling a vaguely remembered past.

When testing the assumptions and details of Esther against data known from elsewhere, we must rely primarily on the Classical Greek historians, in particular Herodotus, Ctesias, and Xenophon, who report on the Persian empire at length—Herodotus at a distance of only 20–25 years from the reign of Xerxes.

a. Arguments Against the Book's Historicity

I. THE LEGENDARY OPENING.   The author looks back to an indefinite, distant past, to the reign of a Xerxes who, though famous, must be identified: "the very Xerxes who ruled from India to Nubia, 127 provinces in all (1:1).[1] These words are certainly not spo-

---

1. There was a short-lived Xerxes II (424). Ezra 4:6 places a Xerxes between Cyrus and Darius (Xerxes I was Darius's son), while Dan 9:1 speaks of a Xerxes (Ahasueros), father of Darius (Xerxes I had a son named Darius, but he was slain immediately after Xerxes' death). There was naturally some confusion in Jewish traditions about the genealogies of the Persian kings. Apparently the author of Esther wants us to know that Xerxes the Great is the king of this story.

ken from Mordecai's point of view, contrary to a Jewish tradition that identifies him as the writer.[2] Identifying the king as "the very Xerxes who ruled" suggests the stance of a writer working in a period when the king of Persia was no longer ruler of the entire East, in other words, the Hellenistic era, some time after Alexander's conquest of Persia in 330 B.C.E. . The phrase "in those days" also suggests the perspective of a later generation. Moreover, the remark in 9:28, "And so these days are celebrated as a memorial and observed in each and every generation," implies a distance of several generations between the report and the events reported.[3]

II. INACCURACIES.   The book of Esther contradicts our best knowledge of Persian history in several ways:

(1) Xerxes is said to have ruled over 127 "provinces," meaning satrapies (see the Commentary on 1:1), whereas there were actually only 20 to 31 satrapies in the Persian empire.[4] Esther (as well as the book of Daniel, which speaks of 120 *satrapies*) exhibits. the propensity of legend to inflate qualities and quantities of ancient times.

(2) Xerxes, according to Herodotus, was married to one Amestris (VII 114, IX 112). She was still his wife in 479, the year Xerxes spent in Ionia after his defeat at Salamis (IX 112)—this was the year *after* he supposedly married Esther—and Ametris remained his wife in her old age (VII 114).

(3) The Scroll has Xerxes marrying an obscure maiden of unknown ancestry, contrary to the rule that the queen of Persia had to come from one of seven noble families. (The practice is reported by Herodotus in III 84. Though embedded in an account with a legendary cast, it accords with what we know of the background of the Persian queens.) Esther, we should note, is not merely one of the harem, but *the* queen, the replacement for Vashti; see 2:17.

---

2. See Commentary on 9:20. The phrase "in those days" in 1:2 would also be inappropriate for a book written by Mordecai, even if we imagine him surviving into the next reign (which began in 465).

3. The verbs are participles and convey a continuous-present tense. Like Mishnaic Hebrew, Esther has a tense system, distinguishing *qatal* for past, *yiqtol* for future, and participles for present, with few exceptions; note the *yiqtol* forms for future tense in 9:28b.

4. According to Her. III 89, Darius I set up twenty satrapies. Darius' own monuments list 23 (Behistun), 24 (Persepolis) and 29 or 30 (Nakhsh-i-Rustam) administrative units. Under Xerxes there were apparently twenty satrapies.

(4) The author is mistaken about the layout of Susa during the Achemenid period. At that time, the royal palace lay on a mound in the north, while the courtiers and officials dwelt on the south-eastern hill. In Esther, on the other hand, the royal palace is on the hill, and various officials live there as well (1:5; 2:5).[5]

(5) There was no principle forbidding the Persians to change their laws; that notion is found nowhere but in Esther and Daniel. It would be impossible to run a government by such a principle.

III. IMPLAUSIBILITIES AND IMPOSSIBILITIES. It is unlikely, if not impossible

(1) that two non-Persians, one after the other, would be selected for the highest office in the empire;

(2) that these two viziers as well as Queen Esther would not be mentioned in historical sources, in spite of the anomaly of their presence in office;

(3) that Esther would be introduced into the harem in 480 B.C.E. (2:16), when Xerxes was away fighting in Greece and hardly likely to be concerned with choosing a new wife;

(4) that the historical Xerxes—who was not a fool—would issue such an inane edict as the one quoted in 1:22. (Such things do happen, of course; but *a priori* they must still be reckoned implausible);

(5) that Xerxes would allow massive, uncontrolled battles, leading to the death of thousands, to take place throughout his empire;[6] and further that this catastrophe would leave no imprint in the historical record;[7]

---

5. Noted by Stiehl 1956:15. Stiehl says that this situation did exist in the time of Antiochus III (223–187 B.C.E.). However, the statement in Polybius V 48.14 hardly proves it, and in any case we do not know how early that arrangement came into being.

6. He would have to have been mad to do this, not merely erratic. The historical Xerxes was an effective monarch, in spite of his failed invasion of Greece. He reaped a series of military victories and retained control over most of the Greeks. He initiated and completed several significant architectural projects at Persepolis (Olmstead 1948:230).

7. An argument from silence is valid when (1) the event in question is of such a magnitude that it could be expected to leave an impression on other sources; and (2) we have an adequate number of other sources that could reasonably be expected to take note of the event. The Greek historians were fascinated by all that was *outré* in the Orient, and it is hardly credible that they would not have heard of this worldwide upheaval. Nor is there so much as a whisper of this event in any other source, Elamite or Babylonian, for example.

(6) that Mordecai, exiled from Jerusalem in 587 B.C.E. (2:6), could still be alive and active in 473 and for some time thereafter, or that he could have a cousin who was still an attractive young virgin.

All the above inaccuracies, implausibilities, and impossibilities argue that the events did not happen as reported—which is to say that *these* events did not happen. They mark a writer working at a much later time who is not familiar with the chronology, geography, and events of the period he is writing about. Such confusions are common in ancient books that tell about earlier times. The book of Judith (second half of the second century B.C.E.) calls Nebuchadnezzar the king of the Assyrians (he was actually king of Babylonia) and says that he ruled from Nineveh (which was actually destroyed before he came to the throne). The author of Tobit (second century B.C.E. or later) tells about a man who was taken into exile in Assyria, yet he has the Assyrian kings out of order and believes that Nebuchadnezzar and Asuerus (Xerxes)—who actually lived centuries apart—together destroyed Nineveh (14:15).

If the Scroll were not canonical, it is hard to imagine scholars arguing for its historicity, or even its "historical core," any more than they now insist that Judith and Tobit were written in the ages they tell about or that they record actual events.

b. Arguments For the Book's Historicity

There are no arguments *for* the book's historicity, that is to say, positive evidence that the events reported actually occurred. There are only arguments asserting the *possibility* that they happened; these are of two sorts: circumstantial and permissive.[8]

I. CIRCUMSTANTIAL ARGUMENTS. Circumstantial arguments assert that many details of the story accord with information from other sources about the world in which the story is set.

(1) There was a king Xerxes who ruled from India to Ethiopia and who liked to give sumptuous banquets.

(2) There was a good system of post riders in the Persian empire.

---

8. For a typical defense of the book's historicity see Wright 1970, which musters most of the following arguments.

(3) There are some actual Persian names and words used (though most cannot be identified with any certainty).[9] No Greek names or words appear.

(4) There seems to be an allusion to the Ab-Kharkha river in Susa (4:17).

Items 1–4 would, however, be known to a later writer both from the Classical historians and from living legend. To the Greeks, Xerxes was notorious as the archetypal Oriental potentate—autocratic, erratic, and sybaritic. Persian names and words and the basic geography of Susa would also be available to a Hellenistic writer, especially one living in Susa, and he could easily distinguish Persian from Greek if he wished to avoid obvious anachronisms.

(5) The picture drawn of the situation of the Jewish community—its acculturation to Persian ways, the antisemitism, and so on—is "entirely credible."[10]

This picture is indeed credible, because the situation is well known from other times and places (including various Hellenistic communities). But for that very reason, this credibility is no evidence for the writer's firsthand knowledge of Achemenid Jewry. Further circumstantial arguments are:

(6) The name Mordecai was actually used in Persia. A text dated (without certainty) to the beginning of the fifth century mentions an official named Mardukâ, in Susa. "That there were two officials with the same name at the same time in the same place is scarcely likely."[11]

Were this supposition valid, it could just as well prove that the Mordecai of our book did *not* exist.

(7) The author refers the reader to the chronicles of the kings of Media and Persia (10:2), and "only a writer acting in good faith would dare extend such an invitation to his readers."[12]

---

9. See Zadok 1986; Gehman 1924; Paton, pp. 66–71; Duchesne-Guillemin 1953. Though many of the names can be explained as derived from Persian words, few of them are found elsewhere as Persian names.

10. Gordis 1981:386–87.

11. Ungnad 1942–43:219; followed by Gordis 1981:384 and Moore 1971:L.

12. Moore 1971:XXXV. On p. 99, Moore interprets the verse as a reference to a "popular historical account of the Persian kings, possibly written from the Jewish point of view." But no such source exists—and if it once did, then *its* account could be legendary as well.

The proto-AT does not mention these chronicles, and they probably were invented by the MT author, who sought—successfully—to create verisimilitude.

This argument assumes that the Persian chronicles did exist and that they were accessible to the public. The same argument would prove the actuality of Lilliput, since Gulliver's (fictitious) publisher assures the reader that he received Gulliver's papers from Gulliver himself.

II. PERMISSIVE ARGUMENTS. To use permissive arguments is to claim that events and data that appear improbable or contrary to known fact could be true. "Could be" arguments are widely invoked in Bible studies, where many scholars assume that if they can stretch their imaginations far enough to cover the implausibilities in a biblical account, they have somehow made a case for its historicity.[13] Such arguments are legion, because possibilities are limitless. Here are a few of the "could be" arguments that have been applied to Esther:

(1) "It is not impossible that 'Esther' represented an apocopated form of the name 'Amēstris.'"[14] Many things are not impossible, but if this one is true, then we know something about the later career of Esther: she devised the ghastly mutilation of a woman who roused her jealousy (Her. IX 112) and was reported to have ordered nine boys and nine girls buried alive in her old age (Her. VII 114). Fortunately, however, the identification is wrong (if the book of Esther is right), because Amestris had Xerxes' third son in about 483, before Esther came on the scene in 480 (according to 2:16).[15]

(2) It is "not totally excluded," Gordis argues, that the restriction on the marriages of Persian kings mentioned by Herodotus (they could only marry within one of seven noble families) was not

---

13. "Could be" arguments are valid only when refuting counter-arguments to a strong hypothesis. When we have good evidence that something *is* (and not merely may be) true, one can rebut objections on the grounds that other explanations are available for the supposedly contrary evidence. But the primary hypothesis itself must be built on likelihoods rather than bare possibilities.

14. Gordis 1981:384.

15. Wright (1970:41–42) claims that *Amēstris* has a "possible linguistic link" to *Vashti*, which comes down to two letters in common (*s* supposedly corresponds to *š* and *t* = *t*). The identification requires assuming that Vashti was not actually deposed immediately in 484–483 (as chap. 1 has it), since Amestris accompanied Xerxes to Sardis in 480 and was still acting very much as queen. Wright's curious exercise is another example of how the defenders of a biblical book's historical accuracy often do so by sacrificing the truth of its statements.

a law but only a custom, or even just an "unsubstantiated report," [16] but (he reasons) if Herodotus is indeed right, it "cannot be totally ruled out" that Esther was a convert to Judaism, or if that is not so, perhaps Xerxes chose to disregard this law, or maybe Esther was not Xerxes' principal wife. These curious suppositions, intended to support the book's historicity, must deny its accuracy in other regards. Esth 2:5–7 shows that Esther was not a convert; for Xerxes to ignore the marriage law would violate the principle on which the drama is based; and to class Esther as a secondary wife contradicts the fact that she replaces Xerxes' principal wife, "reigns," [17] and is called "the queen." Among the possibilities that cannot be "totally excluded," Gordis neglects to include the option that Queen Esther is a fictional character. Herodotus can, of course, be in error, but he has a claim to credibility when writing about the Persian empire of the preceding generation, especially when he is reporting matters that are not inherently fantastic. In this case, he is at least recording a report he heard, and it is a reasonable one, which neither Herodotus nor his informants would have reason to fabricate. As far as information allows us to determine, this rule was in fact never violated.

III. A "HISTORICAL CORE"? Some defenders of historicity retrench by affirming the presence of a "historical core," some central event such as the existence of a plot against the Jews foiled by Mordecai.[18] The best that can be said for this assumption is that it has not been disproved. By the same token we could as well affirm that there is a "historical core" to the book of Judith, such as the decapitation of the Babylonian general. Though this is nowhere hinted at in any other historical record, it "cannot be totally ruled

---

16. Gordis 1981:385.
17. 2:4. The verb *timlok* would not be used of anyone besides the queen proper.
18. Thus Moore 1971:LII-LIII, who follows Bardtke (248–52) in positing that the Scroll is based on an ancient "midrashic" source (namely, the annals mentioned in 10:2). Moore proposes that this source "may reflect an actual event" (p. LII). Possibility glides into fact on the following page, where he claims that "the Book of Esther has a historical core—the story of Mordecai, and possibly even the story of Esther, to which have been added legendary and fictional elements." Similarly Gordis says that "there is nothing intrinsically impossible or improbable in the central incident." (This is true of most fiction). Therefore, he concludes, "we believe that the book is to be regarded as a basically historical account . . ." (1981:388).

out"[19] that a Jewish widow killed an otherwise unknown Babylonian general, leading to the defeat of Babylon in an otherwise unknown battle. In any case, to say that a book has a "historical core" is to grant that it is not historical as it stands.

IV. A CODED HISTORY?   One theory regards the book of Esther as a coded representation of events belonging to another time and place. This is more plausible than some of the possibilities surveyed above, though no one has yet pointed to a historical situation that fits the story more than vaguely. J. Hoschander asserts, strangely, that the book of Esther is both "strictly historical" (1923:11) and also full of erroneous later interpretations, corruptions, and additions and that it refers to events some eighty years later, in the reign of Artaxerxes II Mnemon. Hoschander goes on to describe in detail an event that *could have* occurred in 392 B.C.E., but that most certainly did not. R. Stiehl argues that the book's background is the reign of the Seleucid Antiochus IV, who afflicted both Judeans and Persians—thus the sympathetic portrayal of the Persian king—and who was defeated and driven out of Palestine by the Hasmoneans in 165–163 B.C.E.[20] But the book of Esther does not correlate with that situation even as a code. The gentile king in Esther is portrayed as vaguely sympathetic, while Antiochus IV was hostile and brutal. Also, the afflictions of the Judeans by a foreign power are in no way comparable to a pogrom in which Jews in the diaspora are attacked by their neighbors. Moreover, there is no allusion to the most painful manifestation of the crisis in Judea, the desecration of the Temple in Jerusalem.

A work that is full of legendary features and improbable incidents and that has no external attestation should be presumed to be fictional. To be sure, to read Esther as fictional, while a legitimate critical stance, runs contrary to the intentions of the author, who almost certainly meant us to read the book as a precise report of actual historical events. We must therefore balance two distinct perspectives. As critical readers, viewing the text as an object from a deliberate distance, we can recognize the book as fiction and analyze it in those terms, while as immediate readers, giving ourselves over to the book's own terms, we can respond to its realities—those it creates and those it reflects—as if they were our own. In one

19. As Gordis (1981:385) says of one of this theories.
20. Stiehl 1956, cf. 1963; see esp. 1956:18–22.

138

sense they are: in a fundamental way the legend is very true to history. Its story is an epitome of numerous occasions on which Jewish communities were delivered from threats to their existence.

2. Date

The story of the Scroll is most likely legend. Yet it presents itself as history not fiction, for history provides the grounds for the establishment of the holiday. Hence it could not report events and details that its first readers knew were fictitious. A much later writer, however, could get away with misinformation, and, in fact, might be writing in good faith, contriving a picture of Xerxes' reign confected from legends, romances, and historical romances such as were popular in the Hellenistic world. It is, for example, unlikely that a writer would refer to the 127 satrapies of Persia while the Persian empire was still in existence, any more than a modern work about the United States would be accepted as history if it spoke of the 300 States of the Union. For that reason, I would date the book in the Hellenistic period, as do many modern commentators. The Greek translation (according to a note at its end) was brought to Egypt in 73 B.C.E.,[21] making a date considerably earlier than that probable for the Hebrew. There is nothing to allow a more precise dating.

The book's language is, in our present state of knowledge, of little value in determining the date of authorship. The language is, of course, "late biblical Hebrew" (LBH)—meaning postexilic. We cannot determine how late the language is, for we lack the data for calibrating linguistic dating of works originating between the fifth and second centuries B.C.E. Striedl[22] notes Esther's linguistic similarity to Chronicles (and mistakenly thinks that this shows that the book cannot be earlier than the third century), while R. Polzin distinguishes Esther's language from that of Chronicles, Ezra, and the

---

21. The Greek Esther, according to the colophon, was brought to Egypt in the fourth year of the reign of Ptolemy and Cleopatra. This probably refers to Ptolemy XII Auletos, making the date 73 B.C.E. This is Bickerman's understanding of the colophon (1944:347). Another view identifies the Ptolemy of the colophon with Ptolemy VIII Soter II, ca. 114 B.C.E. (Jacob 1890:279–80).
22. Striedl 1937:81. He says that the Scroll's language gives the impression of being an artificial literary dialect rather than a natural, living language (pp. 82, 98), but even if his impression is correct, that means only that the book was written as literature, not that it was written at a time when there was no spoken Hebrew.

non-memoir portions of Nehemiah.[23] R. Bergey examines a number of linguistic features and concludes that the book's language is composed of a mixture of features characteristic of early (preexilic) BH, LBH, and the Hebrew of the Tannaim (the rabbis of the first to third centuries C.E.), and also that Esther belongs toward the later end of the LBH spectrum.[24]

In conclusion, a third century dating seems most likely. The dating of the Septuagint (see above) requires dating the Hebrew no later than the second century B.C.E. The Hasmonean rebellion (165 B.C.E.) and restoration of the Judean kingdom (completed by 145 B.C.E.) have made no impression on the writer. As for place of origin, the author's knowledge of Persian names and words and of (post-Achemenid) Susan geography, and his special interest in the date of the holiday in Susa, suggest that he was Susan, as does the Susan perspective of 9:19, which assumes the Susan date of Purim (15 Adar) and explains the non-Susan one (14 Adar). These arguments are not conclusive, however, since Hellenistic readers enjoyed local color in descriptions of exotic places,[25] and all the data about Susa could have been learned at a distance to provide just that.

---

23. Polzin 1976:74.
24. 1984, 1988, and, most fully, 1983, esp. pp. 181–86. In brief, Bergey—conceding the tentativeness of his conclusions—argues, first, that Esther has some late features which are not found in other LBH sources but which do appear in the Mishna (and sometimes the Dead Sea Scrolls), and, second, that there are late features in Esther which contrast with earlier equivalents still being used in the other LBH sources (sometimes including the Dead Sea Scrolls). The available data do not allow a more precise dating, but they do make a pre-Hellenistic dating very improbable.
25. Bickerman 1967:206.

CHAPTER IV

GENRES

What *type* of book is Esther? Questions about a text's genre (or "Gattung," or "form"—the terms are poorly distinguished) are the concern of Form Criticism, an important endeavor in Bible studies lately neglected in favor of aesthetic, thematic, and ideological analyses of individual texts.[1] The original concern of Form Criticism was to trace the history of the forms of biblical literature and to ascertain their social functions. This is not, however, a goal of the present monograph, for to do so requires a large number of exemplars of the same types, preferably some of them datable, and these are not available for Esther.

Genre criticism may look at the classification of the text as a whole or of its parts. The problem with classifying the parts is that this quickly becomes an exercise in ad hoc labeling, as is the case with Dommershausen's study (1968), which is the only extensive typology of the Scroll's component genres, that is, of its minimal literary units. As Dommershausen proceeds through the book of Esther, he gives each unit a label he finds appropriate. 1:1–22, for example, is "narration," 2:1–4 is a "servant speech," 2:5–7 is a "biographical note," and 2:21–23 is "short report." None of this is very informative.

Genre identification probably performs its most viable service when it treats the work as a whole and sets it within an appropriate group of texts. Such classification may help us ascertain the author's purposes and strategies and also give us a sense of the way the original audience was supposed to read the text, on the assumption that similar texts reflect and respond to similar needs and interests. Readers approach a text with certain expectations, which the author can reinforce, play upon, or defy. To do a literary work justice, we should try to read it with something like the mind-set the author expected of the readers, and genre criticism may aid in this.

We should observe first of all that although genre criticism

---

1. Coats (1985:7–15) has a clear exposition of genre analysis in the introduction to his anthology on narrative forms in OT literature. This anthology includes a valuable study by Humphreys on the Story of Esther and Mordecai.

tends to ask about *the* genre of a text, with each scholar advocating one candidate and rejecting all others, no text has a single "right" genre. Every text is a member of numerous different sets,[2] each one of which constitutes a different genre. A psalm (Ps 89, e.g.) can be a poem and a liturgical song and a hymn and a national lament and a royal psalm and a prayer for deliverance, and more—not because it is a "mixture" of originally "pure" genres,[3] but because it belongs to overlapping and nested sets. One may choose to approach a text with extremely broad classifications ("poetry," or even "literature," for example) or ones so narrow that the set has only one member. In fact, the act of reading may be conceived of as a progressive narrowing of genre until we arrive at an "intrinsic genre" that determines the meaning of the text being read.[4]

Some genre identifications are more useful than others, and some are just wrong and misleading. In the following, I reject the first three genre hypotheses and accept the others. The latter all place Esther in appropriate groupings, though they are not equally helpful. The most useful are, unfortunately, represented by an inadequate pool of exemplars. To draw conclusions about genre from two or three exemplars (as we are forced to do in the case of Esther) is like describing Elizabethan historical drama on the basis of Shakespeare's *Henry V* and Marlowe's *Edward IV* alone. A few generalizations can reasonably be wagered, but the addition of a new work to the grouping could easily overturn them.

1. Wisdom Literature?[5]

S. Talmon (1963) classified and interpreted the book of Esther as a historicized Wisdom tale. This hypothesis is significant because it places Esther in (or near[6]) a well-known genre and makes asser-

---

2. Genres are in fact *fuzzy* sets. In fuzzy-set theory, an element may belong partially to a set, and there may be gradations of membership and blurred boundaries.
3. As if genres were races that begin "pure" and progressively degenerate. This is the metaphor underlying (and distorting) Gunkel's concept of genre (see, e.g., Gunkel 1925 [1906]: 65–66).
4. The process is well analyzed by Hirsch 1967, chap. 3.
5. "Wisdom Literature" refers first of all to didactic literature—gnomic instructions such as Proverbs and Ben Sira, as well as numerous Egyptian and Mesopotamian texts of similar nature—and secondarily to some speculative, often skeptical, books, in particular Ecclesiastes and Job. Certain Psalms also are closely allied to Wisdom.
6. There are few historicized Wisdom tales. Only the preambles to the Aramaic Ahiqar and the Egyptian (Demotic) Onchsheshonqy clearly belong in that

tions that bear strongly on interpretation. Talmon argues that there are strong similarities between Esther and Wisdom Literature in various regards: the concept of an unspecified and remote deity; the lack of interest in Jewish history or community; the story's anthropocentricity; its static, typological characters; and several of its motifs and ideas, such as adoption by a wise man (cf. the story of Ahiqar), and the notion that the wicked man meets an untimely death (e.g., Prov 26:27).

Talmon's theory has been criticized for overstretching the category of Wisdom and for failing to reckon with non-Wisdom elements in Esther.[7] It seems to me that Esther is not affiliated with Wisdom by even the broadest definition and that few—if any—of its elements are derived from Wisdom. Wisdom Literature by no means conceives of God as vague or remote. In Proverbs and other didactic texts, God is intimately involved in man's life and—in sharpest contrast to Esther—is mentioned repeatedly. And, quite contrary to Talmon, national concerns—Jewish history, community, destiny—are at the center of interest in the Scroll, while these are indeed absent from biblical Wisdom and of secondary importance in other Wisdom literatures. The characters in Esther may be typical, but they are not the types of Wisdom Literature, which, except for those in borderline texts such as Job, are almost all purely stereotypical and designated abstractly—"the wise man," "the righteous man," "the wicked man," and so on. No such epithets, so frequent in all of Wisdom, are employed in Esther. Nor are all the figures in Esther superficial or (as Talmon himself grants [1963:449]) static.

Haman does not quite fit the Wisdom stereotype of the fool (see chap. VIII §3), nor is Mordecai based on the Wisdom ideal of the eloquent sage. The practice of adoption is mentioned in only one Wisdom text (Ahiqar) and can hardly be considered a special feature of Wisdom thought. Many sayings of Wisdom can of course be applied to the Esther story, for example, "He who digs a pit will fall into it," but one can always find a proverb appropriate to any situation—that's what proverbs are for. One could as well say that *Madame Bovary* is a Wisdom Tale because her adultery exemplifies Prov 30:20 (beautifully!).

---

category—not because of their content so much as their collocation with Wisdom Instructions proper. Most of Talmon's comparisons draw upon Wisdom Instructions, such as Proverbs, Ben Sira, and the body of Ahiqar.

7. Crenshaw 1969:140–42.

2. A Persian Chronicle?

R. Gordis put forward another bold hypothesis: the Scroll is a fictitious chronicle from the Persian court, purportedly composed by a gentile scribe and modeled on Persian royal annals.[8] Gordis's task is made easy—and undermined—by the fact that he is comparing Esther to something that is not extant or even secondarily attested; there are not even *fictitious* Persian chronicles to show what one looked like. In any case, the Scroll does not identify itself as an extraction from Persian royal chronicles, which it should do if that is how it is supposed to be perceived. In fact, royal chronicles are mentioned in 10:2 as something *other* than this book; they are the object of an external reference. The Letter of Aristeas, which Gordis musters in support of his contention, does show that pseudepigraphic attribution to gentile courtiers was a possible technique in Hellenistic Jewish literature, but it also shows what such attribution looked like—and it is not at all like Esther. First, attribution is clear in Aristeas; there is, after all, no point in putting on an invisible mask. Second, Aristeas is openly apologetic, inculcating the notion that even gentiles must recognize the truth and nobility of Judaism (see Gordis's description of this work, p. 379). This is the import of the gentiles' prayers and declarations in Daniel as well (2:46–47; 3:28–29; 4:2–3, 34–37; 6:25–27). There is a bare touch of this in Esther (6:13), but the gentiles who are speaking there are not (even by Gordis's thesis) the putative authors of the book. If we follow Gordis's lead and imagine what pseudepigraphic Persian chronicle reports of Jewish salvation would be like, we must conclude that they would be very different from Esther.

3. Historical Novella or Romance?[9]

If the (nearly interchangeable) terms "historical novella" and "romance"[10] are taken to imply essential historicity,[11] they are probably wrong, or at least there is nothing to support that implication

---

8. Gordis 1981:375–82. The idea had been briefly suggested by M. Segal (1960: II, 721).
9. Streane 1922:xv; Myers 1968:92; Moore 1971:LII; Gordis 1981:388; and others.
10. The terms "novella" and "romance" have been used nearly interchangeably; the German "Roman" can be translated "novel" as well as "romance." On the confusion between these terms see Hägg 1983:2–4. We are probably best to think of a romance as a novella with an emphasis on love and eroticism.
11. As is the case explicitly for Myers (1968:92–94), who says that the adjective in

(see chap. III §1). The term as applied to the Hellenistic novella does not, however, assert historicity but only the use of historical personae and events in a fictional tale. If "historical romance" ("geschichtliche Roman") means a wish made into history (Gunkel 1916:75), the term is appropriate, but the grouping is then too vague to have much significance for the individual text. The classification as historical novel/romance is more significant if it is intended to assert Esther's affiliation with the Hellenistic novella, a connection that Stiehl (1956:6–9) has drawn.

The Scroll does show some affinities to the Hellenistic novella and romance. Eduard Schwartz's remark on Ctesias' novella, that it "breathes seraglio and eunuch perfumes, mixed with a disgusting stench of blood,"[12] captures something of the Scroll's atmosphere as well. The romance or novella, however, sought only to provide entertainment and merely used traditional historical personages and events for the framework, without expecting anyone to view the resulting tale as historically accurate.[13]

The book of Esther does have some features of the Hellenistic romance, including attention to the king's love life (such as it is) and a delight in depictions of royal luxury. Still, the Scroll cannot be classed as a romance. It lacks the romance's favorite themes and motifs: sudden and overpowering passions, heavy sentimentality, swooning, separation and reunion, chastity under temptation, and religion—cults, prayers, oracles, and divine interventions. Above all, love is not the Scroll's central concern, as it is in the Hellenistic romance. Xerxes' love for Esther has importance to the story only insofar as it furthers *her* goals, and we are hardly to suppose that she feels much love for him. The scenic description in chapter 1 is only decorative background. In Esther we have at most a few romantic and novelistic features garnered from the broader Hellenistic milieu, but these do not determine the work's basic character.

4. Diaspora Story

A diaspora story deals with crises of Jewish life in the diaspora and the responses to them. Esther and Daniel 1–6 belong in this category; Tobit does as well, though not so clearly. Several scholars

"historical novel" should be given more emphasis; similarly Gordis (1981: 388) and Moore (1971:LII-LIII).
12. Quoted by Hägg 1983:113.
13. Trenkner 1958:23–24; Perry 1967:38.

class Esther as a "diaspora novella."[14] This label is reasonably specific and apt, but the term "novella" may suggest more precision than it actually offers. A novella is just a short novel or long story.[15] The Scroll is neither; it is a short story. So we should call it a "diaspora story." This tag shows that the concept labels the obvious; yet it does point us toward certain salient features of Esther and related works.

The value of this identification is to make us think of these various tales in terms of each other. The following are the most significant affinities between Esther and Daniel[16]:

(a) The setting is the diaspora (for Esther and Daniel 6, specifically in Achemenid times).

(b) Jews arrive at positions of the highest consequence in the royal court.

(c) The Jews are endangered and saved, and their enemies are punished.

(d) Daniel, his companions, and Mordecai are threatened with death.

(e) The foreign kings are not hostile to Jews.

(f) For this reason, the opponents must use tricks and slander to get the king to act against the Jews.

---

14. This concept has been systematically developed by Meinhold (1975, 1976, 1983a: 16–18) and Humphreys (1973, 1985b).

15. If we use a term taken from another literary tradition, we should stay fairly close to its usage in that tradition. The highpoint of the novella was in nineteenth-century Germany. The various definitions of the German novella seem to me equally applicable to a great many short stories or novels and inapplicable to many recognized novellas. None adequately describes the diaspora story. The *Oxford Companion to German Literature* lists the prominent features of the novella as "a concentrated presentation of an action which arouses suspense and contains an element of surprise leading to an unexpected ending. This element of suspense is the 'new' (*novella*) feature of the narrative, exposing seemingly inexplicable aspects of reality which are inaccessible to reason" (p. 674). L. Tieck (1829) (and others) stressed the need for a point (*Wendepunkt*) at which the story took an unexpected, decisive turn (ibid.; similarly Ryder 1971:xx and others).

The above definition fits many short stories while excluding some recognized novellas (such as von Eichendorff's famous "Aus den Leben eines Taugenichts," included in Ryder's anthology of German "Novelle"). It does describe the Scroll nicely but not Daniel. But if "novella" indeed "denotes a literary form standing intermediate between novel and short story" (Humphreys 1985a:83), then Esther must be classed with the short story. The novellas of the nineteenth century were about 50–200 pages.

16. Based on Stiehl 1956: 16–17.

146

(g) The kings believe they are acting against disobedience, not against the Jews as such.

(h) The kings are unhappy to see their Jewish favorites caught in the net.

(i) The kings are themselves trapped by the decrees. They cannot automatically free the Jews.

(j) The kings punish the slanderers.

The genre could be broadened to include Tobit, for it too teaches a way of life for Jews in the diaspora.[17] In Tobit the kings are farther in the background, and the piety of ordinary Jews comes to the fore. The gentile government is viewed as hostile but tolerable. (After all, a Jew—as Ahiqar is here thought to be—becomes vizier.) It is loyalty to one's people and family that earns God's protection. Daniel and Esther are more closely aligned. Their similarities point up the significance of the ideological differences between them, which we will observe when discussing the relevant topics, in particular the Scroll's worldview.

The book of Esther, Daniel 1–6,[18] and Tobit have different concepts of God, history, and the Jews' duty in crisis, but they all propose a similar perception of Jewish life in exile. As far as we know, there were as yet no laws addressing the peculiarities of Jewish life in the diaspora. Instead, Jews in exile used stories to shape behavior and attitudes and to come to grips with certain questions of great urgency: How do we meet the threats to our existence now that we have no state, no king to command us, no

---

17. Meinhold (1975, 1976) would assign the Joseph story to this genre as well, or at least take it as a prototype. He sees close ties between the Joseph and Esther stories, not only in broad features but in details of structure as well. He does not include Daniel in this genre (that would make the close alignment between the Joseph story and Esther immediately untenable). Berg (pp. 133–36) shows that the components and sequences of the Esther and Joseph stories are not as close as Meinhold maintains. There is no doubt, however, that the authors of both Daniel and Esther were influenced by the Joseph story (Rosenthal 1895; Gan 1961–62; Berg pp. 124–36). The Joseph story shows how a Jew can succeed in a foreign country and serve in a foreign administration and so offered a natural model for the Esther story; but I doubt that this lesson was the Joseph story's purpose. That story (in the view of most scholars) is preexilic in origin, and it is in any case an inappropriate model for diaspora life, for if that is what it were, it would imply that Jews should voluntarily choose exile in hard times.

18. Daniel 1–6 is a collection of six tales about Jewish courtiers. The tales were gathered into a book before the time of Antiochus IV Epiphanes (see especially Ginsberg 1954). Chapters 7–12 are later and probably Palestinian in origin.

army to defend us, no territory to localize the defense, no temple to pray and sacrifice in, no priests to instruct us and lead communal prayer? The answer of all three books is that we are thrown upon our inner resources—spiritual, intellectual, and personal—and we must calculate how best to array them in our defense. The diaspora is dangerous but tolerable, in some ways even hospitable, and Jews can, in the spirit of Jer 29:4–7, lead full and effective Jewish lives within it.[19]

One might wonder whether identifying this "genre" means no more than noting that the works within it resemble each other. But it seems to me that there is more to the identification than that. The similarities among the works are fundamental, yet the book of Esther was not produced by direct imitation of Daniel 1–6.[20] There is no similarity in structure, as would be expected if someone were producing an Esther book on the basis of the book of Daniel; their concepts of religion are so different that one cannot be derived from the other even by reversal; and neither Mordecai nor Esther is a permutation of the Daniel-figure. Since the resemblance does not result from influence, it must be shaped by something outside the two texts themselves—and this something—whether social constraints or artistic traditions—is what is meant by genre.

It is not the facts of diaspora existence alone that determine the character of the narrative, but the attitude and goals of the author. After all, Ezra and Nehemiah too were Jews who prospered in the Persian royal service, yet the books that bear their names do not hold up their success as exemplary or promote any ideas for living in the diaspora. This consideration strengthens the hypothesis that "diaspora story" constitutes a cohesive, meaningful category and does not merely label a miscellaneous group of stories that happen to be set in the diaspora.

5. History

Identifying the Scroll's genre as novella or romance incorporates in the label itself a stance—a negative one—on the book's implicit truth claims. Such a stance is quite legitimate; indeed the willingness *not* to take a text at face value is the essence of critical

---

19. See Meinhold 1978:329–30 and Humphreys 1985b:112 and 1973 *passim*.
20. It could not, of course, be the other way around, since Daniel 1–6 includes several independent stories.

scholarship. But we must additionally ask how the book presents itself, what face *it* wishes to show the reader.

Fictionality may be defined in two basic ways. In the common, pragmatic, understanding of the term, fictionality concerns the work's factual validity: fiction reports events that did not happen in reality, or at least it does not try for a correspondence between report and reality. In a semiotic definition, which specifies the conditions acknowledged relevant to interpretation, fictionality refers to a set of conventions governing reading: in fiction, the reader and author have an implicit "fictional contract" to suspend the veridical conventions of nonfictional discourse; they agree that the text is play.[21] Fiction does make statements about the real world, but these are oblique and must be read out of the text by various acts of translation and generalization. In this sense, Esther is not fiction;[22] it is history.

It is notoriously difficult to extrapolate semiotic contracts from the texts of other ages and cultures, but in the case of Esther, the signals that do get through make it very unlikely that the author would have us read his text as fiction, or even that he would be satisfied with the "historical core" theory. I do not see any "once-upon-a-time" clues that would direct the reader to a fictional reading, whereas there clearly is an effort to create verisimilitude, namely the numerous scenic details and the reference to the royal chronicles (10:2), which implies external verification for the facts reported.[23] The precise dating of events and the numeration of secondary personages are also intended to convince the reader that actual persons in a datable time and an actual place did such and such.[24] Nothing in the story is so fantastic as to definitively remove it from the sphere of reality. Nor is the humor of the tale or the carnival atmosphere of Purim in any way meant to detract from the truth claimed for the story in all its details. There are, to be sure,

---

21. On the latter definition see Price 1973:112–58.
22. Morson (1981:39–68) identifies the intriguing category of "boundary works," in which it is uncertain which of two mutually exclusive sets of conventions govern a work. Such texts can be read according to different hermeneutic procedures (p. 48). In a sense, I am viewing Esther as a boundary work: a fictive text meant to be read by nonfictional conventions. But since its fictiveness (judged by historicity) and its nonfictiveness (judged by inherent conventions) reside in distinct domains of definition, it does not, strictly speaking, straddle two mutually exclusive categories.
23. This device has succeeded with several scholars, such as Moore (1971:XXXV).
24. Observed by Gerleman, p. 29.

clues to the text's non-historicity (see chap. III §1), but these apparently escaped the author, and subsequent interpreters found little difficulty in explaining away the difficulties (such as in 2:6).[25] Most fundamentally, the MT-author would not want the book read as fiction because that would undo the authority of the call to observe Purim, which is self-consciously based on the actuality of the deliverance in Adar and the Jewish response to it (9:24–26).

The Scroll's reference to the Persian-Median chronicles is an imitation of the references to the external sources in Samuel-Kings and Chronicles. The author would have us class his book with Ezra-Nehemiah and Chronicles.[26]

A genre-designation of "history" would better accord with the author's intentions.[27] "We call a narrative a history on the basis of its author's perceived intentions in writing, the author's *claim* that the account is accurate in its particulars, the author's sincerity" (Halpern 1988:8).[28] We can assign Esther to a subdivision of history, such as the "historical story," which B. Long defines as "a self-contained narrative mainly concerned to recount what a particular event was and how it happened, but with more literary sophistication than is usually evident in simple reports. . . . We read of characters and events rooted in plausible time and space, but given contours conceived in the writer's particularizing imagination" (1984:7).[29]

---

25. This observation runs contrary to Greenstein's assertion that the story's festival context, humor, and plot contrivances lend it an air of fiction and that these qualities determined from the start that it would be read tongue-in-cheek and not taken seriously as history (1987:226–28).
26. Myers observes that the book of Esther is "cast within the same framework as that of the Chronicler" (1968:95).
27. The book's self-presentation as history is probably not just an intentional falsification. Since most of the story came to the MT-author ready-made (see chap. XIV §3a), it is likely that he saw himself not as fabricating a history but as reworking a factual narrative and drawing (or just highlighting) a connection between it and the popular festivities of Adar. Perhaps the connection already existed in oral tradition and the MT-author believed he was only putting it into literary form.
28. An author may deliberately present lies and distortions as history, but even then the work's genre—at least from the literary standpoint—is history.
29. Long says that historical stories range themselves on a spectrum between fiction and history written with the resources of fiction. But again, although the historical story may be closer to or farther from the historical facts as we know them, the conventions of the historical story call upon the reader to take them all as reliable and accurate reports. (A reader can, of course, refuse to accept the "contract" implicit in the conventions an author proposes.)

6. Festival Etiology

Like "history," the genre identification "festival etiology" is congruent with the author's intention.[30] If we rank genre identifications in terms of intrinsic importance rather than appeal to scholarly interests, then the primary genre of the book as a whole is surely this one.[31] (An etiology is a narrative that explains the origin of some existing phenomenon in society, religion, or nature.)[32] In this regard, the Scroll belongs together with Exodus 12–13 (and, in a sense, the entire Exodus story). Everything in the Massoretic version of Esther leads up to the establishment of Purim as a two-day holiday. (The emphasis is probably on the two-day factor; see the Commentary on 9:20–28.)

If this function does not seem an adequate literary explanation for most of the book (most of chaps. 1–8 is not necessary for making the case for the festival), that is because the Purim theme has been grafted on to an older salvation tale,[33] and consequently the latter tale (without the MT expansion in 3:7 and 9:1–32) calls for another classification (such as "diaspora story"). But in the MT, the story of Esther and Mordecai has been appropriated to the service of the festival etiology: a celebration unsanctioned by divine command is given its justification in historical experience and communal declaration.

The term "etiology" may sound too intellectual, as if the pur-

---

30. Ringgren (p. 375), Gerleman (p. 23), and others call it a "Festlegende" or festival legend. Again, this is accurate, but from the author's point of view the story should not be thought legendary as that term is usually understood, namely as implying fictionality. Most commentators recognize the centrality of this function, whether or not they use it to designate a genre. Würthwein accurately claims that the originally independent Esther novella was secondarily transformed into the etiology of the Purim festival (1969:193).

31. Meinhold 1976:72 f. objects that "festival legend" designates the book's purpose, not its *Gattung* (genre). In fact, however, festival legend *is* its Gattung from the standpoint of its practical purpose. To be sure, that purpose may have been spliced on to an Esther story that originally lacked it (as I argue in chap. XIV §3 a), but it is intrinsic to the *massoretic* Esther.

32. By a tighter definition of "etiology," which requires that the narrative be designed in its basic structure to support the explanation and which excludes tales with an "etiological suffix" (Coats 1983:10), MT-Esther is not etiological. The problem with this tightening is that it classifies the current function of a story on the basis of its prehistory.

33. Some commentators consider 9:20–10:3, or parts thereof, as later additions to the Esther story; see chap. XIV n.12. I hold to a modified form of this theory; see Fox 1991:chap. 2.

pose of the explanation were information for its own sake. An etiology of a religious practice, however, helps shape the practice. It organizes it, gives it meaning, and motivates its continuance. The etiological function of Esther is ongoing, not static; the story cannot disappear once the holiday is accepted, for it is the source of the holiday's meaning.[34] It alone brings past events into the present.

7. Festival Lection

In terms of its present function, the Scroll's genre is festival lection. The primary requirement of the rabbinic Purim observance is to hear the reading of the Scroll.[35] Raba (affirming the argument of R. Jose ben Hanina) went so far as to assert that "between the Temple service and the reading of the Scroll, the reading of the Scroll takes priority" (b. Meg. 3b).

The public reading of the Scroll is not ordained in the book itself, yet the reading is rooted in the book's ideology. The only festival practice the author envisaged was festivities which replicate the Jews' rejoicing of year 12. Jews of subsequent generations, rather than commemorating something that happened to their ancestors, celebrate their ancestors' *experience*. The holiday has a reflexive, inner-directed quality; the people remembers its own experience, and that is accessible only through story, the vehicle of memory.

Memory, as Brevard Childs has shown, was at the heart of Israelite cult in the Deuteronomic understanding. "To remember was to actualize the past, to bridge the gap of time and to form a solidarity with the fathers" (1962:74). Purim, like the Sabbath and the Passover in the Deuteronomic interpretation, not only commemorates the past but also recalls it to actuality. To actualize the joy and respite the ancestors enjoyed on the first Purim entails recalling the events they lived through, and this means retelling the tale. It was an accurate extension of the author's intention when the rabbis took an imperative implicit in the text—"read me"—and made that the prime commandment of the festival.

---

34. That is to say, the holiday in its Jewish form. Whatever its prehistory, Purim as we know it was born with the book.
35. The Mishna (tractate Megilla) does not directly command the reading of the Scroll, but rather assumes this as a recognized obligation and proceeds to discuss the details of the practice.

CHAPTER V

STRUCTURES

1. Structures and Meanings

No one writes at random. Unless a book is an anthology or a collection (like Proverbs 10–31), we can expect to find some logic or system—not necessarily conscious—behind the placement of material, and we can further assume that this placement is supposed to serve the author's goals and control the way the reader perceives the world of the text.

The shape of literary characters is integral to the structure of the text in which they exist.[1] If we altered the course of events in MT–Esther, the characters would inevitably be different. If, for instance, Esther were to accuse Haman at the first instead of the second banquet, her development from timid to bold would be too abrupt to be convincing, and she would also appear a less skilled tactician. Characters are shaped even by the placement of scenes in which they do not appear. If Vashti's story had not been placed before Esther's, Esther's early obedience would be less distinctive and also less necessary; her courage too would be obscured. A study of character, then, cannot confine itself entirely to an analysis of individual figures, but must consider the text's overall shape.

There is no reason to insist on a single structure in each text, a single principle of organization that can be definitively ferreted out. A text, like life in general, is organized—or organizable—into a multitude of domains. The type of organization we perceive depends on what we are looking for. It seems reasonable to expect that the structures should remain distinct and not override one other. The structures need not present neat, symmetrical, or hierarchical designs, for design is not their point. Nor are designs in themselves evidence of artistry; even a hack can write to rule and produce clear patterns. There must simply be enough of a design to do the job assigned it.[2]

---

1. But once the character is created, it is not necessarily inseparable from the structure; see chap. I §3.
2. Y. Radday attempts to show that the entire book is structured in a large chiasm

In Robert Alter's description of biblical narrative, he speaks of elaborately integrated systems of repetition in which repetition becomes a "Jamesian 'figure in the carpet,' half-hidden, subliminally insistent . . ." (1981:94–95). He proposes a scale of repetitive structuring and focusing devices based on leitwort, motif, theme, and sequence of action (p. 95). The second, third, and fourth devices are the significant structuring principles in Esther.

The elements that combine into a structure must be significant and prominent or the structure itself will be trivial. A structure controls perceptions—the way the reader segments a text, reconstructs the sequence of events, draws connections between earlier and later materials, and more. The four structures I survey in this chapter are, I believe, the ones that make the greatest impact. I base the last statement in part on what the commentators have noticed, but mainly on my own experience of reading Esther. Its validation, however, must come from your own experience of the text. A successful structural proposal should elicit a sense of recognition: it expresses your sense of the work's shape either as you have read it or as you will henceforth read it.

2. Sequence and Segmentation of Events

The main principle of design in the Scroll is so obvious that commentators neglect to mention it: the story proceeds in chronological order. With the slight exceptions of the background information in 2:5–7 and the proleptic remark in 9:1, nothing is allowed to override this principle.

a. Tripartite Division

The chronological progression in itself makes for a well-organized, easy-to-follow narrative. The narrative is divided, with classical clarity, into a beginning, a middle, and an end. Not only are these

---

(1973). But this view requires accepting his particular unit division—though it lumps together diverse material in unnatural ways—and interpreting the units in accordance with the labels he gives them—though these were devised to fit the design. For example, he joins chaps. 2 and 3 as a single unit by calling them "the king's first decree," and chaps. 8 and 9 are taken together as a unit summarized as "the king's second decree," which supposedly balances chaps. 2–3.

unequivocally marked by shifts in subject matter, but the events are separated by chronological gaps as well.

BEGINNING   setting the stage: the events that prepared the way for Esther's rise (year 3); Esther's rise to queenship (year 7); Mordecai's service to the king (ca. year 7). 1:1−2:23.

MIDDLE   the narrative proper: the scheme and its defeat (months i-iii and xii, year 12). 3:1−9:19.

END   the establishment of Purim, with an appendix about Mordecai (from some time after year 12 to the indefinite future). 9:20−10:3.

The time allotted to each major division paces the drama. The beginning, extending over six years, proceeds at a leisurely tempo. Nothing urgent is happening; it is a time of preparation and (for Mordecai and the reader) waiting. The middle covers one year, during which the crisis breaks out and is resolved. The height of the drama, the period in which Haman initiates his plot and the two Jews defeat him, rushes forward breathlessly, with five chapters squeezed into eighteen or fewer days. The end—contrary to the book's earlier practice—ceases to date events. It begins when the Jews establish the holiday, presumably in year 13, and extends into the indefinite expanse of time in which the Jews will celebrate the holiday.

b. Acts

The segmentation into acts and scenes is discussed in the Commentary. The three major divisions together with the acts produce this outline:

BEGINNING
Act I: 1:1−22.   Vashti deposed.
Act II: 2:1−23.   Esther becomes queen; Mordecai uncovers a plot.

MIDDLE
Act III. 3:1−15.   Haman's plan and decree.
Act IV. 4:1−17.   Mordecai sends Esther to the king
Act V. 5:1−8.   Esther goes to the king; her first banquet.

155

Act VI. 5:9–6:14.	Haman's humiliation and Mordecai's exaltation.
Act VII. 7:1–10.	Esther's second banquet; Haman's defeat.
Act VIII. 8:1–8.	The grant of authority.
Act IX. 8:9–17.	The counter-decree.
Act X. 9:1–19.	The battles of Adar.

END

Act XI. 9:20–32.	The establishment of Purim.
Act XII. 10:1–3.	Epilogue.

3. A Major Motif: Feasting

A motif is a recurrent action, word, or thing (or an event sufficiently specific to be conceived of as a "thing") that draws attention to itself and forms linkages that help unify the narrative.[3] By creating cross-connections among passages, motifs make the reader think of one passage in terms of the other. In Esther, one motif in particular, feasting,[4] has special importance in shaping our reading.

The book opens with banquets, the denouement occurs at a banquet, and the crisis eventuates in a perennial banquet. This motif, then, is a good place to expect a significant design to emerge. Berg (pp. 31–35), Meinhold (1983b:435–439), and Clines (pp. 36–37). have emphasized the importance of this motif and its function in bringing out irony, though there are some differences in the ways they connect the various banquets. In the following diagram, special similarities among banquets as I see them are marked by lines. It emerges that the banquets are all paired—as is appropriate to a book that establishes a two-banquet holiday.[5]

The movement of the plot is punctuated by ten banquets, which are the sites of important events and which signal shifts of power:

---

3. Cf. Alter 1981:95; similarly Berg, p.16–17, who distinguishes between "governing motifs" and "auxiliary motifs."
4. In the following, both "banquets" and "feasts" translate Hebrew *mišteh*. Of the forty-six occurrences of this word in the Hebrew Bible, twenty are in Esther—a fact that in itself suggests the importance of this concept for the book.
5. I nevertheless do not think that this is entirely the work of the original author. As I trace the Scroll's literary history, the establishment of Purim was not an original part of the story. Banquets ##1, 2, 3, 6, 7 were present in the original, insofar as this can be deduced from proto-AT (see chap. XIV §§2a-b). The MT redactor found the motif in the story he inherited and reinforced it in preparation for adding the Purim etiology in chapter 9.

156

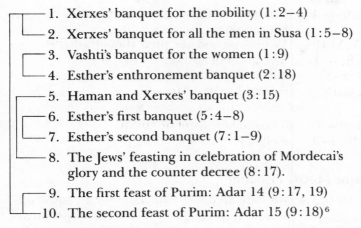

1. Xerxes' banquet for the nobility (1:2–4)
2. Xerxes' banquet for all the men in Susa (1:5–8)
3. Vashti's banquet for the women (1:9)
4. Esther's enthronement banquet (2:18)
5. Haman and Xerxes' banquet (3:15)
6. Esther's first banquet (5:4–8)
7. Esther's second banquet (7:1–9)
8. The Jews' feasting in celebration of Mordecai's glory and the counter decree (8:17).
9. The first feast of Purim: Adar 14 (9:17, 19)
10. The second feast of Purim: Adar 15 (9:18)[6]

The last pair (##9–10, i.e. Purim) corresponds to the first pair (##1–2), though not tightly.[7] #10 is for the Jews of Susa and #2 for all inhabitants of Susa, while #9 is for the Jews throughout the empire and #1 for nobles throughout the empire. This echoing makes the Jewish festival suggest a celebration of imperial splendor.

For refusing to leave her own banquet (#3), Vashti is deposed, opening the way for Esther, whose coronation is celebrated in #4.

The ironic use of the banquet motif is most vivid in the central banquets. While Haman celebrates his supposed victory with the king (#5), the Jews throughout the empire[8] fast (4:3). Then, at Esther's bidding, the Jews fast with her (4:16) as she prepares herself for two banquets, of which the first (#6) will confirm Haman's pride in his own eyes and the second (#7) produce his downfall.

In #8, the Jews rejoice and hold feasts in honor of Mordecai's glory and the counter-decree. This banquet is linked to #5 first by

---

6. Meinhold (1983b:435–39) likewise counts four pairs, corresponding to ## 1–2, 3–4, 6–7, 8–9+10 (the two Purim feasts are taken as one). His schema, however, requires taking the Purim feasts as one, though the author is very emphatic about their duality, calling them "days of feasting" in 9:22, 26–32. This scheme also requires pairing the combined feast, unnaturally, with #8.

7. Berg claims that both sets are hosted by royalty, inasmuch as Mordecai becomes a quasi-royal figure. But this connection seems forced, since Mordecai does not become a king-substitute, and in any case Mordecai and Esther do not "host" Purim.

8. Some regard this as a fast in the provinces (Meinhold 1983b:438); but the Susan Jews could hardly refrain from joining the others. Mordecai, though he is not said to be fasting, is performing mourning acts that are commonly accompanied by fasting (4:1).

its occasion—each celebrates the issuance of a decree—and second by the wording of the sentences joined to them. When Haman feasts, "the king and Haman sat down to feast, while the city of Susa was thrown into dismay" (3:15b), whereas when the Jews celebrate, "the city of Susa rejoiced and was merry" (8:15b).

The banqueting motif is thus the vehicle for the theme of power—its gain and its loss.[9] Banquets belong to the rich and powerful. Such occasions, as the description of #1 shows, are the setting for conspicuous consumption.[10] Banquets are an opportunity to show one's "opulent wealth" and the "splendid honor" of one's greatness. The Jews do not celebrate or display their wealth, but they too employ feasting as a means of display—the display to all generations of the respite earned by victory and of community solidarity.

4. A Major Theme: Reversal

A theme is "an idea which is part of the value-system of the narrative" (Alter 1981:95).[11] A variety of specific elements—statements, images, motifs, events—may convey a theme. The most important structural theme in Esther, one that organizes much of the presentation and wording of events, is the idea that an event intended to harm the Jews eventuates in its opposite. This is the theme of *peripety*: the result of an action is actually the reverse of what was expected.[12] The various reversals, many of which must strike every reader, have been well noted by the commentators. I would maintain that the reversals work together to govern the way we read the book and to convey a particular worldview.

---

9. Berg 1979:34–35.
10. Clines, p. 36.
11. Berg defines theme as a "message or idea which the author conveyed by his use of the story's motifs" (1979:17). A theme is not, however, necessarily composed of motifs, but may appear in various ways, such as statement or unique event.
12. This is not the *most* important theme in Esther. The most important theme is the obligation of all Jews to celebrate the two days of Purim, but that theme seems to have little *structural* function, probably because it was added to the base narrative at a later stage (see chap. XIV §3a).
    C. M. Horowitz (1882) identified peripety as a key principle of the narrative's progression, but he saw its operation only in chapter 6; similarly Feldman (1970:154–55) refers to Haman's disgrace in 6:10 as the book's peripety. But peripety informs the course of the narrative before and after that point as well.

Events in the middle section of Esther are built around two matching series of theses and antitheses. The theses are situations portending disaster for the Jews and success for their enemies, situations which could be expected to lead, in the natural course of events, to the Jews' destruction. But rather than running their natural course, events lead to the antitheses, the mirror opposites of the results intended or apparently portended in the theses.

Repetition of the vocabulary of the theses in the antitheses is the most distinctive marker of their mirror relationship. In a few cases, however, the reversal is not supported by distinctive repetition of vocabulary but is nevertheless manifest. Those passages are given below in virgules.[13]

THESES	ANTITHESES
a: Haman's Authority	a': Mordecai's Authority
(3:10) Thereupon the king took his signet ring off his finger and gave it to Haman son of Hammedatha the Agagite, persecutor of the Jews.	(8:2a) And the king took off his signet ring, which he had taken away from Haman, and gave it to Mordecai.
(3:11) /And the king said to Haman, "The silver I grant you, as well as the people, to do with as you please."/	(8:2b) /and Esther set Mordecai over Haman's estate./
b: Haman's Decree	b': Mordecai's Decree
(3:12) So on the thirteenth day of the first month, the royal scribes were summoned.	(8:9) The royal scribes were summoned at that time, on the twenty-third day of the third month, the month of Sivan,
and it was written in accordance with all that Haman	and it was written in accordance with all that Mordecai

---

13. An earlier form of the following observations was published in Fox 1983. S. Berg (pp. 109–13), who had a prepublication manuscript of that article, adopted its thesis in part and also offered a useful critique of my interpretation of the theme's function, and my current approach has benefitted from her remarks.

had commanded the king's satraps and the governors who were over each and every province, and the princes of each and every people— to each and every province in its own script and each and every people in its own language. In King Xerxes' name it was written, and it was sealed with the king's signet ring. (3:13) And letters were sent by means of couriers . . . to slaughter, slay, and destroy /all the Jews, young and old./	had commanded the Jews and the satraps and the governors and the princes of the provinces from India to Nubia, 127 provinces, to each and every province in its own script and to each and every people in its own language. . . . (8:10a) He wrote this in King Xerxes' name, sealed it with the king's signet ring, (8:10b) and sent letters by the hand of couriers . . . (8:11) to slaughter, slay, and destroy /the forces of every people and province who afflict them./
together with children and women,	together with children and women, with their property as spoil.
on a single day,	(8:12) on a single day, in all the provinces of King Xerxes, on
the thirteenth day of the twelfth month, the month of Adar. with their property as spoil, (3:14) with a copy of the edict to be issued as law in each and every province, made public to all the peoples, that they be ready for that day.	the thirteenth day of the twelfth month, the month of Adar, (8:13) with a copy of the edict to be issued as law in each and every province, made public to all the peoples, that the Jews be ready for that day to take vengeance on their enemies.
(3:15a) Then the couriers	(8:14) Then the couriers, riders of swift horses, steeds *pur sang*,
went forth urgently at the king's command,	went out urgently and hastily at the king's command,

while the law was also issued in the Fortress of Susa.
(3:15b) And the king and Haman sat down to feast, . . .
and the city of Susa was thrown into dismay.
(4:1) /When Mordecai found out all that had happened, he tore his garments and put on sackcloth and ashes. And he went out into the midst of the city and cried out, loud and bitterly./

and the law was also issued in the Fortress of Susa.
(8:15) Then Mordecai went out.
And the city of Susa rejoiced and was merry.
(8:15a) /Then Mordecai went out from the king's presence in royal clothing of violet and white, in a large golden turban and a cloak of linen and purple./

(4:3) And in each and every province,

(8:17) And in each and every province and in each and every city,

wherever the king's word and law reached, there was /severe grief among the Jews with fasting and weeping and lamenting, with sackcloth and ashes being spread out for the masses./

wherever the king's word and law reached, there was /merriment and joy for the Jews, feasting and holiday./

c: *Counsel of Haman's Wife and Friends*
(5:14) And his wife Zeresh and all his friends said to him, /"Have a stake made fifty cubits high and in the morning tell the king to have Mordecai impaled on it. Then come merry with the king to the feast."/

c': *Despair of Haman's Wife and Friends*
(6:13b) And his advisers and his wife Zeresh said to him, / "If Mordecai, before whom you have begun to fall, really is of the Jewish race, you will not overcome him, but will undoubtedly fall before him."/

d: *Haman's Pride*
(6:7) (So Haman answered the king,) . . .

d': *Haman's Disgrace*

(6:8) "Let royal garments be brought—ones the king has worn—and a horse. . . . (6:9) Have them put the garments on the man the king desires to honor, and have them set him on the horse in the city square and cry out before him: 'Thus shall be done for the man whom the king desires to honor!'"	(6:11) So Haman took the garments and the horse and clothed Mordecai and set him on the horse in the city square and cried out before him, "Thus shall be done for the man whom the king desires to honor!"

The thesis-antithesis series runs through the core-drama, which begins in chapter 3, after the preparatory episodes, and ends in 8:17, just prior to the discursive concluding matters in chapters 9 and 10. The battle narrative in 9:1–19 reports on the great reversal but is not itself antithetical to anything that preceded. Chapters 1 and 2 likewise report a reversal—Vashti deposed and Esther crowned—but they lack mirror passages. The effect of confining the linguistic mirroring to chapters 3–8 is to help rivet our attention to the winding and unwinding of events in the intense drama at the heart of the narrative.

The thesis series proceeds to 6:9, at which point the antithesis series begins. The turning point at 6:10 is bracketed between Esther's two banquets, the first of which swells Haman's pride, the second of which crushes him. Haman ironically signals his own downfall by determining Mordecai's reward, so that by his own words he begins the antithesis series that holds his destruction. Haman's wife and friends recognize that this is the turning point, the *beginning* of his fall (6:13).

Berg regards 4:13–14 as the turning point.[14] Now there is no rule that a story must have a single "turning point." If we think of a plot-line as a curve, there can be multiple "turning points." Certainly 4:13–14 is *a* turning point—the crucial one in Esther's development. But the plot takes *its* sharpest turn in 6:10. In 4:13–14 (and, in fact, in 4:1), the danger has been addressed, but there is as yet no sign that it will be overcome. That sign, as Haman's associates recognize (6:13), comes with Haman's humiliation.

---

14. Berg p. 110. She is followed by Meinhold (1983b:439–41), who calls 4:13–14 the book's "spiritual mid-point" ("geistige Mitte"). He observes that 4:13–14 comes between two fasts, the two royal edicts, and the two banquet pairs (I-II and III-IV [= ##1–2+3–4 and 6–7+8-9/10 in my numbering]).

The guiding principle, reversal, is a conscious one. The historical manifestation of reversal is stated explicitly in 9:1:

> Now on the thirteenth day of the twelfth month, the month of Adar, when the king's word and his law were due to be carried out—on the very day when the enemies of the Jews had expected to gain control over them, whereas things would be turned about, in that the Jews would gain control over their adversaries.

This conception of events is again emphasized in Mordecai's epistle: "and the month that turned about for them—from misery to merriment and from mourning to holiday . . . (9:22a). The principle is also expressed on the moral plane by making the punishment the reversal of the evildoer's intentions. In Xerxes' words as Mordecai rephrases them: "let the evil plan that he formed against the Jews recoil back upon his own head (9:25b)."

While the aesthetic value of the antiphony is undeniable, the structure has a function that goes beyond aesthetics. It reflects and communicates the author's worldview. We will examine this in chapter XIII.

CHAPTER VI

VASHTI

One opinion:
"Wicked Vashti . . ."

(R. Samuel ben Naḥmani, in b. Meg. 12b)

1. Vashti's Refusal

Vashti said no. This is the entirety of her direct portrayal, yet her character is an intriguing one. It is drawn in silhouette by the contrast between her "no" and what it negates.

Vashti is a woman of dignity, too proud to allow herself to be put on display alongside other pieces of royal property before a bunch of bibulous males. She consequently loses her queenship. Her independence and dignity are worthy of respect.

Most modern readers would agree with this assessment, but they often think they are reading *against* the text, that they are siding with a character toward whom the author is unsympathetic or even antipathetic, whom he presents as an arrogant female defying rightful male authority.[1]

2. Views of Vashti

Some early Jewish interpreters thought that the author of Esther (whom they identified as Mordecai) viewed Vashti with hostility, since they themselves did so.[2] They thoroughly approved of feminine reserve, of course, but they could not believe that a gentile—the granddaughter of King Nebuchadnezzar—would have

---

1. See the Excursus in chapter X, pp. 205–11.
2. These views are represented in Tar¹, Tar², Est. Rab., and b. Meg. 10b, 12b. In Tar¹ (1:9) she is called "the wicked queen" and in b. Meg. 10b she is identified as the granddaughter of Nebuchadnezzar. According to one view in the Talmud (b. Meg. 12b), because she had taken Israelite maidens and stripped them naked she was punished by herself being summoned naked. R. Jose b. Hanina taught that she refused to come because she was leprous or because Gabriel had made her grow a tail (ibid.).

shown true modesty. They consequently invented less admirable motives for her action. They said that she was ordered to appear naked (as if "in the royal crown" [1:11] meant wearing only the crown), or they opined that she suffered from disease or disfigurement and was ashamed to appear in public (b. Meg. 12b). Such explanations are, of course, entirely ad hoc. The author does not hint that she was wicked or diseased but on the contrary states that she was beautiful (1:11b). Even the opinions disdainful of Vashti, however, did not fault her for disobedience or feminine pride. They looked about for some more significant failing and faulted her for whom they imagined her to be and for crimes they imagined her to have committed.

Some of the early interpreters regarded Vashti's motive to be personal modesty and dignity. Josephus believes that Persian law prohibited wives from being viewed by strangers, and that she refused out of respect for that custom (XI 191).[3] Some rabbis picture her remonstrating with the king in bold words when he ordered her to appear naked.[4] On the basis of an equation of Memuchan and Haman (b. Meg. 12b), Esther is imagined as siding with Vashti and declaring (at 7:4), "This adversary is not worth harm to the king. He envied Vashti and killed her, and now he envies me and seeks to kill me" (b. Meg. 16a). Another opinion held that the king felt remorse because he remembered (in 2:1) that Vashti had acted properly, and that what was decreed against her was contrary to what was right (Est. Rab. V 2).

Some modern commentators are convinced that the author disapproves of Vashti and her action. Paton believes that the author would have us understand her refusal as "merely a whim," since no reason is given for the action. But an absence of stated reasons does not mean there were none at all. The author of Esther (as usually in the Bible) rarely gives explicit motivations for the characters' behavior but leaves us to infer them from words and actions. Paton

---

3. Josephus nevertheless seems to lack sympathy for her. He emphasizes her stubbornness by having her refuse repeatedly, and he has Memuchan accuse her of arrogance toward the king (XI 195), which in Josephus' view is a serious fault; see Feldman 1970: 162–63.

4. Est. Rab. III 13–14. Among other things, Vashti berates him: "You used to be the stable-boy of my father's (Belshazzar's) house, and you were in the habit of bringing in with you naked harlots, and now that you have come to rule you have not left off from your corrupt ways." But Xerxes was too dense "to get her hints ... or feel her pricks." Tar[2] agrees with this sympathetic appraisal of Vashti's motives.

finds another sign of the *author's* hostility in the phrase "conveyed by the eunuchs" (1:12); this supposedly shows that the summons was conveyed in a proper, formal way and thereby heightens the disrespect of Vashti's refusal. But the formality of the summons is actually just another instance of the puffery and pomposity of the court, with which the author is surely not enthralled.

A common view (held, for example, by Bardtke) is that the author is uninterested in Vashti and therefore implies no ethical evaluation of her action. Gunkel thinks that the narrator's silence shows indifference to Vashti's fate, and that he was interested in Vashti only as a device for vacating the queenship for Esther. Similarly, Moore and Gerleman say that the motive of Vashti's act resides in the *author's* need to vacate the queenship. Undoubtedly the episode does prepare the way for the central drama, but if that were its only function, a compressed summary of events would have been sufficient. The author has chosen a more expansive opening to prepare the stage thematically, in ways discussed in the Commentary (see the remarks on Act I scene ii). The scene sets the arena in which Esther will have to operate and exposes in particular the discomfort that the king and the noblemen feel before women of independent will.

3. Evaluation in Objective Narration

Does the author really leave us completely in the dark in regard to Vashti's motivations and moral quality? If so, that is the end of the matter, and Vashti's character is truly indeterminate and we cannot discuss it. There is no "it"; there is not even something that can be called ambiguous or vague. I believe, however, that she does have a character, which the author reveals in ways other than statement. There is, of course, much we are not told and cannot know about her, as is the case with any person, in real life as well as in fiction. But something of her character is both determined and evaluated.

The narrator's formally objective stance, which eschews explicit evaluation of the people in the story, does not show neutrality, and certainly not ill will, toward Vashti. After all, prior to the last two verses of the book, Mordecai is not explicitly evaluated either, and by then we have learned how to view him. Esther is never explicitly judged. Thus the objective viewpoint does not in itself mean that the author had no opinion of Vashti.

One reason for the author's silence on Vashti's motives may be to avoid drawing too much attention to a minor character at the expense of the central issue in this chapter, namely the fate of women—and not necessarily only women—who cross the king's will. Disproportionate attention to that character would result if, for example, the narrator had said, "But Queen Vashti refused to come at the king's word conveyed by the eunuchs, because she would not show herself before the men at the banquet." Instead, the text's silence effects a sort of closure, limiting the attention the reader will give this character. The consequences of Vashti's refusal did not depend on her motives. Whatever the author's attitude toward Vashti, his evaluation is secondary to the bare presentation of the conflict.

An author creates norms and values that are applicable to all persons in the text. Even a scanty presentation of a character can be suggestive of a larger quality and the author's attitude toward it. This is because a literary figure does not exist in isolation, but enters into a complex network of relations with others and is shaped by the pressure of their images. The actions and experiences of one figure, even when these do not affect the outcome of the main action, alter the reader's understanding of other, parallel characters.[5] Hence we can understand Vashti only by pairing her with the characters to whom she is contraposed by conflict (the men of the court) and correspondence (Esther). The same can be said of Esther.

4. Vashti and the Men

The first clash is with Xerxes and his underlings. The nature of the banqueting to which Vashti refuses to come together with the character of the noblemen she enrages constitute an evaluation of her action. Xerxes sought to exhibit her to a mass of party-goers—all the men of Susa. Just by refusing—at obvious risk to herself—she shows that she disapproves of being put on display, at least—or especially—before tipsy men. Xerxes is treating her like the other property he flaunts. The author's sympathy toward Vashti emerges from the way she is made the victim of Xerxes' instability and the princes' insecurity.

---

5. Phelan (1989:56) calls this the principle of Indirect Affective Relevance and shows how it can be used in the foregrounding of a character's thematic function.

Xerxes' quarrel with Vashti is quickly blown up into sexual politics on an imperial scale. Memuchan believes that Vashti's action will set a bad example for all the wives in the empire, making them contemptuous and recalcitrant. His advice creates the very hullabaloo he had wanted to squelch and prevents Vashti from doing precisely what she had refused to do. Only if this is the implied author taking on Memuchan as his persona and speaking through him straight-faced can we conclude that the author, too, views Vashti's refusal as an impudent violation of female propriety. But surely the author is smirking at this spokesman for the wise men of Persia—for his pomposity, his hysterical interpretation of a trivial incident, his nervous concern about female powers, and his self-defeating "wisdom."

Xerxes, as we quickly learn, is weak-willed, fickle, and self-centered. He and his advisers are a twittery, silly-headed, cowardly lot who need to hide behind a law to reinforce their status in their homes. (Persian machismo caught the attention of Herodotus [IX 107], who says that "to call a man 'worse than a woman' is of course, the greatest insult one can offer a Persian.") They fabricate a crisis out of nothing and come up with a proposal that throws the spotlight on their own embarrassment. The author makes Vashti shine by the contrast, though perhaps he is motivated less by respect for Vashti than scorn for the gentile nobility. The satirizing of the nobility can only redound to the credit of the person whom they oppose.

Vashti's indignation is probably motivated by sense of rank rather than any protofeminist ideals. She is, after all, the queen, not a mere concubine to be toyed with. Persian wives could be present at banquets (Neh 2:6) but would leave before the drinking. At Belshazzar's banquet, only harem women and concubines are present (Dan 5:2) until the queen comes in especially to see the writing on the wall (5:10). There were thus circumstances where it was improper for women of rank to be present. In Esther 1, not merely the drinking bout but the entire banquet was segregated. By appearing before males, including commoners—especially when the king himself "was lightheaded with wine"—Vashti would be behaving like a mere concubine.[6] The king's insistence that she wear the

---

6. This explanation is based on Bickerman 1967: 185–86.

royal diadem heightens the degradation by calling attention to her true status, as does the repeated use of the title "Queen."

Vashti does not say anything on her own behalf. This silence too is significant as a foil to Memuchan's verbosity. Her taciturnity resembles Mordecai's, who also refuses an order from above with no excuses that might help him avoid the consequences (3:2). Conversely, Xerxes' wrath at the affront to his dignity is paralleled by Haman's reaction to the affront Mordecai delivers; even the same words for anger are used. This does not mean that Vashti is another Mordecai or Xerxes another Haman, but it does show that the author attributes to Vashti a type of behavior that is elsewhere associated with some clear sympathies.

5. Vashti and Esther

Vashti is a counterpart of Esther. Vashti's recalcitrance contrasts with Esther's docility. Esther comes into Vashti's place, a station whose constraints Vashti tested and demonstrated. Xerxes will, at Memuchan's advice, seek a woman who will be "better than" Vashti (1:19)—and by Memuchan's standards that can only mean one who is willing to subordinate herself to her husband. The matching of Vashti, who refuses to come when bidden, and Esther, who insists on coming though not bidden, is certainly deliberate. But these links and contrasts do not impugn the one behavior or praise the other. It is the Persian men who rate female "goodness" by this standard, and their norms are not the author's.

Esther is contraposed to Vashti not only in her initial obedience and ductility but also in the subtlety of her later efforts to sway the king to her will. The axis of comparison is not moral but practical. Vashti is an example of how *not* to do things, as well as a demonstration of the dangers of running afoul of the king. Her blatant self-assertion, whether or not it is praiseworthy in the abstract, is simply not the way to get along in the Persian court; the men do not choose that approach either. Too many egos, including the massive and tender one of the king himself, are there just waiting to be bruised, and too many laws and regulations block the straight path toward one's goals. The Vashti episode shows what Esther will be up against. Esther must reverse the will of a king who demands subordination to his will—and who is himself subordinated to his earlier decisions.

Vashti's fate was not a disaster; one might consider her rewarded by being forbidden to come where she had refused to go.
But Esther does not have the luxury of standing on her dignity.
Had Vashti's fate befallen her, her people would have perished.
Vashti's example thus provides something of a justification for Esther's pliancy in her early years and for the obliquity and manipulativeness of her later actions.

CHAPTER VII

XERXES

One opinion:
"He was a clever king."

(Rab, in b. Meg. 12a[1]*)*

1. A Soul's Surface

Xerxes is all surface. Other characters have private thoughts: Haman schemes, broods, and fantasizes his own glorification; Mordecai takes precautions and makes plans; Esther fears, takes courage, and devises a strategy of her own. But it is hard to imagine Xerxes having any thoughts not obvious to anyone. His character consists of a few obvious moods and impulses. Indeed, his most dangerous flaw is his failure to think. This adds up to a damning portrayal of autocracy, drawn by an author resigned to living under its sway.

Like Haman—and unlike the two Jews—Xerxes' soul is exposed. But the exposure of Xerxes' soul takes little work—just simple statements of unnuanced pleasures and angers. We are informed that Xerxes was angry (1:12b; 7:7), that his anger subsided (2:1a; 7:10b), that he was pleased (1:21; 2:4b, 9), and that he loved and favored Esther (2:17a). Xerxes' thoughts, unlike Haman's, are never directly quoted; they are all easily available on the surface. His psychology is easily read by the people *in* the story too. His princes (chap. 1), his servants (chap. 2), his vizier (chap. 3), and his queen (chaps. 5–9) are all able to bend him to their wills, for his moods and motives are obvious to all who must live by them, and he has no deeper resources to resist their blandishments. His soul is adequately exposed by simple description of his mental states, which are mostly a collection of impulses.

---

1. Rab deduces Xerxes' cleverness from the fact that he invited his distant subjects first, because he could win the loyalty of the Susans whenever he wished.

171

2. Showing Honor

The first among his impulses is an obsession with honor
(*y⁽qar*)—more precisely, with the display of honor. We see this impulse in an apparently extraneous scene at the start of the book, in
which he flaunts his glorious wealth and "honor" to the entire empire, inviting noblemen and officials from all over Persia, and even
the commoners of Susa, to admire the spectacle of wealth and
extravagance.

Vashti's refusal hits him at the worst time, just when he is putting his honor on display. The offense is a deep one, for the Persian
court conceives of honor not only as ostentatious wealth, but also
as the ability to constrain obedience, as Memuchan demonstrates
by equating wifely obedience as "showing honor [*y⁽qar*] to their husbands" (1:20). Xerxes does not simply order Vashti dragged in. It
is not enough for him to control her body; he must be master of
her will as well. Having her brought by force might prove his mastery as king but not his power as a man. That can only be confirmed
by his wife herself, and for this she needs at least ostensive freedom
of will. Similarly, the princes insist not merely that wives be forced
to obey their husbands, but that they *show* honor to them (1:20).
Power itself does not fill the need; men need a show of honor from
their wives, like kings from their subjects, for they are always reading their images in other people's eyes. This need is what allows
people of lesser powers to manipulate the cumbersome juggernaut
of state. Haman too will prod Xerxes' sensitive ego. He will claim
that the unnamed people are insubordinate, that they "do not obey
the laws of the king" (3:8). Later, an imagined outrage to the king's
masculine honor will facilitate Haman's execution.

3. Showing Generosity

Xerxes tries to buy honor by ostentatious generosity. His mara-
thon banquets lavish hospitality upon those who come to witness
his glory. At Esther's coronation, he gives gifts and ordains tax relief (2:18). Demonstrative generosity accompanies his munificent
grant to Haman, whom he tells (insincerely) to keep the money and
to "do as you please" with the people. The same impulse inspires
him twice to offer half his kingdom to Esther. And after he becomes, willy-nilly, the protector of the Jews, he flatters himself with
that image, claiming—and probably believing—that he executed

172

Haman out of solicitude for the Jews (8:7). Then, having taken the Jews' side, he admires their success at arms (9:12). Their success apparently makes him feel expansive, for he repeats his clichéd offer to do whatever Esther wishes (9:12). In an historical retrospect, Mordecai flatters the king's self-image as protector of the Jews by saying that he pronounced judgment on Haman with the declaration: "Let the evil plan that he formed against the Jews recoil back upon his own head" (9:25)

4. Authority and Irresponsibility

The paradoxical consequence of Xerxes' nervousness about his honor and authority, coupled with his demonstrative generosity, is that the will of others becomes law: Memuchan's (1:21), Haman's (3:12), and finally, Mordecai's and Esther's (8:9).

Though Xerxes is obsessed with the manifestation of authority, he is surprisingly indifferent to its actual exercise. Xerxes *never says no*. The closest he comes to a refusal is when he protests that he cannot rescind his own decree (8:7–8)—but then he immediately grants Mordecai and Esther royal authority by consigning to them his signet ring and empowering them to write whatever they wish (8:8). Earlier he had handed the same prerogative over to Haman (3:10). In both cases, this is an amazing concession, a veritable carte blanche, for the signet is not merely a token of vizierial office, but the king's own ring, and it confers near-royal authority, the right to make laws that will constrain the king himself. In both cases, Xerxes avoids responsibility for the consequence by telling the recipients to do or write as they "please" (lit., "as is good in your eyes"). The decision is theirs; *he* is just being a nice guy. Consequently, both Haman and Mordecai can write their commands into law; but both decrees are officially "the word of the king" (3:15; 8:14).

Thus the all-powerful Xerxes in practice abdicates responsibility and surrenders effective power to those who know how to press the right buttons—namely, his love of "honor," his anxiety for his authority, and his desire to appear generous.

5. The Sin of Laziness

Xerxes is lazy. He does not like to spend energy on thought, so people can get their way by doing his thinking for him. Although

Wisdom Literature praises the value of counsel,[2] Xerxes' need to seek advice in all situations and his alacrity in following it without discussion are suggestive of a man not fond of thinking for himself. His only independent decisions are to allocate power to others—Haman (3:1, 10) and Mordecai and Esther (8:2, 8). In other cases, his subordinates step forward to exploit his moods—anger (1:12–16; 7:7–9), melancholy (2:1–2), or expansiveness (7:2–3; 9:12–13)—by feeding him ideas that he can simply accept.

Memuchan agitates the king by blowing up a marital spat into national crisis, then tells him how to deal with it (1:16–20). Later, Xerxes' servants steer his thoughts away from Vashti and toward a new wife (2:1–4a). Like Memuchan, Haman first creates a dilemma and then, without pause, appends a simple solution (3: 8–9). Harbona channels Xerxes' rage and confusion by calling his attention to the stake Haman had erected, thereby providing a quick and easy way to eliminate the immediate cause of the king's vexation (7:9). (If Harbona had told him what Haman was actually doing at the queen's couch, the counter-plot might have fizzled while the king tried to sort out the conflicting obligations he had taken upon himself.[3]) Esther, strangely, is not quite so helpful. In her second banquet, she just lays the dilemma before the king, who promptly runs out of the room. In her audience afterwards (8:3–5), she begs him to undo Haman's evil by rescinding the edict—a forthright and difficult solution—to which Xerxes answers that he has done all he can and dumps the matter in Mordecai's and Esther's hands.

It is a feature of his laziness that Xerxes acts without quite knowing what he is getting himself into; he does not bother with inquiries. This is the case in his decision to destroy the Jews, in his acceptance of Esther's invitations, in his unintended humiliation of Haman in chapter 6, and in his judgment of Haman in chapter 7.

A later addition in the Septuagint (Addition E) recognizes that the king's intellectual laziness made the entire fiasco possible. In a proclamation canceling the first edict, the king insists that he had been deceived and promises to give no attention to slander in the future but instead to investigate matters more fully (E 8–9). This

---

2. E.g., Prov 11:14; 24:6; 19:20; 8:14.
3. Harbona's intervention is thus more valuable than it might seem at first. It is appropriately recognized in a special blessing after the reading of the Scroll at Purim, in accordance with Est. Rab. X 9.

recognition is accurate but the repentance is unconvincing, because it is a misreading of Xerxes' character. His concession to Haman was no one-time slip of attentiveness; nor was Xerxes entirely deceived. Although Haman had warped half-truths into full lies, Xerxes knew what he was doing—giving Haman a people to destroy. Xerxes' agreement to Haman's request was fully of a piece with his qualities before and after that incident: his fear for his authority, his impulsive generosity, his malleability, and, above all, his abdication of thought to those with more energy for such things. In the canonical Esther, Xerxes never does admit, or even seem aware, that he did anything wrong. He does not even claim that he was tricked (Haman's lies are never refuted; once he loses power, they do not seem to matter). Xerxes is indignant that someone would threaten his queen's (and, perhaps incidentally, her people's) life, and he condemns Haman for apparently seeking to violate his wife. He agrees to the counter-decree because he has put himself into the hands of Jewish advisers. Not a glimmer of recognition that it is wrong to extirpate a people.

Xerxes is not particularly cruel, but he is nonetheless terrifying—such power, with so little thought invested in its employment. His foggy indifference to life is simply the capstone of this laziness. He had not even bothered to ask which people he is consigning to destruction. The offhand quality of his agreement is grotesque, as is his sitting down to feast with Haman right after the murderous decree is published and the capital thrown into dismay (3:15). So little impression does the extermination order make upon him that he does not even recall the incident only a few days after the edict was issued, for he asks Esther who had done such a thing, as if the engineering of genocide were a commonplace in his empire. Nor does the death of myriads of Persians in the consequent battles strike him as anything other than an interesting spectacle.

One expects the force motivating a crime as horrendous as genocide to be a mammoth one, such as the vast tribal and personal animosity that spurred Haman. In this regard, Haman is more comprehensible than Xerxes. Haman's motives, at least, correspond to his actions; the king has no such motives. His decision is driven not by hatred, but by indolence, and reinforced by egotism and cupidity. This combination of petty impulses and mental sloth is what Hanna Arendt called "the banality of evil"—"the strange interdependence of thoughtlessness and evil" (1963:233). Arendt was referring to Adolph Eichmann, the chief bureaucrat of the Holocaust, whose evil was of quite a different sort—more deliberate, conscious, and determined than Xerxes'. But it is important to realize that the concept applies not only to the initiators and perpetrators of iniquity but also to those who facilitate it by agreement and passivity. "Wickedness," Arendt argued in a later work, "may be caused by absence of thought" (1978:13).

Haman is a given; he is always lurking in the background, awaiting the opportunity to pour his malice upon the Jews; the question is whether he will be allowed to have his way. Most rulers, if only from simple self-interest, have not given him free rein; Xerxes did. As Arendt writes, "such remoteness from reality and such thoughtlessness can wreak more havoc than all the evil instincts taken together which, perhaps, are inherent in man" (1978:13).

6. King and Kingdom

That, however, is my evaluation, not the author's. Neither the narrator nor the Jews in the story condemns Xerxes or even seems to resent his indifference to their existence. Xerxes is a lumpish, indifferent mass, not inherently vicious, not anti-Jewish, but erratic, childish, apathetic, and pliable. In this exemplary tale, in which the Persecutor of the Jews is a man of second rank, Xerxes is the epitome of the gentile king, and, as such, he embodies the power of the gentile state. It is a severe, if unintended, indictment of that state that the author does not condemn the king as evil, does not use him as an example of a wicked king, but merely snickers—quietly—at his doltishness and egotism. Beneath the voice that lavishes admiration on the king's wealth and (in 9:25) flatters him for his solicitude toward the Jews, we hear another one, more subtle and insidious, which by *not* denouncing his behavior—by taking it for granted that a despot will be of this sort—damns gentile rule as scarcely worthy of contempt. How frightening, it says, that our "friends" are of this sort; how tenuous our security when it rests upon the fickleness and moral obtuseness of heathen power! But that is what we must live with.

The author does not expect any better of a gentile king. While some of the Persian monarchs can be credited with at least declaring ethical concerns, few were the kings of the Hellenistic kingdoms who warranted higher expectations. Rulers like the Xerxes of Esther were a fact of life; they constituted the world through which Jews had to make their way. The author realizes the perils of a society dependent on such a dangerous man, but he does not envision a better society or criticize the one he describes, except to mock it by careful satire.

The decisions of the gentile state are made on the basis of personal influence, irrational impulses, and selfish desires. The legal system is so rigid that it makes the most whimsical and the most vicious of laws binding even upon the king, yet it does not even provide true law and order. The concept of the legal system of the Persians and the Medes is a fiction known only from Esther and Daniel, but it does represent a reality as perceived by the Jews: they are up against a massive, foreign structure of administration, laws, and custom that is often puzzling, unpredictable, and dangerous, and always inert and indifferent to human needs and higher justice. Clearly, Jews cannot rely on such a state to ensure their existence, but must, like all the other subjects, manipulate its power for their own ends.

CHAPTER VIII

HAMAN

1. Haman's Transparency

Devious though he is, Haman is allowed no mysteries. His motives, drives, and attitudes are transparent, his twisted soul laid bare to all. None of his motives are obscured, and little is left for the reader to wonder about. Evil, the author seems to say, is really quite simple and obvious, however sneaky the evil man may be and however subtle he may fancy himself. To demonstrate this, the author subjects Haman to special treatment: he exposes his thoughts to public view.

Robert Alter (1981, chap. 6) has shown the importance of the interplay of opacity and transparency in the David story, in which Saul's thoughts and feelings are revealed, David's hidden. There is a similar interplay—with very different effects—in the portrayal of Haman and Mordecai.

We are repeatedly informed of Haman's emotions: Haman "was filled with wrath" (3:5b). "Haman went out that day merry and lighthearted. But when he saw Mordecai . . . Haman was filled with wrath against [him]" (5:9); "But Haman controlled himself" (5:10a); "The idea pleased Haman" (5:14b). "Haman hastened home in grief, his head covered" (6:12b); "And Haman shook in terror before the king and the queen" (7:6b); "At this word from the king's mouth, Haman was humiliated" [?] (7:8b). His perceptions too are revealed: Haman "saw that the king was bent on his ruin" (7:7b). Even the nuances of his calculations are bared: "But he thought it beneath himself to strike out at Mordecai alone. . . . So Haman sought . . ." (3:6). His thoughts are even quoted verbatim: "And Haman thought to himself, 'Now whom could the king desire to honor more than me?'" (6:6b).

In addition to the various explicit revelations of Haman's thoughts, two scenes are devoted largely to exposing the way his mind works. In 5:9–14, Haman displays his bloated pride and his obsession with Mordecai's lack of deference. The following scene

(6:1–11) reveals Haman's prideful assumption that he alone can be the man the king seeks to honor. The author tells us exactly how Haman mistook the king's intention and delighted in it. Interestingly, the author refrains from looking within Haman at the moment of his disgrace. It is obvious what Haman's feelings must have been; and the silence suggests his dumbfounded shock and leaves the intensity of that feeling to the reader's imagination.

Haman's motives are everywhere laid bare. His reaction to Mordecai's refusal to bow is more clearly motivated than is Mordecai's action: Haman is simply driven by pride and the hostility this engenders. He excels only in the magnitude of his drives.

No other characters, not even Xerxes, are ever subjected to such direct, deep, and extensive exposure. This is not to say that the personalities of the others are hidden from view, but rather that theirs must be constructed mainly from actions and speech, while Haman's is revealed directly and unambiguously. The contrast between Haman and the other characters shows that the author is deliberately choosing to examine, and to throw a harsh light on, the squalid soul of the antisemite.

2. Haman's Motives

What is revealed in all this is a vast and tender ego. Haman's primary motivation in all his actions is neither racial hatred, though he hardly lacks this, nor undirected spleen, though he is certainly splenetic, but rather the need to confirm his power at every step.

Haman is first enraged by Mordecai's refusal to show obeisance, in other words, to confirm publicly Haman's power and station. Haman does not seek to punish Mordecai alone. One individual would be an inadequate target for Haman's massive rage. Moreover, merely to punish Mordecai would be to allow *him* to define the scope of the conflict: one person punished for an insult to one person. So Haman devises a vengeance embracing the entire people to which Mordecai belongs. When Haman feels he has set this total revenge on an inexorable course, he takes his ease (3:15).

After Esther's first banquet, and flattered by a second invitation, Haman leaves the palace merry, but is devastated to find that Mordecai even now does not fear him (5:9). Haman has discovered that the prodigious vengeance he has in store is not adequate, for it does not secure him the personal victory he needs. He has not forced Mordecai to recognize his power. Nor is Mordecai's impending death a sufficient personal triumph for Haman, because the Jew can still withhold fear and thus trivialize the power Haman does have. (Compare Xerxes' need for Vashti's inner acquiescence to his command.) If Mordecai continues to defy him for the next eleven months, his defiance will endure as a victory that mere murder cannot expunge. Haman's domination must be absolute and it must be universally recognized, otherwise he cannot believe in it himself.

Haman is devoured by this obsession with control. Such an obsession is a single, ineradicable notion that dominates the thoughts and feelings in spite of one's own will. Mordecai's refusal to show fear, indeed his very presence in the King's Gate, proves to Haman that, whatever his might, he lacks control: he cannot govern the Jew's emotions; he cannot even prevent his current presence in the place of power. But ironically and appropriately, Haman's obsession with control in effect imposes Mordecai's presence upon all of his thoughts and gives Mordecai power over his mind, robbing him of all pleasure he might derive from the honor, wealth, and power in which he glories. Haman makes himself miserable. Yet he is still eager for more honors, as if these would confirm his station and salve his wounded pride. Again it is his pride that makes him assume that *he* must be the man the king wishes to honor (6:6).

Such a desperate need for personal confirmation reveals, of course, a painful insecurity. Magonet (1980:175) proposes that Haman's pathetic boasting (5:11) reflects his insecurity as a member of a minority group who must rely on wealth or other signs of power to maintain his position. But the Persian empire comprises many minority groups, and the author does not see this as a problem. Haman's membership in a non-indigenous ethnic group does not seem to cause him any professional difficulties, nor does Mordecai's. The hostility that does exist in some quarters toward the Jews is not due to their being a minority or non-indigenous, but to their Jewishness itself.

The conflict between Haman and the Jews is, as noted above, essentially personal, to be explained primarily as a defect of Haman's psyche rather than as a clash between two races. To be sure, the clash is rooted in an ancient tribal enmity, but this remains in the background. The tribal enmity is not stated, but is only suggested by the genealogies of Mordecai and Haman. The tribal antagonism seems to lie behind Mordecai's refusal to show Haman obeisance, and it probably spurs Haman to encompass all the Jews in his revenge on Mordecai. But the tribal strife is not prominent. Mordecai is not a direct descendant of Saul and Haman is not called an Amalekite, the name by which Israel's archetypal foe was known. Haman, for his part, never mentions the Jews by name (outside the edict, which is written in the king's name). Neither an ancient nor a present conflict between nationalities is mentioned. The Jews, for their part, do not fight against the Amalekites, but against all their enemies, who are mixed in with all the peoples.

In fact, Haman's hatred of Jews is not the direct cause of his murderous scheme. In other words, it was not because of his spite for the Jews that Haman set out to eliminate them. Rather, he makes antisemitism an *instrument* for achieving perfect personal revenge. The tribal conflict is the context for a personal one. Accordingly, the essential victory is won on the personal level and only carried to completion in the mass battles, and even these are not between the Jews and their ancestral enemies, but between Jews and individuals in many nations who choose to assail them.

This is the author's image of the enemy of the Jews. This image is without parallel in the earlier sources. The pharaoh of the enslavement is motivated by fear of the Israelites (Exod 1:9–10)—an irrational and pathological fear, to be sure, but if one were to grant his assumption that the Israelites could become a military threat, his actions could claim to protect his national interest. The numerous enemies that Israel faced during the invasion of Canaan, the period of the Judges, and the monarchy were hostile peoples and states fighting over territory, control, or tribute. Even Amalek was an enemy of this sort; its assault was especially shocking because it was directed against the weaker segments of the population, not because its hostility was fundamentally different from that of Edom or Moab. Haman's hatred, in contrast, does not grow out of a fear of the Jews' power or a greed for something they possess. It is a response to bruised pride; the cause is purely psychological, an offense to a man's self-image. The reasons come later.

Once he resolves to relieve his frustration by an orgy of murder, Haman produces arguments to show that the Jews present a danger to the commonweal. Haman's rhetoric is analyzed in the Commentary to Esther 3 (Act III, scene ii). His arguments are so artfully insidious—spinning lies out of truths and half-truths—that they seem the product of a deliberate craft, shaped just for the purpose of persuading Xerxes.

The qualities Haman ascribes to the Jews are not the cause of

181

Haman's antisemitism but its deliberate product. The author is asserting that the antisemite—and Haman is *the* antisemite, not merely an antisemitic person—is driven by disturbances in his own psyche: a distended pride, a nervous insecurity, and an insatiable thirst for confirmation of his significance—all compounded with a hatred inherited from his ancestors.

3. Haman's Folly and Cleverness

Haman is sometimes thought to epitomize the Wisdom concept of a fool, the uncontrolled braggart who prides himself on his wealth and good fortune and lives in false security, the sort of man condemned in Prov 11:28; 13:3; 14:16; 16:5, 18; 27:1; 28:11; 29:1, 20, and elsewhere.[1] Thus Talmon characterizes Haman as one of the "wicked wise," impetuous, wrathful, impatient, loquacious, and ultimately foolish (1963:444). This description is correct, but it does not prove that Haman's image was drawn from Wisdom Literature. Of course Wisdom Literature condemns traits such as these, but not only that genre is aware of them. Indeed, the "wicked wise" is not a type-figure in Wisdom Literature, though a few proverbs (especially in Ben Sira) may speak of such persons. (Some of the "wicked wise" outside Wisdom Literature are Jonadab [2 Sam 13:3], those who are "wise to do evil" [Jer 4:22], and the unscrupulous "wise men" of the heathen [Ezek 28:2–10; Ob 6–8].) In contrast, Wisdom Literature, as Talmon himself observes, equates the "wise" with the "righteous."

Moreover, Haman does not exhibit his folly in quite the form described in Wisdom Literature. His is of a more subtle sort. First of all, he is able to control himself and seek counsel before acting (5:10)—as advised by Prov 11:14 and 20:18, for example. Also, his pride is not mere smugness, self-satisfaction, or an excessive sense of security. Haman lacks satisfaction in his station and possessions, and his confidence is very fragile. Nor is pride Haman's primary vice. That is hatred, a vice given little attention in Wisdom Literature.

Haman is undoubtedly clever, but his cleverness exhausts itself in his insidious rhetoric when he persuades Xerxes to extirpate the

---

1. See Talmon (1963:443–47), Gerleman (p. 116), and Dommershausen (pp. 83, 91). On the image of the fool in Wisdom Literature see von Rad 1972:64–65.

unnamed people (3:8–9) and in the edict he devises to that end (3:13b-14). Haman is a skilled demagogue, able to fabricate a vast lie out of threads of truths and half-truths, to play upon the king's cupidity and mental sloth, then to write a decree appealing to mass malice and greed. Yet even in this he gives himself away. After arguing the case from the point of view of the king's interests—which have nothing to do with Haman's real motives—he offers a fabulous sum of money to have the Jews destroyed (3:9b), thereby revealing that he is promoting his own, not the king's, interests, for in the latter case the inducement would not be necessary. (Fortunately for Haman, Xerxes is quite obtuse.) Still, Haman *has* gotten his way through cunning. His skills do not, of course, constitute wisdom, but he is at least crafty. Moreover, Haman does have the virtue of self-control, but only in short-range, tactical ways. But all his skills are overwhelmed by his pride, pettiness, and rage.

After the "high point" of his cleverness in chapter 3, everything Haman does is manifestly foolish, as he is buffeted about and driven by his passions and impulses. His anger makes him unable to wait for his revenge and leads him to push fate and try to kill Mordecai prematurely. The consequence is that he erects the instrument of his own death and rushes straight into humiliation. His fatuous assumption that he alone is worthy of the king's honors makes a public fool out of him. He, the vizier and high nobleman, has to conduct his enemy on horseback as his herald through the city square, all this exacerbated to the extreme by the fact that his conflict with Mordecai is well known among the palace officials who are watching the display. His folly finally unmasks itself in his rash fall on Esther's couch, an act which is the immediate cause of his death. Haman is a buffoon, a clever fool.

By making Haman superficial and silly, the author hits him where his sort would most feel it: in his pride. We can imagine how a person such as the one created in this book would feel about the way he is depicted. Haman would not be bothered by being shown to be deeply evil, but he would be mortified to be revealed as an impulsive bungler. I am reminded of Charlie Chaplin's *The Great Dictator*, a satirical attack on Hitler, which showed the Führer to be not only an evil and dangerous power but also a gesticulating, screeching, frenetic ninny. Rather than attacking evil in its own terms, Chaplin, like the author of Esther, denigrated it by exposing it for what it most deeply fears to be: weak within and ludicrous without. It is no surprise that Chaplin's satire hit its target harder than the standard propaganda, so that the German Foreign Office went into high gear to get it banned in Latin America and parts of Europe. Hitler can no longer be ridiculed in this way; perhaps it is a triumph of evil to have descended beyond the reach of satire. But Haman can still be laughed at, as he is every year, because his plan was nipped in the bud, allowing the book to remain, in classical terms, a comedy.

CHAPTER IX

MORDECAI

One opinion:
"Mordecai proves to be a worthy successor to Haman. He
is another version of Haman" ("Haman mit umgekehrtem
Vorzeichen").

(S. Ben-Chorin, 1938:9)

Mordecai is an ideal figure, a repository of virtues, a shining
example of how a Jew of the diaspora should behave. Yet he is not
entirely a bore.

Mordecai is the dominant figure in the book. He is introduced
first (2:5) and praised last (10:2–3), and his glorification lies at the
book's turning point and presages the Jews' victory. His initiative
begins the rescue effort, his edict is the mechanism of deliverance,
and his epistle guides the people in the establishment of the new
holiday. His unalloyed success, personal and public, for himself and
for his people, shows that his behavior is to be taken as exemplary.

1. Mordecai as an Ideal Figure

For Esther's author—though not for all readers—Mordecai is
unblemished. He is consistently wise and knowing. His actions save
his people and later promote their welfare, all the while benefitting
the king and advancing his own career.

The difficulty in discussing an exemplary figure is in getting
behind the obvious. But the obvious is a good place to begin, because an exemplum is supposed to be an unequivocal paradigm
for use in equivocal circumstances. The exemplum must be (or
at least become) an unwavering, unambiguous, even unnuanced
standard of right behavior. What, then, are the components of the
ideal which Mordecai embodies?

A. JEWISHNESS. While Jewishness is not in itself a virtue, a good
quality to be emulated, it is a necessary constituent of this ideal.
Mordecai is identified as a Jew in 2:5 and 3:4 and six times there-

185

after called "Mordecai the Jew." Epithets in the Bible are not incidental identifiers, but clues to the development of the story and integral to it.[1] In this case, the reader does not really need to be informed repeatedly that Mordecai is a Jew, and Esther, who is no less Jewish, is never identified as "the Jewess" (her epithet is "the Queen," for that is closer to her specific function). Mordecai's epithet, then, is a pointer to his special role in the story's development and message: He acts not as an individual but as *the* Jew—the representative and then the leader of the Jewish people. He is introduced as (literally) "a Jewish man" (2:5)—with no comments on other qualities, such as piety, wisdom, courage, or obedience to Torah (contrast the introduction of Ezra in Ezr 7:6, 10). Jewishness, then, is Mordecai's main identifying feature. Later it is not simply Mordecai who enrages Haman, but "Mordecai the Jew" (5:13), just as it is "Mordecai the Jew" who will receive honors from the Agagite (6:10). It is in his capacity as "the Jew" that Mordecai receives the right to compose a royal edict (8:7), confirms the holiday of Purim (9:29, 31), and serves as viceregent (10:3). The ideal typified by Mordecai, then, is of the representative Jew, a man identified first and foremost and finally by his Jewishness.

B. WISDOM.   Mordecai knows just what is happening and—except for one moment[2]—knows exactly what must be done. His wisdom includes foresight, the preparation for dangers before they arise. He has the political savvy to compose a decree that will avert the disaster, and the social sagacity to direct the people in the establishment of a new ritual. He also knows how to play up to the king's ego and encourage a favorable attitude toward the Jews (see the Commentary on 9:24–25).

C. PRIDE.   The author is wholly in sympathy with Mordecai's pride, in particular, his national pride, even though it sparks a dangerous

---

1. The definitive discussion of biblical epithets is Sternberg 1985:328–341. He says that "all formal epithets, in contrast [to redundant epithets that specify character in the interest of realism], enter into tight relations with the patterns that surround them, fulfilling at least one role beyond direct characterization. . . . All these epithets are implicitly proleptic within the dynamics of action" (p. 331). Such epithets "are charged with kinetic power straining for release" (p. 332). They are bound to carry "actional as well as descriptive implications."

2. In 4:8. Esther will take a better approach than the one Mordecai recommends; see the Commentary on Act V (5:1–8).

series of events. Mordecai's is the pride of self-esteem rather than the pride of arrogance.

D. COURAGE. He never varies his course to protect himself.

E. LOYALTY TO THE KING. He is the king's man, and only through him does he serve the kingdom.

F. LEADERSHIP. He uses his influence among the Jews and with the king to instruct the people in establishing and developing their religious institutions.

Mordecai represents a leader of a new sort: the diaspora leader. What does it mean to lead the Jews when you are neither king nor prince, prophet nor priest? The answer is, of course, dependent on the nature of the community to be led, and that issue will await our discussion of the Jewish people (chap. XI §2c-d). The main feature of this personage is that he earns his position by his own deeds; it is not an institutionalized post (Mordecai's viziership is a tool in leadership, not its basis). He is not elected or even acclaimed (no social framework is available for such choices) but simply acts as he sees fit, and his deeds are confirmed by communal accord.

Mordecai is to the diaspora what Ezra was to the Judean community. Both the book of Esther and Ezra-Nehemiah try to define a new sort of leader. According to T. Eskenazi's analysis, "Ezra's chosen method involves persuasion, example, and appeal, rather than coercion. The enormity of the powers in his possession heightens the magnitude of Ezra's restraint, stressing thereby his abnegation of such means. . . . At the core of Ezra's activities is the transfer of power and knowledge from himself to the community as a whole" (1988:138). The book of Esther proposes a very similar model of leadership for a similar reason. Ezra was facing a community in dissolution, lacking authorities or rulers with powers rooted in the people's laws and traditions (Joshua and Zerubbabel having proved dead-ends). Rather than exercise his official authority, which derived from the gentile realm, to impose his will on the community, Ezra sought to harness the communal will and energy in the fulfillment of Torah. Mordecai does much the same. Of both it can be said, in Eskenazi's words, that they exercise "the power of influence rather than coercion, relying on example, embodying the difference between genuine power and force" (p. 140). Ezra is counterbalanced by quite a different model, that of the overbearing and coercive Nehemiah, whom the book of Ezra-Nehemiah treats with a certain ambivalence. But, as Eskenazi shows, it is finally Ezra who embodies the ideal to be emulated (pp. 144–54).

G. LOYALTY TO THE JEWISH PEOPLE. Mordecai's loyalty to his people is his chief virtue. He acts on their behalf, pulling whatever strings he can, wielding whatever power he holds in the cause. In his later career, he speaks up on their behalf and sees to their welfare (*šalom*, 10:3).

H. LACK OF PERSONAL AMBITION. Mordecai does nothing to further his own career. Many commentators assume that as a palace official who reaped success, Mordecai must have been an opportunist. Paton thinks that Mordecai was willing to sacrifice his cousin to his political ambition (p. 173).[3] Bickerman believes that Mordecai refused to bow because Haman had received a promotion that Mordecai considered his due for having saved the king's life.[4] We would indeed expect a palace official to be ambitious; it is all the more significant, then, that Mordecai never strives for personal advancement. Any personal benefit he might have derived from his cousin's position he gives up by insisting on keeping their kinship secret. He certainly could not expect to advance his career by disobeying the king and slighting the vizier, his boss. He claims no reward for informing on the eunuchs. The laurels he does receive fall into his lap without affecting him much. He rises in rank and power without evident effort toward those goals; they accrue to him as incidental rewards for his devotion to his king and his people.

I. DIRECTNESS. Manipulativeness is another quality that many commentators assume must belong to a figure like Mordecai; but it is not there. Mordecai always acts in an entirely forthright manner. He is wise but not cunning, and certainly not devious. He does not, after all, even attempt to get on the vizier's good side; quite the contrary, he is dangerously blunt. He does not manipulate or "run" Esther but gives her direct instructions, as befits his parental

---

3. He had no choice, of course, in the induction of his cousin into the harem. Surely the king did not see himself obligated to obtain parental consent. In any case, Mordecai does not seem to consider Esther unfortunate for having reached royal station (4:14).
4. Bickerman 1967:179. This is part of a hypothetical "Mordecai Story" that Bickerman reconstructs and believes to have been woven into the present book of Esther. Whatever the validity of this theory, the strife between Mordecai and Haman is present in the canonical book as well.

status. When facing the gravest of crises, he sends Esther to the king not to deceive him or finagle her wish out of him, but straightforwardly "to implore and beseech him on behalf of her people" (4:8). In this instance, Esther turns out to be shrewder than Mordecai and chooses a less direct approach, which the situation certainly required.

J. FAITH AND PIETY? One virtue is surprisingly absent in the portrayal of Mordecai. Piety, either as an attribute of spirit or as obedience to Mosaic Law, is not displayed among Mordecai's virtues. Piety is the foremost quality of other ideal figures in Second Temple Jewish literature—the Jews in Daniel, for example, or the heroes of the books of Maccabees—and it is always in plain view. Ideal figures pray, preach, and demonstrate their trust in God and their zeal for the Law and are rewarded accordingly. Mordecai, in contrast, nowhere prays, and when he states his faith, it is not expressly in God. Nor does he show any concern about his ward's marriage to a gentile and the inevitable impingement on her religious duties, though he does worry generally about her welfare (2:11). Given the blatancy of Mordecai's other virtues, the non-mention of this one must be deemed deliberate, not merely a neglect of the obvious. This is not to say that Mordecai was not pious; traditional readers, at least, invariably saw him as such, and there is no suggestion that he deliberately lacks or avoids devotion to God. But the author does not make piety a component of the *ideal*, one of the virtues to be conveyed by Mordecai's example.

Mordecai does have faith—in Jewish survival. He is confident that "relief and deliverance will arise for the Jews from another source" (4:14a). This is a peculiar faith; it seems autonomous, not derivative from any system of belief. It is at its core irrational, for it is not reasoned out from premises, religious or natural.

I will explore Mordecai's faith and the book's religious stance (and it does have one) in chapter XII §3. For now, I observe only that Mordecai's faith is all the more courageous for eschewing rationalization, for assuming its own adequacy. Furthermore, if we respect the book's silences rather than filling them with presuppositions about what an ideal figure must be, we must conclude that the author conceived of a valid Jewish life without the primacy of piety or Law. (He does not say that religion is secondary; he just does not choose to make it primary.) This is not unthinkable. Jews have never all defined their Jewishness in the same way, certainly not in Second Temple times, in spite of the later rabbis' stereotyping of the men they considered their predecessors (picturing Mordecai as the first president of the Sanhedrin). Qohelet (Ecclesiastes), roughly contemporary with the author of Esther, is very concerned with God's role in human life yet holds very unorthodox views of divine providence and says nothing about Torah. Torah itself did not invariably have the primacy for all sectors of Jewish religious life that it later acquired. As Nickelsburg and Collins say of the ideal figures studied in their anthology, *Ideal Figures in Ancient Judaism*,

> The variety of religious expression evidenced in the different types of ideal figures serves, moreover, as a *caveat* for systematic treatments of Jewish religion and theology. . . . While the authority of the Mosaic Torah may in no case be denied, implicitly or explicitly, it is evident that the mentality of the apocalyptist or the visionary or the charismatic allows for, indeed, asserts the value and authority of other complementary and supplementary sources of revelation. . . . In short, while "systematic" studies of ancient Judaism are valid and helpful, they must be carried on in tension with a sensitivity to the unique characteristics of the individual phenomena. Only then do we historians stand a chance of glimpsing the variegated and many-sided edifice of this ancient religion. (1980:10–11)

The virtues that Mordecai displays are quite different from those of other ideal figures of the diaspora. Daniel and his friends exemplify loyalty to God and maintain their piety even in extremes. But they do nothing for the direct benefit of other Jews—besides themselves epitomizing piety. They do not speak up on behalf of their co-religionists; they do not seek the nullification of decrees that force Jews into idolatry and place them in mortal danger. Their virtues are purely individual and spiritual. The first six chapters of Daniel have no sense of community. The Scroll tries to inculcate such a sense and so makes its ideal figures—especially Mordecai but also Esther—communal leaders. We can also contrast Ezra and Nehemiah, whose solicitude for Jews (insofar as this is recorded) is directed only toward those in Palestine. Joseph, who is sometimes thought the model for Mordecai, takes care of his family, but this is quite different from national loyalty; it is motivated more by personal sentiments.

The most important lessons of the book of Esther are not subtle. They are put into the form of a schematic, exciting story, easily understood and remembered, and they are conveyed by clearly etched type-figures. Mordecai is the type of the Jewish courtier in the diaspora, the ideal court Jew: a man of power and courage, favored by the king and beloved of his kin, concerned above all for the welfare of his people. Mordecai's power and position are the best guarantor of security for his people.

2. Mordecai's Reserve

Mordecai is complete at the beginning of the book. He has never wavered and never will. He is exemplary to start with. But he is saved from being a Sunday-school figure by one intriguing trait: he keeps his own counsel, and the author respects his reserve. This reserve—and the author's—saves Mordecai from the flat predictability of perfection.

At certain key points, Mordecai does things that are hard to explain; indeed, one danger-fraught act, the refusal to bow, seems almost irrational. The author's belief in Mordecai's wisdom induces the reader to look for an explanation, but we are never granted entry into Mordecai's psyche. Whereas the author violates Haman's privacy, he respects Mordecai's, even when Mordecai's motivations, reasoning, and responses call for explanation. This evokes curiosity and gives the reader an impression of character-depth: much is going on in Mordecai's mind that we can only guess at. But the author wants us to guess, and so gives us enough clues to make some guesses better than others. Indeed, a discussion of Mordecai's character can proceed by attempting to fill in the silences.

We are not told why Mordecai instructs Esther to conceal her national identity. He is almost certainly preparing Esther as an inside agent in the event of danger to the Jews (see the Commentary on 2:10). Years before the danger materializes, Mordecai is alert and planning for the contingency. He is looking out for his people's interests, taking upon himself the responsibilities of leadership even before the need to do so is evident. The LXX fills the gap by giving Mordecai a dream foretelling the crisis and how it would be met, thereby making him more understandable and less mysterious. The MT-author chooses not to satisfy our curiosity in some such way.

The biggest puzzle is Mordecai's refusal to bow to the new vizier. He was obviously endangering himself. But didn't he realize that he would endanger his people too by publicly defying the haughty vizier—an ancient tribal enemy—while flaunting his own Jewishness? The author must have in mind some reason for such persistent, dangerous, and apparently useless behavior; it cannot be due to a whim, certainly not in a stable, thoughtful character like Mordecai. In the Commentary on 3:2–3 I weigh the various explanations that have been offered and argue that the most likely reason for the refusal is that Haman is an Amalekite, the ancient tribal enemy of Israel. This motive is, however, kept well in the background. The author does not rationalize the act that will endanger the Jews, perhaps because Jewish motives are not relevant to antisemitic malevolence.

Whatever the reason for Mordecai's defiance, it is behavior that the author affirms and admires, for Mordecai's wisdom and heroism are unalloyed and unquestioned. The author never suggests that Mordecai bore any responsibility for Haman's scheme. Unlike some commentators (Paton and Ben-Chorin [1938:8], among others), the author does not blame the hatred on its victim.[5]

Mordecai has already proved his fealty to the king. Only in this regard does he insist on disobeying the king's orders, though the consequences are potentially disastrous. If Mordecai's stubbornness is, as argued, rooted in tribal loyalties, a concession would betray his people (thus Meinhold). Mordecai's first loyalty is to the ancient demands of his people's history. In the diaspora, the Jews, subjugated to the laws and the will of a foreign people, dare not compromise their national honor, even when this stubbornness might imperil their existence. Though beaten in their homeland, they must remain unbowed in exile. Mordecai shows this even in his posture.

Yet I find that I cannot affirm Mordecai's behavior in the way the author does. The only explanation of Mordecai's defiance that saves him from mere arrogance or instability—namely, that his act was due to tribal hostility—does the author no credit. He (like other biblical authors) believes that ancient tribal antagonisms are transmitted from age to age and that Jews in later generations are obliged to express them. Mordecai's flaw is not his pride but his (which is to say the author's) concept of genetic culpability. Nothing suggests that at the time Haman appears on the scene the vizier already bore personal guilt or had otherwise shown himself deserv-

---

5. This is the "Hitler's tailor" theory of antisemitism, the notion that Hitler hated the Jews because he was once cheated by a Jewish tailor.

ing of hostility. He will prove to deserve it, but Mordecai is not a prophet, and even so, no one is responsible for future crimes. The author believes that the dichotomy between good and evil can be encoded in a national-genetic one.[6] To be sure, prostration signals subordination, and Mordecai would not want to imply Israel's subordination to Amalek, but the gesture is individual not tribal, and, after all, Mordecai was in fact Haman's subordinate. If Mordecai found the gesture intolerable, he should not have accepted the reality, but should have quit his job when Haman took office.

Mordecai's silence is again noticeable in 6:11, when Haman leads him about the city in honor and pomp. We may contrast the way this episode is handled in the original AT, in which Mordecai is not imperturbable. When Haman emerges with orders to bestow the honors and tells Mordecai to change his garments,

> Mordecai was disturbed, like one about to die, and he removed the sackcloth in distress, and he put on the garments of honor. And Mordecai thought he saw an omen, and his heart was toward the Lord, and he was beside himself in speechlessness. (AT vii 16–17)

The Midrash, too, pictures Mordecai as fearful at this point (Est. Rab. X 4 = b. Meg. 16a). It is hard, however, to imagine the Mordecai of the MT seized by agitation and fear on his own behalf, or even being struck dumb with amazement. The MT version avoids ascribing such frailties to the hero, but it does not substitute other feelings for them, such as exultation or gratitude to God. The elision of Mordecai's thoughts suggests that he is not overwhelmed by either fear or delight but simply accepts the honors in silence. Afterwards he returns to the gate with no further ado and waits, his composure highlighted by Haman's agitation (6:12).

When Mordecai appears again, after Haman is overthrown, he still maintains silence, while it is Esther who begs the king to rescind Haman's decree (8:1–6).

We are given clear signals to Mordecai's thoughts and feelings only in 4:1, where he goes into public mourning. And even in this limited exposure there is reserve, for we do not know to what extent his behavior is tactical. The closest the author comes to revealing Mordecai's thoughts directly is in reporting that he "found out"

---

6. This schema is overcome in the Talmud, which says that Haman's descendants converted to Judaism and became Torah scholars in the academy of Bney Beraq (b. Gittin 57b).

what had happened (4:1) and that he sought to "learn about" Esther's welfare (2:11) (in both cases the verb *yada^c*, usually translated "know," is used). Both these insights are virtually external data that someone on the scene could have observed (in the latter case Mordecai would have to ask questions about Esther), and they expose little of the depths of Mordecai's mind. It is significant that these slight incursions into Mordecai's mind use the verb *yada^c*. "And Mordecai knew" is an excellent encapsulation of an important facet of his character.

Mordecai speaks very little in the whole book. He is most talkative when persuading Esther to undertake the mission, but even there he is communicating through messengers and is quoted indirectly. (Strictly speaking, we only hear him quoted in 4:13b-14, thirty-one words in all; another sixty-six are phrased as indirect discourse.)[7]

Mordecai retains a hard nub of inscrutability. Esther I feel I can understand. My reading may, of course, be wrong or incomplete, but the point is not the adequacy of my reading but rather my sense (which is to say, illusion) as a reader that I can know all that there is to know about her. Xerxes has no silences. There is nothing there to be silent about; we know this from the exposure of his shallowness in chapter 1. Mordecai, however, I cannot quite decipher. The author has carefully left a few dark spots that invite scrutiny but do not satisfy it. That the author preserves obscurity in such a schematic ideal figure shows a certain delight in developing character for its own sake rather than only for its exemplary value, and thus keeps Mordecai realistic and human in a way that Daniel, for example, is not. Mordecai's portrayal preserves respect for a character who is a creation of ideology by excluding certain areas from the ideology. This technique makes Mordecai always deeper than the reader. And that, in turn, makes him a more effective exemplum.

Nevertheless, an exemplum is what Mordecai remains. Haman is vivid in his evil; Xerxes is predictably unstable; Esther is changeable and human and multifaceted. Mordecai is flat—always presenting one surface to the reader—and unchanging. This is a quality, not a fault: Mordecai is meant to be flat—level, we might say, or

---

7. The forty-four words of the counter-decree (9:21–22) are an indirect quote of something Mordecai composed, but they are formally the king's words and they are meant to be taken that way.

solid—a brick.[8] His perfect wisdom, stability, and loyalty make him reliable. He continues unchanged, powerful, energetic, benevolent, issuing public epistles, and exercising authority through his station as vizier and leader. He will never surprise us. We know we can rely on a leader like that and comfortably adapt our will to his—such is the picture of Jewish leadership that the book projects. But we cannot *approach* him. His completeness, together with his taciturnity, makes him a leader at a distance. We can try to follow his example but cannot easily identify with him. It is otherwise with Esther.

---

8. Responding to E. M. Forster's recognition and definition of "flat" characters, E. Muir says: "In the novel of character, they [flat characters] are to be met in thousands, and it is more reasonable to believe that there is method in their flatness than that they are mistakes which all the great character novelists have had the misfortune to commit. Why, indeed, should not a character be flat? The only real answer to this is that the present taste in criticism prefers round characters" (1929:25). Muir proceeds to elucidate the function of flatness. Many Bible scholars, however, use "flatness" as a reproach to the author of Esther, as if a book populated with variegated, shifting, multifaceted, unpredictable characters would do a better job in achieving the goals of the book of Esther than this one does.

CHAPTER X

ESTHER

One opinion:
"Esther, for the chance of winning wealth and power,
takes her place in the herd of maidens who become
concubines of the King. She wins her victories not by
skill or by character, but by her beauty."

(L. B. Paton, p. 96)

Of the two heroes in the book of Esther, Mordecai is the dominant actor and the more sterling paragon; yet it is appropriate that
the Scroll bears Esther's name, for she too is central.[1] There is no
need to determine for every book a single most important character. A book can have two central characters, equally important but
significant in different ways. In the Scroll, it is Esther who stands at
the center of the book's artistic interest. She emerges as the most
distinct and memorable character in the book, the one with whom
the reader most naturally identifies. Mordecai's character forms a
solid frame around the smaller and more finely executed depiction
of Esther.

The distinctive feature in the portrayal of Esther is change.
Esther alone undergoes growth and surprises the reader by unpredictable developments.[2] She is, in E. M. Forster's influential terminology, "round," having more than a single dominant character
trait and capable of surprising the reader. Her dynamism stands
out in relief against the static nature of the other characters (including Xerxes, who is erratic but is consistent in his instability).
She develops in three stages, from passivity to activity to authority.

---

1. The rabbis called the book simply *hamm'gillah*, "The Scroll." The earliest use of
   the title "Esther" that I can find is the heading given the book in the ancient
   codices of the Septuagint—the Vaticanus and the Sinaiticus (both fourth century C.E.) and the Alexandrinus (fifth century).
2. Several scholars have recognized Esther's development, among them Jones
   (1977:176), Clines (p. 145), Craghan (1986), Meinhold (p. 105), S. White
   (1989:170), and Talmon (1963:449—notwithstanding his statement on
   p. 440 that the dramatis personae remain static).

1. Passivity

Esther's early years—until the first month of the twelfth year—are distinguished by passivity and pliancy. She is introduced incidentally to the identification of Mordecai, as an object of his action: he "had been raising" her, having "taken her to himself as a daughter" (2:7). She was, of course, strictly obedient to him (as we are told retrospectively in 2:20b). The mother would normally be the primary authority, tutor, and model for a girl, but as an orphan raised by her cousin, Esther is from the outset entirely dependent upon and governed by males.

Esther is "taken" (a key word in chap. 2), along with the other beautiful virgins, to the seraglio (2:8), put into the control of a eunuch, processed through a twelve-month beauty treatment, then "taken" for one night to the king, who tries her out in bed. Esther has been criticized for compliance and even opportunism in going along with all this, but of course she had no choice. Contrary to a common notion, there was no beauty contest to choose a new queen. *All* comely virgins were gathered; there was no further selection before they were taken to the king. In any case, the Persians have already proved themselves intolerant of female freedom of choice. (Nor does the royal decision to have the maidens "gathered" leave scope for consulting her guardian's will.) But while Esther's induction into the harem was beyond her and Mordecai's decision (and thus not a matter for censure), the way the induction is described suggests docility of the deepest sort. If she had been dragged off weeping, she would at least have been expressing indignation at having her sexuality—indeed, her whole life—expropriated by the royal authority. Or if she had gone off pleased at her prospects for personal promotion, she would at least have been lending her will to the bargain. But unlike the men at the banquet (1:8b), Esther is not consulted; her will is of no interest. The author does not even hint at how Esther felt about what was happening to her, because her feelings are irrelevant. But this ostensive indifference to Esther's soul is not because the author is indifferent to her as an individual; the contrary will be proved in the course of the book, as in 4:10–16, where her hesitation, fear, and resolution are crucial to the progress of the story. Rather, the author seeks to convey the insignificance of her will and mind *at this stage*. Esther is putty—not because of any personality flaw, but because of age and situation. Nothing has ever challenged her to be anything more.

In the seraglio, Esther spends a year being worked over by cosmeticians. Natural charms apparently do not suffice in this glut of pulchritude; the women must be smeared with odoriferous unguents for a year, then sent to the king's bed bedecked and bedizened like the rest of his possessions. Esther accepts whatever happens to her. So devoid is she of individual will that she does not ask for further aids on her big night—a request that might at least show active participation in the process. Her disinclination to ask for supplemental aids shows only self-effacing receptivity and passivity. Nor does she *refuse* anything, an action that might show a spark of self-assertion—evidence of confidence in her own beauty, perhaps, or indifference to the outcome, or principled repudiation of artificial luxuries. In consequence of these qualities, everyone likes her. It is no surprise when the king "loves" her as well; she has Vashti's good looks without her willfulness. The king—we may assume—also found Esther's sexual talents to his liking, and so he makes her queen.

So far Esther has been nothing more than sweet and pretty, hardly a person you would expect to shoulder her people's fate and engineer its salvation. Her personality seems hardly changed when we next see her, a little more than three years later, just after the publication of Haman's edict. When she learns that Mordecai is in mourning, she responds by sending him fresh clothes, as if to solve a problem—whatever it might be—by improving appearances. Perhaps she is afraid he is making waves; she has, after all, lived in secretiveness for several years. Her focus on superficials is to be expected of a young woman whose daily routine places overwhelming importance on her appearance, and whose excellence in that regard has brought her to what everyone around her views as the ultimate in feminine success.

The exchange with Mordecai is related from Esther's, not Mordecai's, point of view, with the movement of the maids and messengers described from her standpoint. For the first time, we start to identify with her as a person and to see events through her eyes.

At this stage, just before the moment of transformation, Esther does three things that foreshadow her role as national leader: she sends, she commands, she inquires. The sending back and forth of messages and messengers both represents and accomplishes the transition from the centrality of Mordecai to that of Esther, who must now adopt the primary role in moving the plot toward resolution.[3] Her three commands to Hatach (the word "commanded" rather than "sent" is used) hint at her potential authority. And her inquiry about the causes of Mordecai's behavior is her first step in becoming an initiator and planner: she looks behind appearances to causes and asks about the meaning of what is happening around her. In the cumbrous process of communicating with Mordecai she is starting to behave like a leader.

When Mordecai first instructs her to go to the king to plead for the life of the Jews (4:8b), her immediate thought is for her own safety (4:11). This reaction, natural but self-centered, shows that she does not yet fully identify her fate with her people's. This, too, is hardly surprising, for she has lived apart from them for over four years, during which time she has carefully concealed her identity.

In Mordecai's next message (4:13–14) he does not merely command Esther; he argues with her, gives her evidence, and seeks to persuade her. He is beginning to treat her not merely as a former ward but as a partner, an adult and equal who must be persuaded rather than commanded. Not only can he no longer enforce obedience (though Esther, according to 2:20, was still obeying him), but it is also true that mere obedience would not suffice, because once Mordecai sets Esther going, she must think and act on her own. At the very least, she must find the right words and tactics to sway the king. She must be fully and personally involved in the effort; indeed, she must direct it.

2. Activity

The turning point in Esther's development comes at the end of the scene, in 4:15–16. It is abrupt and surprising. She resolves to do her duty, and a change immediately comes upon her. She *commands* Mordecai—in the imperative, with no polite circumlocutions—to assemble the Jews in Susa for a public fast: "Go, gather all the Jews who are in Susa, and fast for me. Do not eat or drink for three days, night and day, and I too, with my maids, will fast in

---

3. These observations draw upon Clines (pp. 33–35). He describes well the subtle art of this scene but attaches too much weight to the significance of the specific objects sent, seeing the copy of the edict as a counterpart of the clothes. In my view, it is not the objects but the content of the messages sent, as well as the back-and-forth communication in and of itself, that moves the scene toward transfer of responsibility.

this way" (4:16). In convening such an assembly and issuing directives to the community, Esther is assuming the role of a religious and national leader, and doing so prior to Mordecai's own assumption of that role. She has taken control, giving Mordecai instructions, enjoining a fast on the Jews, and deciding to act contrary to law. Her resolute behavior marks a woman determined to work her way through a crisis, not one cowed into obedience.

She takes her fate in her hands with a courageous declaration: "And in this condition I will go to the king, contrary to law, and if I perish, I perish" (4:16b). This is the courage of one who must do her duty without certainty of success, without a simple faith that a higher being will protect her.

In the two banquet scenes, she unwinds her strategy patiently, with great control. I trace that strategy step-by-step in the Commentary to chapters 5, 7, and 8. Two points are to be emphasized.

First, the plan Esther executes is of her own devising. Mordecai had merely told her to go to the king and entreat him on behalf of her people (4:8). Of course she has acceded to his demand in essence and has taken his cause to herself. But, with no further consultation, she has chosen to approach the task in a way quite different from what Mordecai and (judging from the commentaries) the reader would expect. After all, it would be natural and acceptable for a pretty young lady to plead with her husband to give her her way. Esther chooses a more circuitous approach, one that involves near-disobedience to the king: even though he virtually orders her in 5:3 to declare her wish, she does not comply until the next day. Strict compliance is no longer Esther's prime virtue.

Second, Esther executes her strategy with skill, control, rhetorical precision, and eloquence. She does not—contrary to a common notion—simply exploit her beauty and erotic charm. To do so in such a fateful cause would be quite justified and would not impinge on her dignity. But these qualities would not be sufficient to the task. Her beauty did help secure her the queenship and the audience with the king, and she does employ meekness and play upon her husband's affection, especially by emphasizing the threat to her person. To some extent Esther does exploit feminine wiles and attractions by displaying meekness and playing up to her husband's ego. When she says, "If I have found favor in your eyes" (7:3), rather than simply "if the idea pleases you," she is playing on the king's affection, as if to say, "if you really love me. . . . " She also gives prominence to her need for personal protection, stressing that she herself is threatened. But these tactics are subordinate to her eloquence and cunning.

Esther cannot simply exploit lust as Judith does. After all, Xerxes, as Esther's husband and king, has free access to her sexuality as it is. Mostly, Esther must draw upon hitherto untested and unexpected intellectual powers.

Esther's undoubted need for cunning and circumspection justifies the interpretation of her speeches and actions as being formulated with careful thought and control, rather than as indecisive and haphazard. As I argue in the Commentary, the best explanation for Esther's delaying her request until the second banquet is that she is unfolding a premeditated strategy; and once we grant this, we are justified in scrutinizing her words for further signs of this plan. Such a scrutiny shows her building up to the accusation with great care: piquing the king's suspense, eliciting a near-promise to fulfill her wish, withholding information that could put the king on the defensive (by making him face his own culpability), delaying other information (the identity of the offender) until she has given full momentum to the king's anger, softening her speech with deferential courtesies and demurrals that play to his ego, cracking out her accusation like a whip, then allowing matters to take their course once she has set Haman careening toward destruction.

In chapters 5 and 7—most notably in 7:4—Esther is indirect, self-effacing, and manipulative. Some commentators find these qualities morally unappealing or offensive as an image of the feminine (see the Excursus below). Such reproaches might appear completely extraneous and anachronistic, except that the author himself seems almost to anticipate them by building rebuttals into the story. The Vashti episode is prefixed to the story to demonstrate that humility and indirection were necessary to Esther's success. Vashti's fate showed that the king may react badly to strong-willed women who do not temper their strength with subtlety. What would a direct and bold demand have achieved, besides giving Esther a self-satisfied feeling of moral virtue as *she* was deposed in turn? Even a straightforward request could founder as the king contemplated the deposal of his favorite official or, perhaps, realized that he could simply protect his wife from the mob without sacrificing his vizier or butting up against the earlier decree. Moreover, the successes of the Persian nobility, including Haman's, in playing on Xerxes' nervous ego show that Esther's tactics are exactly those of everyone else in the Persian court—gaining one's way by manipulating the man in power. These preemptive rebuttals suggest that the author is salving Jewish sensitivities by showing that indirection, cunning, and at least some show of subservience are necessary stratagems in such circumstances and should not offend Jewish pride. That such pride was indeed a factor is demonstrated by Mordecai's refusal to kowtow to Haman. The author respects that pride, certainly, and no way reproaches its manifestation. Yet he recognizes that this is not what is needed to resolve the crisis. We cannot afford an entire nation of Mordecais; Mordecai himself must call upon another type of person for help. Moreover, in the end Mordecai, too, will be forced to act with some indirection, writing a clever counter-edict rather than simply annulling the first one.[4]

At the conclusion of Esther's plea, Haman is exposed and shaking in terror—not only before the obvious power holder, the king, but also before the queen (7:6). She is now a force to be reckoned with in her own right. Haman falls on her bed to plead for his life. Esther's silence gives her a stony, imperious air, but Haman deserves nothing else. He has no claim on pity, and sparing him would leave him around to fight countermeasures and try again.

3. Authority

That very day, Xerxes gives Esther Haman's property, which she transfers to Mordecai's control (8:1–2). This little episode restructures relationships and raises Esther's status. She now is a source and agent of wealth and empowerment for Mordecai.

It seems somewhat incongruous when, immediately thereafter (8:3), she falls weeping at the king's feet, imploring him to annul Haman's decree. This is the approach Mordecai had expected her to use at the start, but she exploits it only subsequent to her initial success and her increase of personal power. As the king's hesitant response shows, this request is a difficult one and thus calls for a greater effort and display of emotion on her part. But even that does not work. The matter is out of the king's hands—as he will betoken by transferring the ring to the two Jews. The result of this temporary setback is an increase in power for the two protagonists, a fact reflected in Xerxes' address to both "Mordecai the Jew" and "Esther the queen" and in his bestowal of power upon them jointly,

---

4. As he does in the AT (viii 16), where his (not Esther's) request for the annulment of Haman's edict solves the problem.

a recognition of their partnership in the handling of the crisis. The Midrash captures this relationship in the emblem of a coin with Mordecai on one side and Esther on the other (Est. Rab. X 12).

On the 13th of Adar, when the Jews have overpowered their enemies and slaughtered masses of them, the king, apparently put into an expansive mood by the body-count in Susa, tells Esther to make another request. With little preamble, she asks that the Jews in Susa be allowed another day of fighting and that the bodies of Haman's sons be impaled (9:13). At this point—and not earlier—Esther seems vindictive. The Jews are in no present danger, for they have massacred their enemies, who in any case would not be allowed to continue fighting beyond the 13th. Even if Esther's request is for a precautionary massacre, it is, literally, overkill.

In this exchange, Esther seems less anxious to get her way than her husband is to give it to her. She does not take the initiative to seek another boon, but simply accepts his offer. She makes her request bluntly, no longer trying to convince him that her request is right and necessary. What is disturbing in this speech is not only her vindictiveness, which is humanly understandable, but also the neglect of persuasion. Her earlier petitions (especially in 8:6) appealed not only to personal affection but also to an ethical value: Do this for me to spare me the pain of seeing, and thus suffering, a great injustice. Here she says merely, "should it so please the king." Now that her main request has been granted, her interest in the process seems somewhat diffuse. She no longer tries to justify her requests, though they involve the death and suffering (however deserved) of many people. It seems enough that she *wants* the opportunity to kill more enemies and to abuse the corpses of her foe's sons.

Esther's personality has evolved into the near-opposite of what it was at the start. Once sweet and compliant, she is now steely and unbending, even harsh. I am not sure the MT-author intended this effect. According to my theory of the book's development (see chap. XIV §3a), all of Esther 9 is an expansion of a few sentences in an earlier version of the Esther story. Literary values are here less important than liturgical purposes. Esther's request for a second day of fighting results more from the need to explain an existing practice than from any literary conception of her personality. Yet whatever the author's intentions, the effect of 9:13 is to introduce a note of harshness and even bellicosity into the picture.

Later in the aftermath, Esther issues an epistle confirming the decision to celebrate two days of Purim (9:29–32). Our understanding of her action depends on whether we accept the MT or read an emended version, a problem discussed in the Commentary on this passage. According to the MT,[5] Esther joins Mordecai in confirming the decision (9:29–31), then issues a further validation (9:32). According to the emended reading (which I prefer), Esther adds her own confirmatory epistle to Mordecai's.[6] In either case, it is finally and unequivocally the proclamation of Queen Esther that validates all the previous layers of confirmation, and her statement is inscribed in a document as a witness to the future (9:32). Her decree or statement is called a *ma'ămar*, the term used of Xerxes' command to Vashti in 1:15 and Mordecai's command to Esther in 2:20. She is, after all, queen of Persia as well as an ad hoc leader of the Jews. This is an appropriate penultimate conclusion to the book. The docile young beauty has risen to truly royal stature. She stands before her people, and not only before the king, as her cousin's partner. Still, her role is to reinforce and support Mordecai's plans, albeit with some independence in their execution. The validation of Mordecai's initiative is Esther's final action. Her authority is additive not essential, but it is her own, independent of her cousin's.

4. Esther as an Ideal

Mordecai is more of an ideal figure than Esther. He is a bundle of constant virtues; she is imperfect—certainly in her beginnings and (though the author would not agree) in her behavior on 13 Adar. For that very reason, she is the more lively, human character,

---

5. "(29) And Queen Esther, daughter of Abihayil, and Mordecai the Jew conveyed in writing all the authority necessary to confirm this second Purim epistle. (30) And he sent letters to all the Jews, to the 127 provinces of Xerxes' kingdom—words of greeting and faithfulness—(31) to confirm the observance of these days of Purim in their set times, just as Mordecai the Jew and Queen Esther had confirmed upon them, in the way that they confirm upon themselves and their descendants matters of fasting and the accompanying laments. (32) And the declaration of Esther confirmed these matters concerning Purim, and it was written in a document."
6. "(29) And Queen Esther, daughter of Abihayil, conveyed in writing all the authority necessary to confirm this Purim epistle. (30) And letters were sent to all the Jews in the one hundred twenty-seven provinces of Xerxes' kingdom—words of peace and faithfulness—(31) to confirm the observance of these days of Purim in their set times, just as Mordecai the Jew had confirmed upon them. . . ."

one with whom we can feel intimacy and identification. Her very ordinariness suggests that ordinary people too can rise to the moment and take on unexpected strengths. Mordecai may be the more unqualified exemplum, but she is the more effective one.

The book of Esther links the issue of national salvation to human character. It raises the question of whether a person of dubious character strength and (initially) unclear self-definition can carry the burden of national salvation. Esther becomes a sort of judge (of the type we see in the book of Judges) without benefit of the Spirit of the Lord. She is a leader whose charisma comes not in a sudden divine imposition of spirit but as the result of a difficult process of inner development and self-realization. The Scroll is exploring and affirming the potential of human character to rise to the needs of the hour by whatever means and devices the situation demands. The Scroll offers an alternative to the book of Daniel as a model for Jewish life in the diaspora. In Daniel, pious constancy is the only defense against danger, and it is an adequate one, for it ensures God's intervention. In Esther, not miracles, but inner resources—intellectual as well as spiritual—even of people not naturally leaders, are to be relied upon in crisis.

EXCURSUS: The Image of Woman in the Book of Esther

The author of Esther has shared the fate of many biblical authors in coming under opprobrium for his attitudes toward women. Such judgments often seem to me to impose extraneous standards and to reproach an ancient Oriental society for not meeting some very recent, very Western, ideals. But in the case of the book of Esther the feminist critique seems more apropos, for the book itself addresses the issues of the status and abilities of women and the relation between the sexes.

The most pungent criticism of the image of woman in the book of Esther has been put forward by Esther Fuchs (1982), whose radical feminist critiques of biblical literature are, in my view, often more to the mark elsewhere than here. Her view of the book of Esther is shared by A. L. Laffey (1988) and many other feminists.[7]

Fuchs believes that the Esther story undergirds the assumptions of patriarchal ideology by showing that a woman should be

---

7. See, for example, the personal Jewish response of M. Gendler (1976) to the characters of Esther and Vashti.

obedient and submissive, by teaching that women can become national heroines only by fulfilling their assigned roles as wives and
mothers, and by showing that women get their way through deceptive and circuitous means.[8] The character of the female protagonist
is wanting in personal and religious strengths. Esther is totally unaware of Yahweh and not inspired by religious faith. Omission of
any direct dialogue with Yahweh is, Fuchs claims, "congruous with
a more comprehensive biblical policy which allows women characters to hold direct discourse with God (or his agent) only in a 'pro-
creative' context" (p. 153). Woman's independence is repudiated
through the example of Vashti, a repudiation Esther fails to oppose. In Laffey's words, "Rather than defend Vashti's decision and
protest the injustice of her banishment, Esther uses Vashti's rejection for her own benefit" (1988:216; cf. Fuchs, p. 156). The literary
prominence given to Esther at the expense of the self-assertive, dignified Vashti embodies the biblical stance on sexual politics. The
author fails even to credit Esther with any particular zeal in her
desire to save her people. Her trepidation at violating court etiquette and entering the inner court is blatantly contrasted with
Mordecai's temerity vis-à-vis Haman. She is pretty, obedient, silver-
tongued and somewhat manipulative, using placatory language
and ingratiating formulas. She waits patiently and obediently until
the king gives permission for an audience and only then speaks.
Though the king invites her to make her request, she procrasti-
nates. Her example teaches that aesthetic grace paves the way for
woman's success, whereas man's power comes from ethical fiber. It
is true that she outwits two rather stupid males, and victory is due
to Haman's falling into the trap, but the pivotal moment occurs in

---

8. Speaking of the Bible generally, Fuchs says: "Celebrated or denigrated, the characters of deceptive women, which constitute the majority of female characters in the Bible, serve as an effective ideological tool that perpetuates the
   suspicion and distrust of women, and that validates women's subordination
   through discriminatory literary techniques" (1985:143). We might note, however, that all three patriarchs, especially Jacob, employ deception or devious-
   ness at times, as do many other men, such as Joab, David, and Adonijah.
   Deception is a constant of human behavior, women's not excepted. And even
   God can deceive (1 Kings 22:20–23; Jer 20:7; Ezek 14:9).
   D. N. Fewell (1987:80 f.) criticizes Fuch's treatment of the deception motif for
   suppressing elements that run contrary to her thesis and failing to observe
   that deception is a response to powerlessness and that others besides females
   must use deception in a patriarchal society. In fact, however, it is not only the
   powerless who deceive, nor is deceptiveness in and of itself stigmatized in the
   biblical narratives.

a *bedroom* scene (Fuchs 1982:150–156). She acts not as Yahweh's agent but as her uncle's [sic], with whom she shares authority when she gets power (pp. 153–54). Since Esther is obviously meant to be exemplary, her flaws are to be blamed on the author's image of woman.

This frank attack warrants a response. We must first of all observe that some of these assessments require overlooking some significant, and rather obvious, facts. Whatever Esther's religious flaws—if that is what they are—they are shared fully by Mordecai and thus do not constitute a denigration of woman's spirituality; but clearly the author does not see lack of dialogue with God as a failing, since he chooses to leave it out of the book altogether. Also, this feminist critique must ignore Esther's growth to a woman of influence and power. It isolates her adolescent pliancy and some of her tactics as her essential features and assumes that the author elevates these all to objects of emulation.

Other conclusions confuse presuppositions with purposes. To describe a woman living a restrictive life in an Oriental court in which she gains her goals through stratagems, rhetoric, manipulation, and ostensive pliancy is not to imply an ideology affirming this as the ideal female situation. That would be the case only if the author identified fully with the attitudes of all the males in the book and considered their society as exemplary. Given Esther's situation, she does what she must, and she does it well. Likewise, the author in no way denigrates Vashti's attitude but only shows that in the strange and silly world that she and Esther must inhabit, Vashti's approach simply does not work. (We could as well say that the author condemns Mordecai's dignity by showing *its* consequences.) Esther is indeed, at least at the start, a "stereotypical woman in a man's world" (Laffey 1988:216); but that does not mean that the book *teaches* (as Laffey would have it) "full compliance with patriarchy." Rather, it teaches that *even* a stereotypical woman in a world of laughably stereotypical males is capable of facing the ultimate national crisis and diverting the royal power to her own ends.

Other aspects of this critique scold the book for not being an entirely different work with entirely different concerns. One wonders what the alternative, more worthy, stories implied by the critique would be like. Could Esther have refused to accompany the officials who were sent to gather the maidens? She would have been dragged off or at best ignored, in which case there would have been no book of Esther. And what if she had approached the throne without waiting for the king to extend his scepter? She, like any man who tried the same, would have been cut down by the guards (4:11).[9] Who, then, would have defeated Haman's plot?

The critique also evaluates the characters by irrelevant, even distorted, standards. Esther is of course obedient to Mordecai; since he stands *in loco parentis*, her early docility is an expression of filial respect rather than sexual status. She does indeed share her power with her cousin, and if a willingness to share power is a flaw, she may be faulted for it. Although she presumably obeys the king and pays him homage in most circumstances, she does not subordinate her will to his. She is, of course, indirect and manipulative—she has to be, like everyone else in the palace. But she is never actively deceptive (an accusation leveled by several non-feminist commentators as well)—unless honesty demands that she come to Haman's defense and set the king straight. (How would events have unwound if she had done *that*?). One may reproach the author for not holding his heroes to a standard of absolute openness and directness (an impossible and quixotic standard, in my view). But this fault, if that is what it is, has nothing to do with his image of woman. Most of the men he shows are far more devious in far less worthy causes. (In fact, none of the biblical authors repudiates indirection or even deception in pursuit of worthy goals.) In my view, Esther behaves with dignity, courage, and good sense. There is nothing demeaning in approaching a king as a suppliant or in using stratagems and personal influence in achieving a valid goal.

One thing that troubles me about the critique—apart from its injustice to the author—is that it is indifferent to the severity of the crisis that stands at the story's heart: the mortal danger to the Jewish people. In effect it blames the author for not dealing with other, supposedly more important issues, such as the dignity and independence of women in the Persian court. The author, like perhaps all readers before modern times, sees Esther's sole moral duty to be the salvation of her people from destruction, and he shows her conforming to the expectations of her environment in accomplishing this. A far less dignified approach than the one Esther takes would have been entirely warranted. On the other hand, it would not have

---

9. Josephus accurately envisions the implication of Esther's words when he adds that guards with axes surrounded the king's throne ready to cut down whoever approached unsummoned.

been justified for her to assert her ego at the expense of her people's existence. A story such as Fuchs and Laffey would consider worthy of respect—in which, perhaps, Esther would stomp into the inner court and issue a series of bold, non-negotiable demands, starting with the restoration of Vashti—would have been a bitter satire on the feminine ego. The book we actually have comes closer to being a satire on the *masculine* ego.

In truth, the author of Esther is something of a protofeminist. This book is the only one in the Bible with a conscious and sustained interest in sexual politics. The concept of sexual politics can be applied precisely and without anachronism to Memuchan's advice and the ensuing decree in 1:16–22. The book certainly does not align itself with the men's side in the conflict. Perhaps alone in the Bible, this author is aware of female subservience and is cynical about the masculine qualities that require it. He sees the reaction of Xerxes and his noblemen to Vashti's refusal as ludicrous and self-defeating. He does not, of course, call for an overthrow of "patriarchy" (which is probably not the best label for the social situation portrayed), but neither does he regard male dominance as part of the inherent moral order of the world. On the contrary, he perceives the cracks in the façade of male dominance. In a true patriarchal society, custom would be the strongest enforcer of the patriarch's will. The author of Esther is very much aware that males, at least in the quirky gentile world, must use political power to enforce their position—and even so they do not really succeed.[10] The harem is the most successful locus of male dominance—and its order is enforced by eunuchs. Surely the description of the harem induction shows an awareness that women were being treated as sex objects (an often misused term that is precisely applicable in this case). The author does not rail against the arrangements as a heavy-handed ideologue, but the awareness itself is noteworthy.

The satire is not, however, directed at male dominance in and of itself, but at male dominance as manifested in the Persian court and, by extension, throughout the gentile realm. The book's irony

---

10. Fewell (1987:83–84) puts it in a nutshell: "The action (or perhaps I should say non-action) of one woman threatens to collapse the entire structure of patriarchy in the entire Persian empire. So much for indomitable patriarchy. So what do the men do? They persuade the king to pass a law that 'every man be lord in his own house.' If the king's laws are not more effective than his commands, I dare say that patriarchy is in big trouble."

is from a Jewish—not a feminist or even a specifically female—perspective, but it does recognize the silliness, if not the deep perniciousness, of one extreme form of sexual politics.

More important than the satire of gentile behavior is the way the author shapes his woman hero. He respects Esther as a woman of courage and intelligence who does not abandon her dignity even when facing an enemy and struggling to influence the erratic will of a despotic husband. Moreover, the author depicts a successful relationship of power-sharing between male and female, in which both attain prestige and influence in the community. In the pivotal scene in chapter 4, man and woman give each other mutual obedience. What is more, the book takes as its hero a woman whose importance to the Jewish people does not lie in childbearing; there are only a handful of such cases in the Bible.[11]

Sidnie Ann White, in addition to making several of the above points, argues that the author affirms the feminine as a model for the Jewish people in the diaspora:

> The Jews in the Diaspora are also in the position of the weak, as a subordinate population under the dominant Persian government. They must adjust to their lack of immediate political and economic power, and learn to work within the system to gain what power they can. In the book of Esther, their role model for this adjustment is Esther. . . . With no native power of her own owing to her sex or position in society, Esther must learn to make her way among the powerful and to cooperate with others in order to make herself secure. (1989:173)

The author does not, to be sure, draw the analogy between Esther and the diaspora Jew or turn Esther into a token. She does not "stand for" the diaspora Jew. But as a Jew who succeeds in the most severe of crises, she (like Daniel and his friends) is a natural model for Jews who find themselves in similar situations. Of course, just because the story takes place in the diaspora does not mean that it is intended to be relevant to the diaspora alone. In any royal court—David's being an excellent example—in fact, in any situation where power is concentrated in one individual, people must pursue their goals by circuitous, if not devious, means. But because the gentile state is essentially indifferent to Jewish existence, and because Jews have no other defense in their dispersion, such expe-

---

11. Noted by Meinhold, p. 105–6.

dients may be more important to Jewish national concerns in the diaspora than in the homeland.[12]

The appreciation of the book of Esther from a feminist standpoint[13] has impeccable credentials in the reading offered by Elizabeth Cady Stanton, the prominent nineteenth-century woman's rights advocate, writing in *The Woman's Bible*:

> Vashti had exercised heroic courage in asserting womanly dignity and the inherent human right never recognized by kingship, to choose whether to please and to obey the king. Esther, so as to save her people from destruction, risked her life. . . . Women as queenly, as noble and as self-sacrificing as was Esther, as self-respecting and as brave as was Vashti, are hampered in their creative office by the unjust statutes of men . . . (1895:92).

These judgments, I have argued, are quite in accord with the author's intentions. There are few books from the ancient Near East that can stand up so well to an assessment by feminist standards.

---

12. For a theological appreciation of the person of Esther see Craghan, 1982 and 1986. It is probably excessive, however, to call her, as Craghan does, a "fully liberated woman." The author is not even aware of the possibility of liberation.
13. See also Fewell 1987: 83.

CHAPTER XI

THE JEWS

One opinion:
"Much more frequent are the bad, even repulsive,
features of this national character—above all the
unrestrained vindictiveness, which with true Oriental
savagery allows its imagination to swim and revel in
the blood of the opponent."

(M. Haller 1925:328–29)

The Jewish people is one of the players in the drama of Esther. Not that its character is a vivid one. It is nearly faceless, devoid of personality, and, until the last chapter, almost entirely passive, taking no initiative but only responding to the initiative of others. Yet its role in the communication of the book's ideology is of great importance.

The Jews function as a single figure in the book; whatever they do, they do as a group. (Hence "the Jews" in this chapter will often refer to the anonymous masses of Jews, as distinct from the two named leaders.) Their unity is absolute. Other than the two heroes, no individual Jews are mentioned, nor is their consensus ever breached. The Jews' main characteristic, the mark of their moral character, is their ready and complete assent to the guidance of their leaders.

This image of the Jews is by no means to be taken for granted. In other biblical narratives, the community of Israel has a sharply etched individuality and a will of its own. It is not meekly led; on the contrary, its salient feature is the refractoriness of its will. The biblical texts—narrative, prophetic, and even psalmodic—present a people in constant opposition to its rightful leaders, whether resisting Moses' efforts to lead them out of slavery, the prophets' attempts to turn them to ethical behavior and exclusive loyalty to Israel's God, or Nehemiah's demands for national-religious exclusiveness. Moreover, they are a mixed lot: many sinners, a few righteous people, and many others who seem tossed about in the

212

shifting winds of history. Many individuals are singled out, for better or worse. Quite different is the Israel we see in the Scroll, where the people is unified, undifferentiated, passive, and responsive.

1. What the Jews Do

Four times only do the Jews as a people appear on stage: when they mourn, when they rejoice, when they fight, and when they create the holiday of Purim.

A. MOURNING. The first Jewish action reported is their mourning in reaction to Haman's decree:

> And in each and every province, wherever the king's word and his law reached, there was severe grief among the Jews, with fasting and weeping and lamenting, with sackcloth and ashes being spread out for the masses. (4:3)

Even in their outburst the Jews remain abstract and impersonal. While Mordecai is the active agent of the sentences reporting his mourning—he tears his clothes, cries aloud, and so on (4:1), the Jews are subject to impersonal events described in impersonal constructions: the royal command reaches the places where they live, and "there was" severe grief among the Jews; there were fasting, weeping, and lamenting; and (in a somewhat unnatural passive construction), sackcloth and ashes "were spread out for" the masses of Jews, as if they themselves were not doing the spreading.[1]

The Jews' mourning and outcry (in 4:3) is reported only after Mordecai's (in 4:1). This is logical, since living in the Fortress of Susa, Mordecai would be among the first to know of the edict, while the Jews elsewhere learn of it only later. Yet the sequence of narration has a literary effect as well: it makes the community's response echo Mordecai's, as if he were their leader even before they are aware of it.

B. REJOICING. The communal action of rejoicing is likewise a response rather than an initiative, and again it is formulated in impersonal constructions ("the Jews had" in 8:16 and 17, is, literally, "there were . . . to the Jews"). After issuing his counter-edict on 23

---

1. Gerleman (p. 102) observes the contrast in the way the actions of Mordecai and the people are described but does not explain its literary-ideological effect.

Sivan, Mordecai emerges from the palace dressed in magnificent clothes. This reversal of his earlier public donning of sackcloth signals his personal victory and his assurance of the Jews' deliverance. The Jews learn that the danger is essentially resolved and reverse their earlier act of mourning by joy, feasting, and celebration (8:16–17). In addition, they now have "honor"—the same word (y^eqar) is used repeatedly of the honor the king gives Mordecai in chapter 6. Mordecai has now vanquished his enemy and issued a decree that holds out hope for the Jews' salvation. His fellow Jews share in their champion's glory, and from being helpless mourners they have become an object of both respect and fear (8:17). The two responses, mourning and festivity, bracket the drama of salvation, during which time the Jews can do nothing but wait while others shape their fate in ways they are unaware of.

c. FIGHTING. The Jewish people comes to center-stage nine months later, on 13 Adar, in chapter 9. On the day set for their obliteration, the Jews come on the scene to save themselves by their own actions, slaughtering myriads of their enemies in the process. For the first time they are spoken of with active verbs—a profusion of them—as they "gain control" (9:1); "gather" (9:2),[2] "slaughter," "slay," "wreak their will" (9:5), and so on. And like the ancient armies of Israel, they paralyze their enemies with fear. The authorities, afraid of the growing power of Mordecai, had been "promoting" or "exalting" the Jews (9:3)—the same verb ($niśśa^{\flat}$) was used of Haman's advancement in 3:1. Finally, after the battles, the Jews "have respite" and "make their day of feasting"—again, with active verbs (9:17–18).

The Jews now act in concert on their own initiative, without waiting for a call to arms from Mordecai, beyond the license that the royal edict gave them. Moreover, they demonstrate a certain independence, diverging slightly from his edict by refusing to take spoil, as he had allowed.

The author might have chosen other ways than battle to resolve the crisis and overcome the danger. In the story as preserved by proto-AT (on which see chapter XIV §2), Mordecai receives the royal seal and is able to revoke Haman's decree with no further ado.

---

2. Technically, this verb ($niqhălu$) is in a passive-reflexive conjugation (the niphal); but semantically it is active, describing something the Jews do, not something done to them.

Subsequently, Esther receives permission to have her enemies "punished by slaughter" (AT viii 18–21). This massacre is a punishment executed by royal grant, not a battle. The MT-author, on the other hand, is interested in more than the cancellation of Haman's edict and the death of the guilty. He chooses to portray a crisis which the state (in the person of the king) could not resolve and in which not even the Jewish queen and vizier could unaided save their compatriots. The MT creates this peculiar situation by introducing the presumption of the immutability of Persian law, a theme lacking in the AT. The MT's resolution allows the Jews to behave in a way analogous to an independent nation, one that can defend itself militarily against its enemies. However, the MT-author does not want to have them violating the state's authority or to show them seeking political independence. The addition of the theme of irreversible law creates a situation in which the Jews prove themselves to be at one and the same time obedient to gentile law and fundamentally self-sufficient.

The Jews act in accordance with the law of the land. The author might have emphasized Jewish self-reliance by telling a tale of brave resistance in the *absence* of royal authorization. Instead, he carefully provides royal sanction for the Jewish action, and makes the winning of this, rather than the actual military resistance, the decisive point of the struggle. The exercise of force is the prerogative of the state, and any unsanctioned resort to it is crime or rebellion. Jewish commitment to the king's law is demonstrated by showing Mordecai and Esther first seeking the cancellation of Haman's decree, and only when denied that route issuing a decree of their own—one which is also the king's. We cannot assume that the Jews were so law-abiding that in the absence of the counter-decree they would have submitted passively to slaughter. After all, when the need arises, they are willing to violate gentile law: Mordecai disobeys the royal ordinance for the sake of national pride (3:2), and Esther does likewise for the sake of national existence (4:16). But when possible, Jews work within the framework of the imperial law. Their action refutes Haman's absolute claim that the Jews "do not obey the laws of the king" (3:8).

The second theme that emerges from the battle report is Jewish self-reliance. If the state leaves the Jews to their own resources, either by denying its support to their enemies' schemes, or (at the very least) by permitting the Jews the right of self-defense, they can take care of themselves. They do not require special protection from the state or the investment of special resources to keep them alive. This is demonstrated by the battles of Adar and is implied by Mordecai's assertion in 4:14 that even if Esther neglects her duty, "deliverance will arise for the Jews from another source." The ideology of self-reliance is suggestive of a self-confidence that Jewry could not have possessed in many diasporas and in many eras. But perhaps it is asserting confidence in *defiance* of reality.

The message of self-reliance is emphasized also by the Jews' refusal to take spoil (9:10, 15, 16). This is not a humanitarian gesture—after all, they slaughter all their enemies anyway. Nor is their restraint a matter of obedience, for Mordecai had authorized the taking of spoil. It is in part a rectification of Saul's failing (1 Sam 15): Saul took spoil although forbidden to take it; the present generation refuses to take it though permitted to do so. Their refusal is, moreover, an assertion of dignity and self-sufficiency; they will not be enriched by their enemies' property (compare Abraham's refusal to partake in spoil in Gen 14:23).[3] The Jews, though fully responsive to Mordecai's leadership, go beyond his requirements and spontaneously show a better way to conduct a war.

D. ESTABLISHING THE HOLIDAY. The Jewish people attains its most important role in the ideological (though not the dramatic) climax—the establishment of Purim (9:20–32). On the 14th of Adar (the 15th in Susa), the Jews, unprompted, celebrate. They celebrate not the victory, but the respite that follows upon it. Mordecai recognizes in their festivities something of value, worthy of fixation as a communal institution. He calls upon them to reenact their celebration in perpetuity. They respond to the call of their leader, who has earned moral authority and who invokes recent events (vv. 22–23), and they consequently undertake certain observances and make them binding on their descendants (v. 27).

The keyword in this process is "confirm" (*qayyem*, discussed in the Commentary to 9:20–21). Through a series of confirmations and reconfirmations, the outbursts of joy after the battles of Adar are regularized and made into a practice incumbent upon all Jews in all generations. And all this is further reinforced by the authority of another leader, the queen (9:29–32).

---

3. This interpretation was suggested by Grotius; see Paton.

2. The Character of the Jewish People

A. JEWISH ATTITUDES TOWARD GENTILES. In the context of the Jewish national character, we should consider how the author envisions the relations between Jews and gentiles.

Many commentators read the book as exuding hatred toward gentiles.[4] The prominent biblicist K. Budde ascribes "rabid hatred against all gentiles" (1906:237) to the book. According to Cornill, "All the hateful and wicked characteristics of Judaism here reveal themselves uncovered" (1905:159). Dommershausen (p. 62) believes that Mordecai's refusal to bow to Haman is rooted in Israel's attitude toward the enemy: "You should love your neighbor and hate your enemy" (Matt 5:43)[5]—an attitude he thinks is reflected in the psalmists' and Jeremiah's calls for revenge. Loretz (1969:317) avers that "the book of Esther describes a world in which the Jews and heathens live in mutual hatred." Gunkel asks what brings the entire world to such a hatred against the Jews and answers that it is their monotheism and peculiar laws, together with a scorn for the pagan religion and customs, which sets them apart from the gentiles and "must necessarily draw the wrath of the entirety of heathendom. . . . Hence one can comprehend that at that time heathen and Jews faced each other in two hostile camps" (pp. 73–74).

Such readings identify the antisemites with the entirety of the gentile world, then blame the author for seeing the world that way. But the book itself does not do this. It defines the enemies of the Jews not as the heathen, not even as a certain hostile nation, but

---

4. The Scroll has been widely excoriated for fanaticism, vindictiveness, xenophobia, intolerance of other beliefs, nationalism, and exclusivism. Interestingly, it is the nineteenth- century Germans who seem most incensed by Jewish nationalism. For a survey of the spite heaped on the book of Esther for its supposedly spitefulness, see Herrmann 1986:19–29. Bickerman (1967:215–18) describes how and why the theologians of the German Enlightenment taught that Esther is a document of Jewish intolerance and hatred toward the human race.

   Some commentators did try to mitigate the repugnant qualities they saw in the book by calling attention to the danger and hostility facing the Jews (Herrmann, pp. 31–35). Others urged that the Jews' actions were typical of the period (ibid., p. 39).

5. It is obviously unfair to deduce a people's attitudes from putative quotations in polemical contexts. In the Hebrew Bible it is sometimes assumed that one does hate his enemies (this is almost a matter of definition), but nowhere is it implied that there is a moral obligation to do so.

(tautologously) as *those who hate* the Jews and *those who seek to harm them* (9:1). There is no schematic, light-and-darkness struggle between Jew and gentile.[6] By refusing to tar all gentiles with the same brush, the author of Esther shows that he does not hate the "heathen."[7] He has no desire for vengeance upon the gentiles, but only upon the Jews' enemies (8:13). By the same token, he does not regard all gentiles as antagonistic toward Jews. There do exist numerous diehard anti-Jewish elements; for the author this is a fact of life, one that can be taken for granted without further explanation. This is antisemitism in the modern sense—not a hatred toward individuals or even a clash between tribes, but an ongoing, widespread, inveterate enmity toward Jews as such: at best, a nasty static buzzing incessantly in the background of the Jews' lives, at worst, an assault on their very existence.

The author does not depict gentiles as inherently or universally anti-Jewish. Mordecai's colleagues in the palace administration do not seem to have been aware that he was a Jew until he informed them of this (3:4). Since Mordecai hardly conceals his Jewishness, their unawareness suggests that there was no attempt to identify the Jews or keep them out of office. Nor is the king himself an antisemite. His knowledge that Mordecai is a Jew (6:10) does not affect the way he treats him. When he consents to Haman's proposal, it is not out of hatred of Jews, for he does not know that the people Haman is describing are the Jews.[8] If hostility toward Jews were a given, Haman would have exploited it. The "city of Susa" is dismayed when the Jews are threatened (3:15) and joyful when the way is opened for Jewish deliverance (8:15). The author's belief in the existence of sympathy among the gentiles is thus not canceled by the presence of enemies in Susa and throughout the empire.

---

6. That notion was added to the book in the Greek translation. In Mordecai's dream (Addition A), as two dragons clash, *all* the nations gather to fight against the "nation of the righteous" (A 6). This polarization was deliberately removed by the editor of the AT, in whose retelling all the nations (and not only the Jews) are terrified by the dragons, and they prepare to fight—but not against the Jews, who, it turns out, save everybody by crying out to God (i 6).

7. As Levenson (1976:443) points out, Haman is not considered typical of all gentiles; on the contrary, his foreign, Amalekite ancestry suggests that he is atypical. Bickerman too observes that the author isolates Haman's act as one of personal vengeance (1967:196, 217–18).

8. Nor is he a philosemite. When the plot is uncovered he does not react against it because the intended victims are the Jewish people, but because his own wife is among them.

Moreover, in the months before the clash, many gentiles become Jews (8:17), and all the officials help the Jews in their struggle (9:3). To be sure, the officials are motivated by fear, but the possibility that they could behave thus shows that they are not malevolent (those who are insist in attacking the Jews anyway). The author also believes that the converts, whatever their initial motive, identify themselves fully with the fate of the Jews and will henceforth celebrate Purim (9:27), as if they themselves had been in danger and were themselves delivered.

The book of Esther is indeed nationalistic—in the sense of affirming Jewish distinctiveness in the diaspora—but it is not narrow, segregationist, or exclusivistic.[9] It portrays Jews living and working in the gentile court as members of one national group among many. Almost as if to disprove Haman's claim of Jewish separateness (3:8), the author in no way repudiates Jewish contact with foreigners. He does not even seem troubled by Esther's marriage to a gentile, though this raises problems even for nonexclusivistic Jews. Nor does the author teach that the Jews should isolate themselves socially, though he does hold that they should maintain their ethnic identity. The author of Esther—contrary to most of the Bible—does not even express contempt for heathen worship or practices. Though he presumably believes Israel's religion to be incomparably superior, he does not choose to make that point.

The author believes that the Jews can and should be of service to the peoples among whom they live, and he seems comfortable with the idea of the Jews living among the nations indefinitely. He assumes that Jews are accepted for the most part as equals. Thus Niditch is mistaken in asserting that "Esther's lowly status is largely defined by her being Jewish. . . . To be a Jew is to have marginal status" (1987:136). Esther's status is in fact a step higher than that of the other girls taken into the harem, and it soon becomes higher than that of any other woman in the empire. Of course, we do not know what would have happened if she had revealed her Jewishness at the outset, but we cannot conclude that her status would have been lower. When her Jewishness is finally revealed, the king does not seem to see anything special in having a Jewish wife.

---

9. Even scholars who write without hostility tend to link nationalism and exclusivism. Humphreys (1973:211), for example, claims that Esther and Daniel are the most "exclusive and nationalistic units within the Bible."

In the world of Esther, as in reality, some gentiles—indeed, a great many—hate all Jews, but the Jews do not hate all gentiles. The world at large is viewed as essentially neutral; some gentiles are helpful and sympathetic, others implacably hostile, most are indifferent. Were it not for the danger posed by antisemitic hostility it would not be at all a bad thing to be a Jew in the world of Esther. This is, of course, the situation Jews have actually known in many lands of the diaspora.

B. THE MORALITY OF THE JEWS' CONDUCT. The conduct of the fighting, both in the form licensed by Mordecai's edict and as it eventuated in Adar, has called into question the moral character of the Jewish people in the book, and thus the ethics of the book itself. Scholars have often judged this character in accordance with their own ethical presuppositions, and this is, in principle, quite legitimate. If one can affirm the values assumed and taught by literature, one can reject them as well. A neutral, value-free reading is an incomplete one, an inadequate response to the text's own terms. The author of Esther, after all, is not merely telling an exciting story. He takes an ethical stance, which includes an implicit affirmation of the morality of the behavior of the two protagonists and the other Jews in this affair, and he expects the reader to grant the validity of that stance. It is appropriate, then, for the reader to respond by weighing the author's own values. Objectivity in such judgments does not mean neutrality but rather the avoidance of extraneous motives in the evaluation, such as the desire to justify one's own hostility toward Jews—or to shield contemporary Jews from accusations against their ancestors.

We should remember that all such judgments are properly directed at the book's author, not at the Jews of Esther's time, for it is he who probably created and certainly validated the actions described. Even if, as some scholars assert, there is an historical "core" to the tale—and there is no evidence for such a thing—it is the author who must be held responsible for the values informing the narration of the events.

Esther's requests, Mordecai's decree, and the people's conduct of the war have been condemned for displaying aggressiveness, brutality, and vindictiveness. Schalom Ben-Chorin (1939:9) described the Jewish action as a pogrom protected by the regime. Ben-Chorin, a former German Jew writing in 1938, feared that the book could only exacerbate gentile hostility and urged that it some-how be decanonized. The Protestant scholar L. B. Paton voiced a feeling common among Christian commentators when he claimed that the Jews were not defending themselves but rather were en-gaging in an aggressive campaign: "All [gentiles] that were known to be hostile . . . were hunted out and killed" (p. 283; he finds this notion in 9:5). In an influential OT introduction, Robert Pfeiffer declared that the battles in Persia were "a massacre of defenseless Gentiles on a given day, within a great peaceful empire, with the connivance of the central government."[10] The biblical theologian Bernhard Anderson believed that the book of Esther was "inspired by a fierce nationalism and an unblushing vindictiveness which stand in glaring contradiction to the Sermon on the Mount."[11] In-deed, he asserts, "the Jews, in their actions, are not essentially dif-ferent from the heathen. Mordecai and Esther merely put Haman's plan into reverse."[12] Such opprobrium is unwarranted, for the Jews' fight was necessary, defensive, and justified.

Haman's edict had proscribed the Jews, making it legal for any-one to kill and rob them. The proscription could not be rescinded but only countered. The Jews' enemies were by no means neutral-ized by Mordecai's edict, which did not even assure the Jews of of-ficial aid. To imagine the foe as "defenseless" (Pfeiffer 1952:741) is a perverse misdirection of pity. It is true that Mordecai's decree instructs the Jews to be ready "to take vengeance on their enemies" (8:13), but vengeance, however it may be viewed from an ethical standpoint, is not gratuitous. "Vengeance" (n^eqamah) means legiti-mate exercise of punitive power outside a judicial context (see the

---

10. Pfeiffer 1952:741. Remarks such as this, maligning the Jews and sympathizing with their enemies, are not rare in Esther exegesis.

11. Anderson 1950:32. He might have found less of a contradiction had he chosen to compare Esther with the book of Revelation (e.g., 14:10–11, 20!).

12. Ibid., p. 41. Anderson speaks as if the Jews attempted to exterminate all the gentiles in the Persian empire. He defends the presence of Esther in the Christian canon as retrospective evidence for God's providence in preserving the Jewish people so that salvation might proceed from them to all the earth (p. 40). Similarly, J. Baldwin assures us that there was a good reason for God to preserve the Jewish nation from extinction, namely that "that nation was being prepared for the honour of receiving his Son" (p. 118). She does not say whether, that purpose accomplished, we are now expendable.

Another theologian might inquire whether the existence of any people or race, regardless of their future role in one's own religion, is not in itself a worthy concern for God and, perhaps, for Christianity as well.

Commentary on 8:13). There can be no vengeance without an unpunished offense. In this case, the revenge is directed against actively hostile, armed enemies. It is not a mere vendetta, vengeance for its own sake wreaked upon a currently pacific party guilty only of past wrong.

Esther, for her part, had not sought hostilities or vengeance prior to 13 Adar. She had not asked that her enemies be punished, but only that Haman's edict be returned, that is, rescinded (8:5). This bloodless solution failed only because the rigidity of the gentile state proved unable to protect the lives of its Jewish subjects.[13]

Mordecai's edict granted the Jews the right of self-defense, "to make a stand for their lives" (8:11). The Jewish action is thus, by the book's presuppositions, defensive. (The Jews presumably did not overstep the bounds of the license; had they done so, they would have rendered the edict pointless and would have risked official sanction.[14]) The edict is not a general license to massacre anyone the Jews did not like.

The Jews are of necessity fighting defensively. The phrase "to make a stand for their lives" (8:11) shows that their lives were in danger. They are not fighting against gentiles as such, but only against the deliberate persecutors of the Jews, "the forces of every people and province who afflict them" (8:11), in other words, armed bands ("forces") of assailants. That is what these people are; they have no other identity. (This definition cannot be dismissed as propaganda, because this *is* the reality in the world of the text, and there are no external facts, such as a historical conflict, against which the definition can be measured.) The assailants are endangering themselves by their own hostility.[15] If they had refrained

---

13. As observed by Meinhold, p. 103.
14. Their refusal to take booty was more stringent than the edict demanded, but it did not violate its terms.
15. S. Goldman tries to distinguish between the morality of the Jews in the book and that of the book itself. With regard to (1) the Jewish *people* (as characters in the book) he asserts that "when one considers the disproportionate gratuitous Jewish attack in the light of Persian pro-Jewish sentiments, the attack becomes a massacre, a Jewish bloodbath against Persians" (1990:24). (2) With regard to the *book* (seen from the perspective of the reader, Goldman claims that, by means of "generative irony," the narrative becomes "an example of Jewish self-criticism, a bold questioning of the Jewish self-image" (p. 24).
     Goldman is wrong in both regards. (1) The Jews did *not* attack; they assembled to withstand attack, and the casualties they afflicted were proportionate to the extent of the attack on them: the fewer gentiles chose to attack, the fewer would have been killed. And whatever the sympathies of most Persians, a

from "afflicting" the Jews, they would have been outside the edict's scope and safe from Jewish vengeance.[16]

The Jews in Esther are not waging a religious or national crusade against the "heathen," nor are they pursuing a conquest along the lines of Joshua's invasion of Canaan (in spite of reminiscences of the holy war ban) or an imperialist campaign like the wars of David, John Hyrcanus, and Alexander Jannaeus. They certainly are not trying to exterminate all gentiles. The Jews in Esther are not even attempting to "blot out the memory of Amalek" as commanded in Deut 25:19.[17] Though tribal antagonisms lie somewhere in the background of the conflict between Mordecai and

---

large number were murderously hostile toward the Jews. (2) He brings no evidence that the author is guiding us toward any negative evaluation of the behavior of the Jews in the book. He argues his case only by pointing to the presence of numerous other ironies in the story (which says nothing about the existence of this particular irony), and by identifying those who "have the most difficulty with an ironic reading of the attack" as "those who share the belief in the *Realpolitik* of a first-strike capability" (p. 24). I am not sure that I do share this belief, but in any case Goldman is obviously begging the question by assuming that I *should* read the attack "ironically."

16. There is a noteworthy exception to the supercilious, censorious responses to Esther typical of Christian exegetes in the nineteenth and the early twentieth centuries. Paul Haupt, in a dry and learned monograph on Esther published in 1906, has an extraordinary note on the Kishinev pogroms, news of which was just reaching the West as he was writing. "A cablegram of Nov. 5, 1905," he informs the reader, "stated that thousands of Jews had been killed in Odessa, and that they had been treated with revolting barbarity. Heads were battered with hammers, nails were driven into the bodies, eyes were gouged out, and ears severed" (1906:34). He goes on to detail some of the horrors that he had learned of, quoting cablegrams from March 1906. He writes in shock and dismay; for him, attacks on Jews are not an archaic abstraction. "The Jew-baiters of Bialystock were supported by the Russian troops and the police. The military attacked the Jews who tried to defend themselves against their assailants. The Jew-baiters committed unspeakable atrocities."
Haupt compares the Russian riots to the dangers facing the Jews in the Esther story and their afflictions at the hand of Antiochus Epiphanes in the second century B.C.E. and insists that the measures taken by Mordecai and the Jews were necessary in self-defense. In a later article, Haupt expresses the belief—perhaps overly optimistic—that "if the Russian Jews had been permitted to organize themselves for defense, the majority of the *pogroms* would never have happened" (1908:158).
It seems to me that Haupt was one of the few Christian commentators to sense on a personal level just what the book of Esther is talking about and to grasp the urgency underlying its humor. The commentators' aloof condemnations of the book and the Jews in it for the marginal ethical imperfections attendant on the fateful struggle—not to mention for major ethical failings not there at all—display an arrogant insensitivity to both ethical and literary issues.

17. Dommershausen (pp. 62–63) finds the motif of Holy War hidden in Mordecai's conflict with Haman, for "Yahweh has war with Amalek from generation to

Haman, the Jews direct no special attention to the Amalekites among their foes.[18]

The Jews' struggle is not, however, without moral blemish. Mordecai's edict is tainted by the permission to kill the enemies' children. The heart of the edict is 8:11aα: "the king has permitted the Jews in each and every city to gather and to make a stand for their lives." The rest is only expansion and closer definition of this license for self-defense. Verse 11aβb, "together with children and women, with their property as spoil," is a continuation of the first sentence and describes actions that are encompassed in the defensive action. Like the saturation bombing of Nuremburg and Dresden, this killing of noncombatants is part of an overall defensive strategy, and, like it, unnecessary and excessive.

The permission to kill the enemies' wives and children is not reported to have been carried into effect. Its importance is to exist in the edict as a counterpart of the same clause in Haman's decree. The clause need not be carried out in order to "work" in this way. Nevertheless, the inclusion of women and children in the scope of the authorization respects literary values—the neatness of the tit-for-tat schema—at the expense of an ethical value: the exclusion of noncombatants from hostilities. To be sure, we might picture the women as belonging to the Jews' active adversaries. Though we can hardly imagine them taking up arms, the antithesis drawn between the Jewish heroine and a gentile female antagonist, Haman's wife Zeresh, deliberately inserts women into the struggle. Their sex does not make them innocent victims. But the children are surely *hors de combat* and can hardly be considered among the "forces . . . who afflict them" (8:11).[19]

The principle of excluding noncombatants from hostilities was not, it must be noted, generally recognized in the ancient world,

---

generation" (Exod 17:16). But even if hostility toward Amalek was Mordecai's reason for not bowing to Haman, he did not set out to eradicate Amalek, and there is nothing to suggest that that was the result.

18. The author does not call Haman an Amalekite, which is the term always used of the hostile tribe. Apparently he uses "Agagite" to allude to the ancient conflict without imposing its pattern too strongly on the present story.

19. Haupt argues that the children could indeed present a danger: "a heathen woman might assault a Jewish woman, a heathen boy might attack a Jewish boy; some heathen children might kill an old Jew, &c." (1908:159). It is, of course, true that children have often joined in pogroms and other kinds of racist mob actions, but they are incidental to the aggression, and repulsing the assault does not require killing them.

including biblical Israel, except for expressions of indignation at an *enemy's* refusal to spare the innocent. In the Bible, women and children are often encompassed in the hostilities or in punishments of men, because a man's wives and children (as well as livestock and material property) were considered an extension of his person, and the punishment that falls upon him may strike them as well. This attitude is not peculiar to the book of Esther. Joshua destroyed Achan's sons and daughters—and livestock and property— along with the guilty man himself (Josh 7:24–25); God obliterated the family (and property) of Korah (Num 16:32); and God commanded the Israelites to exterminate men, women, and children in the conquest of Canaan (Deut 20:16–17; Josh 6:17–24).[20] In the latter case, the women would have been considered guilty of the "sins of the Amorite" that, in one view, justified the conquest (Gen 15:16; cf., for example, Deut 9:4), but the inclusion of children among the authorized victims is, at best, primitive brutality.[21] Again, the casualty reports in Esther do not mention women and children, and there is no reason to assume that the author wished us to understand that they were actually slaughtered. Nevertheless, they are marked for slaughter in Mordecai's decree,[22] and if it is true that "the central issue here is not historicity but theology"[23]— namely the theological doctrine of retributive justice—then it is a theology that must be repudiated.

While the Jews had no choice but to fight on 13 Adar, their moral ground becomes shakier on the 14th, when the danger no longer existed. Haman's edict allowed the Jews' enemies to attack only on 13 Adar, and the entire drama rests on the presumption that the enemies would not, or could not, resort to force without such permission, just as the Jews themselves needed special permission to fight on a second day. The king's agreement to Haman's

---

20. It is strange that Christian theologians, starting with Luther, have been more disturbed by the defensive action of the Jews in Esther's time than by the aggressive and more destructive conquest by the Israelites in Joshua's.
21. In actuality, the inhabitants of Canaan were almost certainly not slaughtered by the Israelites, who themselves descended in large part from the indigenous population. Like the schematic notion of the Israelite invasion of Canaan, the ban is a literary "ideal," an expression of the belief that the people of Israel had to make a fresh start, to live free of all ties with the Canaanite culture. But it is a reprehensible way of expressing that ideal.
22. On the inadequacy of the attempts to explain this phrase away, see the Commentary on 8:11.
23. Moore, p. 81.

scheme and the rigidity of Persian law necessitated a war whose shock waves were to harm the perpetrators of the hostility; but that harm was not sought as an end in itself.

There is, it must be granted, something of a power fantasy in the report of the battles[24]—a certain vehemence and even a gloating tone heard in the emphasis on the Jews' "control" and their ability to wreak their "will" on their enemies, in the heaping-up of terms for slaughter (*makkat hereb weʰhereg weʾabdan*, lit., "a smiting by the sword and killing and destruction"; 9:5), and in the fascination with the body count (9:12, 15), which is not relevant to the rescue of the Jews.

Also disturbing is the schematic character of the war. The righteous nation stands against its foes and slaughters them in great number. There is no sense of the danger, the pain, or even the bloodiness of war. The struggle is reminiscent of the schematic war of the Sons of Light against the Sons of Darkness in the Dead Sea Scrolls.

It is doubtful that the conduct of war, even on the part of the defender, is (if the power balance allows) ever free of vengeance, brutality, and overkill. The battles of Adar certainly were not.[25]

c. HOW THE JEWISH COMMUNITY WORKS. The author of Esther conceives of the Jewish people as a united body which, though scattered through a gigantic empire, can act as a unit. They are expected to weigh arguments, interpret events, reach decisions, and take upon themselves and their descendants obligations as they see fit. Purim grows out of the interplay of interpretation and confirmation between leadership and people. Est 9:29–32 explicitly delineates the dual authority of leadership and community that created the Purim festival.[26]

---

24. As claimed by Gunkel p. 75, Meinhold p. 77, and others.
25. The book's moral faults are not ameliorated by the fact that the book is deliberately hyperbolic or humorous, as B. Jones (1977) thinks: "Surely, the author did not expect his readers to keep a straight face while hearing the great king rejoice that so many of his subjects have been killed . . . The repetition of the ten long names of Haman's ten sons must have added to the pleasure of the listeners" (p. 180). A humorous tone would not justify a repugnant attitude. A story that treated, say, wife-beating with good humor would not be more acceptable just because the author expected the audience to laugh at it. However, the book does not view the battles and the slaughter as in any way funny.
26. See Clines, p. 165.

A modern view of religious history might speak of spontaneous actions taking root in the people and becoming recognized as social practices, and only then being interpreted, post facto, as religious obligations (such may be the actual origins of Purim). By this view, the creation of the practice is diffused among numerous individuals, who may enter into the usage with little thought to its meaning. Est 9:20–32 likewise locates the holiday's origin in the people, but, unlike the history-of-religions model, it envisions the people acting as a deliberative body consciously shaping their own praxis. Such a process, assuming an alert and responsive interaction between people and leadership, is probably an ideal more than a historical reality; certainly no historical context we know of fits the picture.

The ideal is exemplary and didactic. It is contrasted with the law of the Persian (i.e. gentile) realm, in which all formal power is invested in the office of king. His word alone is authoritative, so much so, that even when his decision is only an impulse or whim, it creates a law that binds the monarch himself. In reality, the despot's "servants" may exercise actual power by manipulating him, but that only compounds the confusion, for they too can be silly (chap. 1) or evil (chap. 3). The law that emerges from this tug-of-war between despotism and erratic influence is beyond anyone's control, yet it holds the entire empire in its grasp.

The Jews, in contrast to the Persians, arrive at decisions through a dialectic between leaders and community. Mordecai and Esther do speak from a position of authority, but it is moral authority. Perhaps as vizier and queen they could have imposed their will on their co-religionists,[27] but they do not attempt to do so. When addressing the Jews they do not write "in the king's name" or "seal [it] with the king's signet." Mandating behavior in this way would be a poor foundation for a ritual practice lacking divine sanction or historical background. Rather, Mordecai *extracts* the holiday from the people's unprompted activity and turns it into a permanent, official communal rite. The text is emphatic on the duality of the process: "And the Jews committed themselves to continuing what they had begun doing and what Mordecai had written to

---

27. In the AT, Mordecai does just that: "and the king empowered Mordecai to write whatever he wished. And Mordecai sent word via letters that he had sealed with the king's ring, to the effect that his people should remain each in his own place and hold celebration unto God" (viii 33–34).

them" (9:23). All this is then reconfirmed by Esther. Instead of authoritative prescription, Mordecai and Esther employ authoritative validation.

The source of the holiday is the people themselves, and the festival calendar is shaped to their actions. The holiday reenacts what *they* do. Mordecai only helps them convert their action into an institution. As in the refusal of spoil, there is a wisdom inherent in the people independent of the instructions they receive. A leader formalizes this wisdom and holds it up to their inspection. The basic authority resides in the Jewish people, without whose joy the spontaneous celebrations would not have occurred and without whose consensus the practice would not have become binding. With this consensus, however, the practice becomes as durable as a Persian law and attains a universality and stability that the Persian law does not. All Jews, in all places and in all ages (note the extraordinary emphasis on national unity in 9:28) uniformly celebrate the peace and joy that followed upon their struggle for existence.

The book's ideal of community has a democratic quality insofar as it is based on a notion of a collective will that is the final arbiter of the community's obligations. Legislation, as conceived here, requires the consent of the governed. Yet the community does not choose its leadership, but accepts the leadership that arises through force of circumstances. The appropriate action of the community is to consent to the leaders' direction. The author views the community from on high, from the leaders' perspective, yet respects its inherent authority.

Where are the Jews of the Exile to find their leaders? They no longer have a king, and the priests among them have been rendered irrelevant. Prophets are not mentioned (their validity in exile may have been in doubt). Other nations of the empire have princes (*śarim*; 3:12) and other officials; the Jews do not. They are, in a sense, their own princes. Thus Mordecai's edict is directed to "the Jews and the satraps and the governors and the princes of the provinces" (8:9); in other words, the Jews as a body stand on a par with the officials of the empire, but they apparently lack officials of their own. The priestly and administrative institutions of Judea do not interest the author, who looks to them neither for help nor guidance, not even in matters of ritual. Rather, he envisions a self-sufficient diaspora community.

The author supplies this community with leaders who resemble the premonarchical judges, the *šopʿtim*, a word more precisely translated "leaders."[28] Like all the major judges except Deborah, Mórdecai and Esther do not start from a recognized position of communal authority (Esther's queenship is at first irrelevant to the Jews), but arise to meet a specific crisis. Their authority at the end of the book is buttressed by their stations in the gentile world, but these are not positions within the Jewish community. In other words, Mordecai and Esther are charismatic judges without the benefit of divine appointment or inspiriting. Like Ehud and Samson, Esther and Mordecai act as individuals. Later, like Ehud, Gideon, and Deborah, they rally the people to war, and the people itself completes the deliverance. We may also observe that in the time of the judges, too, salvation and leadership could come from a woman, namely Deborah. The loose institutional, non-hereditary character of judgeship in premonarchic Israel allowed for individual women to come to the fore. Also like Israel in the time of the judges, the Jews in Esther cannot be forced to rally behind its leaders. They do so willingly, as the Israelites did—ideally but not consistently—before the rise of kingship.

Since the Scroll does not clearly allude to the judges, we cannot conclude that the author deliberately chose them as a paradigm of exilic leadership. Rather, the similarity is to be explained as a parallel response evoked by a parallel situation. The situation of the Jews in exile after the fall of the monarchy required institutions similar to those of the premonarchical Israelites in their land.

The author sees the Jews' fate as depending on its leading individuals, whose lives both epitomize and entail the nation's fortunes. Just as a danger to highly placed individuals imperils the people, so does the leaders' personal success entail the people's welfare. Haman's wife and friends recognize this, for they regard the conflict with a Jew as a clash with the Jewish people, and in their view it is a power inherent in the people (rather than Mordecai's personal qualities) that makes the Jew Mordecai invincible. Conversely, Mordecai's triumph demonstrates the people's power. Thus when he goes forth in honor (8:15), the Jews have joy and light and *honor*, for the splendor of his success is reflected upon them (8:16). The Jews see their victory prefigured in their leader's. Thus the connec-

---

28. The "judges" are never shown "judging" in a strictly forensic sense. However, the distinction between administrative and judicial governing is largely artificial for ancient Israel, and the premonarchic "judging" probably included both functions.

tion between his personal success and the people's welfare is integral, and his appearance in pomp brings the narrative tension to its resolution.

Community relations are not, of course, only vertical, between the masses and their leaders. The holiday practices strengthen horizontal bonds by the giving of "portions." The exchange of food symbolically turns the multitude of local and family celebrations into one large communal feast. The portions to the poor are not charitable donations any more than the portions given to one's neighbors. Their point is to encompass everyone in the communal feast.

D. THE NATIONAL STATUS OF THE JEWISH PEOPLE. The author of Esther depicts an empire that, for all its faults, does respect the multiplicity and individuality of national groups within it. Haman's decree is issued not only to "the king's satraps and the governors who were over each and every province" (3:12a), but also to

the princes of each and every people—to each and every province in its own script and each and every people in its own language. (3:12b)

Mordecai's decree is directed to the same groups, except that it also addresses the Jewish people like the others, as a nationality in its own right, and, moreover, addresses them in their own script and language (8:9b). The Jews' language is thus given official status.

The author believes that all peoples are and should be concerned with the preservation of their national languages. The decree banishing Vashti, which was also issued to all languages and all peoples, declares that "every man should be ruler in his household and speak the language of his own people" (1:22). Thus it defines the main mark of a man's domination of his household as the right to use his national tongue in his home. (To be sure, the men who issue this decree are behaving foolishly, but their folly consists in their nervous overreaction to any female assertiveness. The author does not repudiate the validity of male dominance in itself.) The desire to maintain one's national language is viewed as common to all the peoples in the empire and is taken seriously. This concern recalls the tensions reported in the time of Nehemiah, who chastised intermarried Jewish men because their children were speaking their mothers' tongues rather than Hebrew (Neh 13:23–31). The author of Esther reveals a similar concern by having the Persian administration recognize the importance of a man's maintaining his national language.

The notion that the Jews actually did speak their own language in the diaspora and that it was recognized by the Persian chancellery represents an ideal, not any historical reality we know of or that is likely to have existed. The Jews' language in Esther (8:9) must be Hebrew, elsewhere called "Jewish," that is, the language of Judah (Neh 13:24; 2 Kgs 18:26, 28; 2 Chron 32:8; and Isa 36:11, 13). Their language certainly was not Greek, whose foreignness was always recognized, nor is it likely that Aramaic is meant, for though this was the language the Jews most widely used, it was also the lingua franca of the Near East and common to a great many peoples.[29]

In reality, the Jews would not have used Hebrew for secular purposes in the diaspora. Hebrew (alongside Aramaic and, later, Greek) was spoken only in Palestine, especially outside the urban centers, but the book can hardly have a Palestinian provenance, for it totally lacks interest in the Temple, in Jerusalem, and in the autonomous institutions of Judean Jewry, whereas it responds to a diaspora crisis in diaspora terms. During Persian rule the Jews would have used Aramaic for the most part, and later, in the Hellenistic kingdoms, Greek as well (in the East, Greek would have been used mainly in the Hellenistic cities). Certainly no royal documents were ever promulgated in Hebrew or even translated into it, for even if the Jews had been a factor worth attention in imperial affairs, they would have known Aramaic. Even the Judeans communicated with the chancellery in Aramaic. In practice, in the Achemenid empire, royal correspondence was sent out in Aramaic and translated into the local languages upon arrival.[30] The slight inaccuracy in the author's notion of the way in which royal documents were issued may reflect a distance from the Achemenid period, though this is no proof of a late date, because a Jew living outside Persia might see imperial documents in a local language and assume that they had been issued in that language from the Persian chancellery. But the picture we see in Esther of the Jews throughout the empire speaking and receiving official communications in Hebrew is an ideal rather than a reality. It reflects the

---

29. On the languages of the Persian empire see Naveh-Greenfield 1984:115–29, esp. 116–17.
30. Dandamayev, 1984:333; Naveh-Greenfield 1984:116.

wish that the Jews be autonomous (in the sense of controlling their lives within their communities) while enjoying the status of a recognized *ethnos*, like many of the peoples among whom they lived.

Though the Jews are pictured as integrated into the daily life of the empire, Haman was right in describing them as "spread out and unassimilated" (3:8). But Haman meant this as a slander, whereas the author views it as the right condition for the diaspora. The Jews are not alone in being unassimilated; the multiplicity of languages and peoples, each with its own prince, shows that others have maintained their individuality. As for being dispersed, no other nations are explicitly stated to be spread out, but the presence of an Agagite shows that other small, non-native groups did exist within the empire. Only Haman, of foreign ancestry, advocates (by implication) an enforced "Persianization."

The Scroll's political ideology resembles the concept of Jewish nationalism developed by the twentieth century historian and philosopher Simon Dubnow.[31] Dubnow advocated the formation and recognition of a non-territorial Jewish national entity within the states and empires of Europe, particularly the Russian and Austro-Hungarian empires. Jews, like other ethnic groups, were to be subjects of their respective empires while regulating their own internal legal and cultural affairs. They would have a national language (Yiddish), communal bodies, and legal-judicial institutions for the Jewish community. The Jewish national entity would, Dubnow believed, be secular. Many of these institutions and practices had been in place, he pointed out, since the Middle Ages.

There is a significant difference, of course: the Scroll does not speak of any formal political status for Jewish institutions. The similarity lies in the way both envision the Jewish people living and functioning as one *ethnos* among many, seeing to its internal governance and preserving its own culture.[32]

It is difficult to determine the background of the book's national ideal. We cannot fix the Scroll's time and place of origin with

---

31. Dubnow's work is voluminous; the standard presentation of his views is *Nationalism and History*, 1958.
32. J. Levenson (1976:451) objects to applying the notion of nationalism to the book, saying that this is done because critics, Jewish and non-Jewish, try to fit the self-understanding of Israel in the procrustean bed of nation, church, or culture. Levenson says that "it is a strange nationalism which advocates cooperation with a foreign monarch rather than secession from his control" (p. 444). But both Hellenistic nationalism and Dubnow's autonomism did just that. Nationalism does not inevitably require a center in the home territory, though

any precision. It may have originated in an eastern diaspora, perhaps in Susa itself, but we have very little information on the status of Jews in the east (especially east of the Euphrates) before the Talmudic period.[33] If the author's context is in fact Hellenistic, the Persian empire in Esther is not the historical Persian empire, but rather represents an empire (Seleucid or Ptolemaic) that the author himself knew and was writing for.

In the Hellenistic world, the Jews for the most part (but with some painful exceptions) enjoyed a fair degree of autonomy within their localities. In some places, the Jews had rights as an officially recognized corporation of resident aliens. In Antioch, Berenice (North Africa), and Alexandria, as well as in some lesser-known places, this corporation (called the *politeuma, katoikia,* or *sunagogē*) had its own officials and could legislate for its members.[34] In the Seleucid kingdom, the numerous national groupings generally enjoyed considerable autonomy,[35] primarily because the kings were unable to impose strong central control on the sprawling mélange of nations they were trying to govern.[36] (Antiochus III [223–187

---

that is the usual model. While the category of nationalism is not an adequate label for the Scroll's concept of the status of Jews in exile, it seems to me an appropriate one, insofar as the concept of non-territorial nationality was recognized and even codified in the Hellenistic world. It is a nationalism that affirms both integration and ethnic identity.

33. See Schürer 1986: III.1, 3–10.

34. Schürer 1986: III.1, 88. As Schürer points out, other nations too, particularly the Egyptians and Phoenicians, had diasporas and formed communal organizations and assemblies (pp. 107–12). There thus existed other models for understanding the status of Jews as "alien" Judeans. But internally Jews had greater communal autonomy than other aliens. Tcherikover describes their situation thus: "The Jewish community, with its officials and institutions, its synagogues and courts, its economic and social life, was a miniature kingdom; and if, from the point of view of the Hellenistic state, its case was no different from that of every other *politeuma*, from an internal point of view it was more like the autonomous Greek *polis* than an ephemeral group of foreigners from abroad" (1959:302).

Mendenhall (1973:100–101) mentions the *politeuma* in conjunction with the legal system that he believes is created by Mordecai's decree in 8:13—a "state within a state" on a religious-ethical basis. The autonomous status, however, has nothing to do with the counter-decree, any more than Haman's decree founded a *politeuma* of antisemites. And Mordecai's decree certainly did not grant the Jews what Mendenhall calls "a freedom from the regular obligations of the Persian Empire," for allowing oneself to be killed was hardly one of the regular obligations laid upon Persian subjects.

35. On the disunity of the Seleucid kingdom see Tcherikover 1972:24–28.

36. But see Sherwin-White (1987:3), who points out that local autonomy can coexist with strong central supervision.

B.C.E.] tried and failed to impose tight control in the East.) The nations (*ethnoi*) of this empire were to a large extent autonomous and were ruled by dynasts or princes, who were intermediate between their peoples and the king.[37] This situation is congruent with the picture of empire we get from the book of Esther.

The charter granted by Antiochus III to the Jews in 200 B.C.E.,[38] is instructive for the status of the Jews in the Seleucid empire. It ensures the Jews of a recognized national status of the sort enjoyed by other favored nations in the kingdom, as a reward for Jerusalem's having transferred its loyalties to the Seleucid monarch. It continues the precedent of national autonomy set by the Persian kings and maintained by the Ptolemies. It proclaims that "all members of this *ethnos* shall be governed in accordance with their ancestral laws," which means governing their own affairs in accordance with the Law of Moses. The Jews not only *may*, but *shall* worship the God of Jerusalem. A senate (*gerousia*) governs the Jews, alongside which a popular assembly has certain judicial functions.[39]

The Jews in the diaspora would not have had comparable independence, but the assurance of national status in the homeland would, ideally, provide Jews everywhere with a recognized national status, for they were an *ethnos* by virtue of having a home territory. (Thus Mordecai was identified as *hayᵉhudi*, which might be translated "Judean" as well as "Jew.") The book of Esther does not touch upon the governance of the home territory but is concerned only with the status of the Jews in the dispersion. The Jews in Esther, as noted above, do not have "princes" (*śarim* = *archontes*). They do not constitute a *dynastea*, subject to a native prince, nor are they a Greek *polis*. They are an *ethnos* and as such have the right to live by their ancestral laws. These laws can only be the Law of Moses. Haman alludes to it when he says that the unnamed people's laws "are different from those of every other people" (3:8). This is true, but Haman is making a crime out of a national right.

---

37. Ibid., p. 29. The LXX reflects the correct Hellenistic technical usage in translating *śarey ʿam* as *tois archousin tōn ethnōn* (3:12).
38. Preserved by Josephus, XII 138–44. The arrangements the charter proclaims were not an invention of the moment, but a proclamation of what the law is and always (in theory) had been.
39. The above paragraph is based on Bickerman 1935; see also 1988:124–26 and passim.

CHAPTER XII

GOD

One opinion:
" . . . all the romantic glamour of the story cannot
blind us to its religious emptiness and moral
depravity."

(J. E. McFadyen 1906:315)

God is not one of the characters *in* the book of Esther. A person cannot be considered a character in a story in which he never appears and is not referred to, not even by circumlocution. We would not call Godot a character in Beckett's play, although he *is* mentioned in it. Yet neither God nor Godot is simply out of the picture. Somehow their absence gives them a presence in the story, though, of course, in different ways. Godot is often spoken about but certainly does not come; his not coming is of highest importance and calls for interpretation. God is not mentioned in Esther yet *might* be there from start to end. It is this "might be" that is so puzzling, yet it should not be reduced to a comfortable "is" or "is not." The *possibility* of the divine presence demands interpretation.

God should be in, or at least manifestly near, a story of Israel's salvation. We expect him to hear prayer, inspire the faithful, punish the wicked, guide events, guarantee national salvation, and finally receive thanks. Yet in Esther he is not said to do any of these things. Such a violation of expectations is surely no accident. What does this silence say about the book's message? Where is God?

1. God's Absence

Many scholars, all of them modern, assert that the book is "secular," meaning that God plays no role in the events. According to one formulation, the book relates "an entirely profane history in a purely worldly mindset for the sake of satisfying worldly passions and instincts" (Cornill 1891:153). (Most of these scholars have a theological background and tend to view secularity as a moral failing.)

The Scroll's alleged secularity is commonly, and strangely, thought to be an expression of Jewish nationalism. B. Anderson thinks that Esther is "a witness to the fact that Israel, in pride, either made nationalism a religion in complete indifference to God or presumptuously identified God's historical purpose with the preservation and glorification of the Jewish people" (1950:40). R. Pfeiffer alleges that "secular nationalism" is the book's guiding light: the author considered religion a garment to be lightly discarded whenever it hindered worldly aims.[1] But a nationalism that is secular on principle never existed in the ancient world (and probably not before the late eighteenth century C.E.); it is unlikely that such an attitude would have been comprehensible in the ancient world. If the Scroll is indeed "secular," that cannot be because of nationalistic influences. Of course, one might argue that the book of Esther itself is evidence for a secular nationalism,[2] but if so, this ideology is unique, and it would be a tautology to explain its unique secular nationalism as a product of its unique secular nationalism. In any case, nationalism, in its ancient forms[3] and most of its modern ones, never hesitated to invoke and claim divine support for its plans. Nothing in biblical religion could hamper nationalist aspirations—certainly not the aspirations of the Jewish nation in Esther, which are simply to stay alive.[4]

Gerleman argues that the book of Esther is patterned after the Exodus story, but is "detheologized" and "desacralized" (p. 43). In

---

1. Pfeiffer 1952:742–43. Pfeiffer associates this "secular nationalism" with John Hyrcanus. But Hyrcanus is a strange candidate for secularity. He took on messianic features and was high priest (Josephus, *War* I 68–69). Josephus even attributes to him the gift of prophecy and says that he was "closely . . . in touch with the deity. His religious authority was recognized by the Pharisees in the early part of his reign, and certain cultic ordinances were attributed to him (Mishna Sota 9:10). His forcible conversion of the Idumeans shows that his nationalistic policies were not devoid of religious ideology. None of the Hashmonean rulers held to a secular policy.

2. It would be more accurate to say that it envisions a nationalism without speaking of its place in the national religion.

3. Though nationalism is a product of eighteenth-century Western Europe, it has antecedents in the Hellenistic world, where nations (*ethnoi*) were forced to define themselves against the background of the sovereign kingdoms.

4. As Levenson puts it, "If they [Mordecai and Esther] are particularistic, it is because the faith that created them and revered their memory is particularistic. If that particularism is a stumbling-block to us, there is hardly a book in the Hebrew Bible over which we shall not trip. . . . It is clear again that if universalism is our theological goal, our problems do not begin with Esther" (1976:442). Perhaps the theologians would have been less exercised by the book's nationalism if the people were called "Israelites" rather than "Jews."

both the Succession Narrative (2 Samuel 9–20) and Esther, events are described in accordance with their inner-historical causality. But, Gerleman believes, whereas in the former God works within the human heart, in Esther "even that final remnant is lost." Gerleman calls Esther a "theologically coded document" but does not inform us what the code is or how to read it.

Talmon, too, deems the Scroll secular and explains this as a characteristic of its literary genre, which he identifies as a historicized Wisdom tale. "The concept of an unspecified and remote deity devoid of any individual character as is prevalent in the Esther-narrative, is present also in some specimens of biblical wisdom literature" (1963 : 430; see above, chap. IV §1). But the comparison helps little, for whereas God is indeed "unspecified" in Esther, that is hardly the case in Wisdom Literature, in which he appears frequently and prominently. The fact adduced by Talmon, that in Qohelet and most of Job God is referred to by "non-specific" appellations (such as "God" and "Shadday"), serves only to distance Esther from Wisdom, for God does not receive these designations in Esther. In fact, all of Wisdom Literature insists on God's constant and ubiquitous presence in human life. Deity may seem to lack "individual character" in Wisdom Literature, but in Esther he does not even appear.

2. God's Presence

The great majority of commentators consider the book "religious," meaning that it teaches, or at least assumes, that God is active in the events it narrates. This position is commonly intended as a defense of the book's religiosity against its detractors, as if religiosity were in itself a virtue. These commentators would agree with Meinhold's description of Esther as a "religious book in non-religious language."[5]

Traditional readers never doubted that God was guaranteeing Israel's existence and shaping its salvation in Esther's time as always, and hence that this must be the author's belief as well. The absence of God's name was just a curiosity; it evoked explanations but was of no more intrinsic significance than the absence of God's name in, say, Genesis 37.[6] Since they were reading Esther as one segment

---

5. See Meinhold 1983a:99–101.
6. The classical midrashim (including b. Meg. 10b–17a and Tar[2]), as well as most of the medieval commentators, scarcely deal with the problem, but simply

of a larger text, the Hebrew Bible, they were right for their purposes. Meaning depends on context, and in the context of the canon, both Jewish and Christian, the Scroll is part of a larger testimony to God's rule of history.

But Esther was not written as part of the Bible. Not only could the author not have known that there would be a Bible,[7] but the lack of reference to God probably shows that he did not intend his book to be regarded as sacred scripture. If, then, we seek to interpret the author's intention, regarding that as source and determinant of the primary (though not sole) meaning, we must try to read the book as an independent unit, unconstrained by the canonical context it was later to enter. That context can elucidate the authorial meaning of Esther by providing material for comparison and showing something about the author's background, but it cannot determine its meaning, for any book can diverge from its tradition as well as draw upon it.

For most readers, the silence speaks clearly of God. H. Fisch, for example, calls the silence eloquent and quickly translates it into theology: "In the end there is only one ruler whose commands, never officially promulgated, are unchanging and whose will prevails. He lurks behind the costly hangings of the court and whispers in the ear of Ahasuerus in the night. It is of him that the subtext speaks and whose deeds it records" (1988:14). But Fisch, straining to hear through and beyond the silence, is projecting his own faith and ignoring the stillness itself.

The commentators who believe that God is hidden do not think he is very well hidden, for they have no doubts that the author had no doubts that God is nigh. But if he is so clearly on the

---

assume God's omnipresence and guidance of history. Some saw a reference to God in some of the occurrences of the word "king" (e.g., b. Meg. 15b, on Est 6:1). The common identification of "another place" (4:14) with God is not prevalent among the traditional commentators. Targum Rishon (unlike Tar²) seems to make the identification but only implicitly. Ibn Ezra (in his preface) repudiates that understanding of the phrase and offers another reason for the silence: Mordecai sent copies of his scroll throughout the world and these were incorporated in the Persian chronicles. He omitted God's name because he was worried that the heathen would substitute the name of their god for it. (In Ibn Ezra² he attributes this explanation to Saᶜadia. It is found in Midrash Leqaḥ Tov.)

7. At the time of Esther's composition, the Pentateuch and probably the prophets had attained canonical shape. Some other books were recognized as sacred, but they had not been gathered together with the Pentateuch and Prophets into a single collection.

scene, why is he not mentioned? Paton (p. 95) suggests that mention of God's name is avoided to prevent its profanation during the carnival-like festivities of Purim. Similarly, E. Greenstein says that the "frivolous" nature of the Purim festival was no time to pronounce the sacred name (1987:233). But Purim celebrants, even if they become tipsy, are unlikely to blaspheme, and if they were to do so, the presence of God's name in the Scroll (which is read aloud by a lector, who would not be drunk) would not have conduced to it. Moreover, the festivities come after the reading. The Septuagintal Esther shows no hesitation about referring to God, and Jewish liturgy introduces and concludes the reading of the Scroll with blessings which use God's name; and certainly later generations were no less scrupulous about blasphemy than the MT-author. In any case, it is not only the sacred name (YHWH) that is avoided in the Hebrew Esther; neither is there any reference to God by epithet or circumlocution.[8]

A. Meinhold argues that the author seeks to emphasize the responsibility of individual Jews and does not want to have God preempting human action. Hence he keeps divinity at the margins, but definitely present, waiting to act if humans fail.[9] Similarly, S. Berg[10] maintains that the Scroll refrains from any reference to deity in order to accentuate the role of human responsibility in shaping history and also to teach the hiddenness of God's control. But you cannot teach that something is hidden merely by hiding it. If you hide it too well, one cannot know that it is there. The point of teaching that God is "hidden" is really to teach that he is present, in other words, not *truly* hidden. To do so one must show people how to read God's presence in events. This is done often in the Bible. For example, Joseph tells his brothers, "You planned evil against me but God planned it for the best, so as to achieve, as is now the case, the preservation of many people" (Gen 50:20). Likewise: "But [Samson's] father and his mother did not know that it [his request to marry a Philistine woman] was from the Lord, for he was seeking a pretext against the Philistines" (Judg 14:4). Or an author may say simply "and the Lord loved him [Solomon]" (2 Sam 12:24) or "The Lord was with Joseph, and he was successful . . ." (Gen 39:2), thereby reminding us that their success was not the

---

8. Streane (p. xvi) observes that 1 Maccabees, too, avoids God's name. That book, however, refers to God by epithets such as "heaven" or simply by a pronoun.
9. 1978:329–30; 1983a:99–101.
10. 1979:178–79; cf. Berg 1980.

reward of human wisdom alone. If that is the point of the author of Esther, he certainly fails to make it.

According to Clines (p. 153), we do not need a particular "historical" reason for the non-mention of God. He contends that the earlier versions of the story[11] said little (but were not silent) about the divine causality of the coincidences, and the author of the Esther tale ("proto-Massoretic" stage) simply pushed the tendency further. But if Clines is right in his historical reconstruction and there were indeed a few references to God in the earlier form of the story (preserved by proto–AT), we must ask why the author chose to eliminate them instead of adding to them. To remove God from a story is a deliberate, significant act, and cannot be taken for granted.

Four types of evidence have been adduced to demonstrate God's presence and activity in the Esther story.

A. ALLUSIONS. Various statements have been thought to allude to God: The phrase "another place" has sometimes been taken as a locution for God. Both Mordecai (4:14) and Haman's associates (6:13) assert that the Jews will endure and prevail. The Jews fast and cry out—actions whose only function can be to appeal to God's mercy. Especially 4:16, where Esther asks that the Jews fast "for me," implies an act that is not only an expression of grief but an attempt to achieve something external, and fasting can achieve something only by influencing God.[12] The indefinite expression "things would be turned about," lit., "reversed" (9:1), may hint at someone—God—causing the reversal. The Jews rejoice after the victory and decide to observe the festival annually, and such festivities are by their nature intended to give thanks to God.

The identification of "another place" as God is certainly incorrect (see Commentary on 4:14). Mordecai and Haman's advisers do know where events are heading, but they do not indicate just what force ensures Jewish victory. The various hints are indeed significant, but hints are all they are. The author avoids mention of God even when that is most natural. This avoidance is as important as the affirmations it skirts.

B. COINCIDENCES. The most common argument for the religiosity

---

11. That is, the "Mordecai source" and the "Esther source" that he thinks may lie behind the present story, as well as the original AT, on which see chap. XIV §2c.
12. Observed by Loader 1978:418.

of the book, one made in different ways and with different emphases, is that the coincidences reported are so far-fetched that they cannot be mere chance; hence the author must (it is assumed) believe that God brought them to pass. The coincidences include: the timely vacancy of the queenship at the Persian court, the opportune accession of a Jew to queenship, Mordecai's discovery of the eunuchs' conspiracy, Esther's favorable reception by the king, the king's insomnia, Haman's early arrival at the palace, and Haman's reckless plea for mercy at Esther's feet.[13] Clines says that taken together, the chance occurrences have a cumulative effect and show the guiding hand of God. "To the religious believer 'chance' is a name for God."[14] According to Clines (p. 153), divine control of events is not "hidden" or "veiled"; it is stated indirectly but unambiguously, primarily by means of the coincidences.

It is, however, difficult to imagine a better veil than silence. If God is present in Esther he is certainly well-hidden. It may be true for some believers that chance means divine governance, but can we assume that the author was one of these? Perhaps it is only the interpreters for whom the story's coincidences declare God's work. Numerous stories shamelessly heap up improbable coincidences without investing them with theological significance—*As You Like It, The Marriage of Figaro,* and *Bleak House,* for example.[15] Moreover, the coincidences in Esther are not so far-fetched as to be incredible as natural occurrences. The most striking coincidence is the king's fortuitous insomnia together with the reading of the annals that chances upon the right passage; but that coincidence was not necessary for the Jews' salvation.[16] It may be very unlikely that any particular one of these events would occur, but it is quite likely that some improbable events would occur, as they do every day, and it is not unlikely that some such coincidences would provide opportunities for alert people to exploit. Even though the author of

---

13. These coincidences are interpreted as evidence of God's activity by Clines (pp. 153–58), among others.
14. W. E. Beet (1921) also argues that the element of chance disappears as the coincidences reinforce one another.
15. Harvey (1965: 141–42) describes how Dickens employed coincidence, weaving it naturally into the fabric of his stories. Harvey says that coincidence is so extensive in *Bleak House* that it becomes natural and "expresses our sense that real life blends the causal and the casual, that things are connected and contingent, patterned and random, that we are both free and determined. This sense of life's contradictions is a common sense . . ." (p. 142).
16. Its religious significance lies elsewhere—in its signaling a historical pattern; see below.

Esther might be expected to interpret the coincidences as God's doing—many commentators clearly expect this—he does not do so. Rather than making coincidences into comforting signs of divine control, he musters them as evidence of almost the opposite: the unpredictability of the alternatives that an erratic reality forces upon people. He thereby shows the need for alert and courageous Jews to deal with the constraints of an unpredictable reality.

E. Segal finds the key to the Scroll's religion in a particular group of coincidences—those incorporating the motif of anger: Haman's wrath, Xerxes' anger at Vashti and his calming down, the anger of Bigthan and Teresh, the king's anger at Haman—and even the absence of anger on the part of the king when Esther enters the throne room. Segal sees this motif as evidence for "a firm theological conviction that God, while generally allowing the events to take a natural course, is also assumed to be tweaking at the strings at strategic moments in order to ensure that justice will ultimately prevail" (1989:250). Yet the motif of anger is no more a pointer to divine intervention than is any other event or emotion in the story (love, pride, arrogance, and so on). It could serve this function only if it were made to do so, for it is a common human emotion not generally thought to be caused by God. If anger in itself proved God's involvement, then Haman's wrath too would be God's doing—but to what end?

In an often-mentioned variant of the above argument, A. Cohen (1974) finds a clue to the book's religion in the *pur*, the lot that Haman casts. The *pur*, he says, is a symbol of chance-fate. The lottery is Haman's way of demonstrating to the Jews that he can deal with their fate by chance alone. "Haman denies both the possibility and the reality of the divine" (p. 89). Haman's defeat is thus, according to Cohen, evidence of God's providence. But, contrary to Cohen, fate is the opposite of chance; it is its negation, not the obverse side of the same coin. Moreover, the casting of lots in the ancient world had nothing to do with chance; it was an attempt to ascertain the will of the gods, and it presumed their control of events. When, for example, Samuel cast lots to select a king (1 Sam 10:19–24), it was in order to determine whom God wanted to appoint (v. 24), not to choose a lucky winner.[17] There is nothing

---

17. The Bible has many examples of lotteries used to inquire of divinity; for example 1 Sam 14:41 ff.; 1 Chr 24–26; Neh 11:1; Josh 7:10–26; and see Prov 16:33. Nowhere does an Israelite author ascribe a different purpose to foreigners'

to suggest that Haman's lots had a fundamentally different purpose from all others. Haman was consulting his gods, as the AT recognizes.[18]

C. REVERSALS. The book is structured on the principle of peripety—unexpected reversal of human expectations. This is explicit in 9:1: matters were "turned about" for the Jews. The core of the story is organized into a series of theses and antitheses, which use the same or similar language (chap. V §4). In several psalms and proverbs (see chap. XIII, §3), peripety is understood as a manifestation of God's control. In an earlier study (published in 1983), I suggested that the theology of Esther is implied in the structure of reversals. The frustration of human expectations in an orderly, symmetrical fashion—a 180-degree reversal rather than a mere breakdown—portrays (but does not prove) the working of a transcendental force beyond human control and prediction. Similarly, J. Loader (1978:419) asserts that the reversal of relations—the "x-pattern of power relations"—reflects divine intervention.[19] The "deepest" level of the book, according to Loader, is the deliberate "veiling" of God (p. 421).

But as Berg (p. 112) observes, peripety in and of itself, like coincidence, is never used as an argument for God's control, but rather is an expression of confidence in God's justice. Elsewhere in the Bible, when peripety is intended to manifest God's power it is said to do so. The author of Esther could not expect his audience to deduce God's presence from peripety alone. As Loader, intending the opposite, puts it, the reversals show "the same *deus ex machina* without the *deus*" (1978:419).

D. THEMES. Some scholars argue that presence of certain themes in and of itself constitutes a religious statement. According to Meinhold, the story's central concern, the preservation of the Jewish people, is inherently a religious one, for they are the people of

---

lots. The sailors on Jonah's ship cast lots as a way of asking their gods who was responsible for the storm (Jon 1:7). On the meaning of lots see *Ency. Judaica* XI, 510–13. Lotteries had exactly the same purpose in Babylonia—and the Babylonian word for "lots"—*pūrû*—is the origin of the word Purim (Lewy 1939b). On the use of lots in Babylonia see Oppenheim 1964:208–9.

18. "And Haman went to his gods to learn the day of their [the Jews'] death, and he cast lots . . ." (iv 7). This verse is part of the proto–AT and may have been present in the story that the MT–author adapted.

19. He claims that stylistic chiasm, such as "enemies" – "Jews" X "Jews" – "those who hate them" in 9:1, also shows the thematic reversal (p. 419).

God's covenant. The book identifies the survival of the Jews with God's will and, by revealing the flaws of the Jewish protagonists, teaches that the Jews were chosen not because of any superiority on their part but through God's free grace.[20] LaCocque (without explicitly claiming that the book is religious) says that the conflict between the Jews and Amalek adumbrates the Holy War, and that the course of events is patterned after the Salvation History.[21]

As in the case of coincidences and reversals, the themes surrounding Israel's deliverance can be, and usually are, used in the context of religious concerns. But that does not decide the issue of whether in Esther they remain or have been deliberately dislodged from that context. The Scroll is undoubtedly peculiar in avoiding mention of God; it may be peculiar in its theology as well.

3. The Message of Silence

The attention that the Scroll's readers have given to its silence about God shows that the silence speaks louder than a whole string of pious prayers and protestations. But what does it say?

A. WHAT IS (ALMOST) SAID ABOUT GOD. Commentators (and other careful readers) have weighed the evidence and decided for one option or the other: either the story is "secular" or it is "religious." I myself have gone back and forth; I am not even persuaded by my own earlier attempt (1983) to tilt the balance in one direction. Let us consider anew just how religion comes into (but not all the way into) the book.

Although Mordecai avoids referring to God, his confidence that salvation will arise for the Jews has theological implications: "For if you are silent at this time, relief and deliverance will arise for the Jews from another source [lit., 'place']" (4:14a). Such confidence usually derives from and expresses a belief in God's covenantal care for Israel. But it might also assert Jewry's inner strength and potential for self-help. The words of 1 Sam 15:29, *neṣaḥ yiśra'el lo' yᵉšaqqer*, are a popular Zionist motto. When spoken by religious Jews it means "The Eternal One of Israel will not deceive";[22] when used by nonreligious Jews it implies, "The eternity of Israel will not deceive" (or "fail"), in other words, the inner resources of the Jew-

---

20. Meinhold 1978:328; 1983a:101.
21. LaCocque 1987:215.
22. In its biblical context it means either "The Glory of Israel does not deceive" or "The Eternal One of Israel does not deceive," in either case referring to God.

ish people will guarantee its existence. The slogan professes faith, but it can be read two ways. Mordecai's declaration is likewise ambiguous.

Mordecai himself shows how to interpret 4:14a by asking in 14b: "And who knows if it was not just for a time like this that you reached royal station?" "Who knows" both expresses a possibility and grants that it is only that. Mordecai believes that it *might be* precisely for a time (that is, a situation) like the present that Esther has come to the throne. (Note that Mordecai does not regard this surprising coincidence as proof of divine guidance.) He raises the possibility that even before events began sliding toward disaster, some force was preparing the way for deliverance. This notion is teleological and thus assumes the working of some hidden guidance of history beyond human powers. This is not stated as a confident religious affirmation but as a possibility proffered with a hesitancy uncharacteristic of Mordecai. He is confident that the Jewish people will survive but uncertain about how this will come to pass.

The providence that Esther's rise to queenship might show is vaguer than a divine determination of specific occurrences. Mordecai says "for a time like this," not "for this time." He does not view the current situation as unique. There are many "times" like the one they now find themselves in. If providence lies behind Esther's rise to prominence, that does not mean that she was providentially predestined for this particular situation. Rather, she has— perhaps—been placed in her position to meet exigencies "such as this" as they arise. A Jew does not have a fixed destiny so much as an individual opportunity to which he or she can choose to respond. In the same vein, one might believe, for example, that it might have been providential that an eloquent Zionist, Chaim Weizman, happened to be both a talented chemist and working in Manchester during World War I, for these circumstances allowed him access to Lloyd George and David Balfour, just at the moment when Britain was seeking to keep the French out of Palestine as well as ingratiate itself with American Jews—an impressive list of coincidences. Yet such an assertion does not require that God made Weizman a chemist and showed him how to synthesize acetone for explosives so that he could prepare the ground for the Balfour Declaration.

Haman's wife and associates share Mordecai's belief that the Jews are certain to prevail in their historical struggles. They tell him: "If Mordecai, before whom you have begun to fall, really is of the Jewish race, you will not overcome him, but will undoubtedly fall before him" (6:13). They imply that there is something deep in history, some law, natural or divine, that makes Jewish victory unstoppable, at least once it is underway. They see Haman's recent disgrace not as a cause but as a sign of his approaching downfall. There is a logic in history beyond natural causality, and this allows the wise (as Haman's friends are called) to discern the direction history is moving in. Yet awareness of this logic does not require or lead to a particular theology.

B. WHERE IS GOD? In all this, God is not spoken of or heard from. Is he absent or present? The matter cannot be decided. This indeterminacy is not due simply to inadequate information. Less information would have made the book more determinate— unequivocally secular. Nor is it due to a lack of interest on the part of the author. The way he approaches the issue and then veers aside is too deliberate to indicate indifference. Nor does the uncertainty derive from some ineluctable slipperiness inherent in language; on most issues of importance the text is quite univocal, and in this matter ambiguity could have been banished by one word. Rather, the author is carefully creating and maintaining uncertainty.[23] That is why he hints at God's role, but only obliquely, and mentions religious practices yet avoids setting them in a religious context. The author must be aware that readers will be expecting a statement that the Jews fasted and cried out *to God* (as we must imagine them doing), or a declaration of faith that deliverance is from the Lord (from whom else?), or a report that the Jews gave thanks to God after their victory (what else would they do?), or an exhortation to thank God in future Purim celebrations (as Jews have in fact always done). The frustration of these expectations must be purposive. The Scroll's religious attitude is like an optical illusion that shifts orientation as you stare at it, but which (to continue the analogy) can temporarily be fixed in a certain orientation by the viewer's decision to see it one way or the other.

God in Esther is indeed "veiled," as the popular metaphor puts it, but the veil is not stripped away by the few well-noticed hints. On the contrary, the hints *are* the veil, not a hand that strips it away.

---

23. Thus I am not attempting a deconstruction, but rather finding the determinacy on another level. The indeterminacy I have described is (I am claiming) the author's intention.

A veil suggests that there is something behind it and invites us to peer through. But when we look through this one, we do not see the sturdy old faith that so many readers assume *must* be back there somewhere. We see a light, but it shimmers.

This carefully crafted indeterminacy is best explained as an attempt to convey uncertainty about God's role in history. The author is not quite certain about God's role in these events (are *you?*) and does not conceal that uncertainty.[24] By refusing to exclude either possibility, the author conveys his belief that there can be no definitive knowledge of the workings of God's hand in history. Not even a wonderful deliverance can prove that God was directing events; nor could threat and disaster prove his absence. The story's indeterminacy conveys the message that the Jews should not lose faith if they, too, are uncertain about where God is in a crisis. Israel will survive—that is the author's faith—but how this will happen he does not know. Events are ambiguous, and God's activity cannot be directly read out of them; yet they are not random.

There is a tendency to equate religious uncertainty with a stance of skepticism and to view doubt as a willed repudiation of belief. But the question "who knows?" does not foreclose options; it may express an attitude of faith as well as doubt. If anything is excluded it is disbelief. The author of Esther wishes us to hold to faith even when lacking certitude and an understanding of details. To act in such circumstances demands special courage, but the demand is not a rare one. Many people are called upon to act on a faith that is hope more than conviction.

When we scrutinize the text of Esther for traces of God's activity, we are doing what the author made us do. The author would have us probe the events we witness in our own lives in the same way. He is teaching a theology of possibility. The willingness to face history with an openness to the possibility of providence—even when history seems to weigh against its likelihood, as it did in the dark days after the issuance of Haman's decree—this is a stance of profound faith. It is the willingness of the Jew to bear the responsibility that a fickle history lays on his or her shoulders, uncertain of the future yet confident that somehow *neṣaḥ yiśra'el lo' yᵉšaqqer*.

---

24. Using Lasine's typology of indeterminacy (1986:51–56), this is an "epistemological indeterminacy" rather than an "ontological indeterminacy" attributed to God's character. See that article for a valuable clarification of this difficult topic.

CHAPTER XIII

THE WORLD

Every story creates a world of its own. In order to narrate events of a certain sort and describe people in a certain way, an author must imagine a world where such events can occur and where such people can exist and behave as they do; and a part of this world is communicated to the reader. The Scroll too, short as it is, reveals a worldview. Of course, all that I have described so far belongs to the Scroll's portrayal of the world. But in this chapter I will move to a higher level of abstraction and inquire into the book's fundamental conception of what the world is like and how it operates.

The worldviews that authors project into their stories need not be images of their own worlds, but it is fair to assume that Esther's world is meant in some way to reflect life. The recognition that the book's intrinsic genre is history (chap. IV §5) implies that the author is making a statement about the world as he knows it. The picture he gives of the world is not necessarily meant as a "true-to-life," naturalistic replica, but it is at least a schematic or typical representation of the world as the author sees it or wishes it to be seen.

1. Society

The opening scene introduces us to the social setting in which the drama will work itself out. This is identified with the Persian empire which, for the purposes of this story, is the entirety of the known world.

We see a society bound to an unwritten, traditional constitution (called "law"). This society is ruled by a legal order; it is not an anarchy or a brute clash of powers. Whatever game is to be played in this tale will be governed by some strict rules, but these allow considerable room for maneuver and do not determine the outcome.

The empire itself is subject to, if not exactly run by, a spoiled and egocentric—though not malign—despot, whose power stands at the disposal of whoever can exploit his malleability, moral flaccidity, demonstrative generosity, and unsteady temperament. In his denseness, erraticism, and rigidity, he epitomizes his empire. His noblemen are obsessed with status, yet advocate laws that are far from dignified; they are devoted to law, yet show no awareness of justice. Such a world is not inherently pernicious—it is not the hellish exile envisioned in prophetic threats and covenantal curses— but it is fertile ground for terrifying evils.

The social order is precarious, threatened by anxieties and discords. Yet at the start, society is in a sort of stasis, a state of repose celebrated in and symbolized by the king's banquets. The first conflict that breaks out is trite and silly, but it is portentous. Vashti's defiance of the rules disturbs stability, but the stasis, such as it is, is restored—at least to the satisfaction of those who felt disturbed. But soon it is overturned when the vizier exploits the rules in an attempt to extirpate one of the peoples of the empire. Susa itself is thrown into consternation (3:15).

Haman's plot brings to light the most sinister face of this society, one that will not be fundamentally altered by the resolution of this particular crisis. The rule of gentile law does not guarantee security or justice. The Scroll shows Jewish life in the diaspora to be "fraught with anxiety."[1] In spite of the empire's constitutional rigidity, one of its peoples can be destroyed at the whim of an individual, a man who speaks of law but makes decisions on the basis of crude utility—the notion that something is or is not "worth his while."

At the end, the world will return to stasis, but one of a different sort. This will be expressed, as at the opening, with feasts, good will, and at least temporary safety—in a word, "respite." But this is only a moment of repose in a worrisome world. This world is both amusing and frightening; for the Jews it holds both danger and hope. It is no paradise, but it will have to do.

2. History and Freedom

Is the course of events determined or free? The Scroll assumes that it is both.

---

1. Greenstein 1987:235. Greenstein sees the function of the holiday as psychic release. It gives vent to repressed tensions through humor and fantasy, allowing Jews to imagine a reversal that puts them on top of their enemies (pp. 235–39).

On the one hand, the story's dramatic tension requires and presumes the contingency of events, meaning that events are conditional only upon prior decisions, actions and occurrences, rather than being prearranged by some greater force. In other words, it really was possible for the Jews to be destroyed. The message of individual responsibility requires contingency: the decisions individuals make are important to history, not only to their own souls. The narrative dynamics assumes the significance of human choice.

On the other hand, history *is* guided; events are channeled in certain directions, and certain possibilities are foreclosed. It never really was possible that the Jews would be destroyed. This is made clear at the two points where the book offers a general statement about history. First, Mordecai asserts that the existence of the Jewish people is somehow ultimately guaranteed when he insists that "relief and deliverance will arise for the Jews from another source" (4:14). Later, Haman's wife and "wise men" confirm this principle: "If Mordecai, before whom you have begun to fall, really is of the Jewish race, you will not overcome him, but will undoubtedly fall before him" (6:13). Of course, this is stated as opinion, not fact, but wise people on both sides agree. Patterns exist in events independently of their causal interrelations. If history were only the sequence of act and consequence, Haman's associates could not have predicted his fall, for nothing has happened as yet in 6:13 to undermine his scheme. The decree still stands, as does the stake they told him to erect. They do not regard Haman's recent humiliation as the cause of his further decline, but rather as a sign of it. It is Mordecai's identity, his Jewishness, that guarantees the Jew's victory. Somehow, Jewishness is a decisive factor in the course of history; but neither Mordecai nor Haman's people say how, or through whom, this factor works. It seems to be an absolute principle, independent not only of individual decisions but even of the moral condition of Jewry. Jewish existence was truly in danger, yet Jewish victory somehow was, and always will be, written into the script.

In the competition between human efficacy and external control, the former usually gives way. Humans, we learn, may believe that their deeds and decisions determine the future, but this is an illusion. Individuals are free to choose their way, but whatever they do, the outcome is preordained. As in the Joseph story and the Davidic succession narrative, free human choices somehow issue in a conclusion scripted in advance. Joseph informs his brothers of this: "You planned evil against me, but God planned it for the best, so as to achieve, as is now the case, the preservation of many people" (50:20). The book of Esther does not draw this conclusion explicitly, but simply lets the contradiction stand.

3. Order

Even apart from the predetermination of the outcome, history is orderly. (The two factors are independent; we can imagine a story in which a swirl of random episodes is resolved in a preordained conclusion. This does not happen in Esther.) History consists in a sequence of paired and balanced oppositions rather than in a miscellaneous collection of coincidences. This order—progression through reversal—is the principle of peripety. Of course, ironic tit-for-tat reversals are extremely common in literature and do not in themselves constitute a statement about the world order. In Esther, however, this theme is built into a prominent structure, the thesis-antithesis series discussed in chapter V §4. The force of evil is shown turning back on itself by events issuing in their polar opposites. The opposition is usually reinforced by the use of the same phraseology in both the thesis and its antithesis.

Aristotle (*Poetics* 1452a, 24–26) defines peripety as the circumstance in which an action or state of affairs intended or expected to produce a certain result yields the opposite one. Though he regards peripety as an essential component of tragedy, it is not limited to that genre. If the reversal is in the direction of happiness, peripety is comic. Peripety in all cases is ironic. It is ironic that man's best laid plans can produce the opposite of their intended goal. When our sympathies are with the planner, peripety means tragic irony, as we watch the attempts to control one's destiny flounder. When the planner is an object of antipathy, the irony is comic, and we draw a sense of security from the force of benign justice at work in the world. But that sense of security is mixed with an awareness of the inability of human faculties to control the course of events.

History presents a series of either-or possibilities: either the option represented in the thesis will win, or the one represented in the antithesis will. Thematically this means that Haman's plan to destroy the Jews, once it is set in motion, will either achieve its goal or rebound against its initiator. It will not, say, eventuate only in harm to some Jews or be defused in a compromise or stalemate. Peripety restores balance. The theses are overturned and issue

251

in their opposites, the antitheses. The world returns to stasis, to *mᵉnuḥah*—rest or respite. This is, of course, a fragile stasis: danger issues in salvation, but, by the same token, new peril can appear anywhere at any moment.

The world of the book of Esther is a tidy one. The neat structures, especially the pattern of reversals, help give its history a geometrical balance. The world is tidy also in the neatness of the villainy and the virtue. Unlike Israel in the main historical books and in prophecy, Israel in Esther has done nothing to bring upon itself threat, let alone disaster. Evil is balanced by good, plot by counter-plot, attack by victory. Such idealization is foreign to biblical historiography. The idealized view of history makes the story a pattern for all times. This is not only the way things once happened; this is the way they *must* happen.

Ben Sira (Ecclesiasticus) holds a similar concept of balance, which he extends to the cosmos as a whole. He states that the world was created in antinomies: good opposite evil, life opposite death, the good man opposite the wicked man, light opposite darkness (33 [36]:14). The antinomies create harmony in the universe: "Look at all the works of God: they are all in twos, one opposite the other" (33 [36]:15).

Justice through peripety is an important theme elsewhere in the Bible too, especially in Wisdom Literature and Psalms. Some Psalms use it in extolling God's vindictive power and expressing faith in his salvation. In Ps 7:11–14, for example, the psalmist declares that God is a righteous judge who punishes the wicked. This is the judgment:

> 15.   He [the enemy] is in labor with iniquity;
>   pregnant with evil, he gives birth to lies.
> 16.   He digs a pit and excavates it—
>   and falls into the hole he made.

God's judgment here comes about by peripety. Verse 17 explains the image:

> His wicked labor recoils upon his own head.
> his violence falls upon his own skull.

The punishment is here described neutrally, as the natural consequence of the wicked acts. But the psalmist recognizes it as divine judgment, not just fortunate chance. Therefore he praises God for his righteousness (v. 18). For other examples of justice as peripety see Ps 35:7–9; 37:14–15; 54:6–7; 57:7; 141:9–10; Prov 1:16–19; 24:12; Job 5:13; Jer 30:16; Isa 14:2b; Ezek 17:24.

Though God's justice may manifest itself as peripety, the Bible does not use peripety in itself as evidence of divine intervention (chap. XII §2c). In Esther, there is no attempt to muster peripety as evidence for anything beyond itself. The cause and purpose of peripety, like God's presence itself, remain indeterminate.

In Esther's world, God's reality shimmers on the boundary between absence and presence, just behind the screen of phenomena. The story shows an order in events apart from simple contingency but gives no explanation for it. The reader must supply the explanation, if any. We strain to make out the force guiding and structuring events, and it may be God, but the author will not give us certainty. God's rule is, at best, imperfectly evidenced in ambiguous events. Yet history is not chaotic; the world somehow makes sense. Mordecai's faith and Esther's courage *are* justified, dramatically if not theologically. We can be confident enough to laugh.

The book's incongruous humor is one of its strange hallmarks. It mixes laughter with fear in telling about a near-tragedy that is chillingly reminiscent of actual tragedies. We laugh at the confused sexual politicians, the quirky emperor, and, above all, the ludicrous, self-glorifying, self-destructive villain. This is almost literally gallows humor, except that the gallows are finally used on the hangman.

Humor, especially the humor of ridicule, is a device for defusing fear. The author teaches us to make fun of the very forces that once threatened—and will again threaten—our existence, and thereby makes us recognize their triviality as well as their power. "If I laugh at any mortal thing," said Byron, "t'is that I may not weep."[2] Jews have learned that kind of laughter. The book of Esther begins a tradition of Jewish humor.

---

2. Don Juan IV, 4.

CHAPTER XIV

THREE BOOKS OF ESTHER

Like most of the Bible, the book of Esther did not appear out of nowhere, born full-grown in its present Massoretic form; nor did its growth stop with that form. There were earlier versions and later retellings. In the case of Esther we have not only some of the ancient retellings—notably the Septuagint (LXX), Josephus' paraphrase,[1] Targum Sheni (Tar[2]) Aramaic, and the Old Latin (translated from a Greek version)—but also a version that, according to a view that I share, is earlier than or at least independent of the MT. This is the proto-AT, the earliest layer of the Greek Alpha Text (AT). The existence of different versions allows us to trace the growth of the book of Esther and to observe the changes that the characters and ideology underwent in the course of retelling.

1. Three Versions of Esther

This chapter will focus on three versions, the MT, the LXX, and the AT, or more precisely, the proto–AT, the earliest layer traceable in the AT. Targum Sheni comes from a much later period and is too paraphrastic to be a useful object of comparison of the sort undertaken here. The text of the Old Latin is not easily available, and its own history involves considerable historical problems.

My discussion in this chapter largely assumes the conclusions of my monograph, *The Redaction of the Books of Esther* (1990), which should be consulted for full argumentation. My conclusions about

---

1. The ideological thrusts of Josephus' adaptation of the Esther story are detailed by L. Feldman (1970). Josephus emphasizes various features in order to give the story more of the qualities of a Hellenistic novella, including the protagonists' royal origins, female beauty, eroticism, and irony. Josephus tries also to bring out the best in Xerxes, making him into a man of probity, thoughtfulness, and substance, and a true friend of the Jews. Josephus makes several modifications to combat charges of Jewish separatism and hostility toward gentiles, most notably omitting Additions A and F, which present the conflict as a universal one between Jews and gentiles. In general, Josephus seeks to make the book of Esther more attractive to gentile readers and to counteract antisemitic propaganda.

the AT draw on and modify hypotheses put forth by C. C. Torrey (1944:5–21), C. A. Moore (1967), and especially D. J. A. Clines (pp. 85–92).

The following diagram shows my understanding of the development of the Esther story, to be discussed below. "R–AT" refers to the redactor who expanded the proto–AT into the current AT by borrowing material from the LXX; "R–MT" refers to the redactor who produced the current MT from an earlier Esther story; "proto–Esther" is the conjectural ancestor of the extant Esther stories; the "Additions" are the six Additions found in the LXX (described below in §4a).

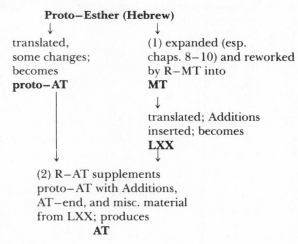

Proto–Esther (Hebrew)

↓   ↓

translated,   (1) expanded (esp.
some changes;   chaps. 8–10) and reworked
becomes   by R–MT into
proto–AT   **MT**

↓

translated; Additions
inserted; becomes
LXX

(2) R–AT supplements
proto–AT with Additions,
AT–end, and misc. material
from LXX; produces
AT

2. The Proto–AT

a. The Recovery of the Proto–AT

The proto–AT is the original form of the AT, which was heavily supplemented by later borrowings from the LXX. Recovery of the proto–AT is a matter of identifying and removing those borrowings.

The AT is preserved in five Greek MSS dating from the tenth to thirteenth centuries C.E.[2] It tells basically the same story as the MT, but in wording and many details it differs considerably from it

---

2. MSS 19, 93, 108, 319, and 392, all from the tenth-thirteenth centuries (see Hanhart, 1983:15–16). The text is available in the Göttingen Septuagint (ed. Hanhart) and the Cambridge Septuagint (ed. Brooke and McLean). For a full translation (together with the Cambridge text) see Clines, pp. 215–47.

as well as from the main Greek version, the LXX, of which it was generally assumed to be a revision.[3] Here are two samples:

(a) LXX 6:6
(6) The king said to Haman, "What shall I do for the man whom I wish to honor?" And Haman said to himself, "Whom can the king wish to honor if not me?"

AT vii 9–10
(9) When he [Haman] entered, the king said to him, "What shall we do to the man who fears the king, whom the king wishes to honor?" (10) And Haman thought, "Whom does the king wish to honor if not me?"

(b) LXX 6:11
(13) Haman took the cloak and the horse, and cloaked Mordecai, and put him on the horse, and led [him] through the squares of the city and cried out, saying, "Thus shall it be to every man whom the king wishes to honor."

AT vii 13–19
(13) When Haman realized that not he, but rather Mordecai, was the one to be honored, his heart was greatly crushed, and his spirit fell into faintness. (14) And Haman took the cloak and the horse, showing respect to Mordecai, whereas he had decided to impale him on that very day! (15) And he said to Mordecai, "Remove the sackcloth." (16) And Mordecai was very agitated, like one dying, and he removed the sackcloth in distress and put on the garments of honor. (17) And Mordecai thought he had seen a sign, and his heart was toward the

---

The AT has its own numbering system, sometimes diverging considerably from the LXX's numeration (which, for its part, is almost identical to the MT's). To distinguish it from the MT numeration (with is used in the LXX, except in the Additions), the chapters in the AT are designated by lower-case roman numerals.

3. In particular, part of a revision carried out by Lucian, the third-fourth century presbyter from Antioch. Moore (1965:133–39; 1967:352–53) disproved this assumption.

Lord, and he was astonished
in speechlessness. (18) And
Haman hurried to put him on
the horse. (19) And Haman
led the horse out and brought
him out, crying, "Thus shall
be done to the man whom the
king wishes to honor!"

In a few sections, the AT follows the LXX almost word for word.
The following passage is from Esther's prayer (Addition C):

(c) LXX C 5–7
(5) You know everything. You
know, O Lord, that I did this
neither in arrogance nor in
haughtiness nor in love of
honor—not bowing to the
haughty Haman—(6) for I
would have been pleased to
kiss the soles of his feet for the
salvation of Israel—(7) but I
did this so that I might not set
the honor of man over the
honor of God.

AT V 14–15
(14) For you know everything,
and you know the race of Israel, (15) and [you know] that
I acted neither in arrogance
nor in love of honor—not
bowing to the uncircumcised
Haman—since I would have
been pleased to kiss the soles
of his feet for the sake of Israel—but I acted so as not to
set anyone before you, O
Master!

There are thus two very different types of material in the AT: sections with precise LXX parallels, such as (c) above, and sections that
differ to a greater or lesser degree from the LXX, such as passages
(a) and (b).[4] This is to be explained by the hypothesis that an editor
(R-AT) has patched parts of the LXX into the AT. The reason for
this editing is easy to imagine: a scribe copying the AT realized that
it lacked some important material present in the LXX, and so he
filled out the gaps with supplements from the LXX. The LXX borrowings are the six Additions (see below on the LXX, §4a), a sec-

---

4. In the sections where AT is close to the LXX, an average of 75% of the words of
the AT have matches in the LXX, and 62% of the words in the corresponding
LXX passages are represented in the AT. In the other parts of the book, an
average of only 35% of the words in the AT have matches in the LXX, and
just 21% of the words in the LXX parallels appear in the AT. There is thus a
gap, not a continuum, between the two types of passages. For further statis-
tical and textual arguments for distinguishing the two stages of development
in the AT, see Fox 1991:I §2.

ondary ending corresponding approximately to MT 8:17–10:3 (viii 39–51), and a few other verses.[5]

The proto-AT is—as can be demonstrated by an examination of its Greek syntax—a translation of a Hebrew text.[6] That Hebrew text was not dependent on the MT. No Jewish editor[7] would have taken the MT and reshaped it into a tale such as the proto-AT, omitting these essentials:

(a) the assumption of the inalterability of Persian law;

(b) the expansion of the battle reports;

(c) the second day of fighting and celebration;

(d) the Purim etiology;

(e) the epilogue in 10:1–3.

The Purim instructions above all would never have been omitted by a Jew for whom the MT was authoritative and the festival of Purim a fact and obligation. All the above elements were added by the editor-author of the MT to an earlier version of the story that lacked them. Further evidence that the proto-AT is not a reworking of MT-Esther is that it has only a few scattered references to God and no moralizing or homiletical additions. A retelling (i.e., a midrash) of MT-Esther would surely have added moralistic messages and significant religious statements of the sort that we find in later retellings such as the LXX, rabbinical midrash, and Targum Sheni.

---

5. Namely AT ii 1a = LXX 1:1a; AT ii 6–8 = LXX 1:6–8; AT iv 9b-11-10a [AT transposes verse order] = LXX 3:9b-11; AT v 4b-5 = LXX 4:8b (missing in MT); AT iv 2 = 3:2; AT v 9bβ (starting with *su*)-10 = 4:14b; AT vi 13–18 = LXX 5:3–8; AT vi 21aβ = LXX 5:10bβ; AT vii 1 = LXX 6:1a.

6. The main argument for the Hebrew origin of the proto-AT uses Raymond Martin's method of syntax analysis (1974, cf. 1975), which provides a way to determine whether a text was composed in Greek or is a translation from a Semitic language (Hebrew or Aramaic). Examining various texts of known origin, Martin looked at seventeen syntactical features and found a sharp difference in the patterns of their distribution in "original-Greek" and "translation-Greek" texts. Application of Martin's criteria (Fox 1991:I §2.10) shows not only that the proto-AT is a translation, but that it is a literal one, preserving Hebrew features that the LXX lacks.
   There are a few additional arguments for a Hebrew base text. For example, the AT's *ektrephōn pistōs*, "raised her faithfully" (iii 7 = MT 2:7), can only be an etymological rendering of Hebrew *ʾōmēn* (the root *ʾMN* also means "be constant, faithful"). The AT rendering is not derived from the LXX's *en toutō pais threptē* (2:7). AT's rendering of this phrase also shows that its base text was in Hebrew rather than Aramaic, since Aramaic would use a form of the root *RBY*, not *ʾMN*, for "raising."

7. Since the creator of the proto-AT was working in Hebrew, he must have been Jewish. Also, there is no suggestion of christology in the AT—proto or final.

Since the proto-AT is not derived from the MT, it represents either a prior version of the Esther story—an "ancestor" of the MT—or (to be safe) a collateral version, a "cousin." To explain the considerable similarities between the two versions, we must posit an earlier Esther story, to be designated "proto-Esther," behind them both. (Calling the proto-AT a collateral version recognizes that there may have been developments between proto-Esther and the proto-AT as well as between the proto-Esther and the MT; but in fact the proto-AT may have been very close to the source R-MT used.) Proto-Esther may have differed from the proto-AT, but it probably lacked the five items mentioned above, as well as a few minor statements and motifs absent in the proto-AT (though these might be proto-AT omissions from an earlier version). In summary, the proto-AT is a different and independent version of the Esther story and is of interest in its own right as well as for its value in tracing the development of the MT.

B. SYNOPSIS. The outline of the story in the proto—AT is close to that of the MT up to 8:3, the transfer of Haman's power and wealth. The story begins with the two banquets and Vashti's refusal. The advisers explicitly call for a woman who will be seen to be obedient (chap. ii). Then the king *ceases* to remember Vashti and proceeds to find a new queen. Mordecai and Esther are introduced, and Esther—without undergoing the elaborate cosmetic treatment—is chosen (chap. iii). There is no mention of Mordecai's discovery of the eunuchs' plot corresponding to MT 2:22–23.[8] As in the MT, Mordecai angers Haman by refusing to prostrate himself, and Haman determines to destroy the Jews. In addition to the arguments he raises in the MT, Haman tells the king that all peoples consider the unnamed people wicked, and that they disregard the king's laws so as to destroy his glory (iv 8). The king allows him to issue an edict of destruction (chap. iv). When Mordecai learns what has happened, he contacts Esther and, in a brief exchange, convinces her to approach the king and "charm him on behalf of me and the people" (v 4a). He continues: "'Therefore, after calling upon God, speak on our behalf to the king and deliver us from death.' And he informed her of the misery of Israel" (v 5–6). When she hesitates he tells her that if she fails to help her people, "God will be a help and salvation for them, but you and your father's house will perish;

---

8. It appears in the present AT in i 12–16, a passage derived from the LXX (Add A).

and who knows if it was not for this very moment that you came to royal station" (v 9–10). Esther then resolves to do her duty and calls a public fast (chap. v).

The story proceeds, much as in the MT, with Esther's first audience, her first banquet, Zeresh's advice to Haman (chap. vi), then the king's insomnia, Haman's humiliation, and Mordecai's exaltation (chap. vii). One notable difference is Mordecai's fear when Haman approaches him to do the honors (quoted above in passage (b)).[9] At the second banquet, "Esther was in anxiety when she replied, for the opponent was before her eyes, but God gave her courage when she called upon him" (viii 2). She states that she and her people have been sold to destruction. The king is angry and says, "Who is this who dared to humiliate the sign of my reign, so as to violate fear of you?" (viii 5). Esther—otherwise than in the MT—is very afraid and says to the king, "Do not be angry, my lord, for it is enough that I have received your mercy. Enjoy yourself, O king, and tomorrow I will do what you have said" (viii 6b). The king, however, insists that she reveal the villain's name on the spot and promises to do what she wishes. She names Haman, whereupon the king leaves the room. When he returns, he finds Haman on Esther's couch and, at the urging of a eunuch (called Agathas), condemns him to hang on the stake he erected for Mordecai (chap. viii).

The proto-AT resolves the crisis quite differently from the MT:

> And the king summoned Mordecai, and he bestowed on him all that was Haman's. And he said to him, "What do you want—I shall do it for you." And Mordecai said, "That you annul the letter of Haman." And the king put into his hands the affairs of the kingdom. (viii 15–17)

Since the proto–AT does not presuppose the unalterability of Persian law, Mordecai's appointment as vizier solves the problem. But there still remain enemies to be punished:

> Next Esther said to the king, "Permit me to punish my enemies by death. And Queen Esther took counsel with the king also against the sons of Haman, that they too might die with their father. And the king said, "So be it." And she[10] smote the enemies *en masse*. In Susa the king came to an agreement with the queen that [the] men would

---

9. The midrash, too, pictures Mordecai as fearful upon Haman's approach (Est. Rab. X 4 = b. Meg. 16a). But it handles the motif quite differently and is not necessarily dependent on the AT tradition.
10. Possibly "he", i.e., the king; the Greek is indeterminate.

be killed, and he said, "Behold, I permit you to hang [them]." And so it happened. (viii 18–21)

The proto–AT concludes with a decree issued by Mordecai informing everybody what had happened and telling the Jews to celebrate in their towns:

> And a decree concerning these matters was issued in Susa, and the king empowered Mordecai to write whatever he wished. And Mordecai sent word via letters, which he had sealed with the king's ring, to the effect that his people should remain each in his own place and hold celebration unto God. And the epistle that Mordecai sent contained the following: "Haman sent you letters saying thus: 'Make haste swiftly to send the disobedient Jewish People to destruction for me.' But I Mordecai inform you that the one who did these things has been hanged before the gates of Susa and his household has been executed, for he sought to kill us on the thirteenth day of the month, which is Adar." (viii 33–38)

c. Character and Ideology in the Proto-AT

The proto-AT is a salvation tale: two Jews clash with a wicked enemy and defeat him. The characters of Mordecai and Haman are very close to what they are in the MT. Esther, however, is different. She is not so courageous or clever as in the MT. She is tremulous when facing the enemy (viii 2), and she almost flinches in fear at the crucial moment of revelation (viii 6). As soon as Mordecai is called in, she disappears, except to ask the king to punish her enemies.

The tale lacks divine intervention and is not strongly religious. There are a few references to God, which were perhaps original but might have been added to the proto-AT by later hands. Even if we accept them as original to the proto-AT,[11] God is given at most a supporting role in the deliverance. The most telling verse is the one which most directly implicates God in the course of events, when Mordecai tells Esther: "If you neglect your people, not helping them, God will be a help and salvation for them, but you and your father's house will perish" (v 9). In this view, God serves as a back-up to human help, entering history only if humans fail. Esther is not perceived as the agent of God's salvation, but as an alternative to it. God is in the background, ultimately guaranteeing Israel's

---

11. As Clines argues (pp. 107–12).

preservation, but also demanding that individual Jews meet their responsibility in the moment of crisis. God will punish those who falter in this mission.

The proto-AT assumes that it is a Jewish duty to respond to national danger and explores human potential to do so. The solution it offers is Jewish influence. Jews become influential by being of value to the crown, through both loyal service and personal attractiveness to the king. Dangers are localized and solutions are specific. The power of the state is essentially reliable. Though it may be deflected from its proper course by lies and deceit, the state possesses the mechanisms to correct itself. The practical problem is how to reach the king, the guarantor of stability who stands at the source of power, for he can then be expected to restore the endangered order.

In the proto-AT, deliverance is implemented by two highly placed individuals alone, with no participation of the people at-large, who are informed of the events when they have passed. There are no battles between the Jews and their enemies. The enemies are "punished by slaughter" *after* the crisis is past. This slaughter seems to be carried out not by the Jews, since they are informed of it only later, but by royal troops following the direct orders from the queen—or the king (the Greek in viii 20 is ambiguous).

The survival of the Jewish people thus depends on a few individuals: their enemies, their friends, and above all their leaders. Salvation is invested in individuals who arise spontaneously to meet the crisis. Victory emerges as the heroes' courage, cleverness, and influence are reinforced by the enemy's stupidity. The Jewish people, other than the protagonists, are spectators to the working-out of their fate. Beforehand they bewail the danger; afterwards they learn about the miracle and—upon instructions from their chief—rejoice in it.

3. The Massoretic Text

a. The Formation of the MT

The MT editor (whom we can also call an author, since he made significant changes) added the five items mentioned above as absent from proto-Esther; to repeat:

(a) the assumption of the inalterability of Persian law;

(b) the expansion of the battle reports;

(c) the second day of fighting and celebration;

(d) the Purim etiology;

(e) the epilogue in 10:1–3.

These are not independent motifs, but are interwoven and inter-dependent. Instead of having the crisis resolved by the appointment of Mordecai, the new theme of immutable Persian law necessitates Mordecai's counter-decree and the battles of Adar. Instead of punitive slaughters (carried out by the grace of the king), the MT has two days of battles in which the Jews must make a stand for their lives. Instead of having Mordecai instruct the Jews to celebrate their victory, the MT has an elaborate dialectical process institutionalizing the annual holiday of Purim.[12]

Other likely MT innovations are the expansive treatment of the beauty regime in 2:12–15 and the eunuchs' plot in 2:21–23. There are numerous variations in wording, but we cannot know which of them were introduced by R-MT.

b. Character and Ideology in the MT

Since the MT has been the topic of the present book, my conclusions need not be repeated. Here I will briefly consider some of the implications specifically of the modifications that the MT editor introduced in his source. I should first observe that if my theory about the internal history of the MT is correct, the "author" I have been referring to so far is really a construct of two writers: the author of proto-Esther, responsible for at least the basic plot of

---

12. Critical commentators of the nineteenth and twentieth centuries have commonly assigned 9:20–10:3, or parts thereof, to a later stage in the book's development. The argument is based on the preception of incongruities and contradictions between that unit and the rest of the book (see Paton p. 57). If this is correct, the Esther story was not originally the etiology of Purim.

Paton (pp. 57–60) argues that 9:20–10:1 was earlier than the narrative proper (1:1–9:19) and quoted from the "Chronicles of Persia and Media" mentioned in 10:2. But there is no particular reason for supposing that these chronicles actually existed or that, if they did, they would have reflected much interest in the holiday of Purim.

Bardtke, who holds that the book was composed from three earlier traditions (a Vashti story, a Mordecai story, and an Esther story), ascribes 9:20–10:3 to the author of the present book of Esther (pp. 249–52 and passim). At one point (p. 385), Bardtke speaks vaguely of two sources in the report of the Jews' defense and the institution of the Purim festival. But the sources he describes in his introduction (pp. 249–52) extend only to the end of chap. 8.

chapters 1–8, and the author (or "redactor") of the MT, who turned this plot into the canonical Esther.

R-MT did not expand the religious dimension of the drama. If the references to God in the proto-AT were present in proto-Esther, R-MT pushed God farther into the background.

The alignment of human forces in the MT differs from that of proto-Esther. The state is not inherently a source of moral order, nor the king a reliable corrective to perversions of justice below him. The state does hold the potential for moral order simply by virtue of its power to restrain anarchic desires and behaviors. But R-MT has little confidence in the stability of the state's power. The law is a morally neutral mass that cannot be dislodged but only circumvented, whether for worse (as by Haman) or for better (as by Mordecai and Esther). The law is unchangeable and so, when the need arises, it must be subverted from within.

Mordecai's role is expanded. Not only does he send Esther to the king to ask for the cancellation of Haman's decree, but he must now also devise a stratagem to counteract it, since it cannot simply be annulled. This variation too augments Jewish self-sufficiency.

Esther is given considerably greater stature in the MT. She is less tremulous than in the earlier version, apparently having overcome her worst fears by 4 : 16. (Admittedly, this conclusion assumes that the author of proto-AT did not add expressions of fear to Esther's personality as it was presented in proto-Esther.) Her strategy in defeating Haman seems more carefully wrought in the MT. She is made the first recipient of Haman's property so that she can appoint Mordecai its steward (8 : 1–2)—an innovation explicable only as a deliberate effort to heighten Esther's independence. By the same token, the expansion of the harem-induction scene increases Esther's later independence and toughness by emphasizing her earlier dependency and pliancy. She is also assigned the task of ar-

---

This, as well as his exegesis of chapters 9–10, seems to indicate that he places the composition of the concluding units later than the three individual source narratives but concurrent with the composition of the present narrative.

Meinhold (pp. 12–14) regards 9 : 20–28 and (subsequently) 9 : 29–32 as later insertions, which required certain revisions in 9 : 1–18 and 3 : 7; he considers 9 : 19 a later gloss. He thinks it possible, however, that the author himself inserted some passages in the Esther tale.

Clines regards all of 9 : 1–10 : 3 as a series of supplements, namely the ending (9 : 1–19), Mordecai's letter (9 : 20–28), Esther's letter (9 : 29–32), and the encomium on Mordecai (10 : 1–3).

For a full discussion and a new approach see Fox 1991:II §3.

ranging for the second day of fighting in Susa. This adds to her power but also (unintentionally) to the impression of vindictiveness. But the latter quality is already present in the proto-AT in her request to have her enemies slaughtered (viii 16–21, quoted above, §2b). Most important, she is made the final authority in sealing the Purim agreement.

The responsibility for national deliverance still rests upon individual, well-placed Jews. But Jewish loyalty and personal attractiveness no longer suffice to resolve the crisis, for there is a momentum in events beyond the king's control; he cannot be counted on to ensure the order. By diminishing the role of the king, the Jewish people are made agents of their own deliverance. Individual initiative and gentile cooperation are preliminary to national self-redemption. The principle of immutable Persian law requires the people to save *themselves*. Their active role in salvation prepares the ground, in turn, for the establishment of the holiday through the interplay between leadership and masses.

The most significant of R-MT's innovations is the use of the Esther story as the rationale for the institution of Purim, which was not mentioned in the original Esther story. In the proto-AT, Mordecai enjoined a one-time celebration of the deliverance that has just been accomplished; he does not add a new festival to the calendar. In the MT, Mordecai urges the nation to continue to celebrate its redemption, covenanting itself and its descendants to a perpetual reenactment of its own rejoicing. In the MT (in contrast to the proto-AT, viii 33–38), Mordecai cannot command public celebration but can only advocate it; the people must confirm his proposal in order to make it binding.

4. The Septuagint

a. The Formation of the LXX

The LXX is a translation and expansion of the MT. Where it is a translation, it is an occasionally free rendering but reasonably faithful to the Hebrew text. In six places, however, there are major supplements with no Hebrew parallels: the Additions A-F. These radically alter the literary and ideological character of the version as a whole. The Additions were not written all at once. Additions B and E were undoubtedly composed in Greek, while F probably was; C and D were probably composed in Hebrew or Aramaic, while A is uncertain.[13] B and E were almost certainly written by a single person (who was not the translator of the LXX). F is a commentary on A, which for its part may have been composed independently of the book of Esther.[14] The disparate origins of the Additions means that the LXX did not have a single writer. The LXX's ideology resulted from the contributions of several persons, starting with the translation of the MT and including the supplementation by the Addition in (probably) four stages.

Translations of the Additions can be found in Catholic translations (following the book of Esther proper), in the Jerusalem Bible, and in many translations of the Apocrypha. For a full translation and commentary see Moore 1977. For our purposes, one may think of the LXX as the MT plus the six Additions:

Addition A: Mordecai's Dream (precedes MT chap. 1). Mordecai, a prominent man serving in the court of king *Artaxerxes*, had a dream. There was a great clamor, thunder, and earthquake, as two dragons advanced for battle. At their roaring, every nation prepared for battle against the righteous nation. In alarm, that nation prepared to die and cried out to God. He sent a tiny spring, which grew into a mighty river. There was light, and the humble were exalted and devoured the eminent.

Later, as Mordecai was dozing in the court, he overheard two eunuchs plotting assassination. He informed on them, they were executed, and Mordecai was rewarded. But Haman sought to harm him for what happened to the two eunuchs.

Addition B: The Decree of Destruction (follows 3:13). In elaborate, intricate language imitating Ptolemaic officialese, Artaxerxes declares that he determined always to act with restraint and moderation to ensure peace and tranquility in the kingdom. When he asked his advisers how this could be accomplished, Haman, a

---

13. Martin 1975.
14. See Moore 1977:165–67; Fox 1991:I §1.8.
   Moore (1977:249) points out various incongruities between the dream and the story and makes the case that the dream was originally a separate entity secondarily adapted to the Esther story. Indeed, if read by itself, Add A has little to do with the story. Add F, on the other hand, was written primarily with attention to the body of the Esther story, not to Add A, as is evident from the fact that (as Bardtke, p. 54, observes) the interpretation is structured according to the sequence of the story rather than according to the pattern of the dream. In other words, the author of this Addition is less concerned with explaining the enigmas of the dream than with showing how the story fulfilled its portents.

man of great loyalty, informed him of a hostile and dangerous people threatening the well-being of the empire. Therefore the king commanded that this people be wiped out, on the *fourteenth* day of Adar, so as to secure the peace of the realm.

Addition C: The Prayers of Mordecai and Esther (follows 4:17). After proclaiming the fast, Mordecai prays (C 1–11). He first praises God for his unopposable power and omniscience. He assures God that it was not out of vanity or arrogance that he refused to bow to Haman—"for I would have been willing to kiss the soles of his feet for the sake of Israel's safety"—but rather out of concern for God's honor. He calls upon God to hear his prayer and save Israel, that they may forever praise him.

Then Esther too prays, after changing her luxurious robes for mourning garb (C 12–30). She asks God to help her, for she is alone. She has heard how God chose Israel for his eternal inheritance. Now they have sinned and are given into the power of their enemies, who are not satisfied to enslave them but wish to destroy them. She beseeches God to reveal himself, to make her words persuasive, and to dispose the king kindly toward her. She assures God that she hates the foreigner's bed and despises her crown as if it were "a menstruous rag," and further asserts that she does not eat the heathens' food or drink the wine of their libations. She asks God to harken to her prayer and protect her from what she fears.

Addition D: Esther's Entry to the King's Throne Room (follows Addition C, just before 5:3[15]). Esther now puts on splendid attire, and, leaning on one maidservant while another holds her train, she approaches the throne, her heart pounding. When the king looks up, she faints in fear and awe at the royal splendor. But God makes the king gentle, and he raises her up in his arms, telling her to be at ease, for the prohibition to approach the king applies only to underlings. Esther tells the king that he seemed like an angel of God to her. She collapses again, and the anxious king, with all his courtiers, tries to comfort her.

Addition E: The King's Decree Counteracting the First (follows 8:12). Again in ornate and convoluted language, the king informs the reader that some men are led by excessive honor to become arrogant and to scheme against their benefactors. Moreover, men in authority are often persuaded to become accomplices in the

---

15. MT 5:1–2 are displaced by the Addition's version of the events.

shedding of innocent blood. This is seen both from ancient records and, more significantly, from recent events. He promises not to pay attention to slanderers in the future.

Haman, he says, sought to kill Mordecai, his benefactor, and Esther, his queen, and all their nation. By this device he would have left the king helpless and transferred power to the Macedonians (to which nation Haman is said to belong).[16] The Jews are innocent and governed by just laws; they are sons of the living God whose providence has governed the Persian kingdom in the past and present.

The king therefore orders his people—on pain of death—to allow the Jews to obey their own customs and to support them in their hour of trial, which their God has already decreed to be a time of rejoicing. Moreover, the Persians too are to celebrate the day as a reminder of deliverance as well as of destruction of enemies.

Addition F: The Interpretation of Mordecai's Dream (follows 10:3). Thinking back to his dream, Mordecai realizes that all that it foretold has been fulfilled. He proceeds to interpret its symbols. The tiny stream that became a river was Esther. The two dragons were Mordecai and Haman. The nations were those who gathered to destroy the Jews. His own nation was Israel, who cried out to God and was saved. The Lord has saved his people!

He goes on to say that God made two lots, one for Israel and one for all the other nations, and these marked the appointed time, the day of judgment. God has delivered his people, and so they shall ever celebrate the fourteenth and fifteenth of Adar.

Among the numerous reformulations, omissions, and insertions in the canonical parts of the LXX, there are a few that bear on character or ideology:

> 2:17b. Mordecai took Esther "for a wife" (rather than daughter); see the Appendix.
>
> 2:20. (Mordecai had instructed Esther) "to fear God and do his commandments, just as when she was with him. And Esther did not change her way of life."
>
> 4:8. (Mordecai tells Esther to beseech the king), "remembering your humble days, when you were cared for by me, because Haman, the second to the king, has sentenced us to

---

16. Greeks in the Hellenistic kingdoms of the East were often called Macedonians and were widely resented by the native populations.

death. Call upon the Lord and speak to the king about us and save us from death."

6:1a. "The Lord removed sleep from the king that night."

6:13b. (Haman cannot withstand Mordecai) "because the living God is with him."

8:11. The king's decree instructs the Jews to act according to their own laws and to help themselves. . . ."

8:13. The Jews "fight against" their enemies rather than "take vengeance on" them.

9:5. Omitted, perhaps because of its vindictiveness.

10:3a. A misunderstanding of *mišneh* ("second to") as (apparently) *meʾšanneh*, produced the strange statement, "And Mordecai succeeded [*diedechato*] King Artaxerxes."[17]

b. Character and Ideology in the LXX[18]

Clines has observed that the effect of the Additions is "to *assimilate the book of Esther to a scriptural norm*," especially as found in the "Persian histories" of Ezra, Nehemiah, and Daniel (p. 169). Like Ezra and Nehemiah, the Additions have God intervening at only a few critical moments in history. They also make explicit reference to the religious activities of the principals, particularly prayer. These prayers strengthen the tale's exemplary function. Mordecai's dream makes the book conform to the precedent of Daniel, where the meaning of history is conveyed through dreams and interpretation. The dream shows God as "an all-seeing designer of history who has already determined the salvation of the Jews," and it shifts the focus to the level of cosmic conflict (p. 172). The addition of the decrees in B and E creates a greater correspondence to the biblical "Persian" books, including Chronicles. The purpose of quotation of Persian documents is not to add an air of authenticity but to serve as "testimony to the impact of the truth of the Jewish religion upon outsiders, neighbors and overlords" (p. 173).

---

17. There are several changes in chapter 9 that do not seem to change the basic facts and ideas—notably a recasting of 9:5, the addition of a sentence after 9:19 (to the effect that the Jews in the large cities also celebrate the 15th of Adar), and the omission of MT 9:30.

18. The following remarks are largely true of the present AT as well, since its ideology is dominated by the Additions transferred from the LXX.

While affirming the validity and importance of Clines' insights, I would give more emphasis to the impact of the introduction of religious themes (which Clines insists are already implicit in the MT) upon the images of God, history, and man conveyed by the LXX.

I. GOD. The LXX brings to the fore the sacral dimension of the tale, making that the arena in which the true meaning of the crisis and the salvation is to be sought. God controls history.

God sometimes works quietly. It was he, we are told, who gave the king insomnia (6:1a), thereby setting events moving toward Haman's disgrace and Mordecai's honor. Even the heathen recognize explicitly the presence of the "living God" in the midst of Israel (6:13b). More fundamentally, the Additions show that salvation is not actually achieved by humans; *in reality* it is the culmination of a divine program. The drama as it plays itself out in the realm of history is the recapitulation of a conflict between cosmic good and cosmic evil that has already been resolved in a temporal reality outside of time and place. This is a "hyperreality" where archetypal cosmic forces clash, as they always have and always will, until the day of God's final victory and uncontested reign. The secrets of this hyperreality can be communicated to the wise man in symbolic images, given in dreams. In this way, the initiate—the wise man in the world of the text and the reader above it—sees the end given at the beginning, so that the dramatic tension is invested in the details of events, not in their outcome. All that is uncertain is how the hyper-real drama will manifest itself on earth, not how it will end.

II. MAN. Before the event, the wise man may be granted a symbolic preview of the earthly drama that lies ahead (Addition A), and afterwards he can decode the cosmic drama by mapping its terms against earthly events (Addition F). However, unlike most dream interpretations, such as those of Joseph and Daniel, the one in Addition F deciphers events of the past rather than the future. Mordecai did gain some prior insight when he happened upon the eunuchs' plot (i 10–11), but this awareness hardly revealed what events lay in store. These could be linked up with the dream only after they had come to pass, when Mordecai could think back and recognize that all its details had been realized (viii 54). The purpose of the dream interpretation is not to give a message about the future, but *to give meaning to the past* by setting it in the context of a higher reality. The decoding of the dream serves to interpret temporal phenomena, and this interpretation then forms a pattern by which future crises are to be understood.

The individuals facing the crisis must act their part in the drama. They abide by Jewish religious practice. The translator is careful to note that Esther did not become lax when she entered the palace (see 2:20a, quoted above). In her prayer Esther assures God that she has avoided the heathens' libation-wine and has not "honored," that is, participated in, the royal banquets (C 28). The task of the Jewish protagonists demands proper attitude no less than appropriate action. Thus they turn to God in prayer, in which they must justify their motivations and behavior as well as asking for divine help (4:8b; Additions C-D). National existence even at the moment of crisis is not truly in jeopardy, for Israel's deliverance is written into the cosmic script. Thus, as in Daniel 7–12 and in apocalypse generally, the drama of history is meant to test the Jews' faith, not the efficacy of their actions.

While victory is the Lord's doing, human actors are still involved—the same ones as in the MT. But the relative importance of their roles shifts against the backdrop of the cosmic drama.

The king is treated respectfully in the LXX, far more than in the MT and even more so than in the proto-AT. Glory radiates from him as he sits on his throne. He is a kindly husband, aiding and reassuring his timorous wife. Though he was led astray, his soul-searching and political moralizing in Addition E (viii 23–24) demonstrate his basic rectitude and ascribe the near-disaster entirely to excessive trust in his right-hand man. The king had followed Haman's advice because he thought to secure the public order, but once truth is made public he can be counted on to straighten things out.

Mordecai maintains his centrality in the palace intrigue but attains a further level of importance. His role, as symbolized by one of the dragons, is to present himself for battle with the other dragon. Yet the dragons do not actually fight, and so the good dragon cannot be said to win the battle. The crucial point of this engagement is not Mordecai's victory, but his willingness to challenge evil; this is prerequisite to God's intervention. Mordecai takes pains to explain his refusal to bow (C 5–6); Addition A (17) explains Haman's enmity as resentment at Mordecai for his loyal deed of reporting on the eunuchs' scheme and thus bringing about their execution.

Esther too remains central. She is the tiny spring from which issue the mighty waters that punish the powerful. This is an image of power, but as the symbolism shows, Esther is the device of salvation, not its author. The human Esther in the LXX is a much frailer, more stereotypically feminine creature than in the MT. Like a delicate Victorian she gasps and faints in anxiety when approaching her powerful, frightening, yet kindly husband (swooning is a favorite device in Hellenistic romance).[19] She is also a more observant Jew, avoiding heathen contamination where possible and hating it where not.

III. ISRAEL. The true human heroes in LXX-Esther are the people of Israel, for in the cosmic drama it was their outcry that turned the tide against the dragon of wickedness (A 9). Their outcry will be replicated in earthly reality before Esther acts on their behalf (C 11). Israel's strength lies not primarily in inner fortitude—they were resigned to death—and not at all in military courage, but in knowledge of prayer. Salvation rests on faith, the faith of the Jewish people as a whole; the protagonists are merely individuals chosen for particular roles in the drama. In the communal outcry, Israel is acting out a response that Mordecai's dream showed that they would act out and hence *must* act out. This too was determined in advance, outside the visible dimension of human events.

The world is divided into two diametrically opposed groups: Israel ("the nation of the righteous") versus all nations (A 6), who, on the day of battle, gather to join the force of evil in war against Israel.[20] The present LXX has an appreciation for the monarchy as

---

19. The atmosphere of Addition D is strongly redolent of scenes from Hellenistic romance such as the following one from Cheriton:

> So he [Chaereas] crossed the threshold, and when he saw her lying there on the ground with her head covered up, the way she breathed and held herself caused his heart to flutter; he became excited, and would certainly have recognized her had he not been quite convinced that Dionysius had recovered Callirhoe. He approached her gently. "Don't be afraid, lady," he said, "whoever you are—we are not going to violate you. You shall have the husband you want." Before he had finished speaking Callirhoe recognized his voice and uncovered her head. They both cried out at once—"Chaereas!" "Callirhoe!"—and embracing each other they fell to the ground in a faint. (8.1.7–8; quoted in Hägg 1989: 14)

> Prayers such as Esther's in Addition C, while they have clear Jewish antecedents, are also at home in the Hellenistic romance, and their inclusion in LXX-Esther likewise helps ally that version more closely to the romance.

20. The editor of the AT introduces a significant change into Addition A, making the nations, too, threatened by the wicked dragon and having them "prepare

a force for stability while showing great suspicion toward gentiles in general.

The overall effect of the Additions on character in the Esther story is to minimize its importance. Instead of Israel's future being dependent on one wise man and one brave woman, its history is now a drama which must turn out the way its Author scripted it. The LXX helps us appreciate why the author of the MT chose to keep God well in the background.

This is not the end of the history of the Esther story. Even after the stage when a new version of the book could claim to be *the* book of Esther, the Esther story remained constantly in movement. Every translation, midrash, and literary re-creation tells the tale differently. Every interpretation too, no matter how scholarly, dry, or literal, projects its own version of the story, envisioning the events and the characters differently, refracting them through the lens of new interests, values, and concerns. My study has done the same. I would claim that my interpretations at least approximate the author's intentions and that my evaluations apply appropriate and ethically valid criteria. But at the same time I do not imagine that my reading alone is a neutral, truly objective description of the work in itself—or that it should be. The book of Esther and its people live on in me as in other readers. These characters are living fictions, with ongoing stories that are reshaped by all who know them, whether or not they choose to put those stories in writing.

---

to fight" rather than prepare to fight against Israel (i 6). Israel's outcry to God thus saves all the nations and not only itself. In the AT, some, but not all, gentile nations are hostile.

PHILOLOGICAL-TEXTUAL NOTES

1:3

The relation between the phrases "his princes and servants" and "the forces of . . ." is unclear because of the absence of a conjunction before "the forces." The second phrase may be appositional, with the princes and royal "servants" being called "the" army, *pars pro toto*. Moore adds וְשָׂרֵי, "officers of," before חֵיל. He regards LXX's καὶ τοῖς λοιποῖς ("and the remainder") as a translation of וּשְׁאָר, a corruption of וְשָׂרֵי. But the LXX is paraphrastic here, as always, and Moore's reading requires too many conjectures.

1:5

חֲצַר גִּנַּת בִּיתַן הַמֶּלֶךְ ("the courtyard in the garden of the king's pavilion"): The people's banquet was out of doors, in the court of the garden next to or surrounding a pavilion meant for banqueting (cf. 7:8). This structure is called the king's בִּיתַן, "little house," "kiosk." The *bitānū* in Mesopotamia was a small kiosk in the garden intended for the use of royalty (Oppenheim 1965:328–31).

1:6–7

These verses form a one-membral sentence in which a long string of nouns is used as a way of predicating existence. The rendering, "And oh the . . . ," is intended to reflect its emphatic tone.

1:8

"No one setting restrictions" for אֵין אֹנֵס: thus Haupt 1908: 106, noting that אַחְאָנֵס in b. Nedarim 27a and b. Ketubot 16b means "be hindered." The point is not that no one was forced to drink, but that no one was prevented from drinking as much as he wanted (hence כִּרְצוֹן אִישׁ וָאִישׁ [8b]), and that this was the *dat*, the king's law (hence כִּי כֵן יִסַּד הַמֶּלֶךְ [8b]).

1:17

Lit., "For the word/matter of the queen will go forth to . . ."

בָּאמָרִם could refer to both men and women, but it probably pertains to the latter, for the quoted sentence speaks of the expected effect on the wives. Non-coordination of gender is common with fem. plurals (GKC § 135*o*).

1:18

The lack of an explicit dir. obj. for תֹּאמַרְנָה has led to the emendation תִּמְר(י)נָה, "will rebel" (Paton, Moore, BHS, e.g.), although, as Paton points

out, that reading would probably also require the emendation of לכל to בכל
(cf. Exod 23:21; Ezek 20:8; e.g.). But the ellipsis of a dir. obj. is common
in BH (GKC §117f; Brockelmann 1956: §§127; 137), and in this case the
object is easily supplied from the preceding sentence, where the words of
the women are quoted as the object of אמר. Note a similar ellipsis with תגיד
in 2:10b.

1:20

כי רבה היא is commonly taken as an adversative clause (e.g., Ibn Ezra, Paton, Moore). Apart from the dubiousness of the existence of the adversative כי (except after negations), the clause is better compared to the
emphatic formation in Gen 18:20 (affirmative-emphatic כי; König 1897:
§351c). The phrase is an incidental courtly interjection.

1:22

להיות כל איש שׁרר בביתו ומדבר כלשון עמו: Many commentators have found
this phrase difficult. Gerleman says that the phrase ומדבר כלשון עמו refers
to the multilingual character of the decree and that the verb should be
read as a pual (m⁼dubbar): "damit jeder Lehnsherr [שׁורר בביתו] in der
Sprache seines Volkes angeredet würde" (that is, in the decree). But that
sense would require וכתוב בלשון כל איש ואיש or the like. Moreover, Gerleman's version leaves the decree without content. Moore and others accept
Hitzig's emendation to ומדבר כל שׁוה עמו, "and say whatever suited him."
But, as Haupt (1908:113) points out, the reading is impossible. To approach that sense, it would be necessary at least to emend עמו to לו, and
that would more precisely mean "talk what is proper to him," implying a
restriction on the men's domestic liberties. Junker rearranges the letters to
read ומדב(י)ר כל נשׁי עמו (1936:173). But not only does this emendation
require drastic changes, it also produces a sentence too harsh for this context: "And crush all the wives of his people" (not "und in Unterwürfigkeit
halten alle Weiber seines Volkes," as Junker translates). הדביר means
"crush, beat down" (an enemy), not hold in subjection, and, in any case,
each man is supposed to control his own wives, not the wives "of his
people."

2:7

The availability of a clear and appropriate Hebrew etymology for "Hadassah"—namely, "myrtle"—makes it unnecessary to derive the name from
Akkadian ḥadašatu, "bride" (Lewy 1939a:129). The name Hadassah is lacking in both Greek versions and may have been added to the Hebrew text
at a later stage.
"As a daughter": Both LXX and b. Meg. 13a state that Mordecai was raising Esther to be his wife (LXX omits "as a daughter" in 2:15). B. Meg. 13a
comes to this conclusion by a play on "daughter" (לבת) and "house" (לבית),
the latter understood as an epithet for wife. LXX's γυναῖκα may be a secondary change motivated by the same sense of propriety as in the case of

the Hebrew interpreters. (LXX MS 93's θυγατέρα, "daughter," supported by the OL, is an adjustment toward the MT.) Though this notion may obviate something of the impropriety of Mordecai taking an unmarried girl into his house, it also makes Esther's involvement with Xerxes tantamount to adultery, since she would have been betrothed to Mordecai. Underlying this interpretation may be the practice of adoption-marriages in the ancient Near East, in which a man would adopt a child with the intention of marrying her when she was old enough (cf. Ezek 16). However, I do not see any hint of this practice in the book of Esther itself.

2:13

בית המלך in this verse, like בית המלך in 5:1 (second occurrence) and בית (ה)מלכות in 2:16 and 5:1, is the royal dwelling, which includes both the king's sleeping quarters and his throne room. The royal dwelling is part of the palace compound, which is designated בית המלך in 2:8; 4:13; 5:1 (first occurrence), and probably 6:4. See Moore on these verses. Context usually makes it clear which sense is meant; thus Esther is brought into the palace complex (בית המלך) in 2:8, then about a year later brought to the king's quarters (also בית המלך). The distinction between the palace proper and the palace compound is clearest in 5:1, where both terms occur.

2:14

בית הנשים שני is a crux. Some commentators read השני and translate "the second harem," pointing to the fact that a different eunuch is in charge (thus Paton, Moore, Meinhold, et al.). Others take שני as adverbial, "a second time," i.e., "again" (e.g. Ibn Ezra, Gordis 1976:54). The verb "return" supports the second explanation. שנית would be the expected adverbial form. The *taw* of שנית may have been lost by haplography with the graphically similar *aleph* in paleo-Hebrew (Talmon 1981:513). A similar shortening occurred in Neh 3:30 as well, also preceding an *aleph*. Ibn Ezra explains the word as elliptical for פעם שני (פעם can be masc.). Gordis says that the word was deliberately abbreviated. It might be just an alternate form of the adverb.

שוב שני(ת) is a pleonasm, like the common שוב עוד (Gen 8:12; Deut 17:16; Jer 22:10–11, e.g.). The idiom שוב שנית occurs in 1 Kgs 19:7 and Josh 5:2.

2:16

"Royal dwelling": thus Moore; see note on v. 13.

2:18

הנחה, an Aramaic haphel infinitive from נוח, "give rest, relief," may mean "amnesty" (LXX, Paton) or "holiday" (Vul, Moore), or "remission of taxes" (Gerleman). The latter is attested as an act of royal grace in Assyria and Babylonia as well as in the Persian empire (Her. III 67).

2:19

Lit., "when virgins were gathered again," Hebrew ובהקבץ בתולות שנית. The difficulty is that a second gathering of virgins seems to have nothing to do with the context and receives no further explanation. Moore (similarly Meinhold), following Ehrlich, reads שׁוֹנוֹת, "various," and regards this verse as a reference to the same gathering as in 2:8. But "various" would be pointless in such a reprise, which would more naturally be expressed ובהקבץ הבתולות. Also, verse 22b shows that Esther is married when this happens, so the "gathering" cannot be the one in which she was inducted into Hegai's seraglio. Gerleman understands שֵׁנִית as meaning, "a second thing [to be said]": "Und betreffs der Sammlung der Jungfrauen (ist noch) ein Zweites (zu sagen)". But this expedient helps little, because the suggested usage is too elliptical and not paralleled elsewhere (certainly not by Gerleman's example, 2 Sam 16:19), and because "a second thing" would be meaningless here—Esther's obedience is not a "second thing" to be said about the gathering of virgins. Moreover, the lack of the definite article makes it unlikely that this refers to the gathering reported in 2:8.

The literal translation, "when virgins were gathered again," in the sense of being brought back again, is to be preferred. It refers to the return of the women to the harem—this time Shaashgaz's harem—after their night with the king—the same event as described in 2:14, which refers to the women "returning" שֵׁנִי to the harem. קבץ can mean "gathered in," "brought in," as in Jer 49:5, Zeph 3:19, and Mic 4:6, where the object of the "gathering" is an individual. These women are gathered "again" (שֵׁנִית) insofar as they are brought back to the seraglio, the "women's house," though they are now in a different division, under the supervision of a different eunuch.

2:20

The lexicons give אָמְנָה as a noun, a hapax meaning "wardship" or the like. Since a possessive seems called for, it is probably best to take the ה as 3 fem. sg. (GKC §91f). The absolute form might be אָמֹן (ʾómen) or a qal infinitive, which can have a passive sense even for transitive verbs (e.g. לטבוח Jer 25:34; ספר Exod 9:16b; במשוך Exod 19:13b; כנשוא Isa 18:3; להמית Est 4:11.

3:2

The question of the meaning of proskynesis is confused by the possibility that proskynesis, at least originally, was probably a formalized hand-kiss "blown" from a distance (as argued by Sachsen-Meiningen, 1960:139, 148, 154, and passim). Προσκυνεῖν translates נשק ("kiss") in 1 Kgs 19:18, where it is used of "kissing" Baal. The verb προσκυνεῖν is, however, the most common Septuagintal rendering of השתחוה, "to prostrate oneself" (in reverence or submission), and is used by the AT, LXX, and Josephus in this passage in Esther.

3:4

The idiom עמד דבר occurs only here. It is a later variant of קם דבר (עמד begins to displace קום in LBH; in MH it is consistently used instead of קום).

קם דבר is used of a prophecy proving true (Isa 40:8; Jer 44:28), of an intention being fulfilled (Isa 8:10), and of a claim being accepted as valid (Deut 19:15). The last sense is closest to that of the idiom in this verse.

3:6

עם מרדכי: עם is commonly repointed ʿim, "with." But the MT's ʿam is correct; the phrase is a case of ultrapositioning, i.e. an apposition separated from its kernel-word, a usage that Thorion-Vardi (1987) has shown to be normal BH syntax, though the separation between the two elements of the apposition here, as in 9:30 ("words of peace and faithfulness"), is unusually great.

3:7

הפיל: "was cast," treating the active form as indefinite.

... [to annihilate the people of Mordecai in one day. And it fell on the thirteenth day of the month]: As it stands, the end of the verse reads, literally, "from day to day and from month to the twelfth month, the month of Adar." Clearly something is missing after "from month," and since the lot is being cast for the day as well as the month, it is likely that the date was lost by parablepsis. Minimally we should restore, after ויפל על :לחדש שלשה עשר יום לחדש, "and it fell on the thirteenth day of the (twelfth) month." The restoration is based on the LXX, in which the verse concludes: "and month from month so as to destroy in one day the race of Mordecai, and the lot fell on the fourteenth of the month, which is Adar." But the translator, it must be granted, may have introduced this clause because the context calls for it. AT has a similar reading, with "thirteenth," which is clearly preferable to "fourteenth." AT's reading might represent the text used by the author of MT, or the phrase might have been transferred from LXX to AT by the redactor.

The dating of the planned pogrom in the Greek tradition is problematic, as the following comparison shows:

vs.	MT	LXX	OL	Jos	AT
3:7	—	14	14	—	13 (iv 7)
3:13	13	—a	—	—	—
B 6	—	14	14	14	14 (iv 18)
8:12	13	13	14	—	—
E 20	—	13	14	13	—b
9:1	13	13	13?	13	—
9:17	13	13c	13?	13	—
viii 38	—	—	—	—	13 (viii 38)

[a] MSS 59, the hexaplaric MSS 58 and 583, and OL (MS L) read the 14th. Its omission in the main LXX tradition may be harmonistic.

[b] AT does not, contrary to Hanhart and the remarks of several commentators, support the OL reading. The AT refers to 14 Adar, but only as a day of celebration, and mentions the 15th as well.

[c] LXX-S (p.m.) adds the 14th.

This is evidence for a tradition setting the pogrom on 14 Adar, partially preserved in the LXX but obscured by incomplete adjustment toward the MT. Fritzsche (1851:87) explains this vacillation as evidence of the uncertainty of the tradition of dating the event and the lack of a unified redaction. Schneider (1962–63:206–7) argues that the 14th of Adar, with the 15th as accessory, was the more original date. But his arguments for this are tortuous and require an affirmation of an "historical kernel" preserved in the text of the decrees in the OL-Greek tradition at the expense of the indisputably earlier MT.

In fact, the MT in Esther 9 seems to be reconciling two traditions of the date of the Purim celebration by combining them. The chapter is an extended argument for celebrating Purim on two days. This reasoning involves introducing a second day of fighting, which 9:12–13 does rather artificially. Hence the dating of the fighting on 14 Adar may indeed reflect a variant practice, though not necessarily a "more original" one. The dating on the 13th in AT iv 7, which was based on neither the MT nor the LXX, shows that the MT-redactor found that tradition in the text he received. The presumably original Greek reading of 14 Adar in various places thus shows an adjustment, either in the Greek or in its vorlage, toward a local tradition. Perhaps, however, no tradition lies behind this dating, but rather the LXX translator was accustomed to Hellenic celebrations falling on the same day as the battle, and simply adjusted the date of the battles to the date of the Purim celebrations (Bickerman 1951:116).

Proto-AT locates the pogrom on 13 Adar; the dating on the 14th in B 6 is taken mechanically from the LXX.

3:8

מפזר: PZR does not occur elsewhere in the pual. In the piel (from which the sense of pual can be directly derived) it means "scatter," "disperse," i.e., break up an assemblage and distance its parts from one another. It is used, for example, of an enemy (Ps 89:11), money (Ps 112:9), and Israel among the nations (Joel 4:2; cf. Jer 50:17—Israel is a "scattered flock" [qal pass.]). Haman thus is implying that the Jews, being widely dispersed, have the insidious power of ubiquity and present a danger in an unexplained way.

מפרד: PRD is not used elsewhere in the pual. It occurs once in the piel, in Hos 4:14, where עם הזונות יפרדו means something like "separate [themselves] [to go with] harlots"; but the sentence is elliptical and unclear. The use of PRD in other conjugations shows its root meaning to be "divide," "isolate," i.e., set one item apart from another or others in the same category. In the niphal it is used of one person moving away or being separated from another (Gen 13:9, 11, 14; 2 Sam 1:23; e.g.), of a river branching into four streams (Gen 2:10), of the genealogical branching of peoples (Gen 10:5, 32), of two nations separating from each other (Gen 25:23), and more. In the hiphil, it refers to God's distinguishing the various nations (Deut 32:8), of dividing sheep into different groups (Gen 30:40), of separating persons from each other (Ruth 1:17), and more. All these usages convey the idea of separation and division between two or more units rather than dispersal. In Job 41:9, the negation of יתפרדו is equivalent to the parallel ידבקו (pual), "cleave together," meaning that there is no separation between the scales of Leviathan's armor (see v. 8), not that they are not "dispersed." In two places the hitpael of PRD does seem to convey the notion of scattering—of evildoers (Ps 92:10) and of lion's whelps (4:11). This nuance may result from the reciprocal notion that the hitpael often conveys: when one thing becomes isolated from others in its group, the group becomes scattered. התפרד used of bones (Ps 22:15) probably means that they become (literally) disjointed, separated from one another, rather than that they are dispersed in various places.

Understanding מפורד as "isolated," "separated from" (other peoples) shows Haman accusing the Jews of isolationism: though thoroughly scattered among the peoples, they keep themselves distinct and removed from them.

3:9

עושי המלאכה, lit., "those who do the work," are not the people who will carry out the massacre, for we learn that that task was given to anyone who wished to attack the Jews. Also, the men called עושי המלאכה are later able to side with the Jews when their enemies attack them (9:3). They are officials, probably revenue officers (Haupt 1908:130; Paton, Moore, et al.). This sense of the term is clearest in 2 Kgs 12:12 and 1 Kgs 11:28 (Jeroboam was not merely a worker, but an official in the king's service who could catch Solomon's eye).

3:15

לשתות, lit., "to drink," is a metonymy for feasting (Paton, Moore), as is the noun משתה (the verbal usage here may be a denominative); cf. the usage in 7:1, where coming לשתות with Esther means coming to her משתה. Compare 1 Kgs 20:12, Job 1:4.

4:5

Lit., "to find out what this is and for what this is." על מה = "for what purpose," "to what end," as in Neh 2:4.

4:7

לשקול ... ביהודיים לאבדם, lit., "to pay for the Jews, to destroy them" = to pay to destroy the Jews.

4:8

A literal translation of verse 8 is "And he gave him a copy of the inscription of the law that was given out in Susa to destroy them to show Esther and to inform her and to command her to come to the king to beseech him and to beg him on behalf of her people."

Haupt (1908:135) observes that the 'atnaḥ at להגיד לה correctly makes this infinitive coordinate with להראות, not with ולצוות עליה. The next verse shows that Hatach was to inform Esther about the situation in general.

4:11

להמית, lit., "to put to death." An infinitive of a transitive verb can be used where the sense requires a passive or intransitive notion, i.e., where the available subject is the object of the action; e.g., 7:4. See the note on 2:20 above.

4:12

MT's plural ויגידו is commonly emended to ויגד (hiphil sing.). The OL and LXX render as "And Hatach informed," a reasonable paraphrase. But it is hard to explain the supposed change from pl. to sing. as a graphic confusion. It is more likely that the author is simply vague about the number of messengers, since Esther's maids too have a role in this scene.

4:14

The negative is not in the Hebrew but is required for the English rhetorical question. See the discussion in Haupt 1908:137–38

5:1

See the note on 2:13.

5:3

The phrase (מה לך (לכם (when it is not part of the idiom מה ל-X ול-Y) always suggests that the listener is disturbed or troubled in some way; thus NJV, correctly: "What troubles you?"

5:11

ואת כל אשר (גדלו המלך): Gordis (1976:54–55) translates the *waw* as "and," "together with," and כל as "all this," comparing Gen 20:16b (which, however, is obscure and probably corrupt), and Job 13:1a, הן כל ראתה עיני (which at most shows that כל means "everything," not "all this").

In fact, ואת כל אשר is a simple expansion of the phrase ואת אשר meaning "the way in which," "in regard to which" (Gen 30:29; Deut 29:15; cf. GKC §157c), as in the next clause, ואת אשר נשאו. The clause כל אשר גדלו המלך is an accusative of respect; the phrase alludes to matters such as the king's placing Haman's chair above those of the other princes (3:1). The literal translation is "and all that with regard to which the king promoted him." This detail recalls Gen 41:40, where Pharaoh says, רק הכסא אגדל ממך, "Only in regard to the throne will I be greater than you," with גדל (qal) governing a noun functioning adverbially. Cf. 10:2a and the comment below.

6:2

MT Bigthana, a variant of Bigthan (2:21).

6:3

יקר and גדולה are genitives dependent on מה (Haupt 1908:143; and cf. Qoh 11:2).

6:8

ואשר נתן כתר מלכות בראשו: the only reasonable translation of this clause is

"and upon whose head the royal crown has been placed," with reference
to the horse. Gerleman, assuming that a crown would not be placed on a
horse, reads אֲשֶׁר (temporal) for וַאֲשֶׁר and translates "while the royal diadem is placed on his [the king's] head," i.e., during an official royal excur-
sion. But the evidence for crowns on horses (see commentary) obviates the
need for an emendation that produces a dubious construction. Nor is there
any reason to think that a horse would be more majestic if the king had
worn a crown while riding it.

6:9

The transitive verbs "have them put the garments on" (וְהִלְבִּישׁוּ), "have
them set him" (וְהִרְכִּיבֻהוּ), and "cry out" (וְקָרְאוּ) may be plural because Haman is thinking of the honored nobleman (i.e., himself) accompanied by
servants who are doing the actual dressing and leading of the horse. Or the
verbs may be indefinite plurals, equivalent to passives.

6:13

"If Mordecai, . . .": This class of conditional assumes the protasis to be a
reality, and the consequence naturally follows. Examples in BH are Job
8:4; 14:5, 14.

7:1

לִשְׁתּוֹת = "to have a מִשְׁתֶּה with"; see note on 3:15.

7:4

כִּי אֵין הַצָּר שֹׁוֶה בְּנֵזֶק הַמֶּלֶךְ: Paton and Moore (among others) consider
this sentence an unsolvable crux. (For a summary of some of the numerous solutions proposed, see Paton.) But it is not really obscure.
MT's הַצָּר (haṣṣār) means "the adversary," which does not give a good sense
in this context. LXX ("the slander"), Vul ("our adversary"), and Syr ("the
enemy") reflect the same consonantal text for this word. The difficulties
are adequately handled by vocalizing the word with a pataḥ: haṣṣar = "adversity, calamity." (Ibn Ezra correctly identifies הַצָּר with צָרָה and compares
Ps 119:143.) The absence of this well-attested word elsewhere in Esther
hardly seems a strong argument against the repointing (contrary to Paton).
As for נֵזֶק, Haupt contends that the root נזק may refer to annoyance as well
as actual damage (1908:147; likewise Ibn Ezra), but in the three Aramaic
sentences he brings as evidence—Dan 6:3; Ezr 4:15, and, most clearly,
Ezr 4:13—נזק refers to damage to the empire's revenue, not to the king's
peace of mind. Gordis (1976:56–57) asserts that courtly etiquette dictates
the use of the strong term נֵזֶק to refer to annoyance to the king. But we
would expect courtly usage to call for a "weak" term, as if to say: our adversity would not be worth causing even a bit of irritation to the king.
In fact, נֵזֶק in Est 7:4 refers to monetary loss, as commonly in MH. שֹׁוֶה
means "be worth," "equivalent to," in other words, "justify." While a hypothetical construction is called for in translation, the construction is not,
strictly speaking, hypothetical. For rhetorical purposes, Esther is asserting
that the adversity just mentioned is not worth a loss to the king's revenue.

7:5

ויאמר המלך אחשורוש ויאמר, lit., "And King Xerxes said, and said to Esther": Some commentators have attributed too much meaning in the repetition of "and said." Dommershausen (following Striedl 1937:106) explains the repeated ויאמר as representing the king catching his breath and starting anew. But such doubling could show no such thing, since it is not the king speaking this sentence. Bardtke says that the doubling is a retarding element to heighten suspense, making us wonder to whom the king will speak, Haman or Esther. Yet the effect is not to retard, but merely to confuse, because we expect a direct as well as an indirect object and do not find it in its proper place. Clines (p. 113) believes that the doubled "he said" is taken from the proto-AT, where two speeches are implied. These speeches are not, however, quoted, and the verb "said" is not used. There is no particular connection between AT viii 7 and the two verbs in MT.

The similar resumption of the word in Ezek 10:2 suggests that the doubling of "and said" was an acceptable idiom, whose effect may have been to control the pacing of the verse. The second ויאמר is not represented in the LXX of either verse, but both are probably cases of smoothing. I similarly have found it necessary to smooth out the idiom in translation by rendering "spoke . . . and said," to suggest the resumption without overemphasizing it.

7:8

MT's ופני המן חפו is commonly translated, "and they covered Haman's face," an action that supposedly marks him as condemned to death. However, the king has not yet passed sentence. Moreover, the evidence for a custom of covering the face or head of a condemned man is thin. The available evidence shows only that it was done on occasion, possibly rare ones, in the Greco-Roman world. Ibn Ezra says that it is a custom "well-known in the books of Persia" for the king's servants to cover the face of a man at whom the king is angry, to spare the king the sight of the hated face. This is possible but, as far as I know, unattested.

Some other suggestions: (1) Gordis (1976:56) takes the verb as an archaic pass. part. (comparing Job 15:22; 41:25), singular by attraction to המן. But the scroll employs the standard form חפוי for the passive (6:12), and moreover does not use morphological archaisms. One might, however, emend to חפוי, a partial haplography with the following וי. It is not a severe objection that elsewhere the idiom uses "head," since covering the head as a gesture of misery involves covering the face as well. (2) Rudolph (1954:90) reads חורו "grew pale." This idiom occurs in Isa 29:22, parallel to יבוש. (3) Gerleman compares an Arabic idiom meaning, lit., "it was covered over him," which has the sense of "lost consciousness." But not only is the Arabic idiom at some distance linguistically and temporally from the phrase in Esther, it also has little in common verbally with the Hebrew phrase. (4) Perles (1895:32) reads חפרו for חפו, "was shamed"; cf. Ps 34:6, ופניהם אל יחפרו.

283

LXX's διετράπη τῷ προσώπῳ (lit., "he was confounded in the face") runs contrary only to explanation (3). I prefer explanation (4), because the disgrace of the wicked (often indicated by the verb חפר) is a hope frequently expressed in the Bible (Ps 40:15; 70:3; 71:24; e.g.), and because a *waw-reš* haplography is more probable graphically than the changes required by reading explanation (2). But the other explanations produce the same general sense.

7:9

אשר דבר טוב על המלך, lit., "who spoke good for the king." Similarly NJV. Haupt (1908:153) is right that the expected meaning of the phrase is "who made kind remarks about the king" (cf. 1 Sam 25:30; Jer 32:42), though few would feel free to insert the verb גמל as Haupt does. Still, pressures of context require understanding this idiom in an unparalleled sense.

8:6

The phrasing of verse 6a echoes Gen 44:34. The non-coordination of gender between ימצא and רעה is perhaps a reflex of that verse, which uses רע.

8:10

The word "this" is supplied in the translation. In the Hebrew, the dir. obj. of "he wrote" in verse 10 is the long "that" clause in 8:11–13.

"Riders of swift horses, steeds *pur sang*" attempts to approximate the general sense of three equine terms whose exact meaning is unknown and which may designate either the horses or the riders; see the commentaries. The French is meant to suggest the foreignness of the Persian words in the Hebrew text. בני הרמכים as pointed in the MT (*hārammākîm*) denotes persons. The Syriac *rammākā'*, though apparently cognate, means "herdsmen," which is inappropriate in this context, so we should probably point *bᵉnê hārᵉmākîm* (Haupt 1908:157), lit., "sons of the herd," i.e., bred with the royal studs for the king. אחשתרנים derives from the Persian term for "realm."

8:11

8:11–13 is one long "that"-clause serving as the dir. obj. of ויכתב in verse 10.

Gordis takes אותם טף ונשים as direct objects of הצרים "attack" (translated above as "afflict") and renders: "and wipe out every armed force of a people or a province attacking them, their children, and their wives." Such a sentence would, however, require a repetition of "their" in Hebrew, i.e., אותם טפם ונשיהם. Gordis draws a distinction between this verse and 3:13 by observing that in the latter, the phrase "all the Jews . . . children" follows immediately upon the verb "destroy," whereas in 8:11, seven words intervene between the verb and "children and women." But this distinction is hardly relevant, since the intervening words are part of the dir. obj. clause, and the words "children and women" could not have been placed earlier in the sentence. Nor is it significant that טף never occurs elsewhere with

נשים alone but is always (with the exceptions Gordis notes) preceded by a noun or a more extended term for adult males (1976:51). The phrase טף ונשים is an appositional extension of the dir. obj. clause . . . כל חיל הצרים אותם, exactly as it is an extension of זקן . . . כל היהודים, which is the dir. obj. of the same verbs, in 3:13.

8:17

מתיהדים: "became Jews" or "pretended to be Jews," a hapax. The word is open to either interpretation, but the first is preferable; see the Commentary.

9:16

"Gaining relief": reading נחום (inf. abs.) for נוח, "to rest" (haplography of *mem* and consequent adjustment of vowel letters); thus Rudolph 1954:90. In Esther נוח is reserved for the respite that takes place *after* the conflict, which would be premature in this verse (it is first mentioned in verse 17). Rudolph understands נחום to mean "avenge themselves," but נחם never clearly refers to the act of vengeance, contrary to a widespread view, though the concepts of vengeance and venting one's emotions are closely related as cause and effect (cf. esp. Isa 1:24; and see Parunak 1975:526, 532).

9:20

Paton believes that "these things" is prospective, referring to the contents of the letter, which are given in verses 21–22. He compares verse 29, where "this second message" refers to what follows. But vv. 21–22 summarize the purpose ("in order to confirm") of Mordecai's letters, not their content. There is nothing in verses 21–22 for "these things" to refer to.

9:25

Commentators are divided on whether to take the suffix of ובבאה as indefinite ("when the matter came . . .") or 3 fem sg. ("when she [Esther] came . . ."). The former interpretation puts Esther out of the picture entirely in this verse, as if Xerxes knew nothing about Haman's plot until he was somehow informed, at which time he took action. In the latter interpretation, Esther's *coming* before the king is the pivotal event, as it is in the body of the book, where the king is swayed by Esther's presence more than by the information about the scheme. It seems best to take the suffix as indefinite, since Esther has not been mentioned for some time.

עם הספר is suspect; it is usually translated "in writing" or "by letters," though there is no parallel to such a use of עם. Haupt (1908:170), followed by Gerleman, says that עם is adversative and that the letter is Haman's; thus: "in spite of the letter." But Haman's letter is not mentioned in this summary, and in any case, Haman's plot cannot be said to have rebounded against him *in spite of* his letter. The above translation follows NJV's "With the promulgation of this decree" in including the phrase in the quotation of Xerxes' words. (NJV also notes that this translation is uncertain.) In both this translation and the usual one the passage maintains that the king issued the decree on his own initiative *before* Haman was executed.

9:28

נזכרים ונעשים = "celebrated as a memorial" (Ehrlich, with reference to his discussion of Exod 13:3).

9:29

ותכתב ... כל תקף: lit., " ... wrote all authority," a difficult expression. Gerleman: "*allerlei Nachdrückliches.*" Haupt (1908:172) places "Mordecai the Jew" after תקף, but this change assumes an unmotivated dislocation and creates an awkward text. Paton translates "with all power", but recognizes that את in the sense of "with" (of manner) is unnatural in this connection (similarly Bardtke, Moore, et al.). תקף means "power" in Est 10:2; Dan 11:17; and often in MH and Jewish Aramaic. Apparently the sentence means that Esther (or she and Mordecai) put into writing the authority necessary to validate the observance. תקף is a trope for *words* of authority.

9:30

If we omit "and Mordecai the Jew" from the previous verse, as seems required (see Commentary), then either the 3 fem. sg. verb of verse 29a (ותכתב) must be emended to the masc., or the 3 masc. sg. act. verb of verse 30a (וישלח, qal) must be emended to one of four possibilities: to 3 fem. sg., 3 masc. pl., 3 masc. sg. niphal, or 3 masc. pl. niphal. Repointing וישלח as niphal requires no change in consonants, and, since non-coordination of number is frequent (e.g., 1:14; 2:21; 9:23a, 27a [ketib]), this form is not ruled out by grammatical considerations. In 9:27a (ketib וקבל, vocalized in qere as pl.), we see the vocalization tradition neutralizing non-coordination of number, essentially the same process as I am presupposing here. The addition of "and Mordecai the Jew" in verse 29 would have made it natural for the Massoretes to point וישלח as active.

דברי שלום ואמת: Gordis (1976:57–58) explains this as the epistolary greeting formula quoted from the "actual letter" sent by Esther and Mordecai. (The letter itself, he believes, is summarized but not quoted). But as a greeting formula (unattested elsewhere), the phrase would hang uselessly in the air. It is better taken as an apposition to ספרים describing the character of the letters sent. This type of apposition (substantive-substantive, separated by adverbial modifiers) is described by Thorion-Vardi (1987:52–56); for another example see the note above on 3:6.

9:29–32

The formidable textual difficulties of this passage are discussed in the Commentary.

The LXX diverges radically from MT in 9:29–32. A possible literal translation of the obscure Greek (using MT numbering) is:

(29) And Esther the queen, the daughter of Aminadab, and Mordecai the Jew wrote what they had done and the strength [στερέωμα =

תקף] of the epistle of Phrourai. (31) And Mordecai and Esther the queen confirmed by [a fast?] themselves for themselves, then confirmed their plan with respect to their health. (32) And Esther confirmed [it] by decree [λόγῳ] for all time, and it was written for a memorial.

MT 9:30 and 32b are not represented in the LXX, while of verse 31a only the words קימו על נפשם [. . .] ואסתר המלכה [. . .] מרדכי are definitely represented in the LXX. The LXX has the appearance of a strained attempt to handle a corrupt and accidentally abbreviated Hebrew text.

9:29–32 is missing in the AT; it is one of several passages in chap. 9 that the redactor of AT did not borrow from the LXX, though it had no parallel in the proto-AT (however, the last two words of viii 49, εἰς μνημόσυνον, are apparently taken from LXX 9:32 [MT 32], showing that the redactor of the AT is deliberately skipping over LXX material he considers unnecessary)

Both Greek versions thus differ too radically from the Hebrew in this passage to be used in retroversion. The lack of verses 30–32 in the OL testifies to their absence in the Greek tradition on which it is based. All that can be deduced from the Greek versions is that the MT was not the only form of this passage in the first century B.C.E. to the second century C.E. But the Greek traditions, especially the AT, are often reductive and offer no evidence for a minus in the Hebrew texts they used. On the other hand, the Syriac to Esther is a highly literal translation, and the absence of the word "second" in it points to its absence in its Hebrew vorlage, which was generally quite close to MT.

10:2

מעשה = "story," "affair," as in MH.

ופרשת גדלת מרדכי אשר גדלו המלך has essentially the same structure as the clause ואת כל אשר גדלו המלך in 5:11a (see the note on that verse above), with פרשת גדלת מרדכי replacing כל. The clause אשר גדלו המלך is almost always taken as modifying "Mordecai," although Mordecai is hardly in need of identification at this point. In fact, the antecedent of אשר is פרשה, which means "details" (just as in 4:7, where it refers to the exact sum of money, not to a report about that money). Thus, literally: "and the details of Mordecai's greatness with respect to which the king promoted him." In other words, Mordecai wrote the details of just how he had been promoted.

10:3

דבר שלום ל–: The closest parallels to this phrase are in Ps 85:9 (where, however, God's "speaking peace" is a matter of declaring what will come to pass rather than attempting to effect it) and Ps 122:8 (with בך). In the latter verse the phrase is parallel to "seek the betterment of," as in Est 10:3). Elsewhere this phrase (Zech 9:10) and variants (Jer 23:17; Ps 35:20; Ps 120:7 [omit כי with Syr, LXX, and so on]) mean "propose peace to," "make peace with."

A DECADE OF ESTHER SCHOLARSHIP

This book first appeared in the Studies in Old Testament Personalities series (University of South Carolina Press), edited by James L. Crenshaw, 1991. In the subsequent decade, numerous new and interesting studies in Esther have been published. This survey brings to the reader's attention some of the most valuable and innovative of the recent books on Esther. (To keep the survey manageable, I do not deal with the periodical literature.) Most of these books have interacted with the present study, accepting some of its ideas and disputing others, thus continuing the scholarly dialectic that I find so fruitful (see above, p. 5).

1. Commentaries

A. Adele Berlin's commentary[1] belongs to a commentary series serving Jewish laity, and as such it draws extensively upon Jewish midrash and exegesis. Nevertheless, like the JPS Commentary series as a whole, it is non-denominational in character. Berlin emphasizes two points: First, the book is a comedy, a burlesque of the Persian court. The comic tone of the book serves its purpose: to establish the carnivalesque holiday of Purim. Second, the author drew heavily on the literary motifs associated with Persia that were current at the time the book was written, which Berlin believes to be Achemenid. These motifs survive almost exclusively in the works of Greek historians but may have been present in other literatures in pre-Hellenistic times. The Greek authors belonged to the same *literary* context from which Esther emerged, and their (sometimes fantastic) views of Achemenid Persia give a sense of the

---

1. Adele Berlin, *Esther* (Philadelphia: Jewish Publication Society, 2001).

world of storytelling from which Esther emerged. Berlin adduces some striking parallels from the Greek historians. I found the following particularly enlightening.

With regard to Vashti's refusal to come to the king's banquet, Berlin points out that Plutarch (and others) believed that when the Persians wished to indulge in drunkenness and lewdness during their banquets, they dismissed their wives. "In this they are right in what they do, because they do not permit their wedded wives to share in their licentiousness and debauchery" (*Moralia* 140 B 16). This parallel demonstrates that, from the author's point of view, what offended Vashti was the affront to her social status, for she was being treated like a concubine. The author assumes that Xerxes was behaving improperly and is thus implicitly siding with Vashti. These considerations supplement and strengthen my remarks on pp. 20 and 168.

Mordecai's refusal to bow to Haman is also best understood against the background of a Greek notion, namely that *proskynesis* before humans was an insult to one's honor. The Greeks viewed the Persian king's demand for this gesture as proof of despotism. They considered it degrading to bow before any human. How much the more so would an author, writing within this social context, consider it humiliating for a Jew to bow before an Agagite. This gives greater clarity to Mordecai's action, discussed on pp. 42-44; 191-92.

B. Jon Levenson's commentary,[2] recognizing that the Hebrew version is not the only canonical Esther, integrates the Septuagintal additions in the translation and commentary, identifying them by italicization. This has the immediate benefit of destabilizing the common and comfortable notion that the MT is the "final form." Whatever version of Esther we choose to read (and whatever text of that version), we are entering the story at a particular moment of its evolution. This dynamism shows the story's vitality and the urgency with which it speaks to every generation.

Levenson vigorously argues that God is clearly present in the MT Esther, contrary to my proposal that the author deliberately preserves ambiguity in this respect (see above, Chapter XII). Levenson discerns evidence of God's presence in "the extraordinary pattern of apparent coincidences that characterizes the narrative and makes possible the deliverance of the Jews from seemingly

---

2. Jon D. Levenson, *Esther.* Old Testament Library (Louisville: Westminster John Knox, 1997).

certain extermination" — and not in the individual coincidences alone, but also in the "highly improbably symmetrical pattern in which they have been imbedded" (Levenson, p. 19). Further indicators are the allusions to a higher power in 4:13-14 and 6:13b, and the implication of deity in the fast Esther calls in 4:16 (Levenson, pp. 18-21). My answer (see above, Chapter XII) is that these things do hint at God's presence — but only hint. When a great many readers (Berlin, among the recent ones) look in that direction they do not see God clearly, if at all. The author's silences too must be interpreted. In my view they leave us with a *maybe* — a "maybe" that demands an even bolder faith than plain statement would.

Levenson (p. 19) challenges me to find examples from Second Temple Jewish literature that heap up coincidences without investing them with theological significance. But *all* of that literature is explicitly theological (except for the Song of Songs, which belongs to a genre unrelated to Esther). This fact itself shows that the book of Esther is doing something unprecedented, and its theological message should not be assimilated to the expected ones. The discussion might be put on firmer ground by an examination of Hellenistic novellas, which exploit numerous coincidences and flukes in part for their surprise value but also to show the hand of fate at work. Perhaps fate has a role in Esther too.

C. Frederic W. Bush's dense and careful commentary[3] approaches the book from a variety of angles. With respect to the formation of the Masoretic version, he proposes that an original work underwent two redactional stages, which together produced a literary and thematic unity that provides the etiology of Purim.

In a literary inquiry (pp. 300-309) Bush argues, primarily on the basis of structural and discourse analyses, that the narrative is controlled by a "problem-based plot" structure. Furthermore, "the genre of the narrative of Esther is at least three-fold. At one level, in its final form, it functions as *the etiology for the festival of Purim* and as its *festival lection*. At a second level, however, its genre is *a short story that reveals the quality of a situation*" rather than "*developing* characters or a situation" (pp. 308-9; italics in the original). For this reason, he classifies the book as a "short story" rather than a "novella." Bush observes that of the four main characters, Esther alone undergoes personal development (p. 308). In my view, this obser-

---

3. Frederic Bush, *Ruth, Esther.* Word Biblical Commentaries 9 (Dallas: Word, 1996).

vation highlights the importance of *her* development to the story's message.

Like Levenson, Bush interprets the book's coincidences and reversals as hints of divine providence (pp. 323-26). Again, I believe that the silence at these very points is deliberate and meaningful.

Bush's insistence that Esther holds out to *all* oppressed communities "the hope that 'relief and deliverance' may indeed be effected by the combination of human effort and the providence of God" (p. 334) is a welcome recognition of the widely ignored universal message of this nationalistic story.

2. Genre

A. Kenneth Craig, Jr.[4] reads the book of Esther in the light of the Bakhtinian category of the carnivalesque. Bakhtin described Rabelais' incorporation of medieval popular-festive forms, which he called the carnivalesque.[5] In the carnivalesque (in actual festival and in literature), the humor of the common folk delights in improprieties and reversals of established structures. Craig proposes that the story grew out a folk celebration of Purim and received its serio-comic character from that *Sitz im Leben*. Such celebrations, living in folk experience and imagination, permit deviations from the norm and revel in the overturning of social hierarchies and proprieties.

Certain complications arise in reading Esther through the Bakhtinian lens. First of all, Bahktin's concept of the literary appropriation of the carnivalesque belongs to a specific historical setting. He believes that the Renaissance mustered the folk humor of the carnival to unseat the official culture of the Middle Ages.[6] The target was a worldview, not a social structure. The applicability of this concept to Achemenid or Hellenistic Jewry is thus very limited. Also, the derivation of the book of Esther from a folk culture may be questioned. Esther is written from the perspective of the most

---

4. Kenneth M. Craig, Jr., *Reading Esther: A Case for the Literary Carnivalesque*. Literary Currents in Biblical Interpretation (Louisville: Westminster John Knox, 1995).

5. Mikhail Bakhtin, *Rabelais and His World,* trans. Hélène Iswolsky (Cambridge, Mass.: MIT Press, 1968), esp. pp. 197-276.

6. Bakhtin, p. 174.

highly placed Jews, not that of the "folk" with their supposed suspicion of the social hierarchy. The "folk" — called simply "the Jews" — are an anonymous mass who do the bidding of their leaders. The book's suspicion and ironic insights are directed at the gentile authorities, not at the Jewish leadership.[7]

Nevertheless, detached from assumptions about the "folk," the carnivalesque is a productive angle from which to approach the book of Esther. (Berlin emphasizes this as well; Introduction, §2.) Much of what Craig describes as carnivalesque does apply to Esther: the banquets, the market (loosely defined), the crown, the mask, "pregnant death," parody, fools, and collective gaiety (Craig, p. 43). To be sure, it is not evident from the description of the festivities after the victory that the celebration of Purim, at least as formalized in 9:22, was intended as a carnival. Ezra's presentation of the Torah — which was far from carnivalesque — was celebrated in the same way; see Neh 8:10-12. On the other hand, one important feature of Purim (unlike the Torah celebration) was its spontaneous origin in the masses (9:17-23). The carnivalesque crowd, according to Bahktin, is "the people as a whole, but organized *in their own way, the way of the people.*"[8] Moreover, Purim had acquired that character by Talmudic times and has maintained it to this day. From medieval times onward, costumes and satirical Purim spiels have teased authority and tested the bounds of propriety. In a general way, overtones of carnival permeate the book of Esther itself, with its farcical treatment of the gentile authorities, its moments of hilarity, and its pattern of reversals.

The comparison of Esther with the carnivalesque inspires some further thoughts. First, the fools in Esther — Haman, the king, and

---

7. For a more fundamental critique of the Bakhtinian concept of the carnival, see David Wiles, "The Carnivalesque in *A Midsummer Night's Dream*," in *Shakespeare and Carnival*, ed. Ronald Knowles (New York: St. Martin's, 1998), pp. 61-82. The carnival belongs to the society as a whole, including the upper reaches. Wiles argues that *A Midsummer Night's Dream* was historically part of an aristocratic festival, and that the play is integrated with a historically specific upper-class celebration. Also intriguing is Wiles's observation of the association of carnival with the rhythm of the calendar, something little considered in Esther studies. "Bakhtin's generalized view of carnival renders him blind to the highly specific way in which festivals organize and give meaning to the passage of time. . . . The carnivalesque [in Bakhtin] is experienced as a textual artefact belonging to a given historical moment rather than as a performance belonging to a specific calendrical moment" (Wiles, p. 67).

8. Bakhtin, p. 255.

the courtiers — are not the fools of carnival, who poke fun at (among other things) the higher ranks. The true *eiron*, who sees through the glossy façades of the gentile authorities, is the author, and he represents the vision of the Jews. From their cultural distance, Jews can see through their masters and smirk at their frivolity and triviality.

Craig rightly underscores the importance of the theme of masking-and-unmasking (Craig, pp. 110-19), to which category we should probably assign the motifs of clothing and changes of dress (pp. 92-100; 110-19). This observation could be developed further: The book of Esther is naturally concerned with the question of identity, the token of which is clothing. Should a Jew boldly reveal his identify without regard to circumstance, as Mordecai did (3:4), or should he or she tactically hide it, as Esther did (2:20)? What, moreover, is the right linguistic "clothing" of the Jew in exile (8:9)?

If the carnival were fundamentally subversive of the social order, as Craig assumes, then the book of Esther would run against its grain. If, however, the carnivalesque is fundamentally conservative and tweaks the holders of power rather than repudiating the power structure, then the humor in Esther is carnivalesque in this regard too. The Jews are threatened not so much by the Persian social order as by its disruption. It is not as if Haman epitomized wealth and power while the Jews were equated with poverty and helplessness. In status, the Jews seem equal to the other nations of the Persian empire. Haman himself is an upstart, a latecomer to power, and he is quite willing to throw the empire into disarray in order to assuage his malice. The Jews maneuver and fight not to overthrow the social order but to restore the *status quo ante*. Like Joseph (Gen 47:13-26), Mordecai ministers to the highest power holder. In the end, the Jews are more secure than before, but their social position has not fundamentally shifted from what it was before Haman's subversive scheme got underway. The book of Esther tacitly but clearly affirms that the social order and governmental authority are essential to Jewish existence,[9] even while nervously eyeing the instability and venality of the men who hold it in their grasp.[10]

---

9. Compare "Pray for the welfare of the realm, for were it not for fear of it, men would swallow each other up alive" (*Avot* 3:2).

10. Compare "Love work and hate authority, and avoid being known to the government" (*Avot* 1:10) and "Be wary of the government, for they bring someone near only for their own purposes. They seem like friends when it is convenient to them, but they do not stand up for a man when he is in difficulty" (*Avot* 2:3).

B. Lawrence M. Wills[11] seeks to define and trace the poetics of "the Jewish novel" as a distinct genre poised between biblical narrative and the Greek novel of the late Hellenic world (200 B.C.E. to 100 C.E.). He cautiously calibrates the affinities of the Jewish novel, including the Hebrew and Greek versions of Esther, with the comparable Greek genre:

> The novels that we are studying are not derived forms of the Greek novel but a series of manifestations of popular art, some predating the Greek novel, that reflect the play of the novelistic impulse. These Jewish writings must bear some distant family relation to the Greek novels. . . . They arise at about the same time, under similar conditions, in parts of the world that are ruled by the same successors of Alexander the Great. (p. 16)

On the basis of the Greek parallels, Wills suggests that the Jewish novel was very likely a genre of popular literature and was meant to be understood as fiction. I am not convinced that the ancient readers would indeed have been cued by the story's improbabilities, such as the choice of a Jew as queen of Persia, to identify the tale as a deliberate fiction; see my remarks above on pp. 148-50. The early readers we know of (especially Josephus and the rabbis in *b. Megilla*) all found these premises credible, and none of the book's historical assumptions runs counter to the historical information available to a Jew of the Hellenistic period. Indeed, only if the readership assumed the historicity of the events could the tale effectively provide an etiology and legal foundation for Purim.

Aptly calling MT Esther "a snapshot of a literary tradition in progress" (Wills, p. 105; and see above, Chapter XIV), Wills discerns three stages in the development of the Hebrew Esther: (1) the "Mordecai/Haman Source," which told of a court conflict; (2) the "*Esther* Source," which elaborated on stage 1 by introducing a female character and extending the threat to all the Jews of Persia; and (3) the MT form, which added the Purim festival, the court descriptions, the exaggerated revenge, and the farcical tone.[12] At

---

11. Lawrence M. Wills, *The Jewish Novel in the Ancient World* (Ithaca: Cornell University Press, 1995). Chapter IV (pp. 93-131) deals with the MT and the LXX Esther.
12. Wills first presented this analysis in *The Jew in the Court of the Foreign King* (Minneapolis: Fortress, 1990), pp. 153-72.
   Scholars widely agree that the Purim etiology was appended to an earlier Esther tale. In my view, the etiology was the major contribution of the editor who reworked the proto-MT into the present book. The book is a unity, but

stage 3, the book was poised on the edge of the novelistic genre. Wills probes the poetics of each stage, in particular its use of focalization in guiding the reader's perceptions of the characters. Wills traces this evolution into the Septuagint, showing its strong ties to the Hellenistic novella. He locates the earliest stages of the story's growth as far back as the fifth century B.C.E., but dates the book as we have it to the Hasmonean period (Wills, pp. 100, 110).

3. Themes

A. Timothy Laniak's *Shame and Honor in the Book of Esther*[13] reads the book through the lens of the double theme of shame and honor. These are not just two themes among many, but pervasive concerns that motivate the characters' moods and actions at every step and govern the book's social interactions. Attention to the dynamics of shame and honor enriches the reading of Esther in numerous regards.

Laniak argues that a crisis of identity lay at the heart of the Jewish experience of diaspora. Exile in the ancient world was a state of shame, a separation from one's sources of identity. Laniak (pp. 138-45) nicely explains how Haman's edict brought shame as well as danger on the Jews, and how the restoration of the Jews' honor required the shaming of their attackers by utterly defeating them.

The need to demonstrate national honor, we might add, is the primary reason that the author constructs premises that require the Jews to defend themselves rather than (as in the proto-AT) simply allowing them to be rescued by noble protectors (see above, pp. 214-16).

To realize the importance of honor in the self-defense motif, one can compare the pride felt by Israelis after the 1948 and 1967 victories in the fact that "for the first time in 2000 years" (as a cliché had it) a *Jewish* army had proved its prowess in battle. (This was particularly true of the generation of Jews who felt firsthand the deepest of the "shame of exile" in the Holocaust.) Members of

---

one created in two main phases. See my study, *The Redaction of the Books of Esther: On Reading Composite Texts*. SBL Monograph Series 40 (Atlanta: Scholars, 1991), chapter II.

13. Timothy S. Laniak, *Shame and Honor in the Book of Esther*. SBL Dissertation Series 165 (Atlanta: Scholars, 1998).

the Jewish Brigade in the British army during the Second World War have expressed the relief and pride, even exultation, they felt when they finally met the Germans (and bested them) in hand-to-hand combat. The ancient diaspora reader of Esther must have read 9:1-15 with a surge of pride unnoted by most commentators.

The book of Esther is concerned with how to maintain honor *outside* the land of Israel, with its traditional repositories of honor: king, army, temple. Through "subversive submission," Esther gains control of the situation (Laniak, p. 91). Esther herself is a personification of life in Exile, a symbol of a marginal community and a model for surviving as a Jew in a foreign land (Laniak, p. 174).

B. Timothy K. Beal's *The Book of Hiding*[14] is a postmodern interpretation, and as such is often cryptic and slippery. Beal sets himself the commendable goals of counteracting Christian hostility toward Esther and resolving the problems the book presents to Christian readers. In Protestant theological discourse, "[t]he book of Esther is Jewish insofar as it is not like 'us,' and within the Christian canon, Esther, in all its Jewishness, comes to represent the antithesis of Christian identity. In this sense, it is the not-us within the us (insofar as the Christian canon serves to define the boundaries of Christian identity)" (Beal, pp. 10-11). Beal also finds problematic the discourse of "woman as other." He proposes to overcome both problems by showing how the book destabilizes ethnic and gender identity.

Beal characterizes the book of Esther as "a literary farce that highlights the impossibilities of locating and fixing the not-self, or other (specifically the woman as other and the Jew as other) over against 'us'" (Beal, p. ix). If this is intended as a statement of what the book does, rather than how a Christian *might* read it, or might *misread* it, it makes no sense. As far as the author of Esther is concerned, "the Jew" *is* the "us," and the reader is assumed to share that identification. Moreover, there is no suggestion that the fact that Esther is a woman makes her an "other" to the author or readers.

Nor does the book of Esther show ethnic or gender identity to be unstable or their boundaries porous. Esther may hide her Jewishness tactically, but (as she learns in chapter 4) her identity as a Jew is indissoluble, even in the absence of external markers (such

---

14. Timothy K. Beal, *The Book of Hiding: Gender, Ethnicity, Annihilation and Esther* (London: Routledge, 1997).

as dietary observances). What is decisive is not the temporary concealment of identity but its ultimate and permanent revelation at the moment of crisis.

Beal discerns ambiguities regarding gender and ethnic identities which, he rather optimistically believes, can subvert anti-Judaism and misogyny. Such "transgressions" are much prized nowadays, and they are easily uncovered everywhere, because if they are not visible, they must be present under "erasure." Whether boundary blurring could have any effect on actual anti-Jewishness or misogyny is very doubtful. Western European anti-Semitism was never diminished by Jewish acculturation or even assimilation. In any case, to impose on the book of Esther the fashionable virtue of boundary transgression is as much a "colonizing" of the text as are the intrusions of Protestant hermeneutics that Beal justly deplores (pp. 4-12).

Beal correctly, if obscurely, points to the importance of the themes of identity and hiding in the book of Esther. (These are explored with welcome lucidity by Laniak and Craig.) Esther, Beal asserts, "is about identity in dispersion. It marks off a space of dislocation in which Jewishness may be more a product of projection by one's enemies than a matter of self-definition" (p. 119). This is certainly not the author's intention. If this is meant as a reader response, it is an idiosyncratic one. Mordecai's title is "the Jew" — no blurring of identity there — and when he tells Esther to hide "her people and kindred" (2:10), she knows exactly what she is supposed to conceal. The author has a very clear notion of ethnic identity, for he regards the Jews as one nation distinct from and comparable to the others in the empire. So powerful is this notion that he even has the Jews using their own script and language (8:9), though that is historically impossible. The author of Esther would have us honor ethnic identity rather than subvert it.

Beal makes some interesting observations. He notes that Vashti is written out of the story but remains a spectral presence in her absence (Beal, pp. 25-32). The author creates a "solidarity" between Vashti and Mordecai (p. 17). Both refuse a command, both provoke rage, and both are "excribed" by royal proclamations, though unsuccessfully in Mordecai's case. Other lines connect Memuchan and Haman, and Haman and the king.

Beal observes, as others have not, the degree to which the identification of Mordecai in 2:6 emphasizes *exile* (the root *glh* "exile" is used four times in that one verse). To Beal this suggests that

"Jewish identity in Esther is always already dispersed, dislocated" (p. 33). I would say instead that it shows Jewish identity holding firm even in national dispersion and dislocation, just as it is indissoluble even when dormant in the apparently oblivious young Hadassah, living under the alias of Esther. Commentators observe that the land of Israel is not referred to in the book except incidentally, when Jerusalem and Judah are mentioned in describing Mordecai's background (2:6). But that is a big exception, for it tells us that Mordecai, the paragon of Jewishness, is identified by where he is *not*. His epithet *hayyᵉhudi* can be translated "the Judean" as well as "the Jew," for although Mordecai's tribal affiliation is Benjamin, he belongs to the community exiled from the territory of Judea in 597. *Yᵉhudi* is an ethnic designation, referring to a "people" (ʿam) like the others in the empire, and parallel to "Agagite."[15] The Jews are indeed "a people scattered and unassimilated" (3:8). They are *displaced* and always away from home. Yet, far from subverting national boundaries, the author of Esther seeks to reinforce them by redrawing them in a non-spatial dimension. This new concept is, I believe, fully at home only in the Hellenistic empires; see above, pp. 230-34.

C. Linda Day's *Three Faces of a Queen*[16] compares the portrayals of Esther in the MT, the AT, and the LXX. Her focus is literary rather than redactional, and she is determined to treat each version as an integral literary work, whatever its prehistory (chapter 1). She examines nine episodes in each version, isolating and interpreting (sometimes overinterpreting) the slightest differences in detail and nuance between the versions, in the best tradition of New Criticism (though not so labeled) (chapter 2). She next undertakes a "Comprehensive Analysis," comparing the portrayals of Esther with respect to ten thematic categories (chapter 3). Since she does not provide a separate summary of each version's picture of Esther, it is difficult to assemble the traits of each portrayal into a coherent portrait. I will synthesize her statements on the character of Esther in

---

15. Ruth Kossmann's careful examination of the terms *yᵉhudi* and *mithyahᵃdim* (8:17) leads to the conclusion that *yᵉhudi* in Esther, as in Nehemiah, is a designation of a group of deportees as viewed from an external perspective and oriented to geography; *Die Esthernovelle: vom Erzählten zur Erzählung.* VTSup 79 (Leiden: Brill, 2000), pp. 294-99. In Esther, the concept is extended to imply the self-understanding of the Jews as a cultic-religious community (Kossmann, pp. 310-13 and 293-313 *passim*).

16. Linda Day, *Three Faces of a Queen: Characterization in the Books of Esther.* JSOTSup 186 (Sheffield: Sheffield Academic, 1995).

the MT, the topic of the present book, with the understanding that this cannot convey the subtleties of Day's descriptions.

In the MT, Esther exercises authority in varying degrees. Her authority is manifested in her royal aspect and demeanor. The degree of her activity and passivity likewise varies. She is level-headed and restrained, outwardly displaying emotion only in 4:4, 8:3, and 8:6. Though her emotions are rarely described, sometimes her silence suggests a certain composure and confidence. She lives in a secular world, but at two points — the fast (4:16) and the Purim letter (9:29-32) — she reveals religious concerns. In her relations with the Jewish people, she moves from being clearly rooted in the community, to being distant from her people in her role as Persian queen, to being solicitous of the Jews and serving as their leader. Her relationship with the king is formal and business-like, with Ahasuerus's feelings developing from affection to respect. With Mordecai, she moves from simple obedience to a relationship of parallel responsibilities. She even attains a certain authority over him, insofar as she has the power to appoint him over Haman's estate (8:2).[17] In her struggle with her enemies, Esther is more focused on Haman than on the Jews' adversaries generally. The formalities of courtly procedures are continually emphasized. In two places, Esther's sexuality is relevant to the plot: when she is chosen queen[18] and when Haman falls on her to request mercy.[19]

Day also assesses the relation of each version to the Hellenistic novella. She agrees that the book of Esther has affinities with the Hellenistic novellas (see my comments above on p. 145 and Wills's study, surveyed above), but she underscores some important differences. In these novellas, unlike in Esther, (1) much attention is paid to the romantic and erotic experiences and feelings of the heroine; (2) women have very little power within their environments, outside the force of sexual attraction; (3) travels in foreign

17. This important point has escaped notice. Esther briefly possesses Haman's wealth and *chooses* to give it to Mordecai. This grant, far from being a surrender of control, is an expression of her queenly status, for royalty honors itself by displaying generosity (Laniak, pp. 44-45).
18. It is, however, doubtful that Esther's "good lovemaking" expresses genuine affection for Ahasuerus, as Day believes (p. 193). Esther had not met him before the night she was summoned to his bed (2:16), at which time the king quickly "fell in love" with her (2:17). The stimulus for this may simply have been her beauty.
19. This passage has nothing to do with Esther's sexuality, but only with the king's jealousy of her sexuality, which causes (or allows) him to grossly misinterpret Haman's motives.

lands are often recounted; and (4) the heroine is largely isolated from intimate contact other than with her beloved (Day, pp. 218-19). The Esther story belongs to a tendency during the Hellenistic period to highlight female characters. "Women are made central to plot development, given more independence, and characterized with greater detail of inner life" (Day, p. 221). This important observation undermines some of the feminist assertions I critique above on pp. 205-11.

4. Literary History[20]

I will treat work done on the formation of the different versions more briefly, since this is not a main topic in the present book.[21]

A. Karen Jobes's study of the Alpha Text[22] proposes an intricate process in the AT's formation. It was the first Greek translation of Esther and was based on a Hebrew (or Aramaic) text that was earlier than but "quite similar" to the MT (Jobes, p. 223). The literary differences are due mainly to pluses and minuses, most of which can be explained as the work of the translator or a redactor. The six major additions (with the possible exception of B and E) were first incorporated in the AT and subsequently copied to the LXX. Later, sporadic attempts were made to adjust the AT to the LXX. Jobes tentatively dates the origins of the AT to the late fourth century B.C.E. and some redaction of the AT to the first century C.E.

I cannot deal with Jobes's complex arguments here, but will only note that the relation of the AT to the MT cannot be reduced to semantic agreement (84%) or formal agreement (54%) between the two texts. There is inevitably much agreement between the two texts, even after the secondary Additions are removed, since they descend from a common ancestor and tell basically the same story. But where they do disagree, the differences are signifi-

---

20. Not read in conjunction with this survey is Kristin De Troyer's *Het Einde van de Alpha-Tekst van Ester* (Leuven, 1997); English translation, *The End of the Alpha-Text of Esther: Translation and Narrative Technique in MT 8:1-17, LXX 8:1-17 and AT 7:14-41.* SBLSCS 48 (Atlanta: SBL, 2000). De Troyer argues that AT 1:1–7:41 (= viii) is a rewriting of the LXX, partially Hebraized by reference to the MT. This is summarized and critiqued by Kossmann, pp. 319f.
21. This was treated in my *The Redaction of the Books of Esther.*
22. Karen H. Jobes, *The Alpha-Text of Esther: Its Character and Relationship to the Masoretic Text.* SBL Dissertation Series 153 (Atlanta: Scholars, 1996).

cant and reflect a different concept of the events and their meaning; see above, pp. 254-61. Day's detailed cataloguing of the impact of the AT-MT differences on the characterization of Esther alone (chapter 2) reveals that though the versions tell the same story, there are still significant divergences between them.

The literary and ideological differences between the MT and the proto-AT are significant even if, as Jobes maintains, the MT pluses arose through excisions by the AT translator/redactor rather than (as I believe) additions by the MT author/redactor. For example, Jobes holds that in chapters 8–10, the AT actively minimizes Esther's role and magnifies Mordecai's (Jobes, pp. 134-37). In my view, the MT author has deliberately enhanced Esther's importance. Jobes finds it difficult to explain why the Esther material would have been added to the Hebrew (MT) text during the Hellenistic period (p. 135). I find it much more unlikely that the heroine's deeds would have been deliberately expunged by a later redactor. A redactor could have augmented Mordecai's glory by augmenting his deeds (as the Midrash did) without reducing Esther's. And it cannot be denied that heroic roles were ascribed to females in Hellenistic Jewish literature — Judith, Asenath, and Susanna being notable examples.

Charles Dorothy's[23] narratological and stylistic analysis of the three versions (in their final forms) concludes that each version has its own textual integrity, each being a discrete tradition deriving from a different community. Neither the LXX nor the AT derives directly from the other (Dorothy, pp. 357f.). Dorothy agrees that the "proto-L" (approximately the same as my "proto-AT") preceded the MT. The AT translates the story in such a way that "segments of the Jewish population (in the homeland or in the Diaspora) could not only read it, but appreciate it as their story, their history, their life" (Dorothy, p. 356). The AT arose within a more Jewishly orthodox, less Hellenized community, possibly in Palestine, whereas the LXX was intended for a Hellenized diaspora audience (p. 355). Day (pp. 226-32) effectively criticizes and virtually reverses these assertions.

B. Ruth Kossmann's *Die Esthernovelle*[24] applies the tools of tradition history and redaction criticism to the different versions of

---

23. Charles V. Dorothy, *The Books of Esther: Structure, Genre, and Textual Integrity.* JSOTSup 187 (Sheffield: Sheffield Academic, 1997).
24. See above, n. 15.

Esther. On the basis of the theory that the AT represents the oldest
witness to the original text of Esther, she builds an intricate theory
of growth and redaction. The basic process (leaving aside details
and subdivisions) was as follows: There were three originally independent components of the Esther story: the Vashti narrative, the
Haman-Mordecai narrative, and the Haman-Mordecai-Queen narrative. Only after they were combined into the pre-Esther did the
story receive the "*Yᵉhudim*-layer" that associated it with the Jews.
The proto-AT is a direct ancestor of the AT, the LXX, and the
proto-MT. Redactional reworking of the proto-MT and the addition of the "Purim layer" produced the MT. This was also a source
for the LXX, and the LXX later fed into the AT. In connection
with "pre-Esther," she carefully refutes J. T. Milik's thesis that the
Qumran fragments 4Q550^{a-f} hold indications of the original
sources, or a sort of prototype, of Esther.

I am still skeptical about the possibility of separating narrative
strands with the "proto-Esther" text. The criteria used to separate
these strands are more plausibly explained in terms of their literary function. The reservations I express about other such theories
in *The Redaction of the Books of Esther* (pp. 97-99) largely apply to
Kossmann's tradition-historical analysis of her "pre-Esther" as
well.

5. Reception and Interpretation

The present commentary uses the Jewish exegetes of late antiquity and the Middle Ages in the same way as it does modern
commentators: It mines them for insights and ideas and help in
understanding the text. Another approach makes the commentators an object of study rather than a tool. Two recent studies do
this, but they too can be read with profit by people interested primarily in the book's original meaning.

A. Eliezer Segal's *The Babylonian Esther Midrash*[25] is a translation
and detailed commentary on the exegetical discussion of Esther in
the Talmudic tractate *b. Megilla*, 10b-17a, which is the only full
exegetical midrash of a biblical book to have been included in the
Babylonian Talmud. Segal's massive study, which includes textual,

---

25. Eliezer Segal, *The Babylonian Esther Midrash: A Critical Commentary.* 3 vols.
Brown Judaic Studies 293 (Atlanta: Scholars, 1994).

philological, historical, and hermeneutic discussions, will be indispensable to future application of this midrash in Esther exegesis.

B. Barry Dov Walfish's *Esther in Medieval Garb*[26] is a comprehensive study of medieval Jewish exegesis in Western Europe. (It is also a fine introduction to medieval Jewish hermeneutics generally.) Walfish shows how Esther-exegesis was shaped by the exegetes' social setting and personal experiences. The book is organized thematically (with chapters such as "Jewish Sources for Exegesis" [1], "Literary Concerns" [3], and "The Jews and the Monarchy" [9]) rather than viewing each commentator in isolation.

The medieval commentators naturally read Esther through the prism of their own experiences. The book spoke with uncommon immediacy to medieval Jews, who were often the targets of slanders like Haman's and who faced dangers much like those that the book recounts. The book's happy ending gave hope and encouragement to the medieval readers. The wise and clever Esther was herself a source of pride (Walfish, p. 202). They admired her mastery of court intrigue (pp. 162-66) and her rhetorical skills, which they described subtly and persuasively, sometimes employing Ciceronian principles, which were the norm in medieval rhetoric (pp. 52-55).

6. In Conclusion

Scholarship of the 1990s showed an increased appreciation for the book of Esther: its artistry, its subtlety, its moral values, its treatment of female characters, the process of its formation. Most important, recent scholarship has been free of the attitudes that tainted much of Esther scholarship in earlier years: contempt for the book and hostility toward the people whose salvation it recounts. The first paragraph of my Introduction (p. 1) must be modified in the light of these welcome developments.

---

26. Barry Dov Walfish, *Esther in Medieval Garb: Jewish Interpretation of the Book of Esther in the Middle Ages* (Albany: SUNY Press, 1993).

BIBLIOGRAPHY

Abbreviations: Journals and Series

AB	Anchor Bible
AJSL	*American Journal of Semitic Languages*
BA	*Biblical Archaeologist*
Bib	*Biblica*
BKAT	*Biblischer Kommentar: Altes Testament*
BZ	*Biblische Zeitschrift*
BZAW	Beihefte zur Zeitschrift für die Alttestamentliche Wissenschaft
CBQ	*Catholic Biblical Quarterly*
ET	*Expository Times*
HAR	*Hebrew Annual Review*
HAT	Handbuch zum Alten Testament
HS	*Hebrew Studies*
HSM	Harvard Semitic Monographs
HTR	*Harvard Theological Review*
ICC	International Critical Commentary
JBL	*Journal of Biblical Literature*
JNES	*Journal of Near Eastern Studies*
JQR	*Jewish Quarterly Review*
JR	*Journal of Religion*
JSOTSup	Supplements to the Journal for the Study of Old Testament
JTS	*Journal of Theological Studies*
MGWJ	*Monatsschrift für Geschichte und Wissenschaft des Judentums*
PAAJR	Proceedings of the American Academy of Jewish Research
RB	*Revue Biblique*
RdQ	*Revue de Qumrân*
SAT	Die Schriften des Alten Testaments
SBLCS	Society of Biblical Literature: Septuagint and Cognate Studies
ThZ	*Theologische Zeitschrift*
VTSup	Supplements to Vetus Testamentum
VT	*Vetus Testamentum*
ZAW	*Zeitschrift für die Alttestamentliche Wissenschaft*
ZTK	*Zeitschrift für Theologie und Kirche*

Traditional Jewish Exegesis and Homiletic Exposition:

Aggadat Esther. See Buber 1897.
Ibn Ezra (Abraham Ibn Ezra). 12th c. (References to "Ibn Ezra" pertain to

his commentary in the Rabbinic Bible; "Ibn Ezra²" refers to his second commentary, for which see Zedner.)

Malbim, see Meier Leibush ben Yechiel Michael

Midrash Abba Gurion. See Buber 1886.

Midrash Esther Rabba. *Midrash Rabbah: Esther*. Translated by Maurice Simon. New York 1983. Compiled ca. 10th c. from much earlier material.

Midrash Leqaḥ Tov (11th c.), by Tobias ben Eliezer. See Buber 1886.

Midrash Panim Aḥerim (12th c. or later). See Buber 1886.

Rashi (Solomon ben Isaac). 11th c. Rabbinic Bible.

Targum Rishon (Tar¹) (First Targum [Aramaic translation] of Esther; in Rabbinic Bible). *The First Targum to Esther*. Translated by Bernard Grossfeld. New York 1983.

Targum Sheni (Tar²) (Second Targum of Esther; in Rabbinic Bible); see Grossfeld, 1991.

Tractate Megilla, Babylonian Talmud (b. Meg.).

The Babylonian Talmud, Seder Moʻed. Translated in the Soncino Edition, vol. IV, by I. Epstein. London, 1938.

Note: Midrashic interpretations commonly appear in several of the midrashic collections. When referring to an interpretation found in several sources, I have noted only one or two of the more important ones, in particular b. Megilla and Esther Rabba. For a synthesis of the aggadic retellings of Esther together with full references see Katzenellenbogen 1933.

Modern Works (including modern editions of classical texts)

* In the text, commentaries and some other frequently-mentioned works (marked with an asterisk) are referenced by name of author only; other works are referenced by author and date.

Albright, William F.

1974 "The Lachish cosmetic burner and Esther 2:12." In *A Light Unto My Path: OT Studies in Honor of Jacob M. Myers*, ed. Howard N. Bream et al., pp. 25–32. Philadelphia.

Allport, Gordon

1937 *Personality*. New York.

Alter, Robert

1981 *The Art of Biblical Narrative*. New York.

Alter, Robert, and Kermode, Frank

1987 *The Literary Guide to the Bible*. Cambridge, Mass.

Anderson, Bernhard W.

1950 "The place of the Book of Esther in the Christian Bible." *JR* 30:32–43.

*1954 "The Book of Esther." *Interpreter's Bible*, vol. III, 821–74. New York.

Arendt, Hanna
1963 *Eichmann in Jerusalem*. New York.
1978 *Life of the Mind*. New York.
Auerbach, Erich
1968 *Mimesis* (first English edn. 1953). Princeton, N.J.
Avi-Yonah, Michael
1984 *The Jews Under Roman and Byzantine Rule*. Jerusalem. (1st English edn. 1972)
Baldwin, Joyce G.
*1984 *Esther*. Tyndale OT Commentaries. Leicester.
Bardtke, Hans
*1963 *Das Buch Esther*. KAT XVII 5. Gütersloh.
1965–66 "Neuere Arbeiten zum Estherbuch." *Ex Oriente Lux* 19:519–48.
Barthélemy, D.; Gooding, D. W.; Lust, J.; and Tov, E.
1986 *The Story of David and Goliath: Textual and Literary Criticism*. Göttingen.
Barton, John
1984 *Reading the Old Testament*. Philadelphia.
Beckwith, Roger
1985 *The Old Testament Canon of the New Testament Church*. Grand Rapids, Mich.
Beet, W. Ernest
1921 "The message of the book of Esther." *Expositor* 22: 291–300.
Ben-Chorin, Schalom
1938 *Kritik des Esther-Buches*. Jerusalem.
Berg, Sandra
* 1979 *The Book of Esther*. SBL Dissertation Series 44. Chico, Calif.
1980 "After the exile: God and history in the books of the Chronicles and Esther." In *The Divine Helmsman* (Festsch. Lou H. Silberman), ed. J. L. Crenshaw and S. Sandmel, pp. 107–27. New York.
Bergey, Ronald L.
1983 "The Book of Esther—its Place in the Linguistic Milieu of Post-Exilic Biblical Hebrew Prose." Ph.D. Diss. Dropsie College. Philadelphia.
1984 "Late linguistic features in Esther." *JQR* 75:66–78.
1988 "Post-exilic Hebrew linguistic developments in Esther: a diachronic approach." *Journal of the Evangelical Theological Society*. 31:161–68.
Berlin, Adele
1983 *Poetics and Interpretation of Biblical Narrative*. Sheffield.
Bevan, Edwyn R.
1902 *The House of Seleucus*. London.
Bickerman, Elias (E. Bikerman)
1935 "La charte séleucide de Jérusalem." *Révue des Etudes Juives* 100:4–35.
1944 "The colophon of the Greek book of Esther." *JBL* 63:339–62.

1951 "Notes on the Greek book of Esther." *PAAJR* 20, 101–33.

1967 *Four Strange Books of the Bible*. New York.

1988 *The Jews in the Greek Age*. Cambridge, Mass.

Booth, Wayne C.

1983 *The Rhetoric of Fiction* (first edn. 1961). Chicago.

1979 *Critical Understanding*. Chicago.

1988 *The Company We Keep*. Berkeley, Calif.

Botterweck, G. Johannes

1964 "Die Gattung des Buches Esther im Spektrum neuerer Publikationen." *Bibel und Leben* 5:274–92.

Brenner, Athalia

1981 "Esther through the looking-glass" (Hebrew). *Beth Mikra* 23: 267–78.

Brockelmann, Carl

1956 *Hebräische Syntax*. Neukirchen.

Brooke, Alan E.; McLean, Norman; and Thackery, H. St. John, eds.

1940 *Esther, Judith, Tobit*. The Old Testament in Greek, vol. III, part I. Cambridge.

Brownlee, William H.

1966 "Le livre grec d'Esther et la royauté divine." *RB* 73: 161–85.

Buber, Salomon, ed.

1886 *Sifrey De'aggadeta 'al Megillat Esther* (Midrash Abba Gorion; Midrash Panim Aḥerim; Midrash Leqaḥ Tov). Vilna.

1897 *Aggadat Esther* (Oxford cod. e. 57). Kråkow.

Budde, Karl

1906 *Geschichte der althebräischen Literatur*. Leipzig.

Cameron, George

1958 "Persepolis treasury tablets old and new." *JNES* 17:161–76.

Carmignac, Jean

1964 "Un Aramaisme biblique et Qumrânien: L'infinitif placé après son complément d'objet." *RdQ* 5:503–20.

Cazelles, Henri

1961 "Note sur la composition du rouleau d'Esther." In *Lex tua veritas: Festschrift für Hubert Junker*, ed. H. Gross and F. Mussner, pp. 17–29. Trier.

Chatman, Seymour

1978 *Story and Discourse*. Ithaca, N.Y.

Childs, Brevard

1962 *Memory and Tradition in Israel*. Studies in Biblical Theology. Naperville, Ill.

Clines, David J. A.

*1984 *The Esther Scroll*. JSOTSup 30. Sheffield.

Coats, George W.

1983 *Genesis*. Forms of the OT Literature, vol. I. Grand Rapids, Mich.

1985 *Saga, Legend, Tale, Novella, Fable*. JSOTSup. 35. Sheffield.

Cohen, Abraham D.
1974 "'Hu Ha-goral': the religious significance of Esther." *Judaism*
23:87–94.
Cook, J. M.
1985 "The rise of the Achaemenids and the establishment of their empire." In *The Cambridge History of Iran*, vol. II, pp. 200–91.
Cambridge.
Cornill, C. H.
1891 *Einleitung in das Alte Testament*. 1st edn. Leipzig.
1905 *Einleitung in das Alte Testament*. 2nd edn. Leipzig.
Craghan, John F.
1982 "Esther, Judith, and Ruth: paradigms for human liberation." *Biblical
Theology Bulletin*. 12:11–19.
1986 "Esther: a fully liberated woman." *Bible Today* 24: 6–11.
Crenshaw, James L.
1969 "Method in determining Wisdom influence upon 'historical' literature." *JBL* 88:129–42.
Curtius (Quintus Curtius)
1946 *History of Alexander*. Trans. John C. Rolfe. Cambridge, Mass.
Dandamayev, M.
1984 "Babylonia in the Persian age." In *The Cambridge History of Judaism*,
ed. W. D. Davies and L. Finkelstein, vol. I: *Introduction; The Persian
Period*, pp. 326–42. Cambridge.
Daube, David
1946–47 "The last chapter of Esther." *JQR* 37:139–47.
Dhorme, Edouard
1984 *A Commentary on the Book of Job*. Nashville. (French orig. Paris 1926).
Dommershausen, Werner
*1968 *Die Estherrolle*. Stuttgarter Biblische Monographien 6. Stuttgart.
Doniach, N. S.
1933 *Purim*. Philadelphia.
Driver, Samuel R.
1967 *An Introduction to the Literature of the Old Testament* (first edn. 1891).
Cleveland & New York.
Dubnow, Simon M.
1958 *Nationalism and History*. Philadelphia.
Duchesne-Guillemin, Jacques
1953 "Les noms des eunuques d'Assuérus." *Le Muséon* 66:105–108.
Eddy, Samuel K.
1961 *The King is Dead*. Lincoln, Neb.
Ehrlich, Arnold B.
*1914 *Randglossen zur hebräischen Bibel*. Leipzig (repr. Hildesheim 1968).
Eissfeldt, Otto
1966 *The Old Testament: An Introduction*. Oxford.

Eskenazi, Tamara Cohn
1988 *In an Age of Prose: A Literary Approach to Ezra-Nehemiah.* SBL Monograph Series 36. Atlanta.

Feldman, Louis H.
1970 "Hellenizations in Josephus' version of Esther." *Proceedings of the American Philological Society* 101: 143–70.

Fewell, Danna Nolan
1987 "Feminist reading of the Hebrew Bible: Affirmation, Resistance, and Transformation." *JSOT* 39: 77–87.

Finkel, Joshua
1961 "The author of the Genesis Apocryphon knew the Scroll of Esther." In *Essays on the Dead Sea Scrolls in Memory of E. L. Sukenik,* ed. Chaim Rabin and Yigael Yadin, pp. 163–82. Jerusalem.

Fisch, Harold
1988 "Esther: Two Tales of One City." In *Poetry With a Purpose,* pp. 8–14. Bloomington, Ind.

Forster, E . M.
1954 *Aspects of the Novel* (first edn. 1927). New York.

Fox, Michael V.
1973 "Jeremiah 2:2 and the 'Desert Ideal,'" *CBQ* 35, 441–50.
1983 "The Structure of the Book of Esther." In the *Isac L. Seeligmann Volume,* ed. A. Rofé and Y. Zakovitch, pp. 291–304. Jerusalem.
1991 *The Redaction of the Books of Esther.* SBL Monograph Series 40. Atlanta.

Fritzsche, Otto F.
1848 ΕΣΘΗΡ. *Duplicem libri textum ad optimos codices emendavit et cum selecta lectionis varietate edidit.* Zurich.
1851 *Zusätze zu dem Buche Esther.* Kurzgefasstes exegetisches Handbuch zu den Apokryphen des ATs, vol. I. Leipzig.

Fuchs, Esther
1982 "Status and role of female heroines in the biblical narrative." *Mankind Quarterly* 23:149–60.
1985 "Who is hiding the truth? Deceptive women and biblical androcentrism." In *Feminist Perspectives on Biblical Scholarship,* ed. A. Y. Collins, pp. 137–44. Chico, Calif.

Gan, Moshe
1961–62 "Megillat Esther Be'aspeqlariyat Qorot Yoseph Bemitzrayim." *Tarbiz* 31:144–49.

Gaster, Moses
1897 "The oldest version of Midrash Megillah." In *Semitic Studies in Memory of Alexander Kohut,* ed. G. Kohut, pp. 167–78. Berlin.

Gaster, Theodor H.
1950 "Esther 1:22." *JBL* 69:381.

Gehman, Henry S.

1924 "Notes on the Persian words in the Book of Esther," *JBL* 43:321–28.

Gendler, Mary
1976 "The restoration of Vashti." In *The Jewish Woman*, ed. Elizabeth Koltun. New York.

Gerleman, Gillis
*1982 *Esther*. BKAT XXI. Neukirchen.

Ginsberg, H. L.
1954 "The composition of the book of Daniel." *VT* 4:246–75.

Goldman, Stan
1990 "Narrative and ethical ironies in Esther." *JSOT* 47: 15–31.

Gordis, Robert
1976 "Studies in the Esther narrative." *JBL* 95:43–58.
1981 "Religion, wisdom and history in the book of Esther." *JBL* 100:359–88.

Greenstein, Edward L.
1987 "A Jewish reading of Esther." In *Judaic Perspectives on Ancient Israel*, ed. J. Neusner et al. Philadelphia.

Grossfeld, Bernard
1983 *The First Targum to Esther*. New York.
1991 *The Two Esther Targums*. New York.

Gunkel, Hermann
*1916 *Esther*. Religionsgeschichtliche Volksbücher II. Reihe, 19./20. Heft. Tübingen.
1958 "Fundamental problems of Hebrew literary history" (German orig. 1906; English trans. 1925). In *What Remains of the Old Testament*, trans. A. K. Dallas, 57–67. New York.

Haelewyck, J.-C.
1985 "Le Texte dit 'Lucianique' du livre d'Esther, son étendue et sa cohérence." *Le Muséon* 98:5–44.

Hägg, Tomas
1971 *Narrative Technique in Ancient Greek Romances*. Stockholm.
1983 *The Novel in Antiquity*. Oxford.

Haller, Max
1925 *Esther*. SAT 2, III. 2nd edn. Göttingen.
*1940 *Esther*. In *Die Fünf Megilloth*. HAT 18. Tübingen.

Hallo, William W.
1983 "The first Purim." *BA* 46:19–26.

Halpern, Baruch
1988 *The First Historians*. San Francisco.

Hanhart, Robert, ed.
1983 *Esther*. Göttingen Septuagint, VIII, 3. Göttingen.

Haran, Menahem

1972 "The graded numerical sequence and the phenomenon of 'automatism' in biblical poetry." *VTSup* 22:238–67.

Hartman, Louis F., and Di Lella, Alexander
1978 *The Book of Daniel.* AB 23. Garden City, N.Y.

Harvey, W. J.
1965 *Character and the Novel.* Ithaca, N.Y.

Haupt, Paul
1906 *Purim.* Leipzig.
1908 "Critical notes on Esther." *AJSL* 24: 97–186 (repr. Moore, *Studies*, 1982, pp. 1–90).

Herodotus
*1968 *Herodotus: The Histories.* Trans. Aubrey de Sélincourt. Baltimore.

Herrmann, Wolfram
1986 *Ester im Streit der Meinungen.* Beiträge zur Erforschung des AT und des antiken Judentums. Frankfurt am Main.

Hirsch, E. D.
1967 *Validity in Interpretation.* New Haven, Conn.

Hochman, Baruch
1985 *Character in Literature.* Ithaca, N.Y.

Horowitz, C. M.
1882 "Ueber die Peripetie im Buche Esther." *MGWJ* 31:50–71.

Hoschander, Jacob
1923 *The Book of Esther in the Light of History.* Philadelphia.

Humphreys, W. Lee
1973 "A life-style for diaspora: a study of the tales of Esther and Daniel." *JBL* 92:211–23.
1985a "Novella." In Coats 1985, pp. 82–96.
1985b "The story of Esther and Mordecai." In Coats 1985, pp. 97–113.

Jacob, B.
1890 "Das Buch Esther bei den LXX." *ZAW* 10:241–98.

Jones, Bruce
1977 "Two misconceptions about the book of Esther." *CBQ* 39:171–81.

Josephus (Flavius Josephus)
[1927] *The Jewish War.* Trans. H. St. John Thackery. Loeb Classical Library. London
[1937] *Antiquities of the Jews.* Trans. R. Marcus. Loeb Classical Library. London.

Junker, H.
1936 "Konsonantenumstellung als Fehlerquelle und textkritische Hilfsmittel im MT." In *Werden und Wesen des AT*, ed. Joh. Hempel et al., pp. 162–74. BZAW 66. Berlin.

Katzenellenbogen, Ilja
1933 "Das Buch Esther in der Aggada." Diss. Würzburg.

Knierim, Rolf
1985 "Criticism of literary features, form, tradition, and redaction." In *The Hebrew Bible and its Modern Interpreters*, ed. Douglas A. Knight and Gene M. Tucker, pp. 123–65. Philadelphia.

Koch, Klaus
1972 "Gibt es ein Vergeltungsdogma im Alten Testament?" In *Um das Prinzip der Vergeltung in Religion und Recht des Alten Testaments*, ed. K. Koch, pp. 130–80. Darmstadt (orig. ZTK 52 [1955]; English trans. in *Theodicy in the Old Testament*, ed. J. L. Crenshaw, Philadelphia 1983, pp. 57–87).

König, Fr. Eduard
1897 *Lehrgebäude der hebräischen Sprache*, vol. II. Leipzig.

LaCocque, André
1987 "Haman in the Book of Esther." *HAR* 11: 207–22.

Laffey, Alice L.
1988 *An Introduction to the Old Testament: A Feminist Perspective*. Philadelphia.

Langen, Joseph
1860 "Die beiden griechischen Texte des Buches Esther." *Theologische Quartalschrift* 42:244–72.

Lasine, Stuart
1986 "Indeterminacy and the Bible." *HS* 27:48–80.

Lebram, J. C. H.
1972 "Purimfest und Estherbuch." *VT* 22:208–22.

Levenson, Jon
1976 "The Scroll of Esther in ecumenical perspective." *Journal of Ecumenical Studies* 13:440–51.

Lewy, Julius
1939a "The feast of the 14th day of Adar." *HUCA* 14:127–51.
1939b "Old Assyrian *puru'um* and *pūrum.*" *Revue Hittite et Asiatique* 5:117–24.

Liddell, Henry George, and Scott, Robert
1968 *A Greek-English Lexicon*. Revised by H. S. Jones. Oxford.

Loader, J. A.
1978 "Esther as a novel with different levels of meaning." *ZAW* 90:417–21.

Loewenstamm, Samuel E.
1971 "Esther 9:29–32: the genesis of a late addition." *HUCA* 42:117–24.

Long, Burke O.
1984 *1 Kings*. Forms of OT Literature, vol. IX. Grand Rapids, Mich.

Loretz, Oswald
1969 "Roman und Kurzgeschichte in Israel." In *Wort und Botschaft des Alten Testaments*, ed. Josef Schreiner, pp. 308–25. Würzburg.

Macrobius, Ambrosius
[1970] *Saturnalia*. Ed. I. Willis. Leipzig.

Magonet, Jonathan
1980 "The liberal and the lady: Esther revisited." *Judaism* 29:167–76.

Meier Leibush ben Yechiel Michael (Malbim)
*1878 *Megillat Esther*. Vilna.

Martin, R. A.
1974 *Syntactical Evidence of Semitic Sources in Greek Documents*. SBLSCS 3. Missoula, Mont.
1975 "Syntax criticism of the LXX additions to the book of Esther." *JBL* 94:65–72.

McFadyen, John Edgar
1906 *Introduction to the Old Testament*. New York.

McKane, William
1961 "A note on Esther IX and 1 Samuel XV." *JTS* 12:260–61.

Meinhold, Arndt
1975 "Die Gattung der Josephgeschichte und des Estherbuches: Diasporanovelle." Part I. *ZAW* 87:306–24.
1976 "Die Gattung der Josephgeschichte und des Estherbuches: Diasporanovelle." Part II. *ZAW* 88:72–93.
1978 "Theologische Erwägungen zum Buch Esther." *ZAW* 34:321–33.
*1983a *Das Buch Esther*. Zürcher Bibelkommentare. Zurich.
1983b "Zu Aufbau und Mitte des Estherbuches." *VT* 33:435–45.

Mendenhall, George E.
1973 *The Tenth Generation*. Baltimore.

Michaelis, Johann David
1783 *Deutsche Uebersetzung des Alten Testaments, mit Anmerkungen für Ungelehrte*. Vol. XIII. Göttingen.

Millard, Alan R.
1977 "The Persian names in Esther and the reliability of the Hebrew text." *JBL* 96:481–88.

Moore, Carey A.
1965 "The Greek Text of Esther." Ph.D. diss., Johns Hopkins University. University Microfilms, Ann Arbor, Mich.
1967 "A Greek witness to a different Hebrew text of Esther." *ZAW* 79:351–58.
*1971 *Esther*. AB 7 B. Garden City, N.Y.
1975 "Archaeology and the Book of Esther." *BA* 38:62–79.
1977 *Daniel, Esther, and Jeremiah: The Additions*. AB 44. Garden City, N.Y.
1982 *Studies in the Book of Esther*. New York.
1983 "Esther revisited again." *HAR* 7:169–85.
1985 "Esther revisited: an examination of Esther studies over the past decade." In *Biblical Studies in Honor of Samuel Iwry*, ed. A. Kort and S. Morschauser, pp. 163–72. Winona Lake, Ind.

313

Morris, A. E.
1930–31 "The purpose of the book of Esther." *ET* 42:124–28.
Morson, Gary Saul
1981 *The Boundaries of Genre*. Austin, Tex.
Motzo, Bacchisio R.
1927 "La storia del testo di Ester." *Ricerche Religiose* 3:205–8.
Muir, Edwin
1929 *The Structure of the Novel*. New York.
Myers, Jacob M.
1968 *The World of the Restoration*. Englewood Cliffs, N.J.
Naveh, Joseph, and Greenfield, Jonas C.
1984 "Hebrew and Aramaic in the Persian period." In *The Cambridge History of Judaism*, ed. W. D. Davies and L. Finkelstein, vol. I: *Introduction; The Persian Period*, pp. 115–29. Cambridge.
Nickelsburg, George W. E., and Collins, John J., eds.
1980 *Ideal Figures in Ancient Judaism*. SBL Septuagint and Cognate Studies, 12. Chico, Calif.
Niditch, Susan
1987 *Underdogs and Tricksters*. San Francisco.
Niditch, Susan, and Doran, Robert
1977 "The success story of the wise courtier: a formal approach." *JBL* 96:179–93.
Olmstead, A. T.
1948 *History of the Persian Empire*. Chicago.
Oppenheim, A. Leo
1964 *Ancient Mesopotamia*. Chicago.
1965 "On Royal Gardens in Mesopotamia." *JNES* 24:328–33.
Oxford Companion to German Literature
1986 *Oxford Companion to German Literature*, ed. Henry and Mary Garland. Oxford.
Parunak, H. Van Dyke
1975 *A Semantic Survey of NHM*. *Bib* 56:512–532.
Paton, Lewis B.
*1908 *The Book of Esther*. ICC. Edinburgh.
Perles, Felix
1895 *Analekten zur Textkritik des Alten Testaments*. Munich.
1922 *Analekten zur Textkritik des Alten Testaments*. Neue Folge. Leipzig.
Perry, Ben Edwin
1967 *The Ancient Romances*. Berkeley.
Pfeiffer, Robert
1952 *Introduction to the Old Testament*. New York.
Phelan, James
1989 *Reading People, Reading Plots*. Chicago.
Plutarch

[1926] *Lives*. Trans. B. Perrin. Loeb Classical Library. (*Artaxerxes*: vol. XI.) London.

Polybius
[1923] *The Histories*. Loeb Classical Library. London.

Polzin, Robert
1976 *Late Biblical Hebrew: Toward an Historical Typology of Biblical Hebrew Prose*. HSM 12. Missoula, Mont.

Pomeroy, Sarah B.
1975 *Goddesses, Whores, Wives, and Slaves*. New York.

Price, Martin
1973 "The fictional contract." In *Literary Theory and Structure*, ed. Frank Brady et al., pp. 151–78. New Haven.

Rad, Gerhard von
1972 *Wisdom in Israel*. London.

Radday, Yehuda T.
1973 "Chiasm in Joshua, Judges and others." *Linguistica Biblica* 27/28:6–13.

Richter, Wolfgang
1971 *Exegese als Literaturwissenschaft*. Göttingen.

Ringgren, Helmer
*1962 *Das Buch Esther*. Göttingen.

Robertson, Archibald T.
1915 *A Grammar of the Greek New Testament*. New York.

Robertson, David
1977 *The Old Testament and the Literary Critic*. Philadelphia.

Rosenthal, Ludwig A.
1895 *Die Josephgeschichte mit den Büchern Ester und Daniel verglichen*. ZAW 15:278–84 (see also 17 [1897]125–38).

Rudolph, Wilhelm
1954 "Textkritisches zum Estherbuch." *VT* 4:89–90.

Rüger, H. P.
1969 "Das Tor des Königs"—der königliche Hof." *Biblica* 50:247–50.

Ryder, Frank G.
1971 *Die Novelle*. New York.

Ryssel, V.
1900 *Zusätze zum Buch Esther*. In *Die Apokryphen und Pseudepigraphen des Ats*, vol. I.

Sachsen-Meiningen, Feodora Prinzessin von
1960 "Proskynesis in Iran." In *Geschichte der Hunnen*, II. Band, ed. Franz Altheim, 125–66. Berlin.

Samuel, Alan
1972 *Greek and Roman Chronology*. Munich.

Sandmel, Samuel
1961 "The Haggada within Scripture." *JBL* 80:105–22.

Sasson, Jack M.
1987 "Esther." In *The Literary Guide to the Bible*, ed. Robert Alter and Frank Kermode, pp. 335–42. Cambridge, Mass.

Schneidau, Herbert N.
1986 "Biblical narrative and modern consciousness." In *The Bible and the Narrative Tradition*, ed. Frank McConnell, pp. 132–50. New York.

Schneider, B.
1962–63 "Esther revised according to the Maccabees." *Liber Annus* 13:190–218.

Scholz, Anton
*1892 *Commentar über das Buch "Esther."* Würzburg-Wien.

Schötz, Dionys
1933 "Das hebräische Buch Esther." *BZ* 21:255–76.

Schürer, Emil
1973–86 *The History of the Jewish People in the Age of Jesus Christ*. Revised by G. Vermes and F. Millar. Vol. I: 1973; vol. II: 1979; vol. III.1: 1986. Edinburgh.

Schwarz, Adolf
1923 "Taanith Esther." Festschrift David Simonsens. Copenhagen.

Seeligmann, Isac Leo
1963 "Menschliches Heldentum und göttliche Hilfe." *ThZ* 19: 385–411.

Segal, Eliezer
1989 "Human anger and divine intervention in Esther." *Prooftexts* 9: 247–56.

Segal, Moshe Hirsch
1960 *Introduction to the Bible* (Hebrew: *Mavo' Hammiqra'*). Jerusalem.

Sevenster, Jan N.
1975 *The Roots of Pagan Anti-Semitism in the Ancient World*. Leiden.

Sherwin-White, Susan
1987 "Seleucid Babylonia." In *Hellenism in the East*, ed. A. Kuhrt and S. Sherwin-White, pp. 1–31. Berkeley, Calif.

Stanton, Elizabeth Cady, et al., eds.
1895 *The Woman's Bible*. Chapters on Esther by Stanton and Lucinda B. Chandler. New York (repr. Seattle, 1975).

Steinsaltz, Adin
1984 *Biblical Images*. New York.

Sternberg, Meir
1985 *The Poetics of Biblical Narrative*. Indiana Literary Biblical Series. Bloomington, Ind.

Stiehl, Ruth
1956 "Das Buch Esther." *Wiener Zeitschrift für die Kunde des Morgenlandes* 53:4–22.

1963 "Esther, Judith, Daniel." In *Die aramäische Sprache unter den Achaimeniden*, by Franz Altheim and Ruth Stiehl, pp. 195–213. Frankfurt am Main.

Streane, A. W.
*1922   *The Book of Esther*. Cambridge Bible. Cambridge.

Striedl, Hans
1937   "Untersuchung zur Syntax und Stilistik des hebräischen Buches Esther." *ZAW* 55:73–108.

Talmon, Shemaryahu
1963   "'Wisdom' in the Book of Esther." *VT* 13: 419–55.
1981   "The ancient Hebrew alphabet and biblical text criticism." In *Mélanges Dominique Barthélemy*, ed. P. Casetti et al., pp. 497–530. Göttingen.

Tcherikover, V.
1959   *Hellenistic Civilization and the Jews*. Philadelphia.
1972   "The Hellenistic environment" and "Hellenistic Palestine." In *The Hellenistic Age*, ed. Abraham Schalit, pp. 5–144. The World History of the Jewish People. New Brunswick, N.J.

Thorion-Vardi, Talia
1987   *Ultraposition*. Judentum und Umwelt. Frankfurt am Main.

Tigay, Jeffrey H., ed.
1982   *The Evolution of the Gilgamesh Epic*. Philadelphia.
1985   *Empirical Models for Biblical Criticism*. Philadelphia.

Torrey, Charles C.
1944   "The older book of Esther." *HTR* 37:1–40.

Trenkner, Sophie
1958   *The Greek Novella in the Classical Period*. Cambridge.

Uchelen, N. A. van
1974   "A Chokmatic theme in the book of Esther." In *Verkenningen in een Stroomgebied*, ed. M. Boertien et al., pp. 132–40. Amsterdam.

Ulrich, Eugene
1988   "Double literary editions of biblical narratives." In *Perspectives on the Hebrew Bible: Essays in Honor of Walter J. Harrelson*, ed. J. L. Crenshaw, pp. 101–16. Macon, Ga.

Ungnad, Arthur
1940–41   "Keilinschriftliche Beiträge zum Buch Esra und Ester." *ZAW* 58:240–44.
1942–43   [Communication]. *ZAW* 59:219.

Wehr, H.
1964   "'Das Tor des Königs' im Buche Esther und verwandte Ausdrücke." *Islam* 39:247–60.

Wellhausen, Julius
1902   [Review of] G. Jahn, *Das Buch Esther*. *Göttingische gelehrte Anzeigen* 164:127–47.

White, James Boyd
1984   *When Words Lose Their Meanings*. Chicago.

White, Sidnie Ann
1989   "Esther: a feminine model for Jewish diaspora." In *Gender and Dif-*

ference in Ancient Israel, ed. Peggy Day, pp. 161–77. Minneapolis, Minn.

Wildeboer, Gerrit

*1898 *Das Buch Esther*. Tübingen.

Wills, Lawrence M.

1987 "The Jew in the Court of the Foreign King." Th.D. diss. Harvard University. Cambridge, Mass.

Wright, J. Stafford

1970 "The historicity of the Book of Esther." In *New Perspectives on the Old Testament*, ed. J. Barton Payne, 37–47. Waco, Texas.

Würthwein, Ernst

*1969 *Esther*. In *Die Fünf Megilloth*. HAT 18 (2nd edn.). Tübingen.

Xenophon

[1914] *Cyropaedia*. Ed. Walter Miller. London.

Anabasis.

Zadok, Ran

1986 "Notes on Esther." *ZAW* 98:105–10.

Zedner, Joseph

1935 *Abraham Aben Ezra's Commentary on the Book of Esther, After Another Version*. London. ("Ibn Ezra²").

Zeitlin, Solomon

1972 Introduction to *The Book of Judith*, ed. M. S. Enslind, pp. 1–37. Leiden.

Zimmermann, Frank

1975 *Biblical Books Translated from the Aramaic*. New York.

INDEX

1. Topics

Actants, 8

Act-Consequence connection: Tat-Ergehen-Zusammenhang, 81

Acts and scenes, 13, 155

Adar, month of: Adar 13: 95, 108, 112, 126, 203, 204, 214, 222, 225, 279; Adar 13, 14, 15: 279; Adar 13–15: 117; Adar 14: 112–115, 216, 225; Adar 14–15: 122; Adar 15: 96, 113, 115; see also Chronology, Nisan

Additions (Greek): 10, 255, 266, 269; translations of, 266; effect on character, 273; see also LXX verse index 10, 255, 266, 269

Adoption-marriages, 276

Advisers, King's; see Servants

Agag, 29, 42

Ahasueros; see Xerxes

Alexandrinus, 196

Allusions, 240

Alpha Text, 9, 10, 90, 139, 193, 215, 227, 240, 243, 254, 255, 277, 278, 287; redactor (R-AT), 255, 257, 272, 287

Amalek, 42, 79

Ambition, 188

Amestris, 68, 132, 136

Amixia, 48

Anger, 242

Antisemitism, 11, 32, 33, 45, 47, 48–50, 54, 55, 111, 179, 180–182, 192, 217, 218, 220, 233

Antitheses, 159, 162

Aramaic, 99, 231

Argumentation, 45, 46; see also Author: technique

Artaxerxes, 14

Artaynte, 68, 77, 91

Artistic interest, 196

Astrologers, 21

Author: his ideal 2–4, 8, 15, 30, 34–36, 38, 42, 47, 55, 57–60, 64, 100, 117, 124, 130, 186, 189, 191–195, 201,209, 219, 226; his technique 16, 18, 19, 22, 23, 69–71, 78, 97, 118, 120, 123, 131, 135, 141, 148–153, 156, 163, 176, 179–183, 185, 186, 189, 191–195, 201–209, 214, 218, 220, 226, 228, 239–241, 243, 246, 247, 253, 263; his context 122, 133, 139, 233; see also Narrator, MT-Author

Authority, 92, 95, 99, 122–125, 127, 128, 150, 164, 172, 173, 175, 202, 227, 228

Authorship, 117, 139

Banquet, 69, 274

Banquets; see feasting

Beauty treatment, 35

Benjaminite lineage, 29

Booty, 100, 115, 222

Bowing: Mordecai's refusal, 42–44, 46, 74

Bribe, 51–53, 60

Chance, 81

Character study: characterization: theory, 2–10, 18, 24–26, 28, 30, 56, 196, 131, 143, 153, 167, 169, 171; character evaluation, 8; character: "real life," 7, 8; character: mimetic component, 6, 7, 18; character: flatness of, 195

Children, 74, 284

Chronicles of Persia and Media: see Persian: chronicles

Chronology, 14, 39, 41, 42, 61, 91, 95–97, 154, 155, 278, 279; see also Adar, Nisan

Clothes, 60, 65, 67, 68, 77, 82, 104, 198, 214, 267

Coincidence, 75, 76, 240, 241, 244, 245

Communication, 65, 66

Concubines, 38; see also Harem

Conflict, 25

Conspiracy, 39, 40

Control, 108; see also will

Conversion, 105, 106

Courage, 187

Cyrus I, 29

Daniel, 194, 210

Darius I Hystaspes, 29

2. Scriptural References

3. Postbiblical Texts
(Apocrypha, New Testament, Rabbinic)

4. Greek Words

5. Hebrew and Aramaic (alphabetized by root)

6. Other Languages

7. Authors and Scholars, Ancient and Modern